Official Guide to Financial Accounting using Tally.ERP9

By

Tally Education

BPB PUBLICATIONS

Distributors:

BPB PUBLICATIONS
20, Ansari Road, Darya Ganj
New Delhi-110002
Ph: 23254990/23254991

MICRO MEDIA
Shop No. 5, Mahendra Chambers, 150
DN Rd. Next to Capital Cinema, V.T.
(C.S.T.) Station, MUMBAI-400 001 Ph:
22078296/22078297

COMPUTER BOOK CENTRE
12, Shrungar Shopping Centre,
M.G.Road, BENGALURU–560001
Ph: 25587923/25584641

DECCAN AGENCIES
4-3-329, Bank Street,
Hyderabad-500195
Ph: 24756967/24756400

BPB BOOK CENTRE
376 Old Lajpat Rai Market,
Delhi-110006
Ph: 23861747

Published by Manish Jain for BPB Publications, 20, Ansari Road, Darya Ganj, New Delhi- 110002 and Printed him at Vijeta Offset printers, New Delhi.

Preface

Tally Education, subsidiary of Tally Solutions (creators and developers of Tally software), has been traversing the journey of an assiduous mission to enhance the employability of learners. We continuously envisage to blend conceptual learning with business applications to develop true professional competence.

Tally Solutions Pvt. Ltd. is a pioneer in the business software products arena. Since its inception in 1986, Tally's simple yet powerful products have been revolutionising the way businesses run. Having delivered path breaking technology consistently for more than 30 years, Tally symbolises unmatched innovation and leadership. Today, it caters to millions of users across industries and continues unchallenged as the industry leader in the enterprise resource planning software domain.

In this age of intense economic competition and rapid technological developments, it has become customary for employers to place a premium on computer skills and abilities to enhance business productivity. This makes it imperative for job seekers and employees to stay abreast of developments in their areas of expertise and constantly update and upgrade their skills to stay relevant in the workplace. Tally Education is committed to bridging the gap between education and employment in the country.

Over the years, the success of Tally software has fueled the demand for Tally trained professionals across the globe. Catering to this demand has always been a priority for us and this courseware is one more step towards the same.

Written as an official guide of the UGC curriculum of Financial Accounting, this book can be adapted to the needs of learners with diverse interests and backgrounds. It shall lead the learner towards varied career goals ranging from entrepreneurship to finance professionals.

Fundamentals of Financial Accounting using Tally.ERP 9 have been explained with the help of diverse business scenarios which provide the learners a clearer insight on the real-life business situations. Thereby preparing the candidates to experience and understand the real life implementation of the theoretical knowledge.

Sections of this book have been kept independent from each other, thus providing additional flexibility to the advanced readers to choose their own way around the book.

Enriched with numerous figures, illustrations and practice scenarios, it enables candidates to understand the intricacies of business operations and nuances of financial accounting with ease and prepares them to handle business transactions in the daily work environment more confidently.

Table of Contents

Chapter 1

Basics of Accountancy

LEARNING OBJECTIVES

After studying this chapter, you will understand:

* Meaning and Purpose of Financial Accounting
* Advantages and Disadvantages of Financial Accounting
* Meaning of Key Accounting Terms
* Convention of Double-Entry System of Bookkeeping
* Different Types of Accounts

1.1   INTRODUCTION

Accounting is the process of classifying, recording and reporting an enterprise's business transactions over a period of time. Financial Accounting is a branch of accounting that is primarily concerned with the preparation of financial statements, based on the business transactions, and communication of the same to person interested in the information.

Financial accounting helps in determining the results (i.e., profit or loss) of business operations during the particular period and the financial position of the enterprise as on a date at the end of the period.

1.2   OBJECTIVES   OF   FINANCIAL   ACCOUNTING

The objective of financial accounting is to keep a record of all business transactions so that:

* The profit earned or loss sustained by the business during an accounting period can be determined;
* The financial position of the business at the end of the accounting period can be ascertained; and
* The financial information required by the owners of business, Government and other interested parties such as employees or investors can be provided.

1.3   ADVANTAGES   OF   FINANCIAL   ACCOUNTING

Financial Accounting has many advantages, the main advantages being:

1. **Record of Business Transactions:** The record of business transactions maintained by an enterprise serves as a permanent record of transactions, and a future reference.
2. **Determination of Profit or Loss:** The availability of the complete record of business transactions, specifically income and expense, helps in the determination of profit or loss of an enterprise.
3. **Determination of Financial Position:** The availability of the complete record of business transactions, specifically information regarding what the enterprise owns, invests and owes, helps in the determination of the financial position of the enterprise. Further, it also helps the enterprise to maintain a clear record of debtors (amounts to be collected) and creditors (amounts to be paid).
4. **Track Progress of Business:** Maintenance of business records on a yearly basis facilitates the comparison of performance over the years. This helps to keep track of the progress made by the organisation year-on-year and over the years.
5. **Compliance with Legal Requirements:** Business concerns are required to comply with certain statutory requirements such as paying and filing of tax returns. Maintenance of financial accounting as per accounting standards, facilitates compliance with such legal requirements.
6. **Documentary Evidence:** Accounting records of a concern can be used as documentary evidence in case of litigation, like seeking claims against debtors.

1.4   LIMITATIONS   OF   FINANCIAL   ACCOUNTING

Financial Accounting has numerous advantages; at the same time, it also suffers from certain limitations. Some of the limitations are:

1. **Record Monetary Transactions:** A major limitation of financial accounting is that, it record monetary transactions only. Non-monetary transactions (i.e., transactions that cannot be expressed in terms of money) are ignored in financial accounting. Thus, important information like technological innovations of the business concern, or competition faced, which have an impact on business are not reflected in financial accounting.
2. **Does Not Provide Exact Information:** Financial accounting reports do not necessarily give exact information. This is because, at times, estimates are used in accounting; thus, the information in such cases is at best, approximate.
3. **Does Not Reflect Present Value of Business:** Balance Sheet, the financial report that reflects the financial position of a business, is prepared by taking into account the historical cost (book value) of assets and not the market value. Hence, financial accounting fails to accurately reflect the present value of a business.
4. **Does Not Provide Timely Information:** The focus of Financial Accounting is provision of information in the form of financial statements for a defined period, normally,

one year. This means that the information is, of a historical nature, that may not be of much use for handling the current situation.

1.5 ACCOUNTING TERMS

Some of the most commonly used accounting terms are:

- **Account:** An account is a statement of transactions affecting any particular asset, liability, expense, or income. Example: cash account, bank account, etc.

- **Accounting Period:** A regular period of time such as a quarter or year, for which a financial statement is generated, is called an accounting period. Example: 01 April 2016 to 31 March, 2016.

- **Chart of Accounts:** A chart of accounts is a list of all account titles used by an organisation. The chart of accounts of the business shows the categorisation and grouping of its accounts.

- **Entity:** An entity is a person, partnership, organization, or business that has a legal and separate existence. Example: Rajesh Jewellers, Vriddhi Traders Pvt Ltd., etc. An accounting system is always devised for a specific business entity (also called accounting entity).

- **Transaction:** A transaction is an event involving some value between two or more entities. Purchase of goods, receipt of money, payments to creditors, expenses, are all examples of transactions. Transactions can be cash transactions or credit transactions.

- **Assets:** Assets are economic resources of an organisation that can be expressed in terms of money. Assets are items of value used by the business in its operations. Example: Deepak Travels owns a fleet of buses. These buses provide economic benefit to the enterprise and so are shown on the asset side of the balance sheet of Deepak Travels. Assets can be broadly classified as:

  o **Fixed assets:** Assets held on a long term basis such as land, buildings, machinery, plant, furniture, and fixtures. Fixed assets are used in regular business operations of a company.

  o **Current assets:** Assets held on a short term basis. Such as, debtors, bills receivables, stock, cash and bank balances.

- **Liabilities:** Financial obligations (amounts which a business owes to others) of a business organisation are called liabilities. Examples include loans from banks or other persons, creditors for goods supplied, bank overdraft etc.

- **Capital:** Capital is the amount invested by the owner/s (proprietor/s) in a business. Capital increases when a company earns profits; and decreases if a company incurs losses or if any amount is withdrawn.

- **Income:** The difference between business revenues and expenses is called income.

- **Expenditure:** Expenditure refers to all the expenses or amounts spent to produce and sell the goods and services. Examples include, purchase of raw materials, payment of salaries, office expenses, etc.

- **Profit:** Profit refers to the excess of revenues over expenses during an accounting period. Profit increases the investment of the owners.

- **Gain:** Gain refers to the profit earned from events or transactions which are incidental to business such as sale of fixed assets, winning a court case, appreciation in the value of an asset, etc.

- **Loss:** Loss refers to the excess of expenses over related revenues during an accounting period. It also refers to money or money's worth lost, without any benefit in return. Examples include, cash or goods lost due to theft, fire, and so on.

- **Discount:** Discount is the deduction in the price of goods on sale. If the deduction is given at an agreed percentage on the list price at the time of the sale it is called a 'trade discount'. Trade discounts are generally offered by manufactures to wholesalers and by wholesalers to retailers.

  Another type of discount is cash discount, which is an incentive that encourages debtors to make prompt payments. In this case, after selling the goods on credit basis, debtors may be given a certain deduction in the amount due if they pay the amount within a stipulated period. Such deduction is given at the time of payment on the amount payable.

- **Voucher:** The documentary evidence in support of a transaction is called a Voucher. Examples include cash memos (when goods are bought for cash), invoices (when goods are bought on credit), receipts (for payments), and so on.

- **Goods:** Goods refer to the products in which a business unit deals or manufactures. For example, for a furniture dealer-chairs and tables are goods, while for others it is furniture and is treated as an asset.

- **Drawings:** Withdrawals of money and/or goods by the owner from the business for personal use is called drawings. Drawings reduce the investment of the owners.

- **Purchases:** Purchase refers the goods procured by a business for use or sale. Purchases may either be cash or credit.

- **Sales:** Sales refers to goods sold after being purchased or manufactured by the business. If goods are sold for cash, they are called cash sales and if goods are sold and payment is not received after sale, it is called credit sales.

- **Stock:** Stock or inventory refers to the goods or merchandise kept in the premises of a shop or warehouse and offered for sale or distribution. In a trading concern, the amount of goods that lie unsold at the end of an accounting period is called closing stock. Similarly, opening stock is the amount of stock at the beginning of the accounting period.

- **Debtors:** Persons and/or other entities who owe an enterprise money, on having bought goods and services on credit are called debtors of the enterprise.

- **Creditors:** Persons and/or other entities who have to be paid by an enterprise for providing goods and services on credit are called creditors.
- **Receivables:** Receivables refer to a business concern's claims to future collection of cash or other assets. In other words, receivables are assets of a concern in the form of debts or monetary obligations owed to it from debtors or customers.
- **Payables:** Payables refer to the debts owed by a business concern to its creditors or suppliers. Payables are liabilities.
- **Journal:** A journal is a book of original entry in which business transactions are entered in chronological order. A record of a single business transaction is called a journal entry.
- **Ledger:** A ledger is the book in which all journal entries, are classified into accounts, are posted.

1.6 SYSTEMS OF ACCOUNTING

An Accounting System refers to the way or method of recording business transactions in the books of accounts of a business concern. Based on the system of recording transactions, accounting systems are classified in two types:

1. Single Entry System, and
2. Double Entry System

A brief explanation of both systems follows:

1.6.1 Single Entry System

Though the Double Entry system of accounting is more popular system of accounting, some small business proprietors still use the single entry system for accounting. It is a system of accounting under which only one aspect (debit or credit) of the transaction is recorded. It is usually used by small concerns which have very few transactions.

The Single Entry system is considered an incomplete and unscientific system of entry, as all business transactions are not recorded under it. Usually, only cash, bank, and a few debtors and creditors accounts are maintained under this system.

1.6.2 Double Entry System

The Double Entry system of accounting is more scientific and systematic method of accounting and hence is popularly used by big and small business organisations all over the world.

This system is based on the premise that every business transaction has two aspects, i.e., the receiving aspect or debit aspect, and the giving aspect or the credit aspect. Each of these aspects of every transaction affects two accounts in opposite ways (increase or decrease in monetary terms). Therefore, under this system, a complete record of both the aspects of every transaction (i.e., debit and credit) is maintained.

Accounting Equation

The double entry system of accounting is based on accounting equations where the relationship between assets, liabilities, and capital can be expressed in form of an equation. The accounting equation signifies that the assets of a business are always equal to the total of its liabilities and capital (owner's equity).

The accounting equation is:

Assets = Liabilities + Capital

As the accounting equation depicts the fundamental relationship among the components of the balance sheet, it is also called the balance sheet equation.

(A detailed explanation of the Double Entry System of Accounting is available in Chapter 3 of this book.)

1.7 CLASSIFICATION OF ACCOUNTS

The essential function of accounting is to record transactions to ascertain the financial status of a company as on a particular date. The usual transactions of a business are:

- Purchase of goods, either as raw material for further processing or as finished goods for resale
- Payment of expenses incurred towards business
- Sale of goods or services
- Receipts, in cash or by cheque
- Other payments, in cash or by cheque

In order to record transactions, ledger accounts are created.

The accounts can be classified into three types, namely, Real accounts, Personal accounts and Nominal accounts.

1.7.1 Real Accounts

Real accounts are accounts maintained as assets owned or possessed by the business. Real accounts include both tangible (things that can be touched) and intangible (things that cannot be touched) accounts. Examples: Buildings, Furniture, Cash, Purchases, Sales, Goodwill, etc.

1.7.2 Personal Accounts

Personal accounts are the accounts of persons with whom the business is required to deal with. Personal accounts are further classified as:

- **Natural Personal Accounts:** Accounts of individuals or natural persons. Examples: Ram's account, Vikram's account, etc.
- **Artificial Personal Accounts:** Accounts of companies, banks or other institutions (not persons). Examples: State Bank of India, Mahendra Club, etc.
- **Representative Personal Accounts**: Represnsentative Personal Accounts refer to accounts that satisfy the following two conditions:
  (i) it relates to the particular head of expenditure or income (nominal account), and
  (ii) it represents persons to whom it is payable or from whom it is receivable. Examples: Outstanding Salaries, Pre-paid Insurance, etc.

1.7.3 Nominal Accounts

Nominal accounts are accounts where income and expenses are recorded. Examples: Sales, Rent expenses, Salary expenses, etc.

Note: All those accounts which are not personal accounts (ie., real and nominal accounts) are called impersonal accounts.

All accounts can be broadly classified under the following **five** groups:

- Assets – Examples: buildings, stock, debtors
- Liabilities – Examples: loan, creditors
- Capital – Example: share capital of Rs. 100,000/-
- Revenue – Examples: commission received, dividend received
- Expenses – Examples: rent, salaries, electricity

Assets, liabilities, and capital are taken to the balance sheet. Revenue and expenditure accounts are shown in the profit and loss statement.

KEY TAKEAWAYS

- Accounting is the process of classifying, recording and reporting an enterprise's business transactions over a period of time.
- Financial Accounting is a branch of accounting that is primarily concerned with the preparation of financial statements, based on the business transactions, and communication of the same to person interested in the information.
- Accounting systems are classified into two types, namely, Single Entry System, and Double Entry System.
- The double entry system of accounting is based on the accounting equation, viz., Assets = Liabilities + Capital
- Accounts can be classified into three types, namely, Real accounts, Personal accounts and Nominal accounts.

PRACTICE EXERCISES

Section A: Review Questions

1. What do you understand by the term 'Financial Accounting'?
2. Discuss the advantages and limitation of accounting information.
3. Explain the three types of accounts with two examples each.
4. Differentiate between the terms 'profit and gain'.

5. Classify the following on the type of Account (Personal, Real or Nominal):

S. No.	Name of Account	Type of Account
1	Building Account	
2	Capital Account	
3	Outstanding Wages Account	
4	Cash Account	
5	Stationery Account	
6	Prepaid Insurance Account	
7	Dr. Ambedkar College Account	
8	Interest Account	
9	Vijay's Account	
10	Sales Account	

Section B: Multiple Choice Questions

Select the most appropriate answer from the choices given below:

1. _____ refers to the difference between business revenues and expense.
   - a. Expense
   - b. Liability
   - c. Asset
   - d. **Income**

2. Canara Bank account is an example of a _____.
   - a. Real Personal Account
   - b. **Artificial Personal Account**
   - c. Representative Personal Account
   - d. Natural Personal Account

3. A _____ is a book in which business transactions are first entered in a chronological order.
   - a. Asset
   - b. Account
   - c. **Journal**
   - d. Ledger

4. If Debtors : Creditors, then Profit :_____.
   - a. Gain
   - b. Expense
   - c. **Loss**
   - d. Income

5. Drawings _____ the investment of owners in a business concern.
   - a. Increase
   - b. **Decrease**
   - c. Double
   - d. Do not affect

Chapter 2

Principles, Concepts and Conventions of Accounting

LEARNING OBJECTIVES

After studying this chapter, you will understand:

- Need for Accounting Principles, Conventions And Concepts
- Fundamental Principles of Accounting
- Concepts of Accounting
- Conventions of Accounting

2.1 INTRODUCTION

Accounting is considered as the language of business. In other words, accounting is the language used by business enterprises to communicate its financial position with the world. So, this language must be understood by all and there are certain uniform guidelines and standards that are followed as a part of accounting practice. Such rules of action are adopted universally, while recording accounting transactions and preparing accounting statements such rules are called 'Generally Accept Accounting Principles' (GAAP).

It may be noted that GAAP differs from country to country based on legislative requirements and accounting practices therefore.

The accounting principles are designed to ensure that financial statements are:

- **Accurate:** i.e., free from errors related to content and principle
- **Reliable:** i.e., represent the information that users consider it to represent
- **Timely:** i.e., available when required to support decision-making, and
- **Relevant:** i.e., applicable to the purpose required.

Accounting principles can be classified into two broad categories:

1. Accounting Concepts, and
2. Accounting Conventions

ACCOUNTING PRINCIPLES	
Accounting Concepts	Accounting Conventions
1. Money Measurement Concept	1. Convention of Consistency
2. Separate Entity Concept	2. Convention of Full Disclosure
3. Going Concern Concept	3. Convention of Conservatism
4. Cost Concept	4. Convention of Materiality
5. Dual Aspect Concept	
6. Periodicity Concept	
7. Objective Evidence Concept	
8. Matching Concept	
9. Realisation Concept	
10. Legal Aspect Concept	
11. Accrual Concept	

2.2 ACCOUNTING CONCEPTS

Accounting assumptions are premises or notions on which the accounting process is based. Also called 'Accounting Concepts', these assumptions form the basis of systematic accounting practices. The following are some important accounting concepts:

1. **Money Measurement Concept:** In accounting, all transactions are measured by using a common unit of measurement, which is money. Under the money measurement concept, only those transactions or events which can be measured or expressed in terms of money are recorded. Hence, factors such as the skill of the human resources, employer-employee relationship cannot be recorded in books of accounts in spite of their importance to the success of a business.

2. **Separate Entity Concept:** The business entity concept views the business as an entity, separate from its owners, i.e. business is assumed to have a distinct entity (existence) other than the existence of its proprietors. Thus, if an owner of a business is interested in playing badminton and so pays a subscription as a member of a local badminton club, this activity will be considered as completely outside the activities of the business. Such personal transactions will be kept separate from the accounts of the business. Based on this concept, a firm can sue and also be sued in its own name.

3. **Going-Concern Concept:** The going-concern concept, also known as the Continue of Activity Concept, assumes that a business concern will continue to exist for a long period. Thus, transactions are recorded on the assumption that a business will remain in operation long enough for all its current plans to be carried out.

4. **Cost Concept:** As per the cost concept or historical cost concept, cost of assets should be recorded at their original acquisition cost (cost price). This is an accounting concept which is used only for fixed assets. For example, if a piece of furniture is purchased for Rs. 50,000, it must be recorded in the books of the company at the invoiced and paid price of Rs. 50,000 even after two years.

5. **Dual-Aspect Concept:** Every business transaction involves a dual or double aspect of equal value. Under the dual-aspect concept, both these debit and credit aspects of a transaction are recorded. For instance, when a business

purchases goods for cash, it receives goods of some value and gives cash of equal value.

6. **Periodicity Concept:** The periodicity concept, also called the time interval concept, requires business enterprises to produce financial statements at set time intervals. As per this concept, financial statements are generated at relatively short periods such as a year or quarter, so that performance can be measured and compared.

7. **Objective Evidence Concept:** According to the objective evidence concept, all accounting entries should be evidenced and supported by business documents such as invoices, vouchers, and so on. Such documents serve as evidence in a court of law.

8. **Matching Concept:** According to the matching concept, the revenue that is reported must be set off against the expenses incurred to generate revenues during the accounting period. This gives a true picture of the profit earned during that period.

9. **Realisation Concept:** The realisation concept deals with how revenue is recognised by a business. Revenue is recognised when goods and services are delivered in quantities/amounts that are reasonably certain to be realised.

10. **Legal Aspect Concept:** According to the legal aspect concept, all accounting records and statements must conferm to legal requirements, i.e. accounting records should be maintained and statements should be prepared as prescribed by law.

11. **Accrual Concept:** Under the accrual concept of accounting, revenue is recognised only when earned rather than when due or collected, and expenses when incurred rather than when paid. Thus, transactions are recorded on the basis of income earned or expense incurred, irrespective of actual receipt or payment. For example, the salary of an employee becomes due from the first of the month, while it is paid at the end of the month.

2.3   ACCOUNTING CONVENTIONS

Accounting Conventions refer to customs and traditions followed by accountants in preparing accounting statements. In other words, these are guidelines for preparing accounting statements.

1. **Consistency:** According to convention of consistency, accounting practices and policies of a business entity must be consistent from one period to another.

2. **Full Disclosure:** According to the full disclosure convention, accounts should be prepared in such a way that all material information, including facts and figures, is clearly disclosed. The disclosure of financial information is useful to different parties interested in the progress and developments of an enterprise.

3. **Conservatism:** The convention of conservatism is related to the policy of playing safe. It states that uncertainties and risks inherent in business transactions should be given proper consideration.

4. **Materiality:** Under the convention of materiality any item should be regarded important (i.e., material) if there is reason to believe that its knowledge would influence the decision of the user of the information. Thus, all unimportant items are either left out or merged with other items.

KEY TAKEAWAYS

- Rules of action adopted universally while recording accounting transactions and preparing accounting statements are called Accounting Principles.

- Accounting principles can be classified into two broad categories called Accounting Concepts and Accounting Conventions.

- Accounting Concepts are assumptions that form the basis of systematic accounting practices.

- Accounting conventions are customs and traditions that guide accountants in preparing accounting statements.

PRACTICE EXERCISES
Section A: Review Questions
1. What is the purpose of Accounting Principles?
2. Differentiate between Accounting Concepts and Accounting Conventions.
3. Briefly explain the Objective Evidence Concept.

Section B: Multiple Choice Questions
Select the most appropriate answer from the choices given below:

1. 'The owners of a business enterprise can rely on the regularity with which the reporting of financial information takes place.' – Which accounting concept does this statement refer to?
   a. Separate Entity Concept
   b. Going Concern Concept
   c. Cost Concept Dual Aspect Concept
   d. **Periodicity Concept**

2. Under which accounting concept can a company sue a debtor?
   a. Going Concern Concept
   b. Legal Aspect Concept
   c. **Separate Entity Concept**
   d. Accrual Concept

3. Anand, an accountant at a company, recorded the cost of land purchased in the year 2013 for Rs. 50 lakh as Rs. 80,000 in 2016, as he felt that it is the current market price. Which accounting concept did Anand violate?
   a. Going Concern Concept
   b. **Cost Concept**
   c. Dual Aspect Concept
   d. Periodicity Concept

4. The _____ is the recording and measurement rule that provides the basis for double entry system of book-keeping.

    a. **Dual aspect concept**
    b. Going Concern Concept
    c. Cost Concept
    d. Accrual Concept

5. The practice of considering bad and doubtful debts in the books of accounts before ascertaining the profit is based on the Convention of _____.

    a. Consistency
    b. Full Disclosure
    c. **Conservatism**
    d. Materiality

Chapter 3

Recording Procedure in Accounting

LEARNING OBJECTIVES

After studying this chapter, you will understand:

- Meaning of Transaction
- Phases of Accounting Cycle
- Meaning and Uses of Voucher
- Different Methods of Recording Business Transactions
- How to Journalise Day to Day Business Transactions
- How to Record Compound Journal Entry
- Meaning of Ledger & Posting
- Rules of Ledger Posting
- How to Post Journal Entries into ledger/Book of Final Entry
- How to Prepare Trial Balance
- Meaning of Subsidiary Books
- Different Types of Subsidiary Books
- How to Record Transactions in Subsidiary Books
- Meaning of Journal Proper
- Type of transactions recorded in Journal Proper

3.1 INTRODUCTION

This chapter deals with the phases of the Accounting Cycle like recording, classifying and summarising of financial transactions. The first step is to identify the transactions that should be recorded and prepare the source documents which are, in turn, recorded in the book of original entry called journal. The transactions are then posted to individual accounts in the principal book called ledger. Finally, the balance amounts from the different ledger accounts are transferred to the Trial Balance.

3.2 DIFFERENT PHASES OF ACCOUNTING CYCLE

Accounting is the art of recording, classifying and summarising the financial transactions and presenting the useful information like financial performance, financial position to internal person like management and external person like owners/stockholders and vendors.

Different phases of the Accounting cycle are:

1. **Recording of Financial Transactions:** Transactions are recorded in the book of original entry called Journal Book.
2. **Classifying the Financial Transactions:** The recorded transactions are next posted to the Ledger.
3. **Summarising the Financial Transactions:** Once the Posting is complete, reports like Trial Balance, Profit & Loss Account and Balance Sheet are prepared.
4. **Analysis of the results:** After preparation of reports financial performance and position of the company is analysed.

3.3 BUSINESS TRANSACTIONS AND SOURCE DOCUMENT

3.3.1 Business Transaction

A Business Transaction is an event or happening which takes place between the business and clients, suppliers and others with whom they do the business and this event will change the financial statements of the business. For example, when you purchase the goods for cash, your cash balance reduces and the stock balance increases. This transaction will involve the aspect of 'give and take'. Thus, business transactions are exchanges of economic consideration between parties and have two-fold effects that are recorded in at least two accounts.

3.3.2 Source Document or Voucher

Business transactions should be evidenced by appropriate documents such as cash memo, invoice, sales bill, pay-in slip, cheque, salary slip, and so on. A document which provides evidence of the transactions is called the source document or voucher.

3.4 RECORDING BUSINESS TRANSACTIONS

Recording of financial transaction is the first step in the accounting cycle. Business concerns everyday are involved in making Purchases, Sales, Payments to Vendors, Receiving Payments from customers on a day to day basis. If any one of the transactions is not recorded then the final financial statements and business financial position of the company will be wrongly interpreted. *For example:* A company sells goods for ₹ 50,000 and receives cash immediately; if this transaction is not recorded, then the income statement will give a wrong picture. Hence, it is very important to record the day to day transactions.

3.4.1 Methods of Recording Business Transactions

Under the double-entry system of accounting, one can record the day to day business transactions in the books of accounts in two ways or methods, based on their size of the business and the number of business transactions recorded by the business concern.

The two methods of recording business transactions are:
- Conventional Method or Theoretical Method
- Modern Method, Practical Method or English Method

3.4.1.1 Conventional Method or Theoretical Method

This method is followed by the small scale business concerns, who have less number of transactions to record in the books of accounts.

Under Conventional Method the following steps are considered while recording the business transactions in books of accounts

Step 1: Firstly, business transactions are recorded in the Journal, which is also called as *Book of Original Entry.*

Step 2: Secondly, the business transactions recorded in the Journal are posted or transferred to the Ledger, which is also called as *Book of Final Entry.* All the ledger accounts are closed periodically

Step 3: Thirdly, by calculating the totals of debit and credit sides of a ledger, the balanced figure or the difference between the sum of credits and debits is listed in the statement called Trial Balance.

Note: The left out amount (Negative or positive) in the ledger account or the difference between the debits and credits in the ledger at the end of the accounting period is known as Closing Balance

---

Step 4: Fourthly, final accounts like Profit & Loss Account and Balance Sheet are prepared from the Trial Balance.

Step 5: After the preparation of Trial Balance, Profit & Loss Account and Balance Sheet, the interpreted Accounting Information is communicated to the end users like Vendors, Customers, Investors and Management etc.

3.4.1.2 *Modern Method, Practical Method or English Method*

This method is followed by large scale business concerns, who have more number of transactions to record in the books of accounts.

Under Modern Method the following steps are considered while recording the business transactions in books of accounts

Step 1: Firstly, business transactions are recorded in the number of books of original entry called Subsidiary Books or Special Journals.

Step 2: Secondly, the business transactions recorded in the Subsidiary Books are posted or transferred to the Ledger, which is also called as *Book of Final Entry.*

Step 3: Thirdly, by calculating the totals of debit and credit sides of a ledger, the balanced figure or the difference between the sum of credits and debits is listed in the statement called Trial Balance.

Step 4: Fourthly, final accounts like Profit & Loss Account and Balance Sheet are prepared from the Trial Balance.

Step 5: After the preparation of Trial Balance, Profit & Loss Account and Balance Sheet, the interpreted Accounting Information is communicated to the end users like Vendors, Customers, Investors and Management etc.

3.4.2 Recording of Business Transactions in Journal/ Book of Original Entry

In accounting systems, transactions recorded in source documents are analysed and recorded for the first time in a journal, also called the book of original entry. Journal is a day book or a daily record wherein the transactions are recorded in chronological order, i.e. as and when they take place.

A **Specimen journal** is shown below in Table 1.1.

Journal				
Date	Particulars	L.F	Dr.	Cr.

Table 1.1 Specimen of Journal

Details of specimen of journal are:

- **Date:** The date column is used to record the date on which a particular transaction takes place.

- **Particulars:** In the particulars column the account title to be debited is written in the first line, beginning from the left corner and the word **Dr.** is written at the end of the column. The account title to be credited is written in the second line, leaving a margin on the left with a prefix **To.** Below the account titles, a brief explanation of the transaction is given which is called **narration**. After the narration, a line is drawn in the particulars column which indicates the end of recording of the specific journal entry.

- **Ledger Folio (L.F):** In the Ledger Folio (L.F.) column, the page number of the ledger book on which relevant account appears is recorded.

- **Debit (Dr.):** The debit column is meant to record the amount against the account to be debited.

- **Credit (Cr.):** The credit column is meant to record the amount against the account to be credited.

The process of recording transactions in the journal is called journalising. The process of transferring a journal entry to individual accounts is called posting. This sequence causes the journal to be called the **Book of original entry** and the ledger account as the **Book of Final Entry**.

3.4.2.1 *Use of Debit and Credit*

Every transaction involves two aspects – give and take. In the double entry system of accounting, every transaction is recorded in at least two accounts. While recording transactions, the total amount debited and credited must be equal. In accounting, the terms debit (abbreviated as Dr.) and credit (abbreviated as Cr.) indicate whether the transactions are to be recorded on the left or right of the account.

3.4.2.2 *Rules of Debit and Credit*

Two fundamental rules are followed to record the changes in these accounts.

For recording changes in assets or expenses (losses)

- **Debit:** Increase in assets, increase in expenses (losses)
- **Credit:** Decrease in assets, decrease in expenses (losses)

For recording changes in liabilities, capital, or revenues (gains)

- **Debit:** Decrease in liabilities, decrease in capital, decrease in revenue (gain)

- **Credit:** Increase in liabilities, increase in capital, increase in revenues (gains). The following table 1.2, summarises the rules applicable to different kinds of accounts.

	Increase	Decrease
Asset	Debit	Credit
Liability	Credit	Debit
Income/Revenue	Credit	Debit
Expense/Losses	Debit	Credit
Capital/Stock Holders' Equity	Credit	Debit
Dividends	Debit	Credit

Table 1.2 Rules of Credit and Debit

The following illustration will help you to understand the Rules of Debit and Credit.

Illustration 1: Application of Rules of Debit and Credit

1. As on 1st April, 2016, Deepak commenced the business with ₹ 50,000

2. As on 1st April 2016, Ashok bought furniture for his business by paying cash ₹ 20,000.

3. As on 2nd April 2016, purchased goods from Pradeep on credit for ₹ 10,000

4. As on 3rd April 2016, sold good to Murthy Traders on credit ₹ 5,000

Solution:

1. Deepak commenced the business with ₹ 50,000

   This transaction increases the capital as well as the cash. Increase in assets is debited and increase in capital is credited. Therefore, record the transaction with debit to cash account and credit to Deepak's capital account.

Journal					
Date 2016	Particulars		L.F	Dr.	Cr.
Apr. 1	Cash Account	Dr.		50,000	
	To Capital Account				50,000
	(Being cash invested by the proprietor)				

2. Ashok bought furniture for his business by paying cash ₹ 20,000.

   This transaction increases furniture (assets) and decreases cash by ₹ 20,000. The increase in assets is debited and the decrease in cash is credited. Therefore, record the transaction with debit to furniture account and credit to cash account.

Journal					
Date 2016	Particulars		L.F	Dr.	Cr.
Apr. 1	Furniture Account	Dr.		20,000	
	To Cash Account				20,000
	(Being furniture bought for business use)				

3. Purchased goods from Pradeep Traders on credit for ₹ 10,000

   This transaction increases purchases (increases assets) and liabilities (Pradeep Traders as creditors). Increase in assets is debited and increase in liabilities is credited. Therefore,

record the transaction with debit to purchases account and credit to Samrat Traders account.

Journal					
Date 2016	Particulars		L.F	Dr.	Cr.
Apr. 2	Purchase Account	Dr.		10,000	
	To Pradeep Traders Account				10,000
	(Being goods purchased from Pradeep Traders on credit)				

4. Sold good to Murthy Traders on credit ₹ 5,000

   This transaction increases sales (decreases assets) and assets (Murthy Traders as debtors). Decrease in assets is credited and increase in assets is debited. Therefore, record the transaction with credit to sales account and debit to Murthy Traders account.

Journal					
Date 2016	Particulars		L.F	Dr.	Cr.
Apr. 3	Murthy Traders Account	Dr.		50,000	
	To Sales Account				50,000
	(Being goods sold to Murthy Traders on credit)				

3.4.2.3 Steps to be followed while recording the Business Transactions in Journal

While recording Business Transactions in a journal, one must follow the below given steps.

1. **Identify Two Accounts Involved in Transaction:** Every Business Transactions involves two accounts. One of the account is the receiver of the benefit and the other account is giver of the benefit **(While identifying the accounts involved in the transactions, ignore the account of the firm because business transactions are recorded in the books of firms)**

2. **Identify Nature of Account Involved in Transaction:** After identifying the two accounts involved in the transaction, next identify the nature or find out to which classes of accounts these two accounts belong.

3. **Apply Rules of Debit and Credit:** Next step is to find out which account should be debited and credited

4. **Recording the Transaction in Journal:** Finally, after identifying the account to be debited and account to be credited, the entry should be recorded in the Journal or Book of Original Entry, by debiting the account which has to be debited and crediting the account which has to be credited.

The journal entry is the basic record of a business transaction. It may be simple or compound. When two accounts are involved to record a transaction, it is called a simple journal entry.

Illustration 2: Application of the Steps to be followed while recording Business Transactions in Journal

1. As on 21st May, 2016, Ashok commenced the business with ₹ 40,000

2. As on 21st May 2016, bought furniture for business by paying cash ₹ 10,000.
3. As on 22nd May 2016, purchased goods from Shuhas on credit for ₹ 5,000
4. As on 23rd May 2016, sold good to TT Traders on credit ₹ 2,000

Solution:

The below given table shows the Steps to be followed before recording the transaction in Journal or book of original entry.

Serial No.	Step 1 Two Accounts Involved in the Transaction	Step 2 Nature of Account Involved in Transaction	Step 3 Rules of Debit and Credit	Accounts to be Debited	Accounts to be Credited
1	a. Cash A/c b. Capital A/c	a. Asset A/c b. Capital A/c	Debit Increase in an Asset Credit Increase in a Capital	Cash A/c	Capital A/c
2	a. Furniture A/c b. Cash A/c	a. Asset A/c b. Asset A/c	Debit Increase in an Asset Credit Decrease in an Asset	Furniture A/c	Cash A/c
3	a. Purchase A/c b. Shuhas A/c	a. Expense A/c b. Liability A/c	Debit Increase in an Expense Credit Increase in a Liability	Purchase A/c	Shuhas A/c
4	a. TT Traders A/c b. Sales A/c	a. Asset A/c b. Income A/c	Debit Increase in an Asset Credit Increase in an Income	TT Traders A/c	Sales A/c

After following the above steps, the entries can be recorded in Journal as shown below:

	Journal			
Date 2016	Particulars	L.F	Dr.	Cr.
May 21	Cash Account Dr		40,000	
	To Capital Account			40,000
	(Being cash invested by the proprietor)			
May 21	Furniture Account Dr		10,000	
	To Cash Account			10,000
	(Being furniture bought for business use)			
May 22	Purchase Account Dr		5,000	
	To Shuhas Account			5,000
	(Being goods purchased from Shuhas Traders on credit)			
May 23	TT Traders Account Dr		2,000	
	To Sales Account			2,000
	(Being goods sold to TT Traders on credit)			

Illustration 3: *TARA Enterprises furnishes the following information regarding transactions for the month of April, 2016.*

Date (2016)	Transactions
Apr 1	Business started with cash of ₹ 5,00,000
Apr 5	Goods purchased from Mohan on credit for ₹ 50,000
Apr 6	Stationery purchased for cash ₹ 4,000
Apr 10	Opened a bank account with Kotak Bank by depositing cash of ₹ 1,00,000
Apr 11	Goods sold to Siva Manufactures on credit for ₹ 50,000
Apr 12	Received a cheque of ₹ 50,000 from Siva Manufactures
Apr 13	Insurance paid by cheque ₹ 10,000
Apr 14	Sold goods to Nidhi Manufactures ₹ 20,000
Apr 15	Nidhi pays ₹ 20,000 cash
Apr 16	Goods purchased for ₹ 30,000 on credit from Gita Traders
Apr 17	Purchased office furniture for ₹ 10,000 in cash
Apr 18	Goods costing ₹ 5,000 given as charity
Apr 19	Paid ₹ 10,000 towards rent by cash
Apr 30	Cash withdrawn for household purposes ₹ 5,000

Record the above given business transactions in Journal

Solution:

	Books of TARA Traders Journal			
Date 2016	Particulars	L.F	Dr.	Cr.
Apr 1	Cash A/c Dr		5,00,000	
	To Capital A/c			5,00,000
	(Being cash used by Proprietor)			
Apr 5	Purchase A/c Dr		50,000	
	To Mohan A/c			50,000
	(Being goods purchased on credit)			
Apr 6	Stationery A/c Dr		4,000	
	To Cash A/c			4,000
	(Being purchase of stationery for cash)			
Apr 10	Kotak A/c Dr		1,00,000	
	To Cash A/c			1,00,000
	(Being opened a bank A/c with Kotak)			
Apr 11	Siva Manufacturers A/c Dr		50,000	
	To Sales A/c			50,000
	(Being goods sold to Siva on credit)			
Apr 12	Kotak Bank A/c Dr		50,000	
	To Siva Manufactures A/c			50,000
	(Being Cheque received from Siva)			
Apr 13	Insurance Premium A/c Dr		10,000	

			Dr.	Cr.
	To Kotak Bank A/c			10,000
	(Being Insurance premium paid by cheque)			
Apr. 14	Nidhi Manufacturers A/c	Dr.	20,000	
	To Sales A/c			20,000
	(Being goods sold to Nidhi on credit)			
Apr. 15	Cash A/c	Dr.	20,000	
	To Nidhi Manufacturers A/c			20,000
	(Being Cash Received from Nidhi)			
Apr. 16	Purchase A/c	Dr.	30,000	
	To Gita Traders A/c			30,000
	(Being goods purchased on credit)			
Apr. 17	Furniture A/c	Dr.	10,000	
	To Cash A/c			10,000
	(Being furniture purchased)			
Apr. 18	Charity A/c	Dr.	5,000	
	To Purchase A/c			5,000
	(Being goods given as charity)			
Apr. 19	Rent A/c	Dr.	10,000	
	To Cash A/c			10,000
	(Being rent paid)			
Apr. 30	Drawings A/c	Dr.	5,000	
	To Cash A/c			5,000
			8,64,000	8,64,000

Note: When there are many transactions recorded in a number of pages in the journal book, then at the end of each page of the journal book, the amount columns are totalled and carried forward (c/f) to the next page where such amounts are recorded as brought forward (b/f) balances.

3.4.3   Compound Journal Entry

A journal entry in which more than one debit account, more than one credit account or more than one of both debit and credit accounts are involved in the transactions on the same date related to one particular account or one particular Nature of account is termed as Compound Entry.

Instead of recording several Journal entries we can record the transaction which involves more than one debit or credit in a single journal entry called Compound Journal Entry.

Compound Journal Entry can be recorded in any one of the following manner.

1. One account will be debited and multiple accounts will be credited.

2. Multiple accounts will be debited and one accounts will be credited.

3. Multiple accounts will be debited and multiple accounts will be credited.

Illustration 4: Recording business transactions in Compound Journal.

1. As on 1st June 2016, payment made to Raghav for ₹ 10,000 and discount received for ₹ 1,000

2. As on 2nd   June 2016, cash of ₹ 20,000 was received from Mohan and discount allowed for ₹ 2,000

3. As on 4th June 2016, running business was purchased by Rakesh and the following assets and liabilities details are shown below.

    Cash ₹ 10,000; Furniture; ₹ 5,000; Land ₹ 20,000; Creditors ₹ 7,000; Bank Overdraft ₹ 2,000; Capital ₹ 26,000

Solution:

Compound Journal Entry					
Date 2016	Particulars		L.F	Dr.	Cr.
Jun. 1	Raghav A/c	Dr.		11,000	
	To Cash A/c				10,000
	To Discount Received A/c				1,000
	(Being payment made to Raghav after discount)				
Jun. 2	Cash A/c	Dr.		20,000	
	Discount Allowed A/c	Dr.		2,000	
	To Mohan's A/c				22,000
	(Being cash received from Mohan and discount allowed)				
Jun. 4	Cash A/c	Dr.		10,000	
	Furniture A/c	Dr.		5,000	
	Land A/c	Dr.		20,000	
	To Bank Overdraft A/c				2,000
	To Creditors A/c				7,000
	To Capital A/c				26,000
	(Being commencement of business by taking over)				
				68,000	68,000

Illustration 5: TARA Enterprises furnishes the following information regarding transactions for the month of July, 2016.

Date (2016)	Transactions
Jul. 5	Purchased goods from Mohan for ₹ 1, 00,000 for cash 80,000 and on credit ₹20,000.
Jul. 6	Sold Goods for ₹ 50,000 to RK Traders for cash ₹ 30,000 and on credit ₹ 20,000.
Jul. 15	Cash payment made to Mohan for ₹20,000.
Jul. 17	Cash of ₹ 20,000 was received from RK Traders.
Jul. 18	Purchased goods from Mohan for ₹ 1, 00,000 for cash and discount of ₹ 5,000 was received.
Jul. 20	Sold goods to TT Traders for ₹ 2, 00,000 for cash and discount of ₹ 10,000 was allowed.

Solution:

Date 2016	Particulars		L.F	Dr.	Cr.
Jul 5	Purchase A/c	Dr.		1,00,000	
	To Cash A/c				80,000
	To Mohan's A/c				20,000
	(Being goods purchased on cash and credit from Mohan)				
Jul 6	Cash Account	Dr.		30,000	
	RK Traders A/c	Dr.		20,000	
	To Sales A/c				50,000
	(Being goods sold on credit and cash to RK Traders)				
Jul 15	Mohan's A/c			20,000	
	To Cash A/c				20,000
	(Being Cash paid to Mohan for the purchases made)				
Jul 17	Cash A/c			20,000	
	To RK Traders A/c				20,000
	(Being cash received from RK Traders)				
Jul 18	Purchase A/c			1,00,000	
	To Mohan's A/c				95,000
	To Discount Received A/c				5,000
	(Being goods purchased from Mohan and received discount)				
Jul 20	TT Traders A/c			2,00,000	
	To Sales A/c				1,90,000
	To Discount Received A/c				10,000
				4,90,000	4,90,000

3.4.4 Opening Entry

Opening entry is the first entry recorded in the Journal, in case of continuous business the assets and Liabilities appearing in the previous year's balance sheet will have to be bought forward to the current year, these details are recorded in the Journal and this is called as Opening Entry.

Even in case of new business when the capital is introduced by the proprietor into the business, this will be the first entry to be recorded in the Journal.

Rule of recording Opening Entry is *all assets accounts are debited* and *all liabilities accounts are credited* and *the excess of Assets or Debits over Liabilities or Credits represents Capital* and it is *credited to the Capital Account*. Thus in an Illustration or question, if the capital Balance is not given then the same can be found out by the following Accounting Equation:

Assets – Liabilities = Capital

The opening entry illustration is given below for clear understanding.

Illustration 6: Record the opening entry as on 1st April, 2016 on the basis of the following information taken from the business of KAR Traders.

Closing Balance as on 31st March, 2016	Amounts (₹)
Cash in Hand	5,000 Dr.
Stock of Goods	10,000 Dr.
Plant	20,000 Dr.
Sundry Debtors	15,000 Dr.
Land and Machinery	20,000 Dr.
Sundry Creditors	25,000 Cr.

Solution:

	Journal				
Date 2016	Particulars		L.F	Dr.	Cr.
Apr 1	Cash A/c	Dr.		5,000	
	Stock of Goods	Dr.		10,000	
	Plant	Dr.		20,000	
	Sundry Debtors	Dr.		15,000	
	Land and Machinery	Dr.		20,000	
	To Sundry Creditors				25,000
	To Capital A/c (Balancing Figure)				45,000
	(Being Balances bought forwards from the last year)				
				70,000	70,000

Note: Capital A/c Balancing figure shows as ₹ 45,000, because Total Asset is ₹ 70,000 and Total Liability is ₹ 25,000. After applying Accounting Equation (Assets – Liability = Capital), we will get the Capital A/c values as ₹ 45,000.

Illustration 7: Record the following transaction in Books of TS Traders as on 1st April 2016

1. The following table shows the closing balance of TS Traders.

Opening Entry	
Closing Balance as on 31st March, 2016	Amounts (₹)
Cash in Hand	10,000 Dr.
Stock of Goods	11,000 Dr.
Plant	10,000 Dr.
Cash in Bank	20,000 Dr.
Sundry Debtors	10,000 Dr.
Land and Machinery	10,000 Dr.
Sundry Creditors	25,000 Cr.
Loan from JK	20,000 Cr.

2. As on 2nd April 2016, purchased goods for cash ₹ 50,000 and discount of ₹ 5,000 was received from the Supplier on the total purchase value.

3. As on 3rd of April 2016, sold goods to TMB traders on credit for ₹ 20,000

4. As on 4th of April 2016, sold goods to TR Traders for cash ₹ 20,000 and discount of ₹ 2,000 was allowed on total sales value.

5. As on 10th of April 2016, received Cash ₹ 20,000 from TMB Traders

6. As on 23rd of April 2016, interest received from Madhukar ₹ 1,000

Journal				
Date 2016	Particulars	L.F	Dr.	Cr.
Apr. 1	Cash in Hand A/c Dr.		10,000	
	Stock of goods A/c Dr.		11,000	
	Plant A/c Dr.		10,000	
	Cash in Bank A/c Dr.		20,000	
	Sundry Debtors A/c Dr.		10,000	
	Land and Machinery A/c Dr.		10,000	
	To Sundry Creditors A/c			25,000
	To Loan from JK A/c			20,000
	To Capital A/c (Balancing figure)			26,000
	(Being balances bought forward from last year.)			
Apr. 2	Purchase A/c Dr.		50,000	
	To Cash A/c			45,000
	To Discount Received A/c			5,000
	(Being Purchased goods for cash and received discount.)			
Apr. 3	TMB Traders A/c Dr.		20,000	
	To Sales A/c			20,000
	(Being goods sold to TMB Traders on credit.)			
Apr. 4	Cash A/c Dr.		18,000	
	Discount Allowed A/c Dr.		2,000	
	To Sales A/c			20,000
	(Being goods sold for cash and discount was allowed.)			
Apr. 10	Cash A/c Dr.		20,000	
	To TMB Traders			20,000
	(Being cash received from TMB Traders.)			
Apr. 23	Cash A/c Dr.		1,000	
	To Interest Received A/c			1,000
	(Being interest received from Madhukar)			
			1,82,000	1,82,000

3.5   LEDGER

Ledger is the principal book of the accounting system and is also called the Book of Final Entry. This Book contains all the accounts of a business or all the accounts of a particular type. In a ledger, the transactions of the same nature are classified and grouped together at one place in the form of accounts. Ledgers may be in the form of a bound register, cards, or separate sheets maintained in a loose leaf binder.

3.5.1   Need of Ledger

A well-maintained accounting system plays a significant role in the growth of an organisation. The ledger, is a record of the transactions, assumes great importance in the process. The net result of all transactions in respect of a particular account on a given date can be ascertained only from the ledger.

For example, the organisation can ascertain the amount due from

a customer only from the ledger. Ledgers, thus act as a reference for the transactions of an organisation on any given date. Accounts are opened in the ledger in a specific order, facilitating easy posting and location. For example, accounts may be opened in the same order as they appear in the profit and loss account or balance sheet.

The format of the Ledger is shown below:

Dr.				Title of the Account				Cr.
Date 2016	Particulars	J.F	Amount (₹)		Date 2016	Particulars	J.F	Amount (₹)

The columns contain the following information:

♦   **Title of the account:** The name of the item is written at the top as the title of the account. The title of the account ends with the suffix, 'Account'.

♦   **Dr./Cr.:** Dr.is the debit side of the account, i.e. the left side and Cr. is the credit side of the account, i.e. the right side.

♦   **Date:** Year, month, and date of transactions are posted in chronological order in this column.

♦   **Particulars:** Name of the item with reference to the original book of entry is written on debit/credit side of the account.

♦   **Journal Folio (J.F.):** It records the page number of the original book of entry on which the relevant transaction is recorded. This column is filled in at the time of posting.

♦   **Amount:** It records the amount in numerical figures, corresponding to what has been entered in the amount column of the original book of entry.

3.5.2 Difference between Journal and Ledger

Journal and ledger are the most important books of the double entry system of accounting. The following table highlights the differences between a journal and a ledger.

Journal	Ledger
It is a Book of Original Entry or Primary Entry, as all transactions are first recorded in the Journal.	It is a Book of Final Entry or Secondary Entry, as all transactions are finally recorded in the Ledger.
It is the book for chronological record.	It is the book for analytical record.
Journal, as a book of source entry, gets greater importance as legal evidence.	Ledger gets lesser importance as legal evidence.
Transaction is the basis of classification of data.	Account is the basis of classification of data.
The process of recording in the journal is known as journalising.	The process of recording in the ledger is known as posting.
In the journal, information related to one particular account is not found in one place.	In the Ledger, the information related to one particular account is found in one place.
In journal, transactions are recorded every day, hence it is a daily record.	Ledger posting is done periodically like weekly, fortnightly, monthly or quarterly based on the requirement of the business concerns.
In Journal the values are totalled not balanced.	In the Ledger the values are balanced.

3.5.3   Classification of Ledger Accounts

Ledger accounts are classified into five categories. They are:

♦   Assets

♦   Liabilities

♦   Capital

♦   Revenues/gains

♦   Expense/losses

All these accounts may further be classified into two groups, namely:

- Permanent accounts (assets, liabilities, and capital accounts)
- Temporary accounts (revenue and expense accounts)

Permanent accounts are balanced and carried forward to the next accounting period. The temporary accounts are closed at the end of the accounting period by transferring them to the trading account and profit and loss account. All permanent accounts appear in the balance sheet.

3.5.4 Posting from Journal

The process of transferring entries from the books of original entry (journal) to the ledger is called posting. In other words, posting is the process of grouping all the transactions in respect to a particular account at one place for a meaningful conclusion and to further the accounting process. Depending on the requirement and convenience of the business, posting from the journal may be done periodically, i.e. weekly, fortnightly, or monthly.

The process of posting from journal to the ledger involves the following steps.

Step 1: Locate in the ledger, the account to be debited as entered in the journal.

Step 2: Enter the date of transaction in the date column on the debit side.

Step 3: In the particulars column, write the name of the account through which it has been debited in the journal. For example, sold books for cash ₹ 25,000. Now, in the cash account on the debit side in the particulars column, 'Books' is entered, signifying that cash is received from the sale of books. In the books account, in the ledger on the credit side in the particulars column, the word, cash is recorded. The same procedure is followed for all the entries recorded in the journal.

Step 4: Enter the page number of the journal in the folio column and in the journal, write the page number of the ledger on which a particular account appears.

Step 5: Enter the relevant amount in the amount column on the debit side. It may be noted that the same procedure is followed for making the entry on the credit side of that account to be credited. An account is opened only once the ledger and all entries relating to a particular account are posted on the debit side or credit side, as the case may be.

3.5.5 Rules of Posting

1. **Separate accounts should be opened:** In journal different accounts are recorded in the chronological manner, while posting these accounts into the Ledger a separate accounts should be maintained or opened. For Example a separate accounts may be opened for Sales, Purchase, Cash, Capital, Sales Returns and Purchases Returns etc.

2. **Particular Account which is debited in the Journal:** The particular account which is debited in Journal, should also be debited in the Ledger and a reference should be made for other account which is credited in the journal. For example, for Cash Purchases, the Purchase account should be debited in the Ledger and a reference should be given of the Cash account, which is credited in Ledger.

3. **Particular Account which is credited in the Journal:** The particular account which is credited in Journal, should also be credited in the Ledger and a reference should be made for other account which is debited in the journal. For example, for Cash Purchases, the Cash account should be credited in the Ledger and a reference should be given of the Purchase account in the Ledger.

From the above details we will come to know that the accounts which are debited and credited in Journal should also be debited and credited in the Ledger while posting and also proper reference should be given for the other account which is credited or debited in the Journal

The following illustration will demonstrate how the transactions are posted to Ledger from Journal i.e., how the transactions are moved from Book of original entry to Book of final entry.

Illustration 8: Record the following transactions in the journal and post them into the Ledger.

1. As on 2nd April 2016, purchased goods for cash ₹ 20,000.
2. As on 3rd April 2016, sold goods for cash ₹ 30,000.

Solution:

The above entries will be recorded in the books of original entry i.e. Journal as shown below;

Date 2016	Particulars		L.F	Dr.	Cr.
	Journal				
Apr 2	Purchase A/c	Dr		20,000	
	To Cash Account				20,000
	(Being purchased goods for cash)				
Apr 3	Cash A/c	Dr		30,000	
	To Sales A/c				30,000
	(Being goods sold for cash)				

In the Ledger three accounts will be opened that is Purchase A/c, Cash A/c and Sales A/c. In the Journal Purchase A/c is debited, hence while preparing the ledger the same account will be debited and the Cash account is credited in the Journal and the same account will be credited in the Ledger as shown below:

Purchase Account

Date 2016	Particulars	J.F	₹	Date 2016	Particulars	J.F	₹
Apr 2	Cash A/c		20,000				

Cash Account

Date 2016	Particulars		₹	Date 2016	Particulars		₹
Apr 3	Sales A/c		30,000	Apr 2	Purchase		20,000

Dr.	Sales Account					Cr.
Date 2016	Particulars		₹	Date 2016	Particulars	₹
				Apr. 3	Cash A/c	30,000

Dr.	Sales Account				Cr.
Date 2016	Particulars		Date 2016	Particulars	₹
			Apr. 23	By Cash A/c	20,000

Note: Purchase A/c is debited in Journal and the same is debited in the Ledger, Cash A/c is credited in the Journal (Purchase transaction) and the same is credited in Ledger.

Sales A/c is credited in the Journal and the same is credited in the Ledger, Cash A/c debited in the Journal (Sales transaction) and the same is debited in Ledger

3.5.6   'To' and 'By' Usage

While posting in the Ledger the words "To" and "By" are used regularly. "To" is used for the accounts which are to be debited in the Ledger and "By" is used for the accounts which are to be credited in the Ledger.

For Example: In the above illustration the first Ledger account shows the Cash A/c on the debit side of the ledger, here we can use "To Cash A/c" instead of Cash A/c, similarly in case of second ledger account purchase is credited in the ledger, here we can use "By Purchase A/c" instead of Purchase A/c.

The following illustration will explain how the word "To" and "By" are used while posting the Transaction into Ledger.

Illustration 9: Recording the following transactions in Journal and Post them into the Ledger, while posting use the words "To" and "By"

1.   As on 22nd April 2016, purchased goods for cash ₹ 10,000.
2.   As on 23rd April 2016, sold goods for cash ₹ 20,000.

Solution:

Journal					
Date 2016	Particulars		L.F	Dr.	Cr.
Apr. 22	Purchase A/c	Dr.		10,000	
	To Cash Account				10,000
	(Being purchased goods for cash)				
Apr. 23	Cash A/c	Dr.		20,000	
	To Sales A/c				20,000
	(Being goods sold for cash)				

Dr.	Purchase Account						Cr.
Date 2016	Particulars	J.F	₹	Date 2016	Particulars	J.F	₹
Apr. 22	To Cash A/c		10,000				

Dr.	Cash Account						Cr.
Date 2016	Particulars		₹	Date 2016	Particulars		₹
Apr. 23	To Sales A/c		20,000	Apr. 22	By Purchase		10,000

3.5.7   Balancing of Ledger Account

Transactions in the ledger Account are arranged in the classified manner. At a certain period like Monthly, Quarterly or Yearly, the business concern will be interested in knowing the position of the particular account, so to know the position of the Particular account we should total up the debits and credits separately and find out the net balance amount, this process of finding the net balance of a particular account after considering debits and credits of an account is termed as Balancing of Ledger Account.

So, there is the need to find out whether the particular Ledger account has received benefit more than it has given or it has given more benefit than it has received as on any particular date. In other words to find out the position of an account, it is very important to balance the account on the given date.

3.5.7.1 *Steps to be followed while balancing the Ledger Account*

1.   **Find out the difference between the debits and credits**: Total up both the sides of the account and find out the difference.

2.   **Enter the difference amount on the side of the account which is smaller with the reference:** Once the difference is found out enter the difference amount on the side of the account which is smaller with a reference stating that To Balance carried forward or carries down (c/f or c/d) to the next period. On the other side in the beginning of the next balancing period a reference is used to state that the opening balance has been brought forward or brought down (b/f or b/d), from the previous period.

Note: A ledger account will have a debit balance or a credit balance. If the credit side of the ledger account is more than its debit side total, then the difference is called as Credit balance. On the other side if the debit side of the account is more than its credit side total, then the difference is called as Debit Balance

The following illustration will demonstrate how the ledger accounts are balanced.

Illustration 10: Record the following transactions in the books of SP Traders and post them into Ledger and balance the accounts on 30th April 2016.

1.   As on 1st April 2016, Ashok started a business with a capital of ₹ 20,000.

2.   As on 2nd April 2016, purchased goods from SK Traders on credit for ₹ 10,000.

3.   As on 10th April 2016, paid cash of ₹ 10,000 to SK Traders.

4.   As on 12th April 2016, sold goods to Shobha Enterprises for ₹ 30,000

5. As on 15th April 2016, received cash of ₹ 30,000 from Shobha Enterprises.

6. As on 16th April 2016, purchase goods from SK Traders for ₹ 20,000

7. As on 17th April 2016, paid cash of ₹ 20,000 to SK Traders.

8. As on 18th April 2016, sold goods to Shobha Enterprises for ₹ 20,000

9. As on 30th April 2016, received a cash of ₹ 20,000 from Shobha Enterprises.

Solution:

Recording the transactions in the books of SP Traders for the month of April 2016.

Journal

Date 2016	Particulars		L.F	Dr.	Cr.
Apr 1	Cash A/c	Dr		20,000	
	To Capital A/c				20,000
	(Being Commencement of business)				
Apr 2	Purchase A/c	Dr		10,000	
	To SK Traders A/c				10,000
	(Being goods sold on credit to SK Traders)				
Apr 10	SK Traders A/c	Dr		10,000	
	To Cash A/c				10,000
	(Being Cash paid to SK Traders for the purchases made)				
Apr 12	Shobha Enterprises A/c	Dr		30,000	
	To Sales A/c				30,000
	(Being goods sold on credit)				
Apr 15	Cash A/c	Dr		30,000	
	To Shobha Enterprises A/c				30,000
	(Being cash received from Shobha Enterprises)				
	Total c/f			1,00,000	1,00,000
	Total b/f			1,00,000	1,00,000
Apr 16	Purchase A/c	Dr		20,000	
	To SK Traders A/c				20,000
	(Being goods sold on credit to SK Traders)				
Apr 17	SK Traders A/c	Dr		20,000	
	To Cash A/c				20,000
	(Being Cash paid to SK Traders for the purchases made)				
Apr 18	Shobha Enterprises A/c	Dr		20,000	
	To Sales A/c				20,000
	(Being goods sold on credit)				
Apr 30	Cash A/c	Dr		20,000	
	To Shobha Enterprises A/c				20,000
	(Being cash received from Shobha Enterprises)				
	Total			1,80,000	1,80,000

Posting in ledger

Dr.			Cash Account					Cr.
Date 2016	Particulars	J.F	₹	Date 2016	Particulars	J.F	₹	
Apr 1	To Capital A/c		20,000	Apr 10	By SK Traders A/c		10,000	
Apr 15	To Shobha Enterprises A/c		30,000	Apr 17	By SK Traders A/c		20,000	
Apr 30	To Shobha Enterprises A/c		20,000	Apr 30	By Balance c/d		40,000	
			70,000				70,000	
May 1	To Balance b/d		40,000					

Note: In the above Ledger Cash Account, we can find out that the cash account is having Debit Balance of ₹ 40,000 because the balance of the account is always known by the side which is greater, in the above account debit side is greater than the credit side.

			Capital Account				
Date 2016	Particulars	J.F	₹	Date 2016	Particulars	J.F	₹
Apr 30	To Balance c/d		20,000	Apr 1	By Cash A/c		20,000
			20,000				20,000
				May 1	By Balance b/d		20,000

Note: In the above Ledger Capital Account, we can find out that the capital account is having credit Balance of ₹ 20,000, because credit side of capital account is more than the debit side.

			Purchases Account				
Date 2016	Particulars	J.F	₹	Date 2016	Particulars	J.F	₹
Apr 2	To SK Traders A/c		10,000	Apr 30	By Balance c/d		30,000
Apr 16	To SK Traders A/c		20,000				
			30,000				30,000
May 1	To Balance b/d		30,000				

			SK Trader's Account				
Date 2016	Particulars	J.F	₹	Date 2016	Particulars	J.F	₹
Apr 10	To Cash A/c		10,000	Apr 2	By Purchase A/c		10,000
Apr 17	To Cash A/c		20,000	Apr 16	By Purchase A/c		20,000
			30,000				30,000

			Shobha Enterprises Account				
Date 2016	Particulars	J.F	₹	Date 2016	Particulars	J.F	₹
Apr 12	To Sales A/c		30,000	Apr 15	By Cash A/c		30,000
Apr 18	To Sales A/c		20,000	Apr 30	By Cash A/c		20,000
			50,000				50,000

			Sales Account				
Date 2016	Particulars	J.F	₹	Date 2016	Particulars	J.F	₹
Apr 30	By Balance c/d		50,000	Apr 12	By Shobha Enterprises		30,000
				Apr 18	By Shobha Enterprises		20,000
			50,000				50,000
				May 1	By Balance b/d		50,000

3.6   TRIAL BALANCE

In Trial Balance, the balances of various accounts (debit balances and credit balances) are listed in a sheet or a statement at the end of the accounting period. In the previous sections you have learnt how to record the transactions in Journal or Book of Original Entry and then posted these transactions in Ledger or Book of Final Entry and balanced the accounts, now to complete the accounting cycle, accounts have to be compiled by preparing a trial balance.

A trial balance is the conclusion of the accounting process. It is the link between primary and final accounting work. The finalisation of accounts cannot be made directly from a journal or ledger as it requires a summary of all ledger account balances of a particular period. The task of preparing the statements is simplified as the accountant can take the account balances from the trial balance instead of looking them up in the ledger.

The trial balance is a statement showing the balances or total of debits and credits of all the accounts in the ledger, with a view to verify the arithmetical accuracy of posting to the ledger accounts.

3.6.1   Objectives of Trial Balance:

1. **Ascertains the Arithmetical Accuracy of the accounting entries:** As per dual aspect concept for every debit, there must be an equivalent credit. Trial balance contains the details of all debit balance and credit balance of all the accounts involved in the transactions, in short it is a summary of all the ledger balances, therefore if two sides of the ledger are equal, then it is an indication that the books of accounts are arithmetically accurate

2. **Helps in preparation of financial statements:** The trial balance is a link between accounting records and financial statements. When preparing a financial statement, the ledger need not be referred. In fact, the availability of a trial balance is the first step in the preparation of financial statements. All revenue and expense accounts appearing in the trial balance are transferred to the trading and profit and loss accounts and all liabilities, capital, and asset accounts are transferred to the balance sheet.

3. **Summarised Ledger:** Trial Balances contains the ledger balances on a particular date, the position of the particular account can be found out by looking at the Trial Balance.

4. **Helps in identifying the errors:** In Trial Balance, when the totals of the debit and credit columns are not equal then this indicates that there is an error.

    The error may have occurred at any of the following stages of the accounting process:

    •   While posting the Journal entries in Ledger.

    •   While balancing ledger accounts

    •   While carrying the ledger account balance to the Trial Balance.

    •   While totalling the Trial Balance debit and credit columns

    •   While totalling of Subsidiary Books

3.6.2   Steps to be followed while preparing Trial Balance

1. Determine the balances of each ledger account

2. Place each ledger account balance in the debit or credit column, as the case may be. (If an account has zero balance, it can be included in the trial balance with zero in the column for its normal balance.)

3. Calculate the total of the debit balances column.

4. Calculate the total of the credit balances column.

5. Verify that the sum of debit balances equals the sum of credit balances. All assets, expenses, and receivables accounts shall have debit balances, while all liabilities, revenues, and payables accounts shall have credit balances.

3.6.3   Methods of Preparing Trial Balance

Trial Balance can be prepared by any one of the below given methods.

1. **Total Method:** In this method, the total of each side in the ledger (debit and credit) is ascertained separately and shown in the trial balance, in the respective columns. The total of the debit column should agree with the total of the credit column as the accounts are based on the double entry system.

2. **Balance Method:** Balances method is the most widely used method in practice. In this method, the trial balance is prepared by showing the balances of all ledger accounts and then totalling the debit and credit columns to ensure that they are correct. The account balances are used because the balance summarises the net effect of all transactions related to an account and helps in preparing financial statements.

3. **Total and Balance Method:** This method is a combination of the totals method and balance method. In this method, four columns are prepared for amount. Two columns are meant for the debit and credit totals of various accounts and the other two are for the debit and credit balances of these accounts.

Sample format of Trial Balance is as shown below:

Trial Balance as on 31ˢᵗ March, 2016			
Particulars	L.F	Debit (₹)	Credit (₹)

Particulars Column: In this column names of various ledger accounts are recorded like Capital Account, Sales Account, Purchase Account, Cash Account etc.

Ledger Folio (L.F): In this column the page number of ledger accounts will be recorded, these are number where a particular ledger is found.

Debit Column: In this column Debit Balance of various ledger accounts are recorded.

Credit Column: In this column Credit Balance of various ledger accounts are recorded.

The following illustration will demonstrate how to prepare different types of Trial balance.

Illustration 11: *Record the following transactions in the books of account of MSK Traders, then post them into the ledger and Prepare Trial Balance based on Balance Method as on 31st May 2016.*

Date (2016)	Transactions
May. 1	Ashok started a business with a capital of ₹ 30,000
May. 2	Purchased goods from SK Traders on credit for ₹ 20,000
May. 10	Paid cash of ₹ 20,000 to SK Traders
May. 12	Sold goods to Shobha Enterprises on credit for ₹ 40,000
May. 15	Received cash of ₹ 40,000 from Shobha Enterprises
May. 16	Purchase goods from SK Traders for ₹ 30,000
May. 17	Paid cash of ₹ 30,000 to SK Traders.
May. 18	Sold goods to Shobha Enterprises on credit for ₹ 30,000
May. 20	Received a cash of ₹ 30,000 from Shobha Enterprises
May. 21	Sold goods to Ramesh Industries for cash ₹50,000
May. 23	Ramesh Industries returned goods of ₹10,000
May. 24	Paid Salaries through cheque for ₹ 20,000
May. 25	Received interest of ₹ 2,000
May. 26	Purchases Stationery for Cash ₹ 3,000
May. 31	Prepaid insurance for cash ₹ 5,000

Solution:

1. Journalising the transactions in the books of MSK Traders for the Month of May 2016

Date 2016	Particulars		L.F	Dr.	Cr.
May 1	Cash A/c	Dr		30,000	
	To Capital A/c				30,000
	(Being Commencement of business)				
May 2	Purchase A/c	Dr		20,000	
	To SK Traders A/c				20,000
	(Being goods sold on credit to SK Traders)				
May 10	SK Traders A/c	Dr		20,000	
	To Cash A/c				20,000
	(Being Cash paid to SK Traders for the purchases made)				
May 12	Shobha Enterprises A/c	Dr		40,000	
	To Sales A/c				40,000
	(Being goods sold on credit)				
May 15	Cash A/c	Dr		40,000	
	To Shobha Enterprises A/c				40,000
	(Being cash received from Shobha Enterprises)				
May 16	Purchase A/c	Dr		30,000	
	To SK Traders A/c				30,000
	(Being goods sold on credit to SK Traders)				
May 17	SK Traders A/c	Dr		30,000	
	To Cash A/c				30,000
	(Being Cash paid to SK Traders for the purchases made)				

Date	Particulars			Dr.	Cr.
May 18	Shobha Enterprises A/c	Dr		30,000	
	To Sales A/c				30,000
	(Being goods sold on credit)				
May 20	Cash A/c	Dr		30,000	
	To Shobha Enterprises A/c				30,000
	(Being cash received from Shobha Enterprises)				
	Total c/f			2,70,000	2,70,000
	Total b/d			2,70,000	2,70,000
May 21	Cash A/c	Dr		50,000	
	To Sales A/c				50,000
	(Being goods sold on cash to Ramesh Industries)				
May 23	Sales Return A/c	Dr		10,000	
	To Cash A/c				10,000
	(Being goods return by the customer)				
May 24	Salaries A/c	Dr		20,000	
	To Bank A/c				20,000
	(Being salaries paid through Bank)				
May 25	Cash A/c	Dr		2,000	
	To Interest Received A/c				2,000
	(Being Interest Received)				
May 26	Stationery A/c	Dr		3,000	
	To Cash A/c				3,000
	(Being Stationery purchased)				
May 31	Insurance A/c	Dr		5,000	
	To Cash A/c				5,000
	Total			3,60,000	3,60,000

2. After journalising the transaction it should be posted to Ledger.

Cash Account

Date 2016	Particulars	J.F	₹	Date 2016	Particulars	J.F	₹
May 1	To Capital A/c		30,000	May 10	By SK Traders A/c		20,000
May 15	To Shobha Enterprises A/c		40,000	May 17	By SK Traders A/c		30,000
May 20	To Shobha Enterprises A/c		30,000	May 23	By Sales Return A/c		10,000
May 21	To Sales A/c		50,000	May 26	By Stationery A/c		3,000
May 25	To Interest Received A/c		2,000	May 31	By Insurance A/c		5,000
					By Balance c/d		84,000
			1,52,000				1,52,000
Jun. 1	To Balance b/d		84,000				

Capital Account

Date 2016	Particulars	J.F	₹	Date 2016	Particulars	J.F	₹
May 31	To Balance c/d		30,000	May 1	By Cash A/c		30,000
			30,000				30,000
				Jun.1	By Balance b/d		30,000

Purchases Account

Date 2016	Particulars	J.F	₹	Date 2016	Particulars	J.F	₹
May. 2	To SK Traders A/c		20,000	May. 31	By Balance c/d		50,000
May. 16	To SK Traders A/c		30,000				
			50,000				50,000
Jun. 1	To Balance b/d		50,000				

SK Trader's Account

Date 2016	Particulars	J.F	₹	Date 2016	Particulars	J.F	₹
May. 10	To Cash A/c		20,000	May. 2	By Purchase A/c		20,000
May. 17	To Cash A/c		30,000	May. 16	By Purchase A/c		30,000
			50,000				50,000

Shobha Enterprises Account

Date 2016	Particulars	J.F	₹	Date 2016	Particulars	J.F	₹
May. 12	To Sales A/c		40,000	May. 15	By Cash A/c		40,000
May. 18	To Sales A/c		30,000	May. 20	By Cash A/c		30,000
			70,000				70,000

Sales Account

Date 2016	Particulars	J.F	₹	Date 2016	Particulars	J.F	₹
May. 31	By Balance c/d		1,20,000	May. 12	By Shobha Enterprises A/c		40,000
				May. 18	By Shobha Enterprises A/c		30,000
				May. 21	By Cash A/c		50,000
							1,20,000
				Jun. 1	By Balance b/d		1,20,000

Sales Return Account

Date 2016	Particulars	J.F	₹	Date 2016	Particulars	J.F	₹
May. 23	To Cash A/c		10,000	May. 31	By Balance c/d		10,000
			10,000				10,000
Jun. 1	To Balance b/d		10,000				

Salaries Account

Date 2016	Particulars	J.F	₹	Date 2016	Particulars	J.F	₹
May. 24	To Bank A/c		20,000	May. 31	By Balance c/d		20,000
			20,000				20,000
Jun. 1	To Balance b/d		20,000				

Bank Account

Date 2016	Particulars	J.F	₹	Date 2016	Particulars	J.F	₹
May. 31	To Balance c/d		20,000	May. 24	By Salaries A/c		20,000
			20,000				20,000
				Jun. 1	By Balance b/d		20,000

Interest Received Account

Date 2016	Particulars	J.F	₹	Date 2016	Particulars	J.F	₹
May. 31	To Balance c/d		2,000	May. 25	By Cash A/c		2,000
			2,000				2,000
				Jun. 1	By Balance b/d		2,000

Stationery Account

Date 2016	Particulars	J.F	₹	Date 2016	Particulars	J.F	₹
May. 26	To Cash A/c		3,000	May. 31	By Balance c/d		3,000
			3,000				3,000
Jun. 1	By Balance b/d		3,000				

Insurance Account

Date 2016	Particulars	J.F	₹	Date 2016	Particulars	J.F	₹
May. 31	To Cash A/c		5,000	May. 31	By Balance c/d		5,000
			5,000				5,000
Jun. 1	By Balance b/d		5,000				

3. Preparation of Trial Balance.

MSK Traders
Trial Balance as on 31st May, 2016

Particulars	L.F	Debit (₹)	Credit (₹)
Cash Account		84,000	
Capital Account			30,000
Purchase Account		50,000	
SK Traders Account		0	0
Shobha Enterprises Account		0	0
Sales Account			1,20,000
Sales Return Account		10,000	
Salaries Account		20,000	
Bank Account			20,000
Interest Received Account			2,000
Stationery Account		3,000	
Insurance Account		5,000	
Total		1,72,000	1,72,000

Note: The above Trial Balance is in the Balance Method format i.e., in the above trial balance the Ledger account balances (Difference amount) are taken and it is widely used format.

In this chapter we have studied about the Accounting cycle like recording the transactions in Journal and posting of the recorded transaction into the Ledger and preparation of Trial balance, which will further help in preparation of Final Statements like Balance Sheet and Profit and Loss Account.

3.7 SUBSIDIARY BOOKS

The business having small number of transactions is easy to record in journal. But, when the business transactions of large numbers are recorded in one journal then it becomes bulk and results in complexities. Therefore, in the modern book-keeping the journal is divided into separate journals, to record the transactions of similar nature together.

These separate journals are known as subsidiary books.

3.7.1 Concept/ Fundamental

These are separate books of original entry, which is based on the earlier practices of **Journal,** where a single book is used to record all the transactions of the business.

In large business enterprises, it would be difficult to record all the business transaction into a single book called journal, hence to avoid the complexity, the concept of subsidiary books were introduced which is the modern approach of book-keeping.

3.7.2 Advantages of Subsidiary Books

- The complexity during recording of transactions is eliminated.
- It saves the time of the accountant.
- It avoids the duplication of transactions.
- Easy to find particular transaction and post it into ledger accounts.
- It helps to rectify the manual errors and mistakes.

3.8 TYPES OF SUBSIDIARY BOOKS & RE-LATED ASPECTS

- Purchase Book/ Register
  - o Purchase Bill Specimen (**Specimen** to be **Prepare** or **Show**)
  - o Purchase Ledger Account
- Sales Book/ Register
  - o Sales Invoice Specimen (**Specimen** to be **Prepare** or **Show**)
  - o Sales Ledger Account
- Purchase Return Book/ Register
  - o Debit Notes Specimen (**Specimen** to be **Prepare** or **Show**)
  - o Purchase Return Ledger Account
- Sales Return Book/ Register
  - o Credit Notes Specimen (**Specimen** to be **Prepare** or **Show**)
  - o Sales Return Ledger Account
- Cash Book/ Register
  - o Single/ Simple/ Only Cash Column
  - o With Discount Column
  - o With Bank Column
- Petty Cash Book/ Register
  - o Imprest System
- Journal Proper

3.8.1 Purchase Books

This book is maintained to record all the credit purchases only, of the company. It is prepared on the basis of purchase bills received from the supplier which contains the details of the purchase transaction which are as follows:

- Date of the transaction
- Inward Invoice Number/ Bill Number
- Description of goods
  - o Quantity
  - o Rate
  - o Amt
- Terms of sales
- Any other references

The purchase book total of a particular period, is transferred to purchase account as **"To Sundries as per purchase book"** and every supplier ledger account is maintained to track the value of goods purchased from purchase account.

Illustration 12: In the books of Garuda Traders Pvt Ltd., record the following transactions in the purchase book and further prepare the respective ledger account and post entries from purchase book.

Below is the transactions details of, 2016-April month

1. On 1-04-16, purchased goods from **Ritin Traders**.

   Quantity: 100   Nos
   Rate: 50   Nos

2. Goods received from **Ammu Wholesaler** dated on 4-04-16.

   Quantity: 200   Nos
   Rate: 40   Nos

3. Goods worth Rs. 800/- were purchased on cash from **Vertical International Traders** dated 13-04-16.

4. Bought goods from Wind Fast Pvt Ltd on 22-04-16

   Quantity: 140
   Rate: 50

5. Computer of Rs. 40000/- were purchased on 30-04-16, for office purpose from Solo Info Systems.

Note: 1. Kindly check the transaction no 3, will not be recorded in the purchase book.
2. Transaction no 5, will not be recorded in purchase book.

Let us see how to prepare the necessary books and applicable ledger accounts

In the books of Garuda Traders			
Purchase Book			
Date	Particulars	Description	Amt
01-04-16	Ritin Trader	Goods	5000
		Quantity: 100 Nos	
		Rate: 50 Nos	
04-04-16	Ammu Wholesaler	Goods	8000
		Quantity: 200 Nos	
		Rate: 40 Nos	
22-04-16	Wind Fast Pvt Ltd	Goods	7000
		Quantity: 140 Nos	
		Rate: 50 Nos	

In the books of Garuda Traders
Purchase A/c

Dr						Cr
Date	Particulars	Amt	Date		Particulars	Amt
	Sundries as per purchase book			By		
01-04-16	To Ritin Traders	5000		By		
04-04-16	To Ammu Wholesaler	8000		By		
22-04-16	To Wind Fast Pvt Ltd	7000		By		

In the books of Garuda Traders
Ritin Trader A/c

Dr						Cr
Date	Particulars	Amt	Date		Particulars	Amt
	To		01-04-16	By	Purchase A/c	5000
	To			By		

In the books of Garuda Traders
Ammu Wholesaler A/c

Dr						Cr
Date	Particulars	Amt	Date		Particulars	Amt
	To		04-04-16	By	Purchase A/c	8000
	To			By		

3.8.2   Sales Book

This book is maintained to record all the credit sales only, of the company. It is prepared on the basis of sales invoices issued to the customers which contains the details of the sales transaction which is as follows:

♦ Date of the transaction

♦ Outward Invoice Number/ Invoice Number

♦ Description of goods

    o   Quantity

    o   Rate

    o   Amt

♦ Terms of sales

♦ Any other references

The sales book total of a particular period, is transferred to sales account as **"By Sundries as per sales book"** and every customer ledger account is maintained to track the value of goods sold from sales account.

Illustration 13: In the books of Harsha Enterprises Pvt Ltd., record the following transactions in the sales book and further prepare the respective ledger account and post entries from sales book.

Below is the transactions details of, 2016-April month

1. On 3-04-16, sold goods to **Swami Electronics,** find the details below.

    Quantity: 70   Nos
    Rate: 80   Nos

2. Sold goods to **Neeta Garments** on 14-04-16 details as follows.

    Quantity: 95   Nos
    Rate: 80   Nos

3. Goods worth Rs. 1,000/- were sold on cash on 14-04-16 to **Nav Jeevan Society.**

4. Sold old office printer @ Rs. 1000/- to **Shantanu Enterprises** on 20-04-2016.

Note: 1.   Kindly check the transaction no 3, will not be recorded in the purchase book.
        2.   Transaction no 5, will not be recorded in purchase book.

Let us see how to prepare the necessary books and applicable ledger accounts

In the books of Harsh Enterprises
Sales Book

Date	Particulars	Description			Amt
03-04-16	Swami Electronics	Goods			5600
		Quantity:	70	Nos	
		Rate:	80	Nos	
07-04-16	Neeta Garments	Goods			7600
		Quantity:	95	Nos	
		Rate:	80	Nos	

In the books of Harsh Enterprises
Sales A/c

Dr						Cr
Date	Particulars	Amt	Date		Particulars	Amt
	To				Sundries as per sales book	
	To		03-04-16	By	Swami Electronics	5600
	To		07-04-16	By	Neeta Garments	7600
	To			By		

In the books of Harsh Enterprises
Swami Electronics A/c

Dr						Cr
Date	Particulars	Amt	Date		Particulars	Amt
03-04-16	To Sales A/c	5600		By		
	To			By		

In the books of Harsh Enterprises
Neeta Garments A/c

Dr						Cr
Date	Particulars	Amt	Date		Particulars	Amt
03-04-16	To Sales A/c	7600		By		
	To			By		

3.8.3   Purchase Return Book

This book is maintained to record all the transactions concerned to return outwards of goods purchased on credit to its original supplier

Some of the common reason for sending back the whole of the goods or partial goods are as follows:

♦ Damage

♦ Defective

♦ Delay

♦ Not up to the mark or unsatisfied

♦ Incompatible

The debit note is issued mentioning remarks (**reason for goods returned**) and sent along with goods to its original supplier, stating that supplier accounts is debited respectively. Hence on the basis of this debit note, the transaction is thus recorded in the purchase return book.

Illustration 14: In the books of Vivek Enterprises Pvt Ltd., record the following transactions in the purchase return book and further prepare the respective ledger account and post entries from purchase return book.

Below is the transactions details of, 2016-April month

1. On 2-04-16, some goods were returned to **Ritin Traders** along with **debit note no: 001**, mentioning **remarks** stating the reason – goods were found damaged on reception.

Quantity:	20	Nos
Rate:	50	Nos

2. On 6-04-16, partial goods were returned to **Ammu Wholesaler** along with **debit note no: 002**, mentioning **remarks** stating the reason – goods were not up to the mark.

Quantity:	110	Nos
Rate:	40	Nos

3. On the same day of 22-04-16, whole of goods were returned to **Wind Fast Pvt Ltd** along with **debit note no: 003**, mentioning **remarks** stating the reason – all goods were defective

Quantity:	140	
Rate:	50	

Let us see how to prepare the necessary books and applicable ledger accounts

In the books of Vivek Enterprises Pvt Ltd.
Purchase Returns Book

Date	Particulars	D/N No	Description			Amt
02-04-16	Ritin Trader	001	Goods			1000
			Quantity:	20	Nos	
			Rate:	50	Nos	
06-04-16	Ammu Wholesaler	002	Goods			4400
			Quantity:	110	Nos	
			Rate:	40	Nos	
22-04-16	Wind Fast Pvt Ltd	003	Goods			7000
			Quantity:	140	Nos	
			Rate:	50	Nos	

In the books of Vivek Enterprises Pvt Ltd.
Purchase Returns A/c

Dr						Cr
Date	Particulars	Amt	Date	Particulars	Amt	
	To			Sundries as per purchase returns book		
	To		02-04-16	By	Ritin Traders	1000
	To		06-04-16	By	Ammu Wholesaler	4400
	To		22-04-16	By	Wind Fast Pvt Ltd	7000
	To			By		

In the books of Vivek Enterprises Pvt Ltd.
Ritin Trader A/c

Dr						Cr
Date	Particulars	Amt	Date	Particulars	Amt	
02-04-16	To Purchase Returns A/c	1000	01-04-16	By Purchase A/c	5000	
	To			By		

In the books of Vivek Enterprises Pvt Ltd.
Ammu Wholesaler A/c

Dr						Cr
Date	Particulars	Amt	Date	Particulars	Amt	
06-04-16	To Purchase Returns A/c	4400	04-04-16	By Purchase A/c	8000	
	To			By		

3.8.4 Sales Return Book

This book is maintained to record all the transactions concerned to return inwards of sold goods on credit from the original customer

Some of the common reason for getting back the whole of the goods or partial goods are as follows:

- Damage
- Defective
- Delay
- Not up to the mark or unsatisfied
- Incompatible

The credit note is provided to the customer as a confirmation, that the return inward goods given by the customer is accepted, mentioning remarks (**reason for goods returned**) and stating that, the customer accounts is credited respectively. Hence on the basis of this credit note, the transaction is thus recorded in the sales return book.

Illustration 15: In the books of Keerthi Trader Pvt Ltd., record the following transactions in the sales return book and further prepare the respective ledger account and post entries from sales return book.

Below is the transactions details of, 2016-April month

1. On 5-04-16, partial goods were returned by **Swami Electronics** hence a **credit note no: 101**, were issued to the customer, mentioning **remarks** stating the reason – customer found goods damaged on reception.

Quantity:	4	Nos
Rate:	80	Nos

2. On 8-04-16, goods were returned by **Neeta Garments** thus a **credit note no: 102**, were issued to the customer, mentioning **remarks** stating the reason – goods were found damaged due to poor packaging.

Quantity:	5	Nos
Rate:	80	Nos

Let us see how to prepare the necessary books and applicable ledger accounts

In the books of Keerthi Trader Pvt Ltd
Sales Returns Book

Date	Particulars	C/N No	Description			Amt
05-04-16	Swami Electronics	101	Goods			320
			Quantity:	4	Nos	
			Rate:	80	Nos	
08-04-16	Neeta Garments	102	Goods			400
			Quantity:	5	Nos	
			Rate:	80	Nos	

In the books of Keerthi Trader Pvt Ltd
Sales Returns A/c

Dr						Cr
Date	Particulars	Amt	Date	Particulars	Amt	
	Sundries as per sales return book					
05-04-16	To Swami Electronics	320		By		
08-04-16	To Neeta Garments	400		By		
	To			By		

In the books of Keerthi Trader Pvt Ltd
Swami Electronics A/c

Dr						Cr
Date	Particulars	Amt	Date	Particulars	Amt	
05-04-16	To Sales A/c	5600	01-04-16	By Sales Return A/c	320	
	To			By		

In the books of Keerthi Trader Pvt Ltd
Neeta Garments A/c

Dr					Cr
Date	Particulars	Amt	Date	Particulars	Amt
03-04-16	To Sales A/c	7600	08-04-16	By Sales Return A/c	400
	To			By	

3.8.5 Cash Book

In any business when a transaction involve flow of cash due to payments or receipts, by means of liquid cash or through bank cheque or any other negotiable instrument, hence to record cash transactions cash book is used. It is opened with a cash or bank balance at the beginning of the period. The entries are balanced on a monthly basis. Cash book, also known as book of original entry, is maintained by all organisations, big or small, profit or not-for-profit. It serves the purpose of both journal as well as the ledger (cash) account. When a cash book is maintained, transactions of cash are not recorded in the journal and no separate account for cash or bank is required in the ledger.

Cash book is maintained in three kinds

- Single Column
- With Discount Column
- Bank Column

Single Column Cash book

It is very simple in form where receipts amount column is maintained in the debit side of the cash book and payments amount column is maintained in credit side of the cash book

With Discount Column

This is a separate column included in the cash book to records all the discounts, the discount allowed column is in the debit side and the discount received column is in the credit side.

With Bank Column

This is an additional column included in the cash book, to record all the cash receipts deposited in the bank are recorded in the debit column and all the cash payment withdrawals from bank are recorded on credit side

Illustration 16:

Single Column Cash book

In the books of SP Enterprises Pvt Ltd., record the following transactions in the cash book. Below is the transactions details of, 2016-June month.

1. Cash in hand as at 1-6-2016 is Rs. 10000/-
2. On 2-6-2016, Payment made for Printing & Stationery Rs 800/-
3. Loan taken from Maxis Fin Corp of Rs 25000/- dated 14-06-2016.
4. Paid for Tea & Snacks of Rs 5000/- dated 22-06-2016.
5. Bank Interest Received on Bank Deposits of Rs 1900/- 30-06-2016.
6. Office Maintenance Charges per month is Rs 4000/- on 30-06-2016.

In the Cash Book of SP Enterprises Pvt Ltd

Dr					Cr
Date	Particulars	Cash Column	Date	Particulars	Cash Column
1-6-16	To Balance c/f	10000	2-6-16	By Printing & Stationery	800
14-6-16	To Loan from Maxis Fin Corp	25000	22-6-16	By Tea & Snacks Expenses A/c	5000
30-6-16	To Bank Interest Received A/c	1900	30-6-16	By Office Maintenance Expenses A/c	4000
			30-6-16	By Balance c/d	27100
	Total	36900		Total	36900

With Discount Column

In the books of Neeraj Traders Pvt Ltd., record the following transactions in the cash book. Below is the transactions details of, 2016-July month.

1. Cash in hand as at 1-7-2016 is Rs. 27100/-
2. On 10-7-2016, Cash purchases of goods worth Rs. 8000/- were made with Virat Traders with a Trade Discount of 5% on purchases.
3. Goods were purchased on cash of Rs 15000/- from Deepak Traders on 12-07-2016, were made with a cash discount received @ 10% on purchases.
4. On 12-07-2016, cash paid to supplier Ancient Tech for the outstanding amount of Rs 5000/- and got 5% cash discount.
5. On 13-07-2016, Sales of goods Rs 12000/- were done and 5% cash discount were provided on total sales
6. Purchased goods worth Rs 10000/- on 14-07-2016, from Virat Traders and received trade discount of 5% and cash discount of 5%.
7. Sold goods worth Rs 25000/- on 18-07-2016, to Yash Mesh Retailers with 2% trade discount allowed and 5% cash discount on total sales.
8. On 31-07-2016, received cash of Rs. 5900 from customer Kenben Traders for outstanding account Rs 6000/-

In the Cash Book of Neeraj Traders Pvt Ltd

Dr							Cr
Date	Particulars	Discount Allowed	Cash Column	Date	Particulars	Discount Received	Cash Column
1-7-16	To Balance c/f		27100	10-7-16	By Purchase of Goods A/c		7600
13-7-16	To Sales of Goods A/c	600	11400	12-7-16	By Purchase of Goods A/c	1500	13500
18-7-16	To Sales of Goods A/c	1225	23275	12-7-16	By Ancient Tech A/c	250	4750
31-7-16	To Kenben Traders A/c	100	5900	14-7-16	By Purchase of Goods A/c	475	9025
				14-7-16	By Balance c/d		32800
	Total	1925	67675		Total	2225	67675

With Bank Column

In the books of Vinod Traders Pvt Ltd., record the following transactions in the cash book. Below is the transactions details of, 2016-August month.

1. Cash in hand as at 1-8-2016 is Rs. 32800/- and Bank Balance of Rs 10,000/-
2. Sold goods worth Rs 20000/- on 2-08-2016, to Yash Mesh Retailers with 5% trade discount allowed and 1% cash

discount on total sales. Payment is received by cheque and deposited to bank

3. Purchased goods worth Rs 12000/- on 5-08-2016, from Virat Traders and received trade discount of 10% and cash discount of 5%, payment were done by issuing bank cheque.

4. On 10-08-2016, cash withdrawn from bank for office maintenance of Rs 4000/-

5. For tea and snacks amount of Rs 7000/- were paid through cash on 12-08-2016.

6. On 31-08-2016, bank charges of Rs 500/- were recognised

7. Cheque deposited by one of the customer named Wilson Traker were recognised on 31 - 08 - 2016 of Rs 15000/-

In the Cash Book of Vinod Traders Pvt Ltd

Dr									Cr
Date	Particulars	Dis Allw	Cash	Bank	Date	Particulars	Dis Rec	Cash	Bank
1-8-16	To Balance C f		32800	10000	5-8-16	To Purchase of Goods A c	540		10800
2-8-16	To Sales of Goods A c	190		18810	10-8-16	To Office Maintenance A c			4000
31-8-16	To Wilson Traker A c			15000	12-8-16	To Tea and Snacks A c		7000	15000
					31-8-16	To Bank Charges			500
					31-8-16	To Balance c d		25800	13510
	Total	190	32800	43810		Total	540	32800	43810

3.8.6 Petty Cash Book

In any business, there are various small cash payments which are very often or recurring in nature, hence it is very difficult to record these petty transactions in main cash book which results in complexities for the cashier. To overcome this a special book is maintained which is called as petty cash book, thus this book is maintained by petty cash

Imprest System

In this a fixed amount is allocated to the petty cashier in advance at the beginning of the specific period, usually a month, to meet various small expenses of the business.

At the end of a particular period when the petty cashier is running out of cash balance, petty cashier is reimbursed with the remaining balance of fixed amount for the next month.

Examples of common often and recurring expenses

* Postage and Telegram
* Printing and Stationery
* Carriage Charges
* Local Travelling Conveyance
* Sundry Expenses
* Personal Account

Illustration 17: In the books of Suraj Enterprises record the following transactions in the cash book. Below is the transactions details of, 2016-May month.

Petty Cash is fixed to Rs 1000/- per month

1. Cash in hand as on 1-5-2016 is Rs. 100/-

2. Petty cashier received Rs 900/- on 1-5-2016

3. Paid on 2-5-16, for Postage/ Courier and Telegram of Rs 80

4. Paid on 5-5-16, Local Travelling Conveyance of Rs 50/-

5. Paid on 8-5-16, for Postage/ Courier of Rs 150/-

6. Paid on 11-5-16, for Carriage Charges of Rs 100/-

7. Paid on 15-5-16, Local Travelling Conveyance of Rs 70/-

8. Paid on 19-5-16, Miscellaneous office expenses of Rs 100/-

9. Paid on 26-5-16, for Postage/ Courier and Telegram of Rs 150

10. Paid on 28-5-16, Local Travelling Conveyance of Rs 40/-

11. Paid on 31-5-16, Mohan for Conveyance of Rs 50/-

In the Petty Cash Book of Suraj Enterprises

Dr			Cr					
Receipts	Date	Particulars	Payments	Postage and Telegram	Carriage Charges	Local Travelling Conveyance	Sundry Expenses	Personal Account
100	1-5-16	To Balance b d						
900	1-5-16	To Cash						
	2-5-16	By Postage	80	80				
	5-5-16	By Local Travelling	50			50		
	8-5-16	By Postage	150	150				
	11-5-16	By Carriage	100		100			
	15-5-16	By Local Travelling	70			70		
	19-5-16	By Misc office expenses	100				100	
	26-5-16	By Postage	150	150				
	28-5-16	By Local Travelling	40			40		
	31-5-16	By Mohan A c	50					50
1000		Total	790	380	100	160	100	50
210	31-5-16	By Balance b d						
	1-6-16	To Balance c d	210					
790	1-6-16	To Cash						

3.9 JOURNAL PROPER

The transactions which are different in nature and cannot be recorded in any regular subsidiary books, such transactions are recorded in the book called as Journal Proper. It is also known as Modern Journal or Miscellaneous Journal.

The following is a list of transactions which can be recorded in a Journal Proper:

* Opening Entries & Closing Entries

- Transfer Entries
- Rectifying Entries
- Adjusting Entries
- Credit Sales (other than goods)
- Credit Purchase (other than goods)
- Withdrawal of Goods or Assets by the owner or proprietor
- Loss of Goods or Assets (by fire, flood, accident, theft etc.)
- Joint Venture Transactions
- Consignment Transactions
- Dishonour of Promissory Notes
- Dishonour of Bills of Exchange

3.9.1   Difference between Journal and Journal Proper

The main difference between Journal and Journal Proper is given bellow:

Journal	Journal Proper
This is maintained under conventional or traditional methods of accounting.	This is maintained under practical or modern method of accounting.
All the transactions are recorded in journal.	Only those transactions are recorded which cannot be recorded in the subsidiary books.

Illustration 18: Record the following transactions in the Journal Proper.

Date (2016)	Transactions
Jul. 1	Furniture of ₹ 10,000 was lost by fire.
Jul. 3	Goods withdrawn by owner for his personal use ₹ 5,000
Jul. 4	Bought office furniture from SKC Mart for ₹ 10,000
Jul. 5	Bought Machinery from NC Trading Company for ₹ 10,000
Jul. 6	Sold Furniture to Shubhashine for ₹ 5,000
Jul. 7	Net Profit of ₹ 1,000 is transferred to Reserve
Jul. 8	A Debit Balance of ₹ 3,000 from CK account to be transferred to M&M account.
Jul. 18	Goods given away as charity for ₹ 2,000
Jul. 19	Goods given away as sample for ₹ 3,000
Jul. 20	Interest on capital ₹ 4,000

Solution:

Journal

Date 2016	Particulars	L.F	Dr.	Cr.
Jul. 1	Loss of furniture A/c Dr.		10,000	
	To Furniture A/c			10,000
	(Being the furniture lost by fire)			
Jul. 3	Drawings A/c Dr.		5,000	
	To Purchase A/c			5,000
	(Being the goods withdrawn by the owner)			
Jul. 4	Furniture A/c Dr.		10,000	
	To SKC Mart A/c			10,000
	(Being furniture bought from SKC Mart)			
Jul. 5	Machinery A/c Dr.		10,000	
	To NC Trading Company A/c			10,000

	(Being machinery bought from NC Company)			
Jul. 6	Shubhashine A/c Dr.		5,000	
	To furniture A/c			5,000
	(Being furniture sold to Shubhashine)			
Jul. 7	Profit & Loss A/c or Profit & Loss Appropriation A/c Dr.		1,000	
	To Reserve A/c			1,000
	(Being goods sold on credit to SK Traders)			
Jul. 8	M&M A/c Dr.		3,000	
	To CK account A/c			3,000
	(Being debit balance transferred from CK A/c to M&M A/c)			
Jul. 18	Charity A/c Dr.		2,000	
	To Purchase A/c			2,000
	(Being goods given away as charity)			
Jul. 19	Free Sample A/c Dr.		3,000	
	To Purchase A/c			3,000
	(Being goods given away as sample)			
Jul. 20	Interest on Capital A/c Dr.		4,000	
	To Capital A/c			4,000
	(Being interest allowed on capital)			
	Total		53,000	53,000

KEY TAKEAWAYS

- Business Transactions are first recorded in the Journal.
- Recording of transactions in Journal is known as Journalising.
- Journal Transactions are posted in Ledger.
- Ledger is also known as Book of Final Entry.
- Trial Balance is the listing of Balances Ledger Accounts.
- In modern book-keeping, a journal is divided into separate journals, to record the transactions of similar nature together. These separate journals are known as subsidiary books.

Trial Balance Format

Balance as on _____			
Particulars	L.F	Debit (₹)	Credit (₹)
Cash Account		xxxx	--
Capital Account		--	xxxx
Purchase Account		xxxx	--
Sales Account		--	xxxx
Sales Return Account		xxxx	--
Wages Account		xxxx	--
Land and Building		--	--
Plant and Machinery		--	--
Bills Receivable		xxxx	--
Bills Payable		--	xxxx
Opening Stock of Raw Materials		xxxx	--
Work in Progress		xxxx	
Salaries Account		xxxx	--
Bank Account		xxxx	--
Interest Received Account		--	xxxx
Advance from customers		--	xxxx
Stationery Account		xxxx	--
Insurance Account		xxxx	--
Total		xxxx	xxxx

PRACTICE EXERCISES

Section A: Review Questions

1. What is a Business Transaction?
2. What is a Journal?
3. What is a Ledger posting and why it is needed?
4. What is the Difference between the Journal and Ledger?
5. What is a Trial Balance and list down the objectives of Trial Balance?
6. Write down the different methods of preparing trial Balance.
7. What is the difference between Journal and Ledger?
8. Why journal is known as Book of Original Entry?
9. What is a Compound Journal Entry?
10. What is a Journal Proper?
11. Record the following transactions in the books of Mani Enterprises for the Month of April.

Date (2016)	Transactions
Apr. 1	Business started with cash of ₹ 10,00,000
Apr. 5	Goods purchased from Karthik for cash ₹ 2,00,000
Apr. 6	Stationery purchased for cash ₹ 10,000
Apr. 10	Opened a bank account with SBI Bank by depositing cash of ₹ 5,00,000
Apr. 11	Goods sold to Ram & Sons Manufacturers on credit for ₹ 80,000

12. Record the following transactions in a Journal:

Date	Transactions
Apr. 12	Received a cheque of ₹ 50,000 from Ram & Sons Manufacturers
Apr. 13	Insurance paid by cheque ₹ 20,000
Apr. 14	Sold goods to Nandini Manufacturers ₹ 2,00,000
Apr. 15	Nandini pays ₹ 2,00,000 through cheque
Apr. 16	Goods purchased for ₹ 3,00,000 from GG Traders and paid through cheque
Apr. 17	Purchased office furniture for ₹ 50,000 in cash
Apr. 18	Goods costing ₹ 30,000 given as charity
Apr. 19	Paid ₹ 50,000 towards rent through cheque
Apr. 20	Cash withdrawn for household purposes ₹ 20,000
Apr. 21	Damaged goods returned to GG Traders ₹ 30,000
Apr. 30	Salaries paid ₹ 30,000 through Cash

Date (2016)	Transactions
Jun. 6	Payment made to Sugnu for ₹1,00,000 and discount received for ₹10,000
Jun. 7	Cash of ₹ 2,00,000 was received from Star Traders and discount allowed for ₹ 20,000
Jun. 9	Running business was purchased by Rakesh and the following assets and liabilities details are shown below: Cash ₹ 50,000; Furniture 25,000; Land ₹ 2,00,000; Creditors ₹70,000; Bank Overdraft ₹ 20,000; Capital ₹ 66,000

13. Record the Following Transaction in Journal and then post them into the Ledgers for the month of May 2016.

Date (2016)	Transactions
May 1	Triveni started a business with a capital of ₹ 2,00,000
May 2	Purchased goods from KS Traders on credit for ₹ 1,00,000
May 3	Paid cash of ₹ 50,000 to KS Traders
May 10	Sold goods to S&S Enterprises for ₹ 3,00,000
May 15	Purchase goods from KS Traders for ₹ 2,00,000
May 16	Returned damaged goods to KS Traders for ₹ 5,000
May 18	Salaries paid for ₹ 20,000 through cheque

14. Record the Following Transaction in Journal and then post them into the Ledgers and prepare the Trial Balance.

Date (2016)	Transactions
May 1	Bhuvan started a business with a capital of ₹ 5,00,000
May 2	Purchased goods from TT Traders on credit for ₹ 2,00,000
May 3	Paid cash of ₹ 30,000 to TT Traders
May 10	Sold goods to SWOS Enterprises for ₹ 6,00,000
May 15	Purchase goods from TT Traders for ₹ 2,00,000
May 16	Returned damaged goods to TT Traders for ₹ 50,000
May 18	Salaries paid for ₹ 30,000 through cheque
May 31	Purchased furniture for ₹ 1,00,000 and the payment I made through cash

Section B: Multiple Choice Questions

Select the most appropriate answer from the choices given below:

1. _____ is the Book of original Entry.
   a. Ledger   b. **Journal**
   c. Trial Balance   d. Balance Sheet

2. _____ is the Book of Final Entry.
   a. **Ledger**   b. Journal
   c. Trial Balance   d. Balance Sheet

3. _____ is the base of Financial Statements.
   a. Balance Sheet   b. Profit & Loss Account
   c. **Trial Balance** d. Cash Balance

4. _____ entry is recorded in the beginning in Journal.
   a. Closing Entry   b. Purchase Entry
   c. Sales Entry   d. **Opening Entry**

5. "To" word will be used by the account which will be?
   a. **Debited**   b. Credited
   c. Balanced   d. Removed

Chapter 4

Bank Reconciliation

LEARNING OBJECTIVES

After studying this chapter, you will be able to:

♦ Understand to examine bank balance as per statements and company cash book

♦ Correcting the difference between bank account funds and company cash book

♦ To prepare bank reconciliation statement

4.1 INTRODUCTION

Every business organisation maintains a cash book in which it records both cash and bank transactions. The cash book shows the balance of both cash and bank transactions at the end of a given period. Once the cash book is balanced, the business must check the details with the records of its bank transactions. For this purpose, the cashier needs to update the cash book and obtain a recent statement from the bank. The balance shown in the passbook must tally with the balance shown in the cash book. Invariably, there is a difference between these balances and it is necessary to ascertain the reasons for such a difference. Once the difference is known, a bank reconciliation statement is prepared to reconcile the balances

4.2 MEANING

A bank reconciliation statement is prepared by a customer (i.e. account holder) to ascertain the items or reasons responsible for the difference between the bank balance shown in the cash book and the bank balance shown in the passbook as on a particular date

4.3 CAUSES OF DIFFERENCE IN COMPANY CASH BOOK AND BANK PASS BOOK

The differences which occur between company cash book balances and bank pass book are as follows

1. **Cheques issued but not presented for payment**

   Cheques issued by a company to its suppliers or some party are immediately entered on the credit side of the cash book. However, the cheques may not be immediately presented to the bank for payment by the receiving party. The bank will debit the company's account only when it actually honors these cheques. Hence, the time gap between the issue of a cheque and it to be honored by the bank causes the difference between the balance as per the cash book and the balance as per the passbook.

2. **Cheques deposited into the bank but not cleared and credited.**

   When a company receives cheques from some party or from its customers (debtors), these cheques are immediately recorded on the debit side of the cash book. This increases the bank balance as per the cash book. However, the amounts on the cheques will only realised, when bank credit the funds to customer's account. Clearing of cheques usually takes a few days, especially in case of outstation cheques or when the cheques are paid-in at a branch other than the one wherein the business has an account. This causes a difference between the balances.

3. **Interest gained and dividend collected and credited by bank but not recognized thus remains unrecorded in company cash book**

   The company is unaware when the dividend are collected by bank, or when bank provide interest by crediting sum of money into company's account, until it confirm the bank statement, Hence this transaction is not recorded in company's cash book. As a result, the balance shown in the bank passbook will be more than the balance shown in the company's cash book.

4. **Bank Charges or Interest charged and debited by bank but not recognized thus remains unrecorded in company cash book**

   The bank interest and any other charges of the company are debited to the company's bank account, the company will acknowledge these transactions and record those in its cash book, only when it receives a bank statement, until then the balances will differ.

5. **Direct payment by the bank on behalf of company's standing instructions.**

   Sometimes, the company may give directions to the bank to make specific payments regularly on particular days to third parties. For example, telephone bills, insurance premiums, rent, and taxes, and so on are directly paid by the bank on behalf of the company and debited to the company's bank account. As a result, the balance as per the passbook would be less than the one shown in the cash book.

6. **Direct deposit by the customer**

   At times, debtors (customers) of the business may directly deposit money into the company's bank account. But, the company is unaware and does not receive the intimation until it confirms the bank statement. In this case, the bank credits the amount in the company's account, but the same is not recorded in the company's cash book. As a result, the balance shown in the bank passbook will be more than the balance shown in the company's cash book.

7. **Dishonor of Cheque or Bills discounted with the bank**

   If a cheque deposited by the company is dishonored or a bill of exchange drawn by the business organisation, discounted with the bank, is dishonored on the date of maturity, the same is debited to the company's account by the bank. As this information is not immediately available to the company, hence there will be no entry in the company's cash book reflecting the same. This will be known to the organisation only when it receives a statement from the bank. As a result, the balance as per the passbook would be less than the balance as per the cash book.

8. **Errors caused in recording transaction by the company**

   Any omission or incorrect recording of transactions relating to cheques issued/cheques deposited and wrong totaling by an organisation while recording entries in the cash book can cause a difference between cash book and passbook balances

9. **Errors caused in recording transaction by the company**

   Any omission or incorrect recording of transactions relating to cheques deposited and wrong totaling by the bank while posting entries in the passbook can also cause differences between passbook and cash book balances.

4.4   HOW TO PREPARE A BANK RECONCILIATION STATEMENT

To prepare a bank reconciliation statement, the bank balance as per the cash book and cash balance as per bank passbook or statement as on a particular day are required along with transaction details of both the books.

1. Compare the values in the bank column on the **debit** (**receipts**) side in the **cash book** with the values of the bank **pass book** or **statement** on **credit** (**deposit**) side.

2. Compare the values in the bank column on the **credit** (**payments**) side in the **cash book** with the values of the bank **pass book** or **statement** on **credit** (**withdrawals**) side.

Bank Over-Draft:

This is a facility provided by banking institution only for those who holds current account in the bank. With this facility the current account holder can withdraw money in excess of their balance in the account in simple these type of account holder can overdraw the money from their account

Proforma of Bank Reconciliation Statement

Date	Effect	Ref	Particulars	Amount
			Balance as per	XX
	Add			
		(a)	Total	XXXXX
	Less			
		(b)	Total	XXXXX
		(c) = (a-b)	Balance as per	XXXX

4.4.1   Using Bank Balance as per Company Cash Book Method

When bank balance of the cash book is available as base then

Add these below items

a. Anything which is **not debited** (**withdrawals**) in the bank

b. Anything which **have credited** (**deposits**) in the bank and not observed/ unknown

Deduct these below items

c. Anything which is **not credited** (**deposits**) in the bank

d. Anything which **have debited** (**withdrawals**) in the bank and not observed/ unknown

4.4.1.1   Illustration

In the books of Premsung Pvt Ltd, prepare **bank reconciliation statement** as on 30th September 2016, with the following details of **September** month.

* **Bank balance** as per company's **cash book** is Rs. 9000/- as on 30th September 2016.

  1. 05-09-2016 – Cheque of Rs. 4000/- was issued to the vendor, Mr. Ram, which he has not presented in the bank.

  2. 06-09-2016 – Cheque of Rs. 1200/- deposited in the bank account was dishonored.

  3. 09-09-2016 – Mangal Motors is customer of the, company has deposited sum of Rs. 5000/- in company bank account which was not yet accounted in cash book.

  4. 21-09-2016 – Rs. 50/- was debited by the bank in the company's account, for bank charges which was unknown and not recorded in cash book.

  5. 25-09-2016 – Sum of Rs. 900/- was late fee towards credit card was debited in the bank account.

  6. 30-09-2016 – Bank credited sum of Rs. 450/- as quarterly interest, this was not identified.

Bank reconciliation statement of Premsung Pvt Ltd as on 30th September 2016

Date	Effect	Ref	Particulars	Amount
			Balance as per cash book	9000
	Add:		Anything which is not debited in the bank	
05-09-16		(i)	Cheque issued to Mr Ram not presented	4000
	Add:		Anything which have credited in the bank and not observed	
09-09-16		(ii)	Mangal motors deposited cheque not identified	5000
30-09-16		(iii)	Quarterly interest credited in the account	450
		(a)	Total	18450
	Less:		Anything which is not credited in the bank	
06-09-16		(i)	Cheque deposited but dishonored	1200
	Less:		Anything which have debited in the bank and not observed	
21-09-16		(ii)	Bank charges debited	50
25-09-16		(iii)	Credit card late fee debited	900
		(b)	Total	2150
		(c) = (a-b)	Balance as per pass book	16300

4.4.2   Using Cash Balance as per Bank Pass Book Method

When cash balance of the bank pass book is available as base then

Add these below items

a. Anything which is **not credited** (**deposits**) in the bank

b. Anything which **have debited** (**withdrawals**) in the bank and not observed/ unknown

Deduct these below items

c. Anything which is **not debited** (**withdrawals**) in the bank

d. Anything which **have credited** (**deposits**) in the bank and not observed/ unknown

4.4.2.1 Illustration

In the books of **Tim-Tom Traders**, prepare **bank reconciliation statement** as on 30th June 2016, with the following details of **June** month.

- **Cash balance** as per bank **pass book** is Rs. 16300/- as on 30th June 2016.

1. 01-06-2016 – Insurance premium of Rs. 699/- and bank charges of Rs. 251/- was debited by the bank directly.

2. 08-06-2016 – Dividend of Rs. 3500/- was directly credited by bank account which was not identified.

3. 15-06-2016 – Cheque payment of Rs. 1300/- were made to C.A. Kotwal Associates towards auditing services were not yet cleared.

4. 20-06-2016 – Cheque Rs. 1200/- received by the customer was deposited in bank was got dishonored.

5. 22-06-2016 – Company had issued cheque of Rs. 2700/- to the supplier M/s Karmel Electronics, was not presented in the bank.

6. 30-06-2016 – Bank credited sum of Rs. 1950/- as quarterly interest, this was not identified.

Bank reconciliation statement of Tim-Tom Traders as on 30th June 2016

Date	Effect	Ref	Particulars	Amount
			Balance as per Pass Book	16300
	Add		Anything which is not credited in the bank	
20-06-16		i	Deposited cheque of customer got dishonored	1200
			Anything which have debited in the bank and not observed	
01-06-16		ii	Insurance premium debited by bank directly	699
01-06-16		iii	Bank charges debited for the month	251
		(a)	Total	18450
	Less		Anything which is not debited in the bank	
15-06-16		i	Cheque issued to C.A. Kotwal Associates not cleared	1300
22-06-16		ii	Cheque issued but not presented by the supplier	2700
			Anything which have credited in the bank and not observed	
08-06-16		iii	Dividend collected by bank directly	3500
30-06-16		iv	Bank interest credited unidentified	1950
		(b)	Total	9450
		(c) = (a-b)	Balance as per Cash Book	9000

4.4.3 Using Overdraft Balance as per Company Cash Book Method

When overdraft balance of the cash book is available as base then

Add these below items

a. Anything which is **not credited** (**deposits**) in the bank

b. Anything which **have debited** (**withdrawals**) in the bank and not observed/ unknown

Deduct these below items

c. Anything which is **not debited** (**withdrawals**) in the bank

d. Anything which **have credited** (**deposits**) in the bank and not observed/ unknown

4.4.3.1 Illustration

In the books of **Ekta Enterprises**, prepare **bank reconciliation statement** as on 31st August 2016, with the following details of **August** month.

- **Bank Overdraft/ credit balance** as per **cash book** is Rs. 6700/- as on 31st August 2016.

1. 01-08-2016 – Bank credited sum of Rs. 3200/- towards refund from IRCTC, which was not recorded in the cash book.

2. 03-08-2016 – Subscribed Govt investment scheme of Rs. 1000/- were auto debited by bank.

3. 11-08-2016 – Bonus of Rs. 500/- on share trading was directly credited by bank which was not identified.

4. 16-08-2016 – Company issued cheque of Rs. 5000/- to a supplier, which was not presented in the bank.

5. 21-08-2016 – Amount of Rs. 1500/- was wrongly debited by the bank.

6. 27-08-2016 – Cheque of Rs. 4000/- was deposited by the company was dishonored due to insufficient funds in the customer's bank account.

7. 31-08-2016 – Commission of Rs. 350/- was credited by bank into company's bank account.

8. 01-09-2016 – Bank has rectified the wrong debited entry and reversed the value of Rs. 1400/- by crediting it.

Bank reconciliation statement of Ekta Enterprises as on 31st August 2016

Date	Effect	Ref	Particulars	Amount
			Overdraft balance as per Cash Book	6700
	Add		Anything which is not credited in the bank	
27-08-16		i	Cheque deposited got dishonored due to insufficient funds in customer bank account	4000
			Anything which have debited in the bank and not observed	
03-08-16		ii	Investment in Govt Scheme debited	1000
21-08-16		iii	Bank wrongly debited, reason not yet validated	1500
		(a)	Total	13200
	Less		Anything which is not debited in the bank	
16-08-16		i	Cheque issued but not presented by the supplier	5000
			Anything which have credited in the bank and not observed	
01-08-16		ii	Refund from IRCTC credited in bank	3200
11-08-16		iii	Share Trading bonus credited in bank	500
11-08-16		iv	Commission credited by bank	350
		(b)	Total	9050
		(c) = (a-b)	Overdraft balance as per Pass Book	4150

4.4.4 Using Overdraft Balance as per Bank Pass Book Method

When overdraft balance of the bank pass book is available as base then

Add these below items

a. Anything which is **not debited** (**withdrawals**) in the bank
b. Anything which **have credited** (**deposits**) in the bank and not observed/ unknown

Deduct these below items

c. Anything which is **not credited** (**deposits**) in the bank
d. Anything which **have debited** (**withdrawals**) in the bank and not observed/ unknown

4.4.4.1 Illustration

In the books of **Roshni Com**, prepare **bank reconciliation statement** as on 31st November 2016, with the following details of **August** month.

- **Bank Overdraft/ credit balance** as per **pass book** is Rs. 4150/- as on 31st November 2016.

  1. 02-11-2016 – Company received cheque from its customer of Rs. 1900/- which was deposited in the bank but not yet cleared.
  2. 06-11-2016 – Cheque of Rs. 2000/- issued to a vendor was not yet cleared.
  3. 11-11-2016 – Bank charges of Rs. 500/- was debited by bank was not recorded.
  4. 15-11-2016 – Bank collected dividend on behalf of the company, sum of Rs. 4000/- and credited it into company bank account, which was not identified.
  5. 22-11-2016 – Cheque of Rs. 2100/- was deposited by the company was dishonored due to insufficient funds in the customer's bank account.
  6. 25-11-2016 – Company issued cheque of Rs. 3000/- to a supplier, which was not presented in the bank.
  7. 28-11-2016 – Bank had wrongly credited sum of Rs. 50/- in the company's bank account
  8. 30-11-2016 – Insurance premium of Rs. 2000/- was auto debited by bank.
  9. 04-12-2016 – Bank has rectified the wrong credited entry and reversed the value of Rs. 50/- by debiting company's bank account.

Bank reconciliation statement of **Roshni Com** as on 31st **November 2016**

Date	Effect	Ref	Particulars	Amount
			Overdraft balance as per Pass Book	4150
	Add:		Anything which is not debited in the bank	
06-11-16		(i)	Cheque issued to vendor not yet cleared	2000
25-11-16		(ii)	Cheque issued to supplier not yet presented	3000
			Anything which have credited in the bank and not observed	
15-11-16		(iii)	Dividend collected and credited by bank	4000
28-11-16		(iv)	Bank wrongly credited	50
	(a)		Total	
	Less:		Anything which is not credited in the bank	
02-11-16		(i)	Cheque deposited of the customer not yet cleared	1900
22-11-16		(ii)	Deposited cheque got dishonored	2100
			Anything which have debited in the bank and not observed	
11-11-16		(iii)	Bank charges debited was not recorded in cash book	500
30-11-16		(iv)	Insurance Premium debited by bank not recorded	2000
	(b)		Total	
	(c) = (a-b)		Overdraft balance as per Cash Book	6700

PRACTICE EXERCISE

In the books of **Magnatus Int**, prepare **bank reconciliation statement** as on 31st December 2016, with the following details of **December** month.

- **Cash balance** as per **pass book** is Rs. 6250/- as on 31st December 2016.

  1. 03-12-2016 – Cheque of Rs. 2000/- issued to a vendor was not yet cleared.
  2. 05-12-2016 – Bank charges of Rs. 500/- was debited by bank was not recorded.
  3. 09-12-2016 – Customer of the, company has deposited sum of Rs. 5000/- in company bank account which was not yet accounted in cash book.
  4. 21-12-2016 – Rs. 50/- was debited by the bank in the company's account, for bank charges which was unknown and not recorded in cash book.
  5. 25-12-2016 – Sum of Rs. 710/- was late fee towards credit card was debited in the bank account.
  6. 15-12-2016 – Bank collected dividend on behalf of the company, sum of Rs. 4000/- and credited it into company bank account, which was not identified.

7. 27-12-2016 – Cheque of Rs. 5000/- was deposited by the company was dishonored due to insufficient funds in the customer's bank account.

8. 31-12-2016 – Commission of Rs. 250/- was credited by bank into company's bank account.

9. 20-12-2016 – Cheque Rs. 3100/- received by the customer was deposited in bank was got dishonored.

10. 28-11-2016 – Bank had wrongly credited sum of Rs. 900/- in the company's bank account, which was got reversed in next month.

11. 22-12-2016 – Company had issued cheque of Rs. 2700/- to the supplier, which was not presented in the bank.

12. 31-12-2016 – Bank credited sum of Rs. 550/- as quarterly interest, this was not identified.

Chapter 5

Preparation of Final Accounts

LEARNING OBJECTIVES

After studying this chapter, you will understand:

- Meaning of Final Accounts
- Trading Account and Profit and Loss Account
- To Prepare Trading Account and Profit and Loss Account
- Balance Sheet
- To Prepare Balance Sheet

5.1 INTRODUCTION

Final accounts are the statements prepared at the end of a year, which present the final results of the operations of a business, in financial terms. The two important aspects of the final results of a business include ascertaining the profit or loss made by the business and determining the financial position of business as on the last date of the accounting period. Final accounts include the following two reports:

- Income Statement or Trading and Profit and Loss account: It is prepared to ascertain the results of a business operation, i.e. the net profit or net loss of the business for an accounting year.
- Position Statement or Balance Sheet: It indicates the financial position, i.e. the assets, liabilities, and owner's capital of a business at the end of an accounting year.

The final accounts prepared at the end of a year are useful for most of the stakeholders in an organisation. Stakeholders can be classified into two broad categories namely i) Internal Stakeholders such as management, shareholders or owners and ii) External Stakeholders such as creditors, employees, consumers, government etc.

While management gets to assess performance and progress of the organisation and decide the future course of action, shareholders or owners use the information to ascertain profits and credit worthiness of the concern.

5.2 OBJECTIVES OF PREPARING FINAL ACCOUNTS

The primary objectives of preparing Final Accounts are as follows:

a. To provide a fair and clear view of the Financial Performance of the business for the accounting period, which includes information about the profit or loss made by the business.

b. To provide a fair and clear view of the Financial Position of the business as on the last date of the accounting period, which includes information about the assets, liabilities and the capital.

5.3 TRADING AND PROFIT AND LOSS ACCOUNT

Profit and loss account is an accounting statement that shows an organisation's trading position over a given period of time, usually the financial year. A profit and loss account has two sections namely trading account and profit and loss account.

At the organisation's discretion (trading or manufacturing), these two accounts may be put together in one account or shown separately. However, the usual practice is that a single account is prepared with two sections, viz. trading account and profit and loss account.

5.3.1 Trading Account

A trading account merely indicates the result of buying and selling of goods, i.e. the gross profit or gross loss on trading, without considering administration, selling and financial expenses incurred in running the business.

The format of trading account is given below:

Trading Account

Trading Account for the year ending _____ (e.g. 31st March, 2016)					
Particulars		Amount (₹)	Particulars		Amount (₹)
To opening Stock		xxxxx	By Sales	xxxxx	
To Purchase	xxxxx		Less: Returns	xxxxx	xxxxx
Less: Returns	xxxxx	xxxxx	By Closing Stock		xxxxx
To Direct Expense (Eg: Wages, Carriage Charges, Octroi, Import Duty etc.)		xxxxx	By Gross Loss*		xxxxx
To Gross Profit*		xxxxx			
		xxxxx			xxxxx

Explanation of the items in the above format

Opening stock: It is the first item on the debit side of the trading account. In case of manufacturing business, opening stock includes the stock of raw materials, partly finished goods, and finished goods at the beginning of the trading period. In case of trading business, it includes only the stock of finished goods at the beginning of the trading period.

Purchases and purchase returns: Purchases refer to finished goods purchased for resale or raw materials purchased for manufacture. It includes both cash and credit purchases. Net purchases are entered in the outer column by deducting the purchase returns from the total purchases.

Cartage, carriage inwards, and freight: The details of transportation charges incurred for the movement of goods are entered in these fields. They may be inwards or outwards. Carriage, carriage inwards, and freight incurred on the goods purchased are entered on the debit side of the trading account. When these expenses are incurred on goods sold, they are entered in the profit and loss account. When it is not stated whether cartage, carriage, and freight are inward or outward, the common practice is to treat them as inwards.

Import duty, Excise duty, Octroi: The import duty, export duty, and octroi paid on the goods purchased are shown on the debit side of the trading account. Such duties paid on goods sold are entered in the profit and loss account. If there is no specification as to whether these duties are paid on purchases or on sales, it is considered to have been paid on purchases.

Wages: Wages incurred while manufacturing goods or making purchased goods ready for sale are considered direct expenses and entered on the debit side of the trading account. Indirect and non-manufacturing wages are entered in the profit and loss account. The wages, of which the nature (direct or indirect) is not mentioned, are treated as direct wages. Certain organisations combine wages and salaries. They treat them as direct expenses and enter the details on the debit side of the trading account.

Other factory expenses: Other factory expenses such as factory rent, factory insurance are direct expenses. They appear on the debit side of the trading account.

Sales and sales returns: Sales is the first item on the credit side of the trading account. Sales include both cash and credit sales. Net sales are entered in the outer column by deducting the sales returns from the total sales.

Sales tax: Sales tax refers to the tax paid by a businessman to the government on the sales made by him. It can be deducted from sales on the credit side of the trading account. Alternatively, it can also be treated as a selling expense and entered on the debit side of the profit and loss account.

Closing stock: Closing stock represents the stock of finished goods in case of a trading business. Whereas in case of a manufacturing business, it represents the stock of raw materials, partly finished goods, and finished goods at the end of the trading period. Closing stock generally does not appear in the trial balance but it has to be calculated and brought into the books of accounts

5.3.2 Objective of Trading Account

The Main objectives of trading account are:

i. To ascertain the gross profit or gross loss as a result of trading (sale and purchase) goods during the current period.

ii. To furnish information about the direct expenses like wages, cartage, freight etc.

5.3.3 Preparation of Trading Account

The trading account shows only the gross profit or gross loss. The gross profit or gross loss is the difference between net sales (sales – sales returns) and the cost of goods sold.

The cost of goods sold refers to the cost of the portion of goods actually sold during the year rather than the cost of goods purchased during the year.

Cost of Goods =

Opening Stock + Net Purchase (Purchase – Purchase Returns) + Direct Expenses – Closing Stock

Here, Direct Expenses refer to the expenses incurred in obtaining the goods and in converting and maintaining the goods into saleable condition such as freight, wages, electricity, rent etc. Net sale is arrived at by subtracting the sales returns from gross sales. Gross profit or gross loss is determined by the excess of net sale over cost of goods and vice-versa.

Opening stock, net purchase, and direct expenses are taken in debit side of the trading account whereas net sale and closing stock appear on the credit side.

Credit side exceeding debit side results in "gross profit" while the debit side exceeding credit side results in "gross loss". The gross profit or loss as shown by the trading account is transferred to the profit and loss account.

5.3.4 Illustrations

Illustration 1

Let's prepare the trading account for the year ended 31.03.2016 from the following particulars.

Particulars	Amount
Opening stock	15,000
Purchases	80,000
Sales	1,25,000
Sales returns	8,000
Fuel	500
Freight	1,000
Octroi	800
Wages	7,000
Electricity	1200
Premises rent	8,500
Packing materials	2,000
Closing stock on 31.03.2016	12,000
Purchase Returns	5000

Trading Account for the year ending 31st March, 2016					
Particulars		Amount (₹)	Particulars		Amount (₹)
To opening Stock		15,000	By Sales	1,25,000	
To Purchase	80,000		Less: Returns	8,000	1,17,000
Less: Returns	5,000	75,000	By Closing Stock		12,000
To Direct Expense (E.g: Wages, Carriage Charges, Octroi, Import Duty etc.)		21,000	By Gross Loss*		
To Gross Profit*		18000			
		1,29,000			1,29,000

Illustration 2

Let's prepare the trading account for the year ended 31.03.2016 from the following particulars.

Particulars	Amount
Opening stock	20,000
Purchases	1,20,000
Sales	75,000
Sales returns	5,000
Fuel	800
Freight	1,200
Octroi	900
Wages	9,000
Electricity	1600
Premises rent	7,000
Packing materials	1,500
Closing stock on 31.03.2016	20,000
Purchase Returns	2000

Trading Account for the year ending 31st March, 2016					
Particulars		Amount (₹)	Particulars		Amount (₹)
To opening Stock		20,000	By Sales	75,000	
To Purchase	1,20,000		Less: Returns	5,000	70,000
Less: Returns	2,000	1,18,000	By Closing Stock		20,000
To Direct Expense (E.g: Wages, Carriage Charges, Octroi, Import Duty etc.)		22,000	By Gross Loss*		70,000
To Gross Profit*					
		1,60,000			1,60,000

5.3.5   Manufacturing Account

A business which manufactures goods would require to know the cost of goods manufactured by them before ascertaining the gross profit or loss acquired by selling the goods. Such businesses have to prepare an additional account called manufacturing account in addition to the trading account.

The format of manufacturing account is as follows:

Manufacturing Account for the year ending (e.g. 31st March, 2016)

Particulars	Amount (₹)		Particulars	Amount (₹)
To Raw Materials Consumed			By Work-in-Progress (Closing)	XXXX
Opening Stock of Raw Materials	XXXX			
Purchase of raw materials	XXXX			
Carriage and freight on purchase of raw materials	XXXX		By Cost of Goods Manufactured transferred to Trading Account	XXXX
Less: Closing Stock of Raw Materials	XXXX			
		XXXX		
To Manufacturing Wages		XXXX		
To Factory Expenses:				
Electricity bill	XXXX			
Factory Rent	XXXX			
		XXXX		
Opening work in progress		XXXX		
		XXXX		XXXX

5.3.5.1 Illustrations

Illustration 3

Let's prepare the manufacturing account for the year ended 31.03.2016 from the following particulars

5.4 PROFIT AND LOSS ACCOUNT

Profit and loss account is an accounting statement that shows the organisation's trading position. It helps in ascertaining the net profit or net loss of a business for a given trading period, usually a financial year. It is the profit earned or loss incurred after charging all business expenses including all depreciation and provisions.

Particulars	Amount
Opening stock of raw materials	15,000
Purchase of raw materials	90,000
Closing stock of raw materials	7,500
Carriage and freight on purchase of raw materials	15,000
Manufacturing wages	37,500
Factory Rent	7,500
Electricity bill	22,500
Opening work in progress	12,000
Closing work in progress	8,500

Manufacturing Account for the year ending 31st March, 2016

Particulars	Amount (₹)		Particulars	Amount (₹)
To Raw Materials Consumed			By Work-in-Progress (Closing)	8,500
Opening Stock of Raw Materials	15,000			
Purchase of raw materials	80,000			
Carriage and freight on purchase of raw materials	12,000		By Cost of Goods Manufactured transferred to Trading Account	1,70,000
Less: Closing Stock of Raw Materials	8,000			
		99,000		
To Manufacturing Wages		37,500		
To Factory Expenses:				
Electricity bill	22,500			
Factory Rent	7,500			
		30,000		
Opening work in progress		12,000		
		1,78,500		1,78,500

The format of Profit and Loss account is as follows:

Profit & Loss Account for the year ending _____ (e.g. 31st March, 2016)			
Particulars	Amount (₹)	Particulars	Amount (₹)
To Gross Loss b/d	xxxxx	By Gross Profit b/d	xxxxx
To Selling and Distribution Expenses		By Discount Received	xxxxx
Advertisement	xxxxx	By Commission Received	xxxxx
Travellers' Salaries, Expenses and commission	xxxxx	By Income from Investments	xxxxx
Bad Debts	xxxxx	By Rent From Tenants	xxxxx
Godown Rent	xxxxx	By Income from Investments	xxxxx
Export Expenses	xxxxx	By Miscellaneous Revenue Receipts	xxxxx
Carriage Outward		By Interest Received	xxxxx
Bank Charges	xxxxx	By Apprenticeship Premium	xxxxx
Agent's Commission	xxxxx	By Interest on Debentures	xxxxx
Upkeep of Motor Lorries	xxxxx	By Income from any other source	xxxxx
To Management Expenses		By Net loss Transferred to Capital Account	xxxxx
Rent, Rates and Taxes	xxxxx		
Heating and Lighting	xxxxx		
Office Salaries	xxxxx		
Printing Stationery	xxxxx		
Postage and Telegrams	xxxxx		
Telephone Charges	xxxxx		
Legal Charges	xxxxx		
Audit Fee	xxxxx		
Insurance	xxxxx		
General Expenses	xxxxx		
To Depreciation and Maintenance			
Depreciation	xxxxx		
Repairs and Maintenance	xxxxx		
To Financial Expenses			
Discount Allowed	xxxxx		
Interest on Capital	xxxxx		
Interest on Loans	xxxxx		
Discount on Bills	xxxxx		
To Extraordinary Expenses			
Loss by Fire (Not covered by insurance)	xxxxx		
Cash Defalcations	xxxxx		
To Net Profit to Capital A/c	xxxxx		
	xxxxx		xxxxx

5.4.1 Classification of Incomes and Expenses

Income is defined as the amount a business receives in exchange of providing a service or good. Expenses are defined as the economic costs a business incurs to earn revenue.

Explanation of a few important items in the above format

Office and Maintenance Expenses

Salaries: This refers to the salaries paid to office staff.

Rent and taxes: Rent and taxes refers to municipal taxes and the rent paid for the office building.

Insurance: This refers to the premium paid for insuring buildings, machinery, stock, and so on against risks.

Office lighting and heating: This refers to lighting and heating expenses incurred in providing lighting and heating for the office.

Printing and stationery: This indicates the printing and stationery expenses incurred in the office.

Repairs and renewals: This refers to repair charges incurred for repairing the properties of the business.

Depreciation: Depreciation refers to the wear and tear, i.e. the reduction in the value of an asset, resulting out of its use.

Selling and Distribution Expenses

Carriage outwards or Freight outwards: It refers to the transportation expenses incurred in carrying the goods to the market for sale.

Bad debts: Bad debts refers to the debts that are considered to be irrecoverable.

Commission paid: This is the commission paid to the salesmen and distributors for their services.

Financial Expenses

Discount on sales or Discount allowed: This indicates the cash discount allowed to the debtors for the prompt payment made by them.

Interest paid: This refers to the interest paid on loans.

Interest on capital: Interest allowed to the proprietor on his capital is entered under interest on capital.

Incomes

Non-trading incomes: It refers to all incomes other than trading incomes, such as rent received, commission received, interest received, and so on.

Interest on drawings: It refers to the interest charged on the amount withdrawn by the proprietor from the business for his personal use. It is an income of the business and appears on the credit side of profit and loss account.

Note: Personal expenses such as life insurance premium, income tax, and so on, incurred by the business owner should not be included in the profit and loss account. Such expenses are treated as drawings, which has to be deducted from the capital

---

5.4.2 Objective of Profit and Loss Account

The main objectives of Profit and Loss Account are as follows:

i.   To get the final profit or loss (net profit or net loss) of the business for the current period

ii. To provide information on different classes of indirect expenses of the business such as financial expenses, maintenance expenses, office expenses etc.

5.4.3 Preparation of Profit and Loss Account

Preparation of profit and loss account can be performed in the following steps:

i.   The gross profit or gross loss as shown in the trading account is entered in the profit and loss account. Gross profit is entered on the credit side whereas the gross loss is entered on the debit side.

ii   All indirect expenses of the business such as rent, repairs, depreciation, electricity bills, taxes etc. are entered on the debit side of the profit and loss account

iii. All indirect or non-trading incomes such as interest or commission received, bad debts recovered etc. are entered on the credit side of the profit and loss account

After all the indirect incomes and expenses are entered in the profit and loss account, the account is balanced. If the total of the credit side of the profit and loss account is more than the debit side, the balance is called 'net profit'. Conversely, if the debit side is higher than the credit side, the balance is called 'net loss'.

5.4.4 Illustrations

Illustration 4

Let's prepare the profit and loss account for the year ended 31.12.2016 from the given particulars

Particulars	Amount
Gross profit	2,25,000
Salaries	37,500
Commission received	2,700
Rent paid	15,000
Office lighting	3,750
Advertisement	8,400
Printing and stationery	4,500
Repairs and Maintenance	6,300
Interest Received	2,700
Interest on loans	1,350
Discount allowed	3,000
Interest on Debentures	375
Bad debts	3,300
Carriage outwards	1,800
Travelling outwards	2,775
Telephone Charges	825
Discount received	900
Insurance	1,000
Depreciation	2,000

Profit & Loss Account for the year ending 31ˢᵗ March, 2016				
Particulars	Amount (₹)	Particulars		Amount (₹)
		By Gross Profit b/d		2,25,000
To Selling and Distribution Expenses		By Discount Received		900
Advertisement	8,400	By Commission Received		2,700
Travellers' Salaries, Expenses and commission	2,775	By Interest Received		2,700
Bad Debts	3,300	By Interest on Debentures		375
Godown Rent	15,000			
Carriage Outward	1,800			
To Management Expenses				
Heating and Lighting	3,750			
Office Salaries	37,500			
Printing Stationery	4,500			
Telephone Charges	825			
Insurance	1,000			
To Depreciation and Maintenance				
Depreciation	2,000			
Repairs and Maintenance	6,300			
To Financial Expenses				
Discount Allowed	2,000			
Interest on Loans	1,350			
To Net Profit to Capital A/c	1,41,175			
	2,31,675			2,31,675

Illustration 5

Let's prepare the profit and loss account for the year ended 31.12.2016 from the given particulars:

5.5   BALANCE SHEET

Balance sheet is a quantitative summary of a business organisation's financial condition at a specific point of time presenting a complete picture of a company's assets, liabilities, and net worth. In other words, it is a statement of the total assets and liabilities (including capital) of an organisation as on a particular date - usually the last date of an accounting period.

The first part of a balance sheet shows all the productive assets a company owns, and the second part shows all the financing methods (such as liabilities and shareholders' equity). It is also called the statement of condition.

Particulars	Amounts
Gross profit	3,15,000
Office Salaries	52,500
Commission received	3,780
Office lighting	5,250
Advertisement	11,760
Printing and stationery	6,300
Repairs and Maintenance	8,820
Interest Received	5,000
Interest on loans	1,890
Interest on Debentures	525
Bad debts	4,620
Carriage outwards	2,520
Travelling outwards	3,885
Telephone Charges	1,155
Discount received	1,260
Insurance	1,400
Depreciation	2,800

Following is a format of Balance Sheet:

Balance sheet as on		(e.g. 31ˢᵗ March, 2016)	
Liabilities	Amount ₹	Assets	Amount ₹
Capital	xxxxx	Fixed Assets:	
Fixed Liabilities:	xxxxx	Plant and Machinery	xxxxx
Long-Term Loans	xxxxx	Land and Building	xxxxx
Long-Term deposits	xxxxx	Furniture & Fixtures	xxxxx
Long Term Liabilities:			
Loan From Bank	xxxxx	Vehicles	xxxxx
Debentures	xxxxx		
Current Liabilities:		Goodwill	xxxxx
Bills Payable	xxxxx	Patent	xxxxx
Sundry Creditors		Copyright	xxxxx
Bank Overdraft		Current Assets:	
Income received in advance		Cash in Hand	xxxxx
Short Term Loans		Cash at Bank	xxxxx
		Floating Assets:	
		Sundry Debtors	xxxxx
		Investments	xxxxx
		Bills Receivables	xxxxx
		Stock in Trade	xxxxx
		Prepaid Expenses	xxxxx
		Profit & Loss A/c	xxxxx
	xxxxx		xxxxx

5.5.1 Objective of Balance Sheet

A balance sheet is prepared with a view to ascertain the financial position or soundness of a business as on a given date. The assets and liabilities of the organisation reflect its financial position or soundness. A business can be called sound when its assets are more than its liabilities. On the other hand, if the liabilities are more than its asset, it is considered unsound.

5.5.2 Classification of Assets & Liabilities

Assets are defined as any item of economic value owned by an individual or corporation, provided it can be measured in terms of money. In other words, assets are the properties owned by an organisation and the debts (i.e. amounts) due to an organisation from other parties. Examples are cash, securities, accounts receivable, inventory, office equipment, and other properties.

From an accounting perspective, assets are divided into the following categories namely current assets (cash and other liquid items), long-term assets (real estate, plant, equipment), prepaid and deferred assets (expenditures for future costs such as insurance, rent, interest), and intangible assets (trademarks, patents, copyrights, goodwill).

Current assets, circulating, floating or fluctuating assets: These refer to cash or other temporary assets which can be converted into cash in a short period. Examples are cash in hand, cash at bank, bills receivable, and other liquid items.

Liquid assets: Liquid assets are the current assets which are either in the form of cash or can be converted into cash immediately without incurring high losses. Examples are cash in hand, cash at bank, and sundry debtors.

Investments: This refers to the amount invested by the business on government bonds, on shares and debentures of companies for the purpose of earning interest and dividends.

Investments may be for a short-term or long-term. Short-term investments are grouped with current assets and long-term investments are shown as a separate item.

Fixed assets: These are the assets held by a business organisation for its use, and not for sale. These are relatively permanent in nature. Examples are buildings, furniture, and machinery.

Wasting assets: Wasting assets are the fixed assets lost through use or exhausted. Examples are mines and quarries.

Intangible assets: Intangible assets are the fixed assets which do not have a physical existence, i.e. it cannot be seen or touched, but the possession of which yields benefit to the business or the possessor. Examples are copyright, patent, and goodwill.

Fictitious assets: Fictitious assets are the debit balances, i.e. expenses and losses, carried forward from one accounting period to another. These are fictitious and not represented by any tangible or concrete property. Examples are heavy advertisement expenses not written off and preliminary expenses.

Liabilities are amounts owed by a business to other parties. This amount can be owed for various reasons such as purchase of assets on credit, services received on credit or purchase of goods on credit. Examples of liabilities are sundry creditors, loans borrowed, bills payable etc. Liabilities of a concern may be classified into the following categories:

Current Liabilities are those liabilities that require to be repaid in a short period. Examples of current liabilities include bills payable, short term loans borrowed, sundry creditors etc.

Fixed Liabilities are those liabilities which are more permanent in nature and require to be repaid after a long period which may extend the current accounting period.

5.5.3 Preparation of Balance Sheet

Balance sheet is prepared only after the trading and profit and loss account has been prepared since the net profit or loss requires to be added to or subtracted from the capital. The liabilities are put on the left hand side of balance sheet while the assets are put on the right. The sides of balance sheet are not called debit or credit side since it is a statement and not an account. There are multiple ways in which the assets and liabilities are arranged on a balance sheet. Assets can be arranged

either in the order of liquidity or order of permanence. The first method puts current assets on the top and fixed assets at the end whereas the second method puts fixed assets on the top and current assets at the end. Liabilities can be arranged either in the order of urgency of payment or in the order of permanence. The first method puts current liabilities on the top whereas the second one puts the fixed liabilities at the beginning.

5.5.4 Illustrations

Illustration 6

Let's prepare a balance sheet as on 31.03.2016 using the particulars given below.

Particulars	Amount
Capital	1,05,000
Long term loan	70,000
Sundry creditors	28,000
Sundry debtors	52,500
Investments	35,000
Bills receivable	8,750
Plant and machinery	39,375
Land and building	43,750
Goodwill	17,500
Patents	8,750
Bills payable	22,750
Cash in hand	9,800
Cash at bank	18,200
Net profit	26,250
Closing stock	27,125
Bank overdraft	8,750

Balance sheet as on 31st March, 2016				
Liabilities	Amount ₹	Assets		Amount ₹
Capital	1,05,000	*Fixed Assets:*		
Fixed Liabilities:		Plant and Machinery		39,375
Long-Term Loans	70,000	Land and Building		43,750
		Goodwill		17,500
Current Liabilities:		Patent		8,750
Bills Payable	22,750			
Sundry Creditors	28,000	*Current Assets:*		
Bank Overdraft	8,750	Cash in Hand		9,800
Income received in advance		Cash at Bank		18,200
Short Term Loans				
Profit & Loss A/c	26,250	*Floating Assets:*		
		Sundry Debtors		52,500
		Investments		35,000
		Bills Receivables		8,750
		Closing Stock		27,125
	2,60,750			2,60,750

Particulars	Amount
Capital	1,84,000
Long term loan	56,000
Sundry creditors	22,400
Drawings	10,000
Sundry debtors	42,000
Investments	28,000
Bills receivable	7,000
Plant and machinery	31,500
Goodwill	14,000
Patents	7,000
Bills payable	18,200
Cash in hand	7,840
Cash at bank	14,560
Net profit	21,000
Closing stock	21,700
Bank overdraft	7,000

Illustration 7

Let's prepare a balance sheet as on 31.03.2016 using the particulars given below.

KEY TAKEAWAYS

♦ Final accounts are the statements prepared which indicates the final results of the operations of a business organisation, in financial terms.

♦ Final accounts include trading and profit and loss account and balance sheet.

♦ Profit and loss account is an accounting statement that shows an organisation's trading position over a given period of time.

♦ Trading account indicates the result of buying and selling of goods.

♦ Balance sheet is a quantitative summary of an organisation's financial condition at a specific point of time, including assets, liabilities, and net worth.

♦ Assets can be defined as any item of economic value owned by an individual or corporation, especially that which could be converted into cash.

♦ Liability can be defined as any item of economic value owed by an individual or an organization.

Balance sheet as on 31st March, 2016				
Liabilities	Amount ₹	Assets		Amount ₹
Capital		Fixed Assets:		
Opening Capital	1,84,000	Plant and Machinery		31,500
Less Drawings	10,000	Land and Building		43,750
	1,74,000	Goodwill		14,000
		Patent		7,000
Fixed Liabilities:				
Long-Term Loans	56,000	Current Assets:		
		Cash in Hand		7,840
Current Liabilities:		Cash at Bank		14,560
Bills Payable	18,200			
Sundry Creditors	22,400	Floating Assets:		
Bank Overdraft	7,000	Sundry Debtors		42,000
		Investments		28,000
		Bills Receivables		7,000
		Closing Stock		21,700
		Profit & Loss A/c		60,250
	2,77,600			2,77,600

PRACTICE EXERCISES

1. From the following trial balance of Smart Electricals, prepare trading and profit and loss account for the year ending 31.03.2016, and a balance sheet as on that date:

Particulars	Debit	Credit
Owner's drawings	24,500	
Furniture	9,100	
Land and buildings	70,000	
Opening stock	77,000	
Debtors	65,100	
Purchases	3,85,000	
Sales returns	7,000	
Discount	5,600	
Taxes and insurance	7,000	
General expenses	14,000	
Salaries	31,500	
Commission	7,700	
Carriage	6,300	
Bad debts	2,800	
Owner's capital account		1,05,000
Bank overdraft		14,700
Rent received from tenants		58,800
Sales		5,25,000
Discount received		7,000
Provision for doubtful debts		2,100
Total	7,12,600	7,12,600

2. Use the trial balance of Surekha Enterprises below and prepare the trading and profit and loss account for the year that ended on 31.03.2016.

Particulars	Debit	Credit
Opening stock	1,20,000	
Purchases	3,30,000	
Purchase returns		12,000
Sales		5,85,000
Sales returns	19,500	
Carriage inwards	5,250	
Wages	24,000	
Freight	3,600	
Factory rent	15,000	
Water and electricity	2,400	
Salaries	40,500	
Rent	18,000	
Advertisement	3,600	
Carriage outwards	2,400	
Discount allowed	2,250	
Discount received		3,600
Bad debts	3,000	
Rent received		7,200
Bad debts recovered		3,300
Lighting and heating	2100	

Particulars	Debit	Credit
Telephone expenses	4,350	
Building	1,35,000	
Furniture	36,000	
Goodwill	45,000	
Patents and trademarks	24,000	
Secured loan		60,000
Debentures		1,50,000
Capital		6,00,000
Sundry creditors		72,000
Sundry debtors	1,20,000	
Bills receivable	1,49,400	
Bills payable		27,000
Cash in hand	36,000	
Cash at bank	84,000	
Bank overdraft		15000
Investments	3,09,750	
Total	15,35,100	15,35,100

3. From the following trial balance of Hinduja and co., prepare trading and profit and loss account for the year ending 31.03.2016, and a balance sheet as on that date:

Particulars	Debit	Credit
Opening stock	85,000	
Purchases	2,51,000	
Purchase returns		25,000
Sales		6,50,000
Sales returns	12,000	
Carriage inwards	4,000	
Wages	23,000	
Freight	3,500	
Water and electricity	3,000	
Salaries	56,000	
Rent	24,000	
Carriage outwards	3,500	
Discount allowed	2,600	
Discount received		4,000
Bad debts	4,000	
Rent received		8,500
Telephone expenses	4,200	
Building	2,50,000	
Furniture	40,000	
Goodwill	1,00,000	
Capital		7,00,000
Sundry creditors		93,300
Sundry debtors	1,10,000	
Bills receivable	75,000	
Bills payable		34,000
Cash in hand	15,000	
Cash at bank	94,000	
Bank overdraft		45000
Investments	4,00,000	
Total	15,59,800	15,59,800

Chapter 6

Computerised Accounting Systems using Tally.ERP 9

PART A

LEARNING OBJECTIVES

After studying this chapter, you will understand:

- Creating a Company
- Configurations and Features
- Creating Accounting Ledgers and Groups
- Creating Stock Items and Groups
- Voucher Entry

- Generating Reports – Cash Book, Ledger Accounts, Trial Balance, Profit and Loss Account, Balance Sheet, Funds Flow Statement, Cash Flow Statement
- Banking
- Cost Centres and Cost Categories
- Order Processing & Pre-closure of Orders

6.1   INTRODUCTION

Tally.ERP 9 is one of the most widely used financial software. Tally.ERP 9 reports can help a business owner make informed decisions to increase efficiency, reduce costs, and organise business operations.

With Tally.ERP 9, accurate, up-to-date business information is available at your fingertips anytime. It provides a comprehensive solution for the accounting and inventory needs of a business.

It provides the capability to extract, interpret and present financial data.

6.1.1   Getting started with Tally.ERP 9

Tally.ERP 9 can be started by double clicking the Tally.ERP 9 icon on desktop.

Components of Gateway of Tally

The Gateway of Tally is Tally.ERP 9's main screen. It appears as shown in Figure 6.1.

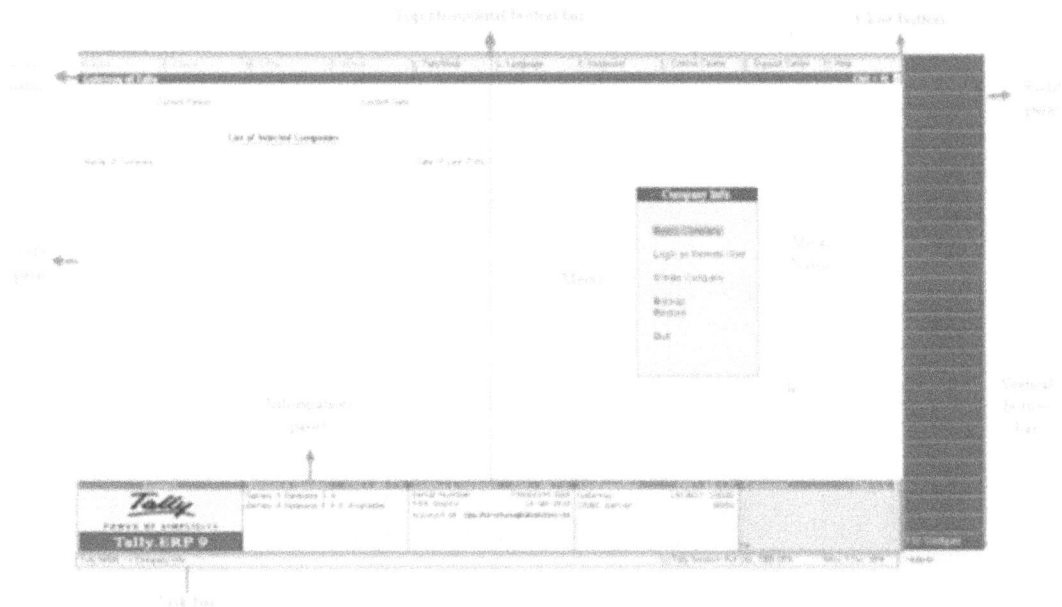

Figure 6.1: Gateway of Tally

The Gateway of Tally displays menus, screens, reports and options that you select. The components of a Tally.ERP 9 screen are as listed below:

- Top horizontal button bar: This is a collection of buttons that provide quick interaction, and is placed above the title bar.

- Close button: This button allows you to exit the current screen. If you are at the Gateway of Tally, this button allows you to exit the application.

- Right Pane: The right part of the Gateway of Tally screen, where the menu is displayed. The shortcut key for each menu option is a letter from the option's name, which will be highlighted in red.

♦ Vertical button bar: This is a collection of buttons which provide quick interaction with Tally.ERP 9, placed on the extreme right of the screen.

♦ Calculator Pane: This can be used for extrapolations.

♦ Information Panel: This displays details of Product, Version, License, and Configuration.

Mouse/Keyboard Conventions	
Action	Particulars
Fn	Press the Function key
Fn	Press ALT + Function key
Fn	Press CTRL + Function key

6.1.2 Mouse/Keyboard Conventions

While working with Tally.ERP 9, use the following conventions:

Switching between Screen Areas

When Tally.ERP 9 first loads, the Gateway of Tally screen will be displayed. To switch between the main screen area and the Information Panel or calculator at the bottom of the screen, press CTRL+N or CTRL+M as indicated on the screen.

6.1.3 Closing Tally.ERP 9

You can exit the program from any Tally.ERP 9 screen, but all screens need to be closed before it shuts down. To exit Tally.ERP 9,

♦ Press Esc until you see the message Quit? Yes or No? Press Enter or Y, or click Yes to exit Tally.ERP 9.

♦ Alternatively, to exit without confirmation, press CTRL+Q from Gateway of Tally.

♦ You can also press Enter when the option Quit is selected from Gateway of Tally.

6.2 CREATING A COMPANY IN TALLY.ERP 9

The first step towards working with Tally.ERP 9 is to create a 'company'. A 'company' in Tally.ERP 9 is a central repository where you can maintain all the financial records of your business, and from where you can extract the required financial reports and statements.

The procedure to create a company is explained below.

Scenario

Create a company named 'Surya Traders' with the financial year beginning 1st April 2016 and book beginning 1st April 2016
Go to Gateway of Tally > Company Info. > Create Company
The Company Creation screen appears as shown below (Figure 6.2):

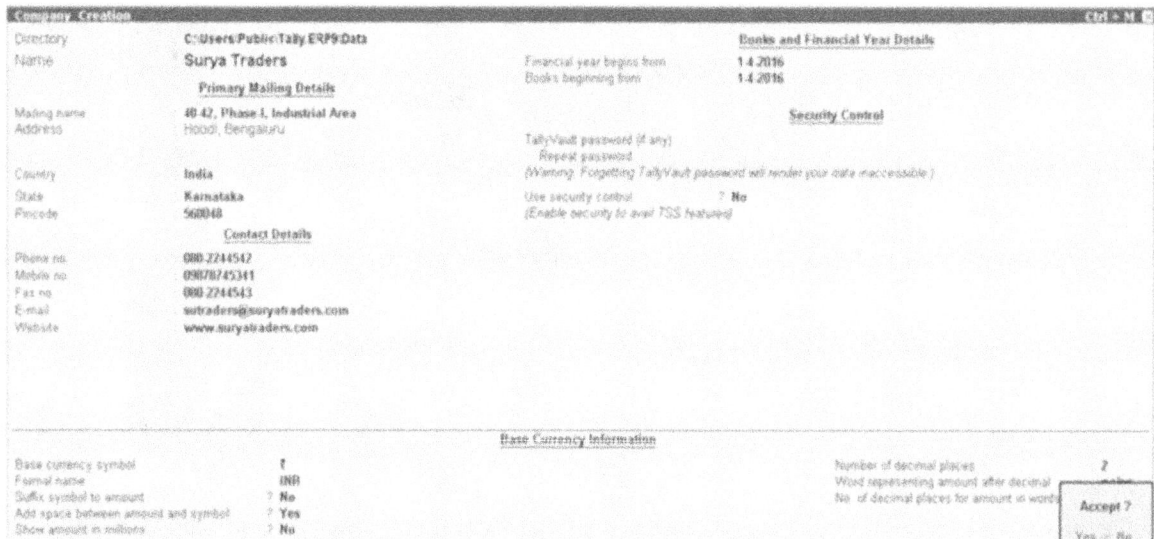

Figure 6.2: Company Creation screen

The message Accept? **Yes** or **No** will be displayed. Press **Y** or **Enter** to save the details.

The fields in the Company Creation screen and the information to be filled in each of them are explained below. To navigate between the fields, use the Enter/Tab/arrow keys, or mouse clicks.

♦ Directory: The path to the location of Tally.ERP 9 data is displayed here. By default, the path provided while installing Tally.ERP 9 will be displayed. However, you can press Backspace and specify the location in which you want the data to be stored.

* Name: Provide a name for the company that is being created. In this example, we are creating a company named National Traders.

* Primary Mailing details: The mailing name and address details of companies are picked from here for any report such as balance sheet and Statements of Accounts.

* Contact Details: We can maintain all the contact details in this section like Telephone Number, Mobile Number, Email, Website

* Books and Financial Year Details:
  o Financial Year from: This refers to the twelve-month accounting period of the company. For Surya Traders, the financial year begins on 1-4-2016.
  o Books beginning from: The date provided in the aforesaid field will be automatically displayed here. In the example, the date is retained. However, if you have started with maintaining your books of accounts with Tally.ERP 9 mid-year, the required date can be set accordingly.

* Security Control:
  o TallyVault Password (if any): Once you enter a password here, you will need it to open your company each time. The name of a company that is locked using TallyVault will be hidden with the asterisk '*' symbol. You need to provide the TallyVault password to open and access the company.
  o Repeat Password: Here, enter the password in the TallyVault field, as a confirmation
  o Use Security Control: Setting this option to 'Yes' will allow you to define the access rights for each user who will access your company. This feature is explained in forthcoming volumes.

* Base Currency Information:
  o Base Currency Symbol: The base currency symbol will

be filled as per the country selected.
  o Formal Name: The currency's formal name will be filled here. In this example, it is ₹ INR(Indian Rupees).
  o Is Symbol SUFFIXED to Amounts: For some countries, the currency symbol is specified after the amount. This option can be enabled for such countries, so that the currency symbol may be printed after the amount. However, National Traders is an Indian company and hence this option is set to 'No'.
  o Add Space between Amount and Symbol: Tally.ERP 9 will provide a single space between the amount and the currency symbol, if this option is set to 'Yes'. For e.g.: Rs. 5,000. Notice the space between symbol and the amount
  o Show amounts in Millions: If the company's financial statements need to have their values expressed in terms of millions, set this option to Yes.
  o Number of Decimal Places: By default, the number of decimal places for the base currency is set to 2. However, you can have up to 4 decimal places. The Indian currency has 2 decimal places whereas certain other countries require 3 decimal places and so on.
  o Word used to print decimal portion of amount: The symbol for amounts expressed in decimals will be set by de- fault. For India, it is paise.
  o Decimal Places for printing amounts in Words: You can specify the number of decimal places for printing the amount in words. This number should be equal to or lesser than the number specified in Number of Decimal Places field. For example, if the currency has up to 3 decimal places, the value to be printed in words can be restricted to 2 decimal places.

Note: Base currency information is set to the default based on the country selected.

The Gateway of Tally screen will appear with the company's name displayed on the left pane as shown below (Figure 6.3):

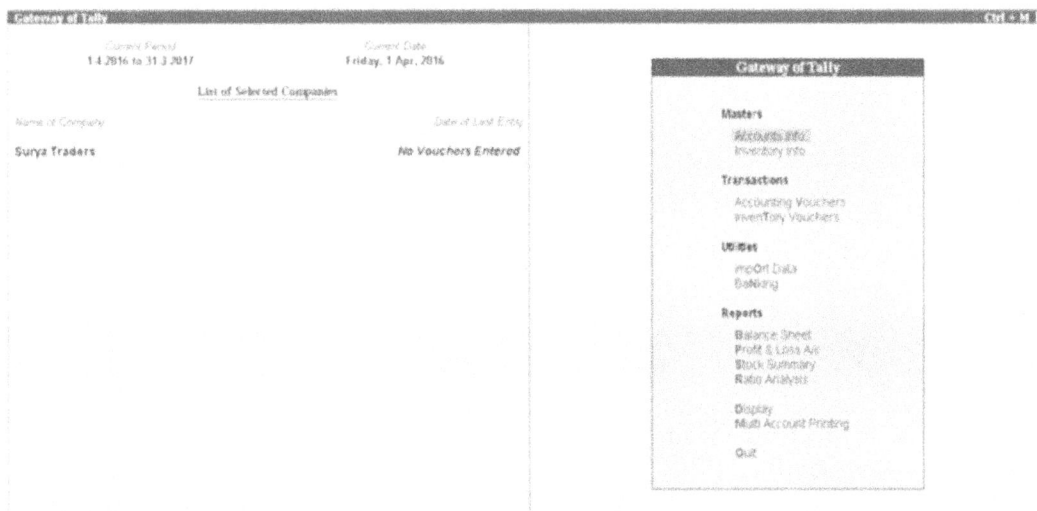

Figure 6.3: Gateway of Tally

This indicates that the company is currently open in Tally.ERP 9.

Activity

Create a company - Radhika Enterprises, with the financial year beginning on 1st April, 2016 and books beginning from the 1st April, 2016. You may enter the company details as required.

6.2.1   Select a Company

By 'selecting' a company, you are essentially opening it in Tally.ERP 9.

1. Go to Gateway of Tally > F3 Company Info. (ALT + F3)
2. Click Select Company, or press S. Tally.ERP 9 displays the Select Company screen, with a List of Companies that are available in the location specified. You can also press F1 to get to the Select Company screen.

6.2.2   Shut a Company

By 'shutting' a company, you are essentially closing a company.

1. Go to Gateway of Tally > F3 Company Info. (ALT + F3)
2. Click Shut Company. Tally.ERP 9 displays the Close Company screen, with the List of Companies that are open. You can also use ALT + F1 from the Gateway of Tally to get to this screen

6.2.3   Alter Company Details

By 'altering' a company, you are modifying the details which you have provided in the Company Creation screen.

1. Go to Gateway of Tally >F3 Company Info. (ALT + F3)
2. Click Alter or press A. Tally.ERP 9 displays the Select Item screen, with a List of Companies that are available in the location specified. Select the company which you need to alter and press Enter to view the Company Alteration screen. Alter the company details as required and accept the screen.

6.3   FEATURES AND CONFIGURATIONS

Once you have created a company in Tally.ERP 9, the next step would be to setup Tally.ERP 9's 'Features' and 'Configurations'.

The 'Features' in Tally.ERP 9 are a set of capabilities, provided as options, that enable you to maintain financial records as per your business needs. The Company Features menu can be found by clicking F11: Features on the vertical button bar. The effect of these options will be reflected only in the company for which they are enabled.

The Company Features section in Tally.ERP 9 is divided into the following major categories:

*   Accounting Features
*   Inventory Features
*   Statutory & Taxation
*   Audit Features
*   TSS Features
*   Add-On Features

You can press **F11** from any screen of Tally.ERP 9 or you may also click the **F11**: Features button available in the button bar, to enable the required features. The features are specific only to the company currently in use (for which the said feature is enabled), thereby allowing flexibility of independently enabling different features for each of the companies.

Go to **Gateway of Tally** > press **F11: Features**

The Company Features screen appears as shown below (Figure 6.4):

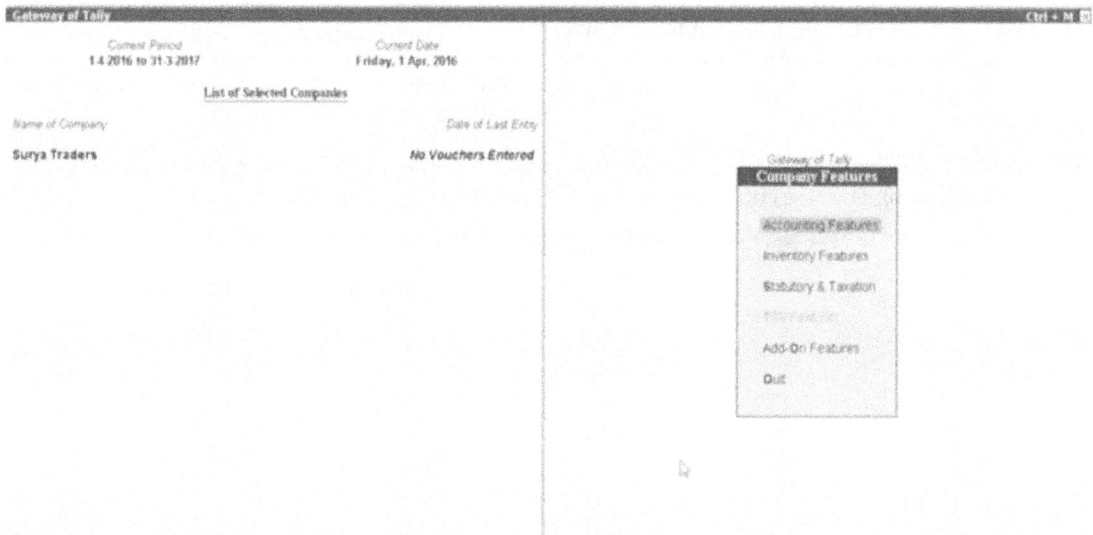

Figure 6.4: Company Features

Note: Audit Features and TSS Features appear only after activating administrator security.

The 'Configurations' in Tally.ERP 9 are options that help you to modify the way a feature works. The Configuration menu can be found by clicking F12: Configure on the vertical button bar. The options when enabled, will have an effect on all the companies in the data directory.

In Tally.ERP 9, the **F12: Configurations** are provided for Accounting, Inventory & printing options and are user-definable as per the business' requirements.

The **F12: Configurations** are applicable to all the companies residing in the Tally.ERP 9 Data Directory. The **F12:**

Configuration options vary depending upon the Context, i.e., if you press **F12: Configure** from Voucher entry screen, the respective **F12: Configurations** screen is displayed.

Go to **Gateway of Tally >** click **F12: Configure**

The **Configuration** menu appears as shown below (Figure 6.5):

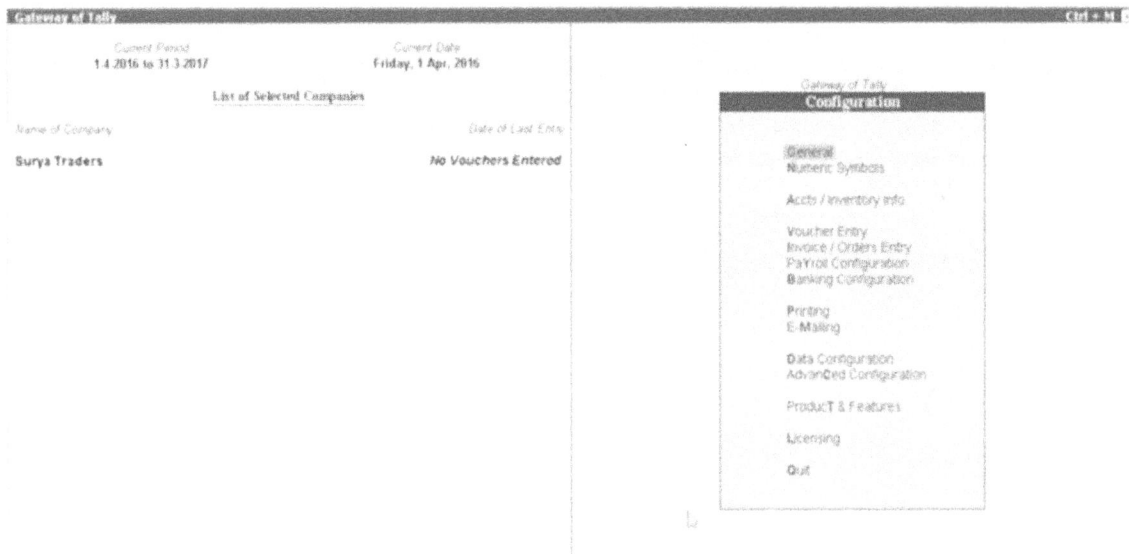

Figure 6.5: Configuration

There are numerous settings available under various menus in the **F12: Configuration** screen, which may be configured for any additional information required to be entered during master creations, voucher entry and printing.

6.4 CREATING ACCOUNTING LEDGERS AND GROUPS

Ledger

A 'Ledger' is an account head. For instance, the sales account head will be called a 'Sales Ledger' in Tally.ERP 9. Similarly, a customer would be an account head, and will be called a 'party

ledger'.

You can create ledgers specific to your business transactions.

For a newly created company, there are two pre-defined ledgers available in Tally.ERP 9:

1. Cash

2. Profit & Loss A/c

To view the list of ledgers, go to **Gateway of Tally > Accounts Info. > Ledgers > Display (Multiple Ledgers).**

The **Multi Ledger Display** screen appears as shown below (Figure 6.6):

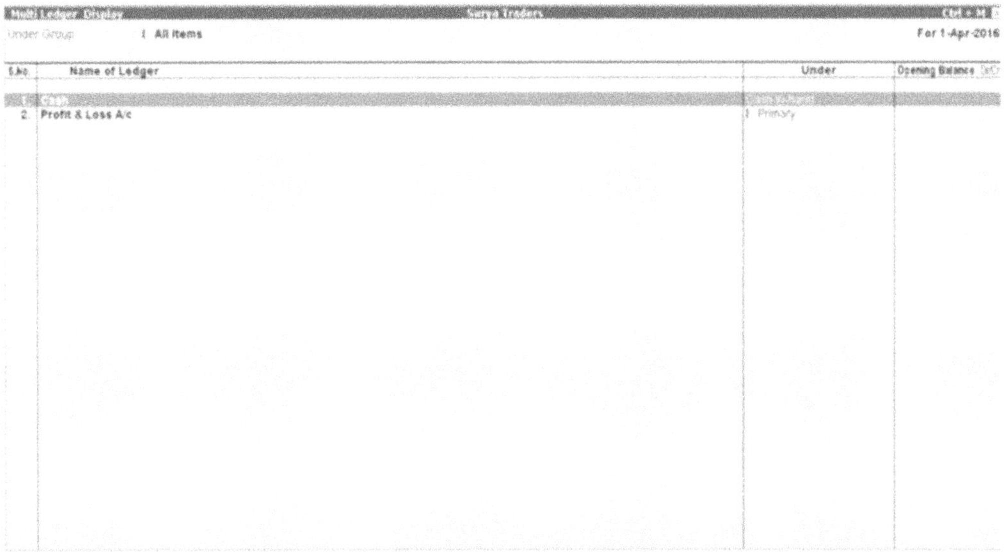

Figure 6.6: Multi Ledger Display

Group

A 'Group' is the accounting group under which ledgers of the same nature can be classified. For instance, Tally.ERP 9 has a default Group 'Sales Accounts', under which all the sales ledgers will be classified.

There are 28 pre-defined groups in Tally.ERP 9, which feature in the Chart of Accounts of many organisations. Out of these, 15 groups are primary groups and the remaining 13 are sub-groups.

Among the 15 primary groups, 9 groups are Balance Sheet items and the remaining 6 groups are Profit & Loss A/c items. You can use these groups to build your chart of accounts, as well as create and use groups specific to your business transactions. However, you may also alter the nomenclature of these 28 groups.

To view the list of the 28 groups, known as the **List of Accounts**, go to **Gateway of Tally > Accounts Info. > Groups > Display (Multiple Groups)**.

The **Multi Group Display** appears as shown below (Figure 6.7):

Figure 6.7: Multi Group Display

6.4.1 Ledger Creation

The ledgers to be created, the opening balance to be provided for them, and the groups under which they have to be classified, are specified in the table below:

Illustration 1

On 01-04-2016 Surya Traders having Capital Rs. 45,000 and Land & Building Rs. 80,000

Creation of Capital Account ledger

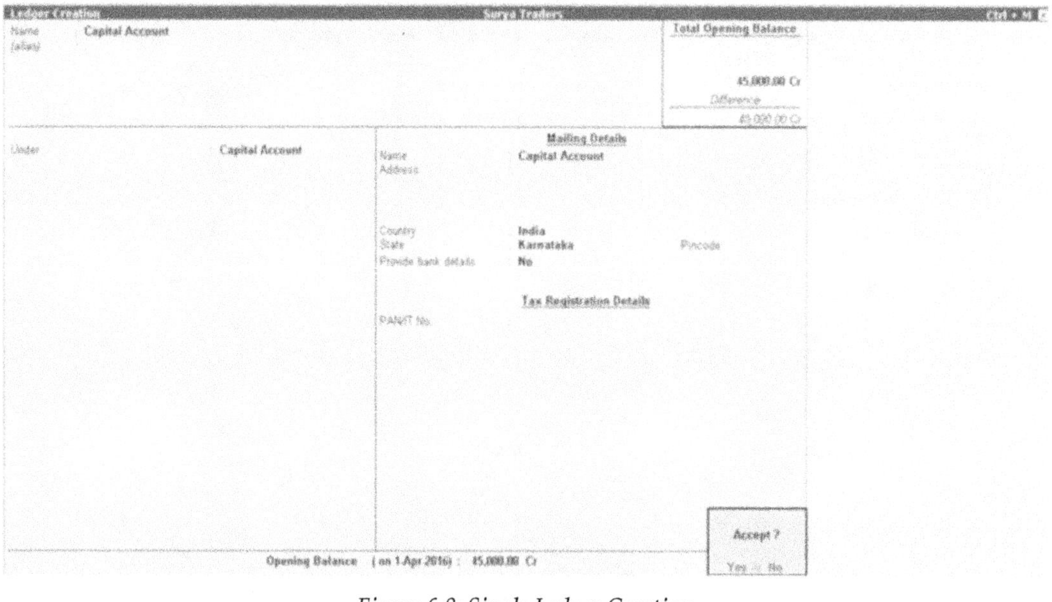

Figure 6.8: Single Ledger Creation

1. Go to **Gateway of Tally > Accounts Info. > Ledgers > Create**
2. Enter **Name** as **Capital Account**
3. Select **Capital Account** from the **List of Groups**
4. Enter Rs. **45,000** in the **Opening Balance (1-Apr-2016)** field

   The completed **Ledger Creation** screen appears as shown (Figure 6.8):
5. Press **Y** or **Enter** to accept the screen

Creation of Land & Building ledger

1. Go to **Gateway of Tally > Accounts Info. > Ledgers > Create**
2. Enter **Name** as **Land & Building**
3. Select **Fixed Assets** from the **List of Groups**
4. Enter Rs. **80,000** in the **Opening Balance (1-Apr-2016)** field

   The **completed Ledger Creation** screen appears as shown below (Figure 6.9):

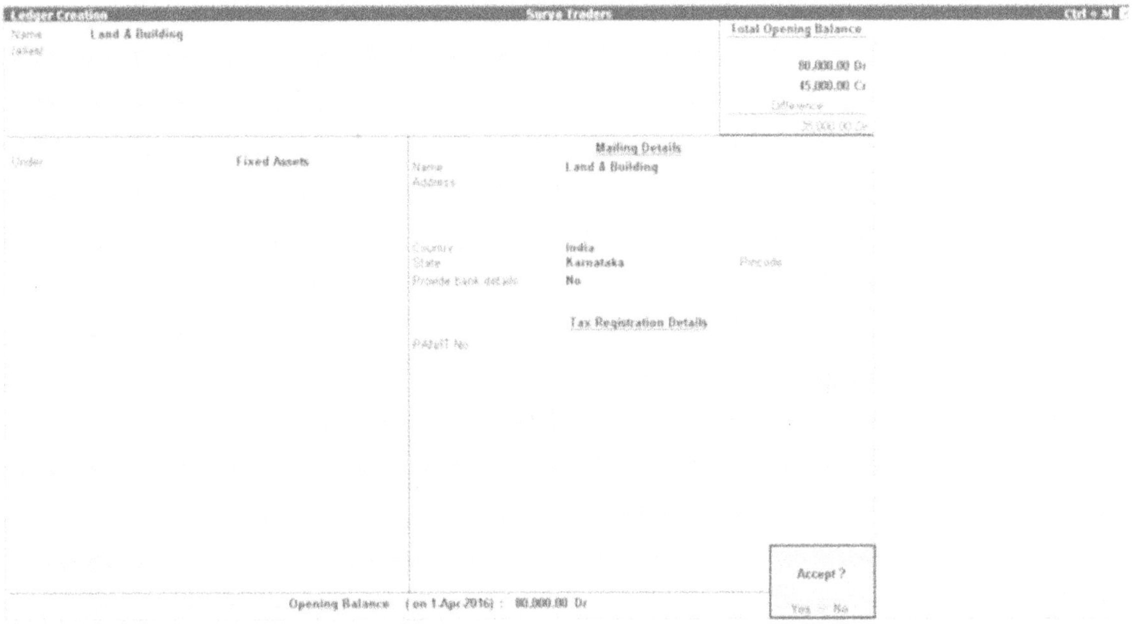

Figure 6.9: Single Ledger Creation

1. Press **Y** or **Enter** to accept the screen.

Tally.ERP 9 displays the total debit and credit opening balances while the ledgers are being created in the Ledger Creation screen. This is to avoid differences in the opening balance.

6.4.1.1 Multi Ledger Creation

Illustration-2

On 01-04-2016 Surya Traders having loan account in Axis Bank.

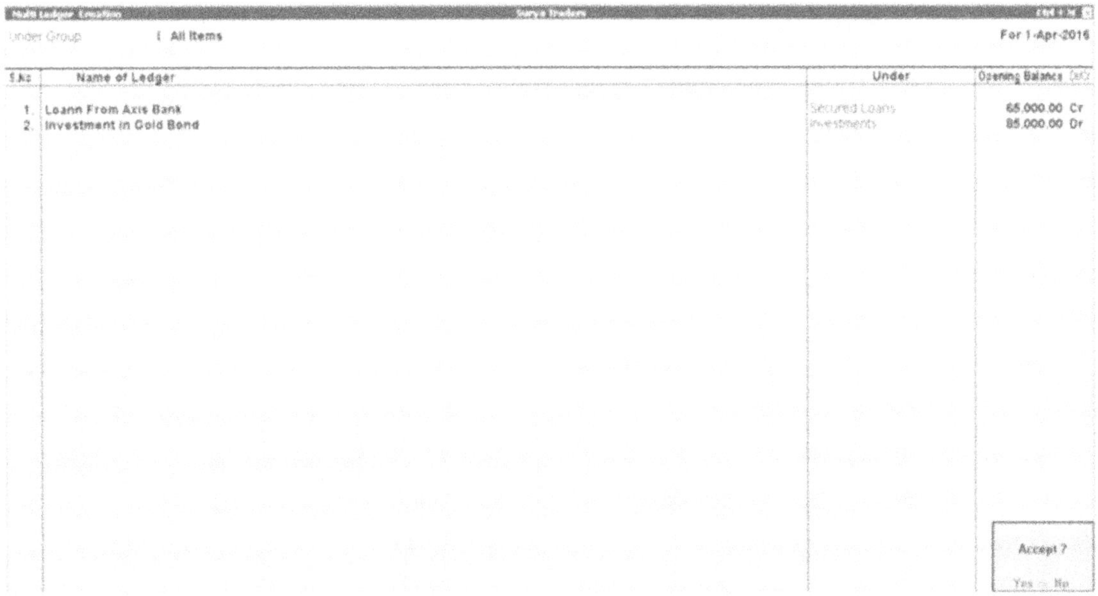

Figure 6.10: Multi Ledger Creation

Opening balance of Axis Bank Loan account is Rs. 65000. Company having investment in Gold Bond. Opening balance of Investment in Gold Bond Rs. 85,000.

Creation of Axis Bank Loan Account and Investment in Gold Bond through Multi Ledger Creation

1. Go to **Gateway of Tally > Accounts Info. > Ledgers >Multi Ledger Create**
2. Select **All Account**
3. Enter name Loan from Axis Bank, select Secured Loan from Group List
4. Enter the Opening amount Rs. 65,000
5. Enter name Investment in Gold Bond, select Investment from group list
6. Enter the opening balance Rs. 85000

   The **Multi Ledger Creation** screen appears as shown (Figure 6.10):
7. Press **Enter** to accept the screen

Activity

Create below ledgers with their opening balance in Surya Traders

- **Raxson Ltd.** Under **Sundry Creditors,** with an opening balance of **Rs.** 95,000
- **ICICI Bank** under **Bank Accounts**, with an opening balance of **Rs.** 55,000
- **Furniture** under Fixed Assets, with an opening balance of Rs. 50,000
- **Sunny Electronics** under **Sundry Debtors,** with an opening balance of Rs. 45000

6.4.1.2 *Altering and Displaying Ledgers*

The procedures for altering and displaying ledgers are similar to those of groups. Now try this out on Surya Traders by altering

the Tally.ERP 9 pre-defined ledger for Cash to Petty Cash and entering the opening balance:

1. Select **Alter** from the **Single Ledger** option.
2. Select **Cash** from the **List of Ledgers.**
3. Change the **Name** from **Cash** to **Petty Cash.**
4. Enter the **Opening Balance** of Rs. 1000.
5. Press **Y** or **Enter** to accept the screen.

If you use **Display** in **Single Ledger** now, you will see that the **List of Ledgers** shows Petty Cash instead of Cash. You can also Alter ledgers from **Accounts Info. > Ledgers > Alter (Multiple Ledgers).**

6.4.1.3 *Deleting Ledgers*

You can delete a ledger, by pressing **Alt+D** in the **Ledger Alteration** screen.

You will not be able to delete a ledger, once the financial transactions (vouchers) have been entered (excluding the Opening Balance). If there is a need to delete a ledger with any financial transactions, all the transactions must be deleted first by pressing **Alt+D.**

6.4.2   **Group Creation**

The group to be created, and the primary group under which it has to be classified, is specified in below:

Group to be created in Surya Traders - Debtors North

Classification- Sundry Debtros

To create the group,

1. Go to **Gateway of Tally > Accounts Info. > Groups > Create**
2. Enter **Name** as **Debtors - North**
3. Against the field **Under** select **Sundry Debtors** from the **List of Groups**

   The **Group Creation** screen appears as shown (Figure 6.11):

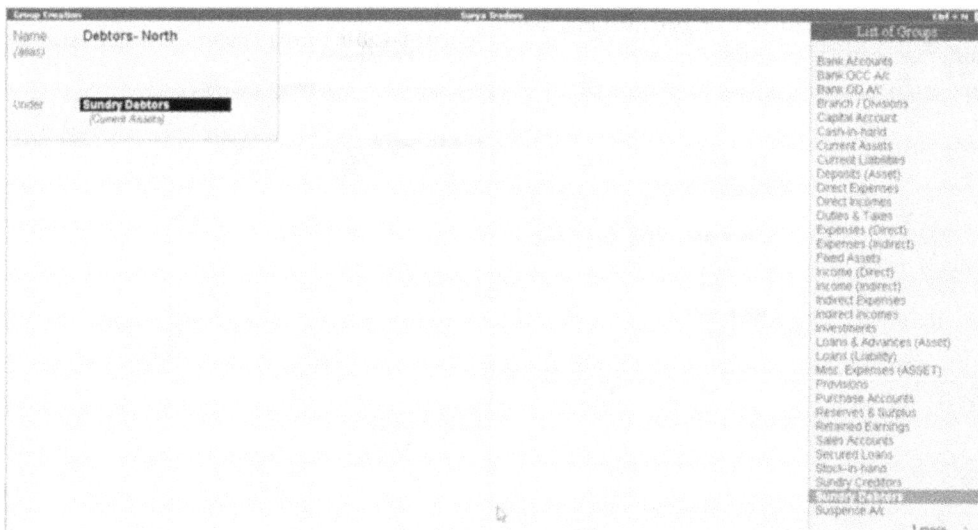

Figure 6.11: Group Creation

4. Press **Y** or **Enter** to accept the screen

Activity

Create the following group in Surya Traders :

1. **Debtors – South** under **Sundry Debtors**
2. **Bengaluru Debtors** under **Debtors – South**
3. **Hyderabad Debtors** under **Debtors – South**

4. **Indore Debtors** under **Debtors – North**

5. **North Delhi Debtors** under **Debtors – North.**

Tally.ERP 9 allows you to create any number of groups under all the default groups. Two sub- groups viz. **Debtors - North** and **Debtors - South** have now been created under **Sundry Debtors.** Additionally, two sub-groups each have been created, under **Debtors - North** and **Debtors - South.**

6.4.2.1 *Altering Groups*

Once created, groups can be altered by selecting the **Alter** option for single or multiple groups. The procedure is the same as used earlier to display groups, except that, here the data can be altered.

You can also Alter groups from **Accounts Info. > Groups > Alter (Multiple Groups).**

6.4.2.2 *Deleting Groups*

You can delete a group via the Group Alteration (Single Mode) screen by pressing Alt+D. However, you cannot delete Tally.ERP 9 predefined groups, or groups with sub-groups or groups containing ledgers. The lowest level must be deleted first.

6.5   INVENTORY MASTER CREATION

The inventory system operates in much the same way as the accounting system. In the place of accounting groups, 'Stock Groups' and 'Stock Categories' are used, and in the place of ledgers, 'Stock Items' are used.

Inventory Masters in Tally.ERP 9

Stock Item

A Stock Item is a unit of the goods that a business trades in. For instance, National Traders deal in electronic goods. 'Television' will be a 'Stock Item' for them.

Units of Measure

Stock items are purchased and sold on the basis of quantity. The quantity in turn is measured by units. In Tally.ERP 9, such goods are quantified using 'Units of Measurement'. Units of Measure can be 'simple' or 'compound'. Examples of simple Units of Measure are: numbers, metres, kilo- grams, pieces etc. Examples for compound Units of Measure are: a box of 10 pieces etc.

Stock Group

A Stock Group is similar to the Groups we create for accounting. Stock Items of similar nature, brand, etc. can be classified under a single Stock Group. In the example above, the Stock Group for 'Television' can be the brand, like 'Sony', 'Videocon', 'Philips', etc.

Godowns/Locations

A place where Stock Items are stored is referred to as a "Godown". For example, a warehouse. You can obtain stock reports for each Godown and account for the movement of stock between Locations/Godowns.

6.5.1   Creating Inventory Masters

Let us take the example of **Surya Traders** who sell **Computers and electronics devices .** Given below is the structure of items being sold:

Main Stock Group- Dell , Samsung , Sony

Stock Item: Dell I3, Dell I5 (Under Dell)
Samsung I3, Samsung I5 (Under Samsung)
Sony I3, Sony I5 (Under Sony)
Pendrive 16GB (Under Sony)
CD Player (Under Samsung)

Surya Traders has two Godowns, the Shop Godown and the Warehouse Godown. The Unit of Measure will be Numbers (Nos)

To facilitate easier understanding, we have illustrated the creation of the aforesaid inventory masters for Surya Traders, in the following order:

1. Stock Groups
2. Godowns
3. Units of Measure
4. Stock Items

6.5.2   Creating a Stock Group

The grouping structure in Tally.ERP 9 is as follows:

1. **Dell** (main stock group, to be grouped under **Primary**)
2. **Samsung** (main stock group, to be grouped under **Primary**)
3. **Sony** (main stock group, to be grouped under **Primary**)

Create the Stock Group – Dell under Primary in Surya Traders

1. Go to **Gateway of Tally > Inventory Info. > Stock Groups > Create (under the Single Stock Group)**
2. Enter the **Name** for the stock group as **Dell**
3. Classify the group under **Primary**
4. Set the option **Can Quantities be ADDED to Yes**

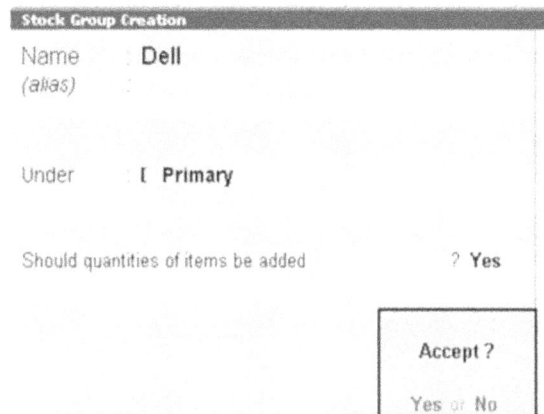

Figure 6.12: Stock Group Creation — Dell

5. Press **Enter** to accept the screen (Figure 6.12)

Activity

Create Samsung and Sony stock group in Surya Traders

6.5.3   Creating a Godown

Locations/Godowns are places where Stock Items are stored. You can monitor the location-wise movement of stock by creating multiple

Tally.ERP 9 has a default Godown named Main Location. You can alter Tally's default godown and create a new one. Tally.ERP

9 permits the creation of any number of godowns, under groups and subgroups to match the structure you need. You can create Locations/Godowns only if Maintain Multiple Godowns is enabled in **F11: Features > F2: Inventory Features> Storage and classification> Maintain multiple godowns.** Go to **Gateway of Tally > Inventory Info. > Godowns > Create.**

The complete Godown creation screen is given below (Figure 6.13):

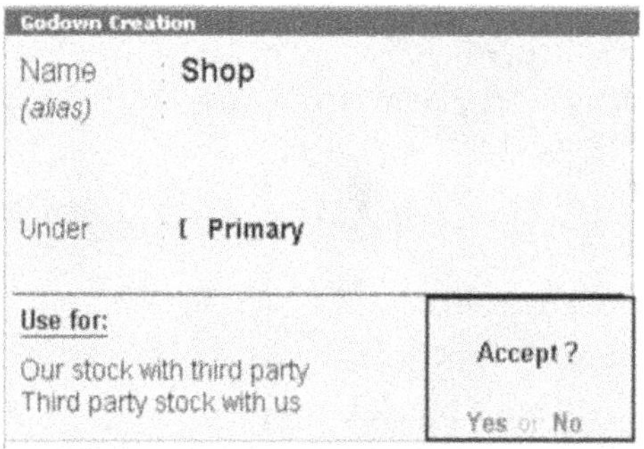

Figure 6.13: Godown creation screen

Activity

Create Warehouse Godown under primary in Surya Traders

6.5.4   Creating a Unit of Measurement

As mentioned in the example, the **Unit of Measure** will be **Numbers (NOS)**

To create the Unit of Measure,

1. Go to **Gateway of Tally> Inventory Info.> Unit of Measure> Create**
2. Enter the Symbol to used for the Unit of Measure, that is Nos
3. Enter the Formal Name, that is Numbers
4. Specify the number of decimal places. Here, it is zero

The completed Unit Creation screen appears as shown below (Figure 6.14):

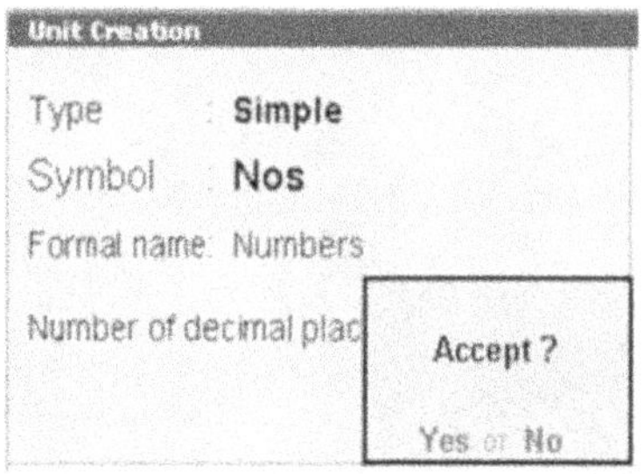

Figure 6.14: Unit creation screen

6.5.5   Creating a Stock Item

As per the example, create the Stock Item Dell I3. To create the same,

1. Go to **Gateway of Tally > Inventory Info. > Stock Items > Create**
2. Enter the **Name** for the stock item, that is Dell I3
3. Group the **stock item** under Dell
4. Select the units as **Nos** (Figure 6.15)

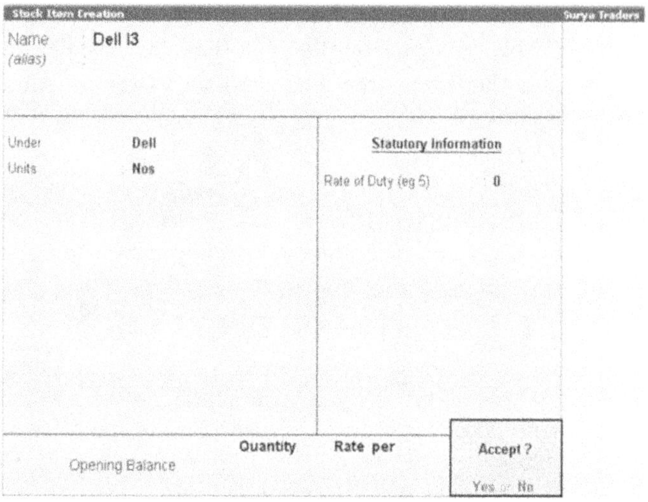

Figure 6.15: Stock Item Creation — Dell I3

Activity

Create the following Stock Group and Stock Item in Surya Traders

Stock Group- Hardware, Software
Godowon- Onsite (Under Primary)
UOM- Nos.
Stock Item- CPU, RAM, Keyboard, Mouse (Under Hardware) Tally, Adobe, MS-Office (Software)

Note: The term Locations is displayed in the Inventory Info. menu, if International is selected under Use Accounting Terminology in General Configuration (Gateway of Tally > F12:Configure) screen. If India/SAARC is selected, the term Godowns is displayed.

Activity

Create following Inventory Master in Surya Traders

Godowns – Onsite, Warehouse under Primary.				
Stock Item	Group	QTY	Rate	Amount
Samsung Galaxy Tab	Samsung	10	Rs. 5,500	Rs. 55,000
Samsung Smartwatch	Samsung	20	Rs. 2,000	Rs. 40,000
Dell Inspiron Desktops	Dell	15	Rs. 12,500	Rs. 1,87,500
Sony Xperia Tablet	Sony	10	Rs. 8,500	Rs. 85,000

6.6 VOUCHER ENTRY

In accounting terms, a voucher is a document containing the details of a financial transaction. For example, a purchase invoice, a sales receipt, a petty cash docket, a bank interest statement, and so on. For every such transaction made, a voucher is used to enter the details into the ledgers to update the financial position of the company. This feature of Tally.ERP 9 will be used most often.

Tally.ERP 9 follows the Golden Rules of Accounting:

Golden Rules of Accounting		
Type of Account	**Debit Aspect**	**Credit Aspect**
Personal	The receiver	The giver
Real	What comes in	What goes out
Nominal	All Expenses and losses	All incomes and gains

Type of voucher

It is essential to check if you are using the right voucher for the transaction. You can change the voucher type by selecting a new type from the button bar, if required. For example on the selection of a payment voucher, Tally.ERP 9 automatically displays the List of Voucher Types you have created. You can select the voucher type required.

Voucher number

Tally.ERP 9 automatically sets the voucher number for you. You can change the voucher number manually, if required.

Reference

You can enter a reference of your choice. A purchase order number or an invoice number can be entered as a reference.

Date of voucher

The date of the voucher you enter is displayed at the top-right of the Voucher Creation screen. The date is taken initially from the Gateway of Tally - Current Date and you may need to change it frequently to ensure that the vouchers are dated as you want.

Effective date

A voucher type can be configured to allow for an Effective date. The line below the date of voucher displays the date when the **voucher will be effective.**

Particulars

This is where you enter the ledger names and the debit and credit amounts. Each line displays a prompt of Dr or By for debit entries and Cr or To for credit entries.

Depending on the Voucher Type, Tally.ERP 9 selects either **'Dr'** or **'Cr'** for the first prompt, which you cannot change. Thereafter, you can change the prompt (if necessary) by typing over it with a **'D'** or a **'C'**. To select a ledger, type the first letter of its name. Tally.ERP 9 then displays a List of **Ledger Accounts** beginning with the letter highlighted. Only ledgers suitable for the voucher type are displayed. The revised current balance is shown after the amount is entered. On selecting the next ledger, Tally.ERP 9 suggests the balancing amount as the value to be entered, which may be accepted or typed over. The voucher entry cannot be completed until the debits equal the credits.

6.6.1 Voucher Type

Tally.ERP 9 is pre-programmed with a variety of accounting and inventory vouchers, each designed to perform a different job. The standard Accounting and Inventory Vouchers are:

Accounting Voucher

- Contra Voucher (F4)
- Payment Voucher (F5)
- Receipt Voucher (F6)
- Journal Voucher (F7)
- Sales Voucher /Invoice (F8)
- Credit Note Voucher (CTRL+ F8)
- Purchase Voucher (F9)
- Debit Note Voucher (CTRL+F9)

Inventory Voucher

- Purchase Order (ALT+F4)
- Sales Order (ALT+F5)
- Rejections Out (ALT+F6)
- Rejections In (CTRL+ F6)
- Stock Journal (ALT+F7)
- Delivery Note (ALT+F8)
- Receipt Note (ALT+F9)
- Physical Stock (ALT+F10)

You can alter these vouchers to suit your company, and also create new ones. Read ahead to understand the function of each Voucher Type. The following exercises are sample entries for understanding voucher entry in Tally.ERP 9.

Let us understand how to record transactions in Tally.ERP 9, with examples from the books of accounts of National Traders.

6.6.1.1 Contra Voucher (F4)

A 'Contra Entry' is an entry in a business' books of accounts, indicating transfer of funds from:

- Cash account to bank account
- Bank account to cash account
- One bank account to another bank account.

Illustration-3

Surya Traders withdrew an amount of Rs. 7,000 towards petty cash, from their account in ICICI Bank on 1st April, 2016.

Let us record a Contra Voucher with the details below.

Contra Voucher Entry

Account	Debit	Credit
ICICI Bank Account		7,000
Petty Cash	7,000	

To record the transaction in Tally.ERP 9,

1. Go to **Gateway of Tally > Accounting Vouchers > F4: Contra**
2. In Voucher Creation screen, press **F12: Contra Configuration** and set the following to **Yes:**
   o **Skip the Date field in Create Mode (faster entry!)**
   o **Use Cr/Dr instead of To/By during entry**
   o **Warn on Negative Cash Balance**
   o **Show Ledger Current Balances**
   o **Show Balances as on Voucher Date**
3. Select the Bank Ledger – ICICI Bank **in Particulars** to **Credit**
4. Enter the amount as **Rs. 7,000**
5. Select the **Petty Cash** Ledger to **Debit**
6. Enter the **Amount** to be debited
7. Enter the details in the field **Narration,** if required

The completed **Contra Voucher appears** as shown below (Figure 6.16):

Figure 6.16: Contra Voucher

8. Press **Y** or **Enter** to accept

6.6.1.2 *Payment Voucher (F5)*

Payment entry is a transaction which is passed to record all payments made by cash or bank.

Illustration-4

On 1st April, 2016, Surya Traders paid a bill raised by Raxson Ltd. By issuing a cheque for Rs. 5000. Let us record a Payment Voucher with the details below:

Payment Voucher Entry

Account	Debit	Credit
Raxson lrd. (Sundry Creditors)	5000	
ICICI Bank		5000

To record the transaction in Tally.ERP 9,

1. Go to **Gateway of Tally > Accounting Vouchers > F5: Payment**
2. In **Voucher Creation** screen, press **F12: Payment Configuration** and set **Use Single Entry mode for Pymt/ Rcpt/ Contra to No**
3. Select the Party **Ledger - Raxson Ltd.** in **Particulars** to **Debit**
4. Enter the amount as **Rs. 5000**
5. Select the Bank ledger – ICICI Bank to **Credit**
6. Enter the **Amount** to be credited
7. Enter the details in the field **Narration,** if required

The **completed Payment Voucher** screen appears as shown below (Figure 6.17):

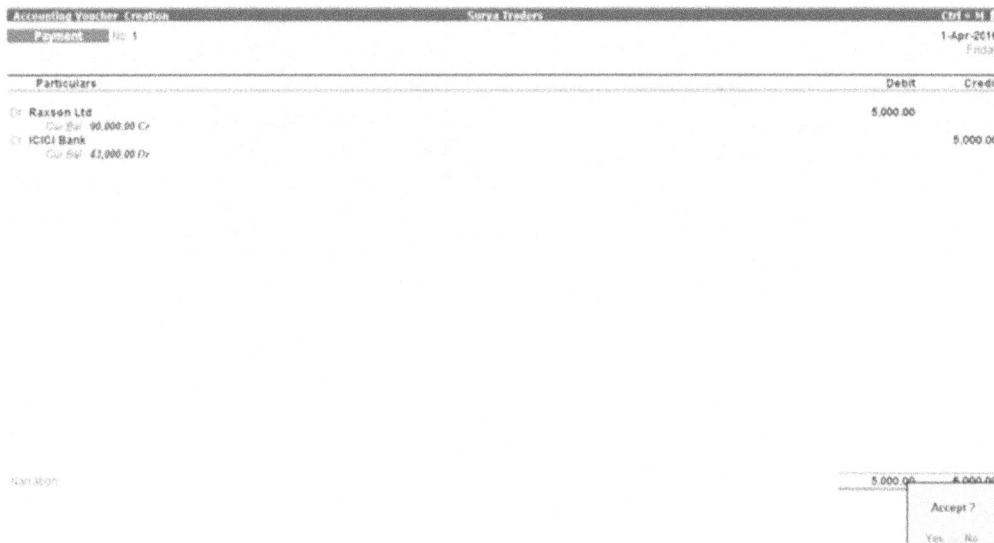

Figure 6.17: Payment Voucher

8. Press **Y** or **Enter** to accept

Recording a payment in Single Entry Mode

Illustration-5

On 1st April,2016, Surya Traders paid Rs. 400 towards Stationery expenses, and Rs. 700 towards postage expenses from their Petty Cash account.

Let us record a **Payment Voucher** with the details below: To record the transaction in Tally.ERP 9,

1. Go to **Gateway of Tally > Accounting Vouchers > F5: Payment**

2. In Voucher Creation screen, press **F12: Payment Configuration** and set **Use Single Entry mode** for **Pymt/**

Rcpt/ Contra to **Yes**

3. In **Account** field select **Petty Cash**

4. Under **Particulars,** select the Conveyance from the **List of Ledger Accounts**

5. Enter **Rs. 400** in the Amount field

6. Under Particulars, select Stationery **expenses** from the **List of Ledger Accounts**

7. Enter **Rs. 700** in the **Amount** field

8. Enter the details in the field **Narration,** if required

The completed **Payment Voucher** made in the single entry mode appears as shown below (Figure 6.18):

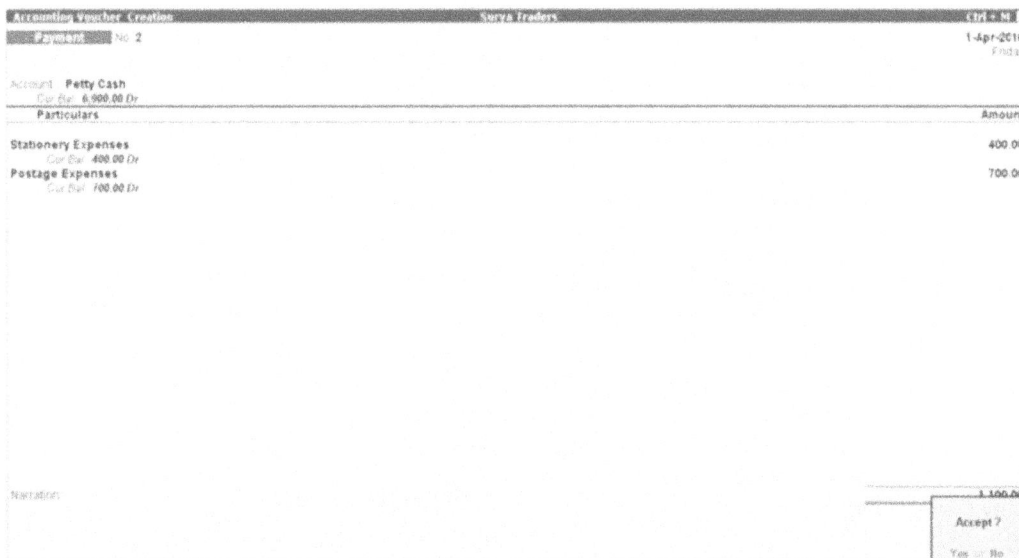

Figure 6.18: Payment Voucher with Single Entry Mode

9. Press **Y** or **Enter** to accept

The advantage of a single entry mode is that you can select multiple debits or credits depending on the type of entry. Similarly the transactions can be recorded in single entry mode even in Receipt and Contra vouchers.

6.6.1.3 Receipt Voucher (F6)

Transactions involving receipt of cash and through bank are entered in the Receipt Voucher. For example, on 1st April, 2016, Surya Traders received interest of Rs. 1,500 on a deposit account maintained by them with ICICI.

Let us record a Receipt Voucher with the details below:

Receipt Voucher Entry

Account	Debit	Credit
Bank Interest (Indirect Income)		1,500
Bank Deposit Account (Deposit-Assets)	1,500	

To record the transaction in Tally.ERP 9,

1. Go to **Gateway of Tally > Accounting Vouchers > F6: Receipt.**
2. In **F12: Payment Configuration**, set the option **Use Single Entry mode for Pymt/Rcpt/Contra** to **No**
3. Select the ledger **Bank Interest** in **Particulars** to **Credit**
4. Enter the amount as **Rs. 1500**
5. Select the ledger **Deposit Account** to **Debit**
6. Enter the **Amount** to be debited
7. Enter the details in the field **Narration**, if required The completed **Receipt Voucher** appears as shown below (Figure 6.19):

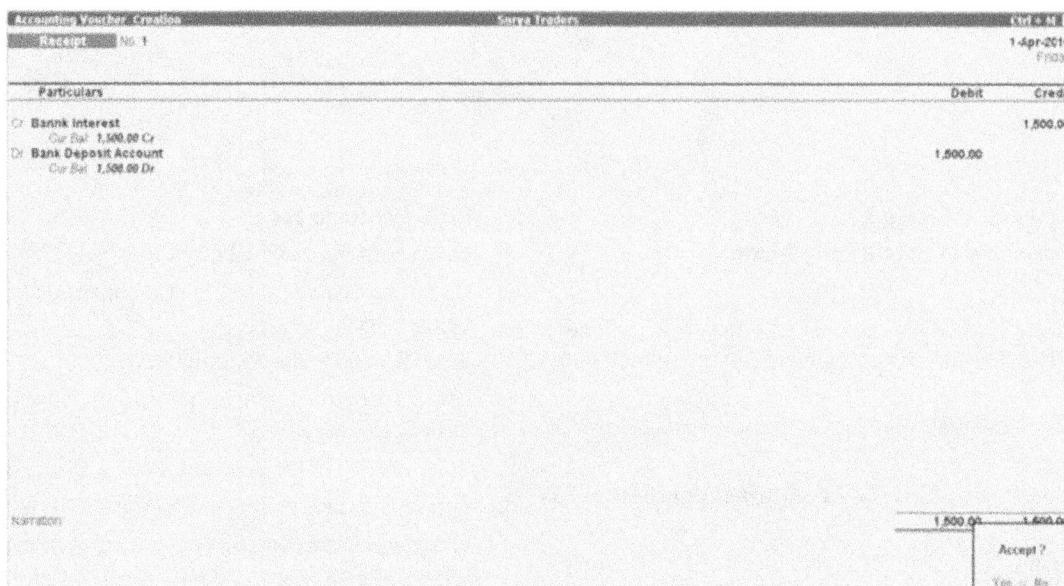

Figure 6.19: Receipt Voucher

8. Press **Y** or **Enter** to accept

6.6.1.4 Journal Voucher (F7)

In accounting and bookkeeping, a journal is a record of financial transactions in order by date. A journal is often defined as the book of original entry. The definition was more appropriate when transactions were written in a journal prior to manually posting them to the accounts in the general ledger or subsidiary ledger. Manual systems usually had a variety of journals such as a sales journal, purchases journal, cash receipts journal, cash disbursements journal, and a general journal.

With today's computerised bookkeeping and accounting, it is likely to find only a general journal in which adjusting entries and unique financial transactions are entered. In other words, accounting software has eliminated the need to first record routine transactions into a journal.

Illustration-6

Surya Traders has entered some expenditure on Repair & Maintenance, amounting to Rs. 2,500, Which should have actually been posted to the Ledger Office Maintenance. To account for the correct entry, a journal voucher has to be created.

First a payment voucher has to be created for the expenditure

(using Petty cash) and then the Repair and Maintenance is accounted as Office Maintenance using a Journal voucher.

Step 1: Create Payment Voucher

1. Go to **Gateway of Tally > Accounting Vouchers > F5: Payment Voucher**
2. Record the voucher as shown below (Figure 6.20):

Let us record a Journal Voucher with the details below:

Journal Voucher Entry

Account	Debit	Credit
Office Maintenance (Indirect Expenses)	2,500	
Repairing & Maintenance		2,500

To record the transaction in Tally.ERP 9,

1. Go to **Gateway of Tally > Accounting Vouchers > F7: Journal**
2. In **Voucher Creation** screen, press **F12: Journal Configuration** and set the following to **Yes**:
   o Skip the Date field in **Create Mode** (faster entry!)
   o Use **Cr/Dr** instead of **To/By** during entry

Figure 6.20: Payment Voucher

o   Warn on **Negative Cash Balance**

o   Show Ledger **Current Balances**

o   Show Balances as on **Voucher Date**

3. Select the **Expense Ledger – Repair and Maintenance** in **Particulars** to **Debit**

4. Enter the amount as **Rs. 2500**

5. Select the **Expense ledger - Office Maintenance** to **Credit**

6. Enter the **Amount** to be credited

7. Enter the details in the field **Narration**, if required

The **completed Journal Voucher** appears as shown below (Figure 6.21):

Figure 6.21: Journal Voucher

8. Press **Y** or **Enter** to accept.

6.6.1.5 Sales Voucher (F8)

Sales voucher is used when the company sells some goods to the customers either by cash, cheque or on credit basis.

Illustration-7

On 1st April, 2016, Surya Traders made credit sales worth Rs. 6,000 to Supriya & Co.

Let us record a Sales Voucher with the details below:

Sales Voucher Entry

Account	Debit	Credit
Supriya & Co (Sundry Debtors)	6,000	
Local Sales (Sales Account)		
		6,000

To record the transaction in Tally.ERP 9,

1. Go to **Gateway of Tally > Accounting Vouchers > F8: Sales**
2. In **Voucher Creation** screen, press **F12: Configure** and set **Accept Supplementary Details to No**

3. Press **CTRL+V (V: As Voucher)** to enter in Voucher Mode
4. Select the Buyer's Ledger - **Supriya & Co.** in **Particulars** to **Debit**
5. Enter the **Amount** as **Rs. 6,000**
6. Select the Sales ledger - **Local Sales** to **Credit**
7. Enter the **Amount** to be credited
8. Enter the details in the field **Narration,** if required

The **completed Sales Voucher** appears as shown below (Figure 6.22):

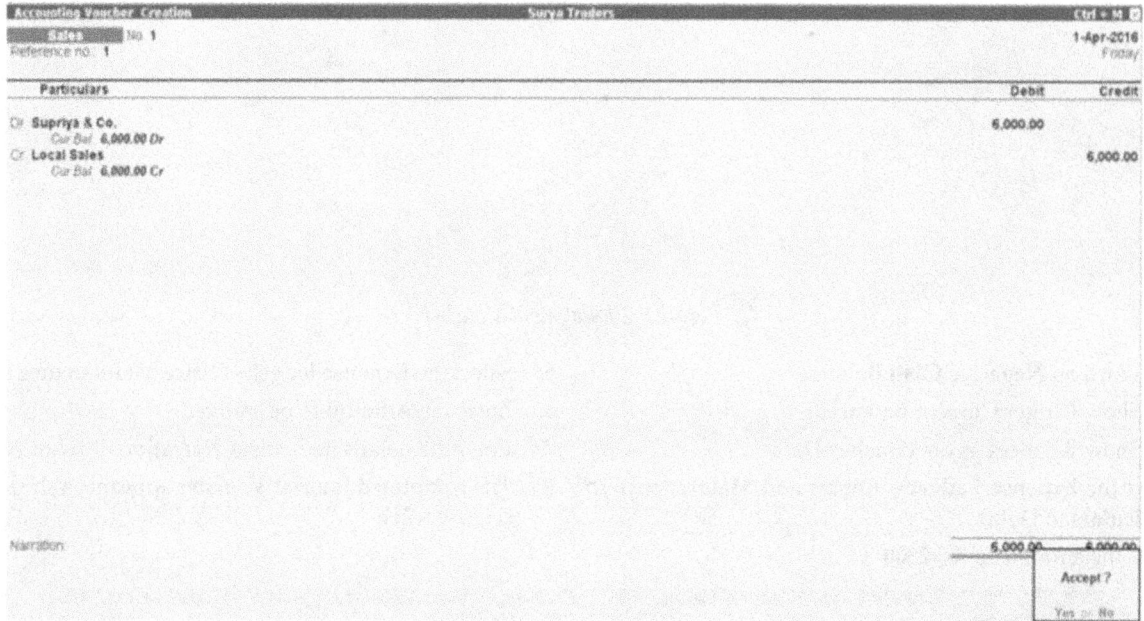

Figure 6.22: Sales Voucher

9. Press **Y** or **Enter** to accept

6.6.1.6 Credit Note Voucher (CTRL + F8)

Credit note entry is passed to account for return of goods sold, and is generally issued by the seller to the buyer.

Illustration-8

On 1st April, 2016, Supriya & Co. returned goods worth Rs. 5000.

Let us record a Credit Note with the details below:

Credit Note Voucher Entry

Account	Debit	Credit
Supriya & Co. (Sundry Debtors)	5,000	
Local Sales Return (Sales Account)		5,000

This voucher type is made available when the option **Use Debit/**

Credit Note to is set to **Yes** in the **F11: Features (F1: Accounting features).**

To record the transaction in Tally.ERP 9,

1. Go to **Gateway of Tally > Accounting Vouchers > F8: Credit Note.**
2. Mention the Original Invoice No. and date of the Purchase invoice which is returned
3. Enter the **amount** as **Rs. 5000**
4. Select the Sales ledger - **Local Sale Return (Sales Account)** to **Debit**
5. Enter the **Amount** to be debited
6. Enter the details in the field **Narration,** if required

The completed **Credit Note** appears as shown in (Figure 6.23):

9. Press **Y** or **Enter** to accept

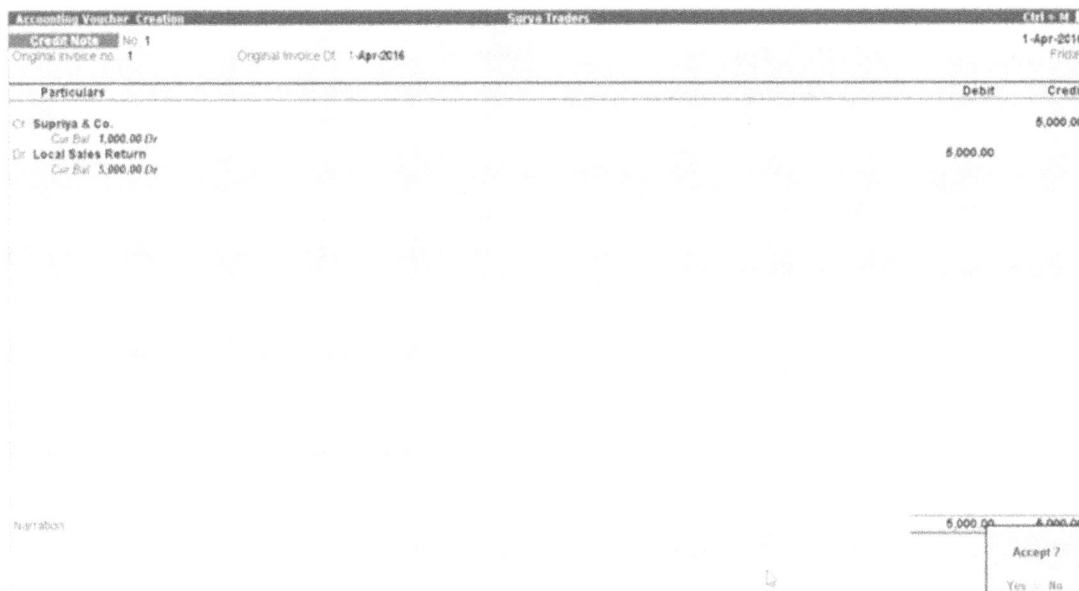

Figure 6.23: Credit Note Voucher

6.6.1.7 Purchase Voucher (F9)

Purchase voucher is used when the company purchases some goods from the suppliers either by cash, cheque or on credit basis.

Illustration-9

On 1st April, 2016, Surya Traders made credit purchase worth Rs. 4,500 from Jakson Ltd.

Let us record a Purchase Voucher with the details below:

Purchase Voucher Entry

Account	Debit	Credit
Jakson Ltd. (Sundry Creditors)		4,500
Local Purchase (Purchase Account)	4,500	

1. Go to **Gateway of Tally > Accounting Vouchers > F9: Purchase**
2. Press **CTRL+V (V: As Voucher)** to enter in Voucher Mode
3. Select the Supplier's Ledger - Jakson **Ltd.** in **Particulars** to Credit
4. Enter the **Amount** as **Rs. 4,500**
5. Select the Purchase ledger - **Local Purchase** to **Debit**
6. Enter the **Amount** to be debit
7. Enter the details in the field **Narration,** if required

The **completed Sales Voucher** appears as shown below (Figure 6.24):

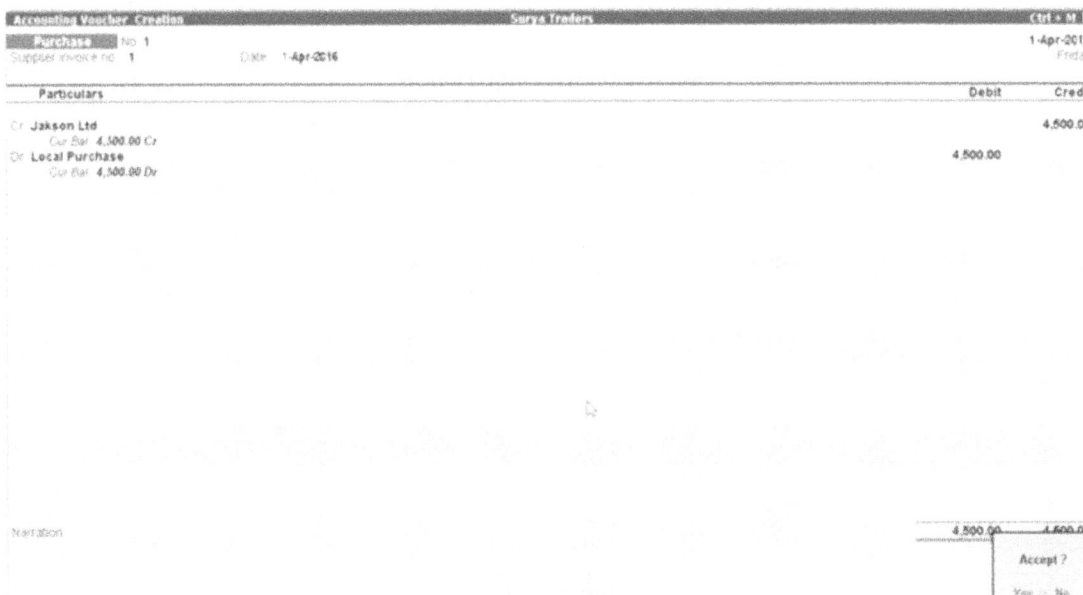

Figure 6.24: Purchase Voucher

10. Press Y or Enter to accept

6.6.1.8 Debit Note Voucher (CTRL + F9)

Debit note entry is passed for purchase returns or for any change in price consideration.

Illustratio-10

On 1st April, 2016, Surya Traders returned goods worth Rs. 1000 to Jakson Ltd.

Let us record a Debit Note with the details below:

Debit Note Boucher Entry

Account	Debit	Credit
Jakson Ltd	1,000	
Local Purchase Return (Purchase Account)		1,000

This voucher type is made available when the option **Use Debit/**

Credit Notes is set to **Yes** in the **F11: Features (F1: Accounting Features).**

To record the transaction in Tally.ERP 9,

1. Go to **Gateway of Tally > Accounting Vouchers > F9: Debit Note**
2. Mention the **Original Invoice No** and **date** of the Purchase invoice which is returned
3. Select the Supplier's Ledger - **Jakson Ltd in Particulars** to **Debit**
4. Enter the amount as **Rs. 1000**
5. Select the Purchase ledger - **Local Purchases Return (Purchase Account) to Credit**
6. Enter the **Amount** to be credited
7. Enter the details in the field **Narration,** if required

The completed **Debit Note** appears as shown below (Figure 6.25):

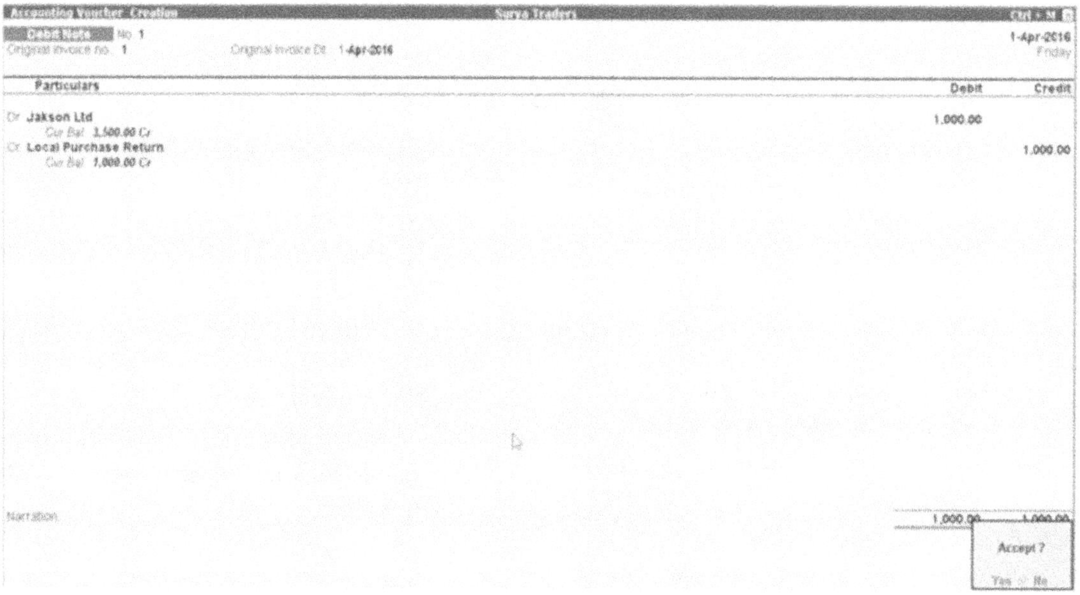

Figure 6.25: Debit Note Voucher

8. Press **Y** or **Enter** to accept.

6.6.2 Creating a New Voucher Type

Surya Traders wants to record bank and petty cash payments differently and needs two new voucher types to replace the pre-defined Payment voucher. In order to do this:

Create a **Bank Payment** voucher.

Go to the **Gateway of Tally > Accounts Info. > Voucher Types > Create**

1. Enter a name for the **Voucher Type.** Here, it is **Bank Payment**
2. Select the Type of Voucher whose functions the new voucher should copy. Here, it is **Payment**
3. Enter an abbreviation for the new voucher. The abbreviation will be used to denote this new voucher in reports
4. Set the Method of Voucher **Numbering** to **Automatic**

You can choose one of the following methods for numbering:

Method of Numbering	Purpose
Automatic	For Tally.ERP 9 to automatically number the vouchers sequentially
Manual	This will require you to manually enter the number of the voucher
None	To disable numbering for this Voucher Type

5. Set **Use Advance Configuration** to **No**

6. Set **Use EFFECTIVE Dates** for **Vouchers to No**

7. Set **Make 'Optional' as default** to **No**

8. Set **Use Common Narration** to **Yes**

9. Set **Narrations for each ledger in voucher** to **No**

10. Set **Print after saving Voucher** to **No**

11. Skip the field **Name of Class**

The completed **Voucher Type Creation** screen appears as shown below (Figure 6.26):

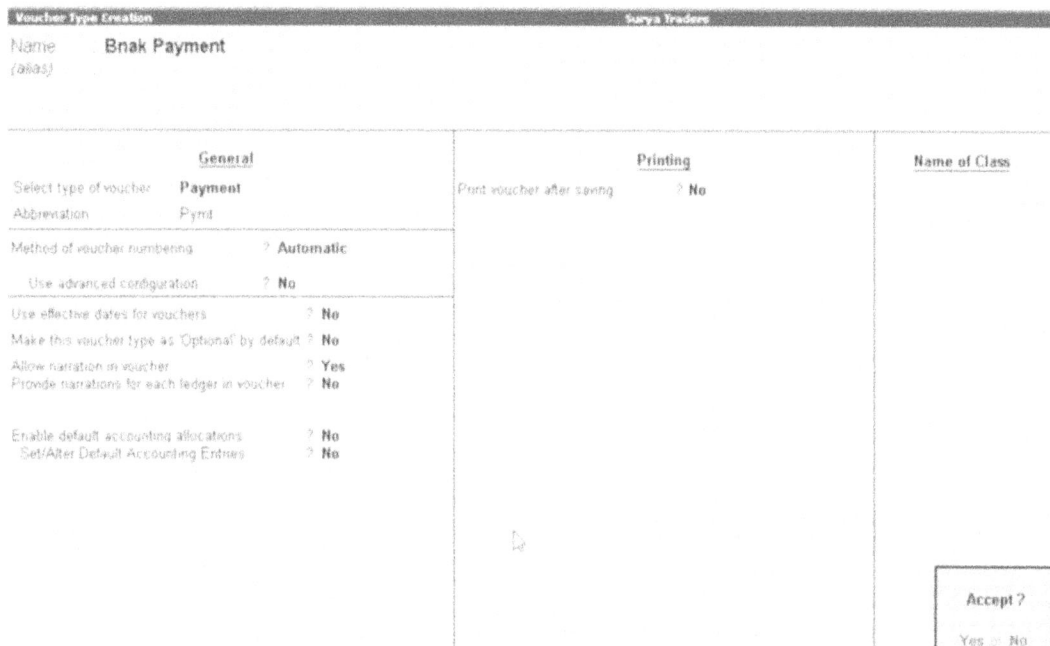

Figure 6.26: Voucher Type Creation Screen — Bank Payment

12. Press **Y** or **Enter** to accept

Note: • The voucher date is taken from the current date mentioned at the Gateway of Tally. However, the **effective date** for the voucher may be different. For example, entering a post-dated cheque.

• Tally.ERP 9 displays the narration field which applies to the whole voucher. By setting **Use Common Narration** option to **No,** we can have separate narration fields for each line on the voucher.

• The **Name of Class** field enables the creation of Voucher Classes for the respective voucher types. (The Voucher class is a template to customise voucher data entry).

6.6.2.1 *Displaying and Altering a Voucher Type*

Observe the menu, you will notice that you can also display and alter voucher types. Selecting these options brings up a List of Voucher Types, from which you can select the one you want to view or work on. Apart from the heading, the Voucher Type Display/Alter screens are identical to the Creation screen.

Activity

Create a Payment Voucher Type for Petty Cash transaction in Surya Traders and pass following entries

Date	Transaction details
08-5-16	Bank Advice received for bank interest of Rs. 800 credited to the deposit account.
10-5-16	Telephone bill for Rs. 600 received from A to Z Mobile. Paid entire amount on same day
20-5-16	Salaries of Rs. 4,500. Amount paid through Bank Account.
25-5-16	Paid commission to Suresh Rs. 1,250 through Cheque
28-5-16	Paid office maintenance Rs. 750 through petty cash
02-6-16	Paid carriage charges of Rs. 250 from Petty Cash.
03-6-16	Paid advertisement expenses Rs. 2,500 through cheque
09-6-16	Transferred Rs. 6,000 from Bank Account to Deposit Account.
15-6-16	Cheque for Rs. 45,000 received from Sony Electronics.

6.6.3   Inventory Vouchers

Purchase Order (ALT+F4): is an order placed by a business entity with a supplier for the delivery of specified goods at a given price and at a predetermined time.

Receipt Note (ALT+F9): Receipt note voucher type is used for recording goods received from the supplier.

Rejections Out (ALT+F6): The Rejections out Voucher records goods that are rejected and returned to a supplier.

Sales order (Alt+F5): Sales Order is an order placed by a customer for the delivery of specified goods at a given price and at a predetermined time.

Delivery note (Alt+F8): This Voucher is used for recording goods delivered to a customer.

Rejection in (Ctrl+F6): This Voucher is used to record goods that are rejected and returned by the customer.

To use Inventory vouchers:

- Enable Delivery Note, Receipt Note and Rejections voucher, set Yes to Use Tracking Numbers (Delivery/Receipt Notes) and Use Rejection Inward/Outward Notes in F11: Features (F2: Inventory Features)

- Go to **Gateway of Tally > F12: Configuration > Invoice/ Orders Entry** – Set Complete Accounting Allocations in Order/Delivery Note to **Yes**

- Make sure that Inventory Values are affected? is set to '**Yes**' in all ledger accounts under the groups Sales Accounts and Purchase Accounts

Let us understand how to record inventory transactions in Tally.ERP 9, with examples from the books of accounts of Surya Traders.

6.6.3.1 Stock Journal (ALT+F7)

To record the consumption and adjustment of goods, a stock journal voucher is used. For example: the company transfers items of stock from the warehouse to the shop.

Illustration-11

On 07-09-2016, Surya Traders transferred 2 Nos of Samsung Galaxy Tab to Shop from On-Site Godown.

To record the transaction:

1. Go to **Gateway of Tally > Inventory Vouchers > F7: Stock Journal**

2. Press **F2** and change the date to 07-09-2016.

3. Under Source (Consumption),
   - o Select Name of Item
   - o Select Godown from which the transfer is being made
   - o Enter Quantity being transferred
   - o Enter Rate. The amount will be calculated automatically

4. Under Destination (Production),
   - o Select Name of Item
   - o Select Godown to which the transfer is being made
   - o Enter Quantity being transferred
   - o Enter Rate. The amount will be calculated automatically

5. Enter **Narration**, if required

The completed Stock Journal appears as shown below (Figure 6.27):

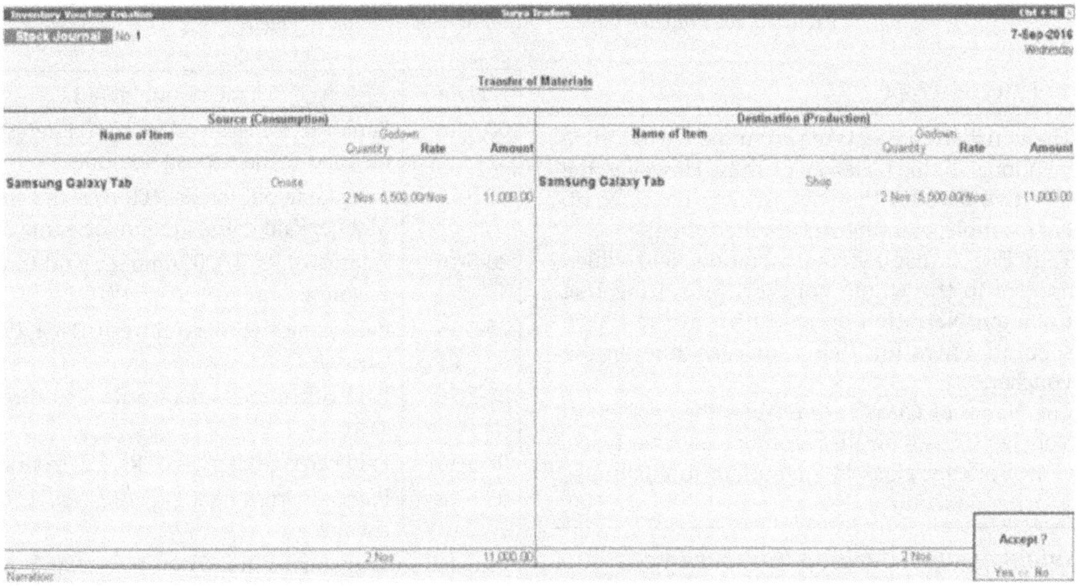

Figure 6.27: Stock Journal

6. Press **Y** or **Enter** to accept.

6.6.3.2 Delivery Note (ALT+F8)

Goods that are being delivered to a customer are recorded in a Delivery Note voucher.

- To enable Delivery Note voucher, set Yes to Use Tracking Numbers (Delivery/Receipt Notes) in F11: Features (F2: Inventory Features).

- Ensure in F12: Configure, F12 more configuration (Delivery Note Configuration), set Complete Accounting Allocations in Order / Delivery Note to Yes.

Illustration-12

On 07-09-2016, Surya Traders delivered one Samsung Galaxy Tab from their shop, to Sony Electronics

To record the transaction:

1. Go to **Gateway of Tally > Inventory Vouchers > F8: Delivery Note**

2. Press **F2** and change the date to 07-09-2016.

3. Enter the reference number SR/DN/456 in the Ref. field

4. Party's A/c Name: Select the party ledger Sony Electronics from the List of Ledger Accounts, to whom goods are delivered and press Enter to view Order Details sub-screen. Accept the default details

5. Name of the Item: Select the stock item Samsung Galaxy Tab that needs to be delivered, from the List of Stock Items. The Item Allocations sub-screen is displayed. Enter the details as shown below:

   o Tracking No: Select Not Applicable

   o Godown: Select Shop from the List of Godowns

   o Enter the Quantity to be delivered as 1

   o Enter Rate as Rs. 6,500 and the Amount is automatically displayed

6. In Accounting Allocations for: Create Computer Sales (**Under Sales Accounts and activated Inventory Values are effected**) You can create directly from Accounting Details screen with the help of ALT+C (Online Ledger Creation)

The completed Delivery Note appears as shown below (Figure 6.28):

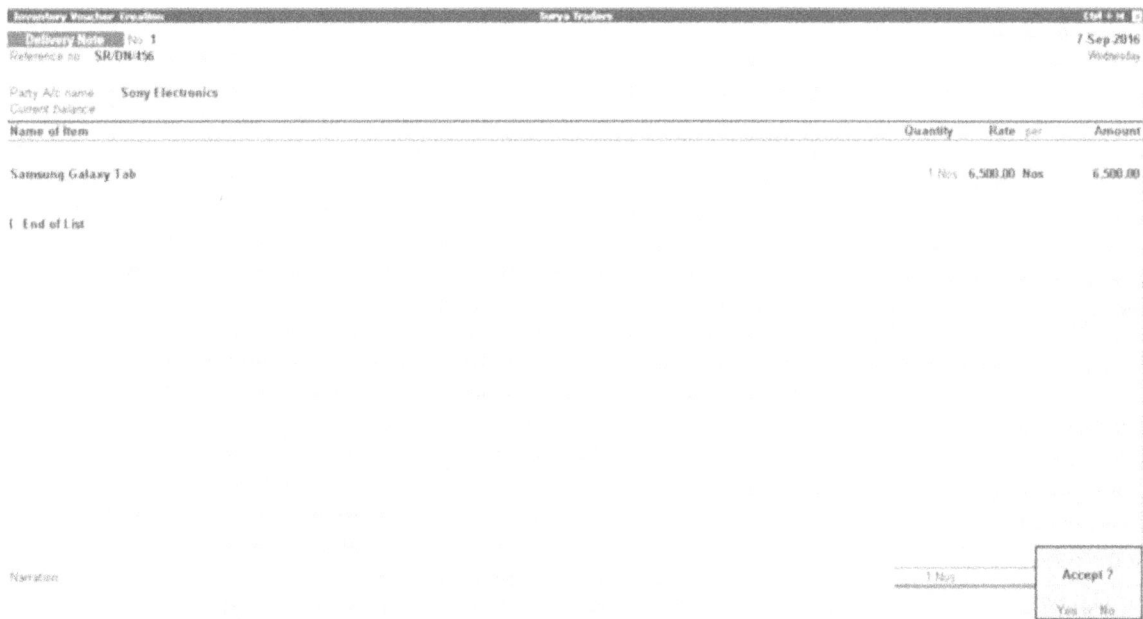

Figure 6.28: Delivery Note Voucher

7. Press **Y** or **Enter** to accept

6.6.3.3 Receipt Note (ALT+F9)

Goods that are received from the supplier are recorded in a Receipt Note (Goods Receipt Note – GRN) voucher.

Illustration-13

On 08-09-2016, Surya Traders received 2 Sony Xperia Tablet from New Computer Ltd. at Rs. 8,500 each and stored them in Shop godown.

To record the transaction:

1. Go to **Gateway of Tally > Inventory Vouchers >F9: Receipt Note**

2. Press **F2** and change the date to 08-09-2016

3. Enter the reference number NCL/045/222 in Ref.. field

4. Party's A/c Name: Press Alt+C and create the party by name New Computers Ltd. under Sundry Creditors and save the ledger creation screen

5. Name of the Item: Select the Stock Item Sony Xperia Tablet that needs to be delivered, from the List of Stock Items. The Item Allocations sub-screen is displayed. Enter the details as below:

   o Tracking No: Select Not Applicable

   o Godown: Select On-Site from the List of Godowns

   o Enter the Quantity to be received as 2

   o Enter Rate as Rs. 8,200 and the Amount is automatically displayed

6. In Accounting Allocations for: Press Alt+C and create Computer Purchase (create this ledger under Purchase Accounts and activate Inventory Values and save the ledger creation screen)

7. Enter the Narration, if required

The completed Receipt Note appears as shown below (Figure 6.29):

Figure 6.29: Receipt Note Voucher

8. Press **Y** or **Enter** to accept

6.6.3.4 Rejections Out (ALT+F6)

A Rejections Out entry is passed to record the instance of rejection of goods by the buyer, for the goods purchased. This is a pure inventory voucher..

Illustration-14

On 14-09-2016, Surya Traders returned one Sony Xperia Tablet to New Computers Ltd.

To record the transaction:

1. Go to **Gateway of Tally > Inventory Vouchers > F6: Rejections Out**

2. Press **F2** and change the date to 14-09-2016.

3. Select the New Computers Ltd. as the **party ledger**

4. Enter **Supplier's Name and Address**, if any

5. Select the **Item** as Sony Xperia Tablet.

6. Set Tracking No. to Not Applicable

7. Select the **Godown** as Shop

8. Enter the Quantity as 1 and Rate as Rs. 8,500. The Amount gets calculated automatically

9. Enter **Narration** if required

The completed Rejections Out voucher appears as shown below (Figure 6.30):

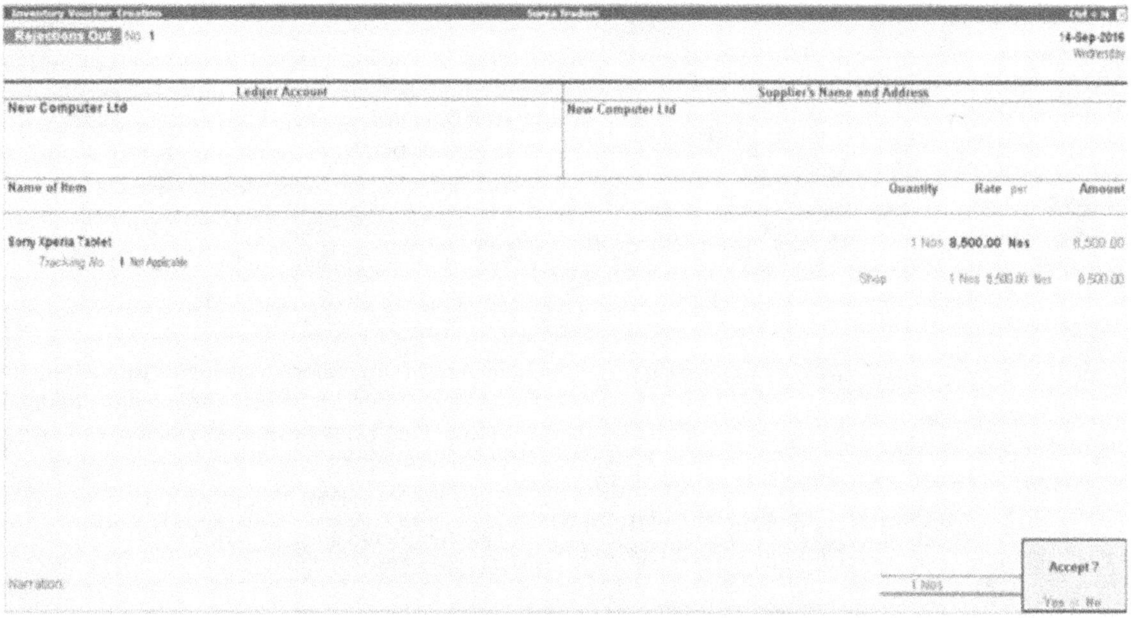

Figure 6.30: Rejections Out Voucher

10. Press **Y** or **Enter** to accept

6.6.3.5 *Rejections In (CTRL+F6)*

A Rejections In entry is passed by the seller to record the instance of receipt of rejected goods. The Rejections In entry is a pure inventory voucher.

Illustration-14

On 16-09-2016, Sony Electronics returned one Nos Samsung Galaxy Tab. To record the transaction,

1. Go to **Gateway of Tally > Inventory Vouchers > F6: Rejections In**

2. Press **F2** and change the date to 16-09-2016.

3. Select Sony Electronics as the **party ledger**

4. Enter **Customer's Name and Address**, if any

5. Select the **Item** as Samsung Galaxy Tab

6. Set tracking number to Not Applicable

7. Select the **Godown** as Shop

8. Enter the Quantity as 1 and Rate as Rs. 6,500. The amount gets calculated automatically

9. Enter **Narration** if required

The completed Rejections In voucher appears as shown below (Figure 6.31):

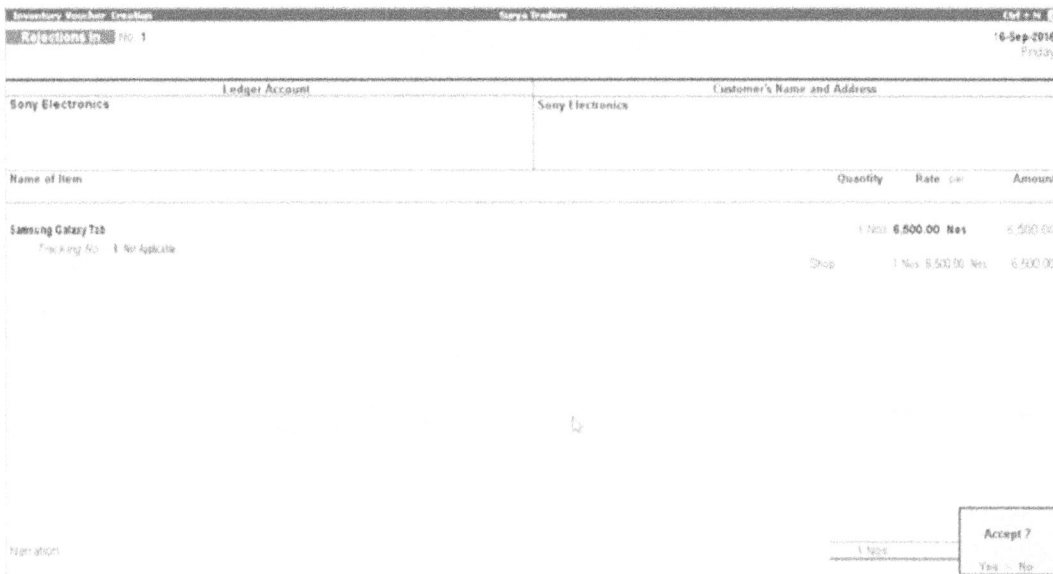

Figure 6.31: Rejections In Voucher

10. Press **Y** or **Enter** to accept

6.6.3.6 *Physical Stock Voucher (ALT+F10)*

Tally.ERP 9 considers the stock available based on the entry made in a physical stock voucher. For example, on conducting a stock-check, the company finds a discrepancy between the actual stock and the recorded stock figure. In such cases, a Physical Stock voucher can be recorded.

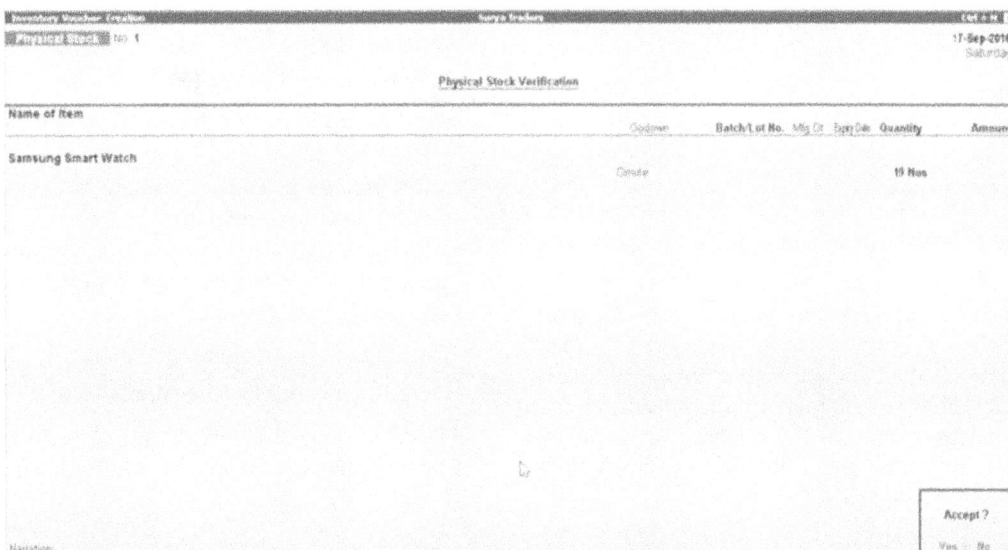

Figure 6.32: Physical Stock Journal

Illustration-15

On 17-09-2016, stock check revealed the physical stock of 19 Nos. of Samsung Smart Watch in Onsite Godown.

To record the transaction:

1. Go to the **Gateway of Tally > Inventory Vouchers > F10: Physical Stock**
2. Press **F2** and change the date to 17-09-2016.
3. Select the **Name** of the Item
4. Select the **Godown**
5. Enter the **Quantity**
6. Enter **Narration**, if any

   The completed Physical Stock Journal appears as shown (Figure 6.32):

7. Press **Y** or **Enter** to accept

Activity

Record further entries for Surya Traders

Transaction from the Books of Surya Traders

Date	Transaction details
10-10-2016	Delivered 2 Nos of Samsung Smart Watch from Onsite to Sony Electronics (Ref: SR/DN/2543)(Hint: Select Computer Sales.)
18-10-2016	Received 2 Nos of Dell Inspiron Desktop from Raxson Ltd. (Ref: RX/12124/056). Store it in Shop Godown
19-10-2016	Returned 1 Nos Samsung Smart Watch (damaged) by Sony Electronics.
02-11-2016	Received 4 Nos of Samsung Galaxy Tab from Smasung World Ltd. (Ref :SWL/1220/210) Store it in Onsite Godown(Hint: Create new Ledger with the name of Samsung World Ltd. under Sundry Creditors) .
02-11-2016	Delivered 2 Nos Dell Inspiron Dektop from Onsite to Disha Computers (Ref: SR/DN/021)(Hint: Select Computer Sales and Create new Ledger with the name of Disha Computers under Sundry Debtors)
04-11-2016	Stock check reveals physical stock of Sony Xperia Tablet is 6 Nos.
07-11-2016	Transferred 1 Nos of Dell Inspiron Desktop from onsite to Shop.

6.6.4 Entering Inventory Details in Accounting Vouchers

Assume that the inventories have to be updated at the same time as entering the accounting vouchers. This is particularly useful for organisations that send and receive goods with a bill or invoice only. In other words, they do not want to update stocks with only a delivery note, neither do they want to do this with just a Goods Receipt Note. Tally.ERP 9 permits stock movement along with invoice. Therefore, you need to select the stock items that come in or move out at the time of purchase or sales voucher entry.

Apart from the Sales and Purchase Vouchers that record the inventory movements, the following vouchers are used to record the stock movements.

- Debit Note for goods rejected and returned to supplier
- Credit Note for goods rejected and returned by customer

Tally.ERP 9 permits the entries of these vouchers in voucher mode as well as in invoice mode. In this section, you will learn how to enter them in Voucher Mode.

To record inventory details in accounting vouchers:

- Set Yes to Use Debit/Credit Notes in F11: Features (F1: Accounting Features). Do not activate the invoice mode.
- Make sure that Inventory Values are affected? is set to Yes in all ledger accounts under the groups Sales Accounts and Purchase Accounts.
- Set Use Tracking Numbers to No in F11: Features (F2: Inventory Features).
- Ensure that in F11: Features (F1: Accounting Features) Allow Invoicing is set to No.

Given below are examples of Purchase, Sales, Debit Note and Credit Note vouchers from the books of Surya Traders, with inventory details:

6.6.4.1 Purchase voucher

Illustration-16

On 08-11-2016, Surya Traders purchased 6 Nos. of Keyboard at Rs. 450 from New Computer Ltd., delivered to their Onsite godown.

To record the transaction:

1. Go to **Gateway of Tally > Accounting Vouchers > F9: Purchase**
2. Press **F2** and change the date to 08-11-2016.
3. Press F12 Configuration> Show Inventory Details **No**
4. Select New Computers Ltd. from the List of **Ledger Accounts** to credit
5. Enter the amount as **Rs. 450**
6. Select **Computer Purchases** from the **List of Ledger Accounts** to **debit**
7. In the **Inventory Allocations screen**, select **Keyboard** as the item and press **Enter**
8. In the Item Allocations screen, select **Godown** as Onsite, Quantity as 6, Rate as Rs. 450 and the Amount will be calculated automatically
9. Accept the **Item Allocations** screen
10. Accept the **Inventory Allocations** screen
11. Enter **Narration** if required

    The completed Purchase Voucher appears as shown in (Figure 6.33):

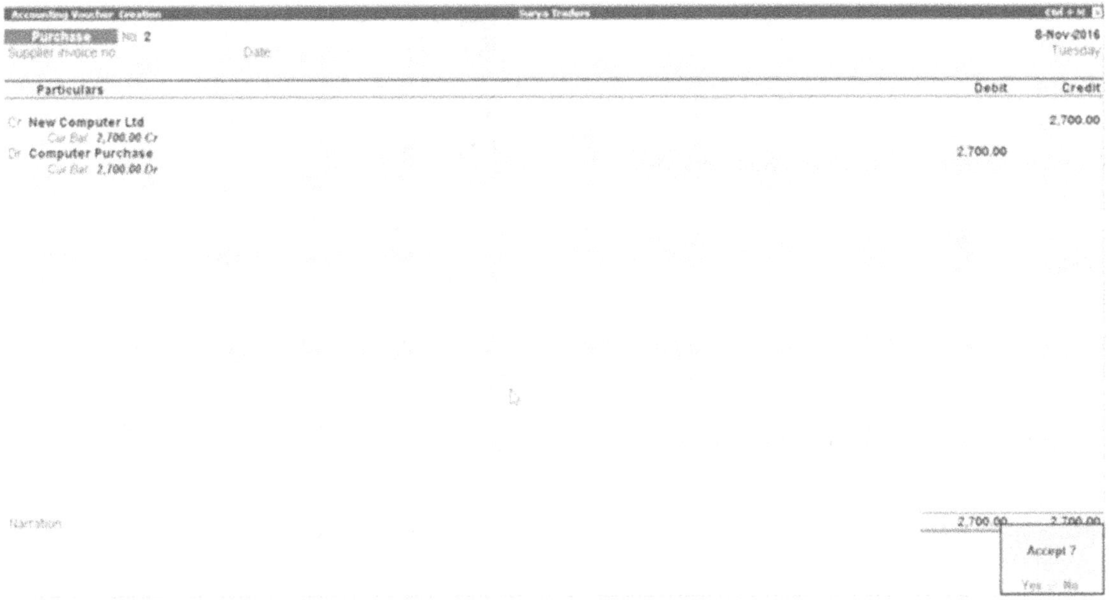

Figure 6.33: Purchase Voucher

12. Press **Y** or **Enter** to accept

6.6.4.2 Sales Voucher

Illustration-17

On 08-11-2016, Surya Traders sold 2 Nos of Samsung Smart Watch at Rs. 2,800/Nos. to Supriya Traders, delivered from their Onsite godown.

To record the transaction:

1. Go to the **Gateway of Tally > Accounting Vouchers > F8: Sales**

2. Press **F2** and change the date to 08-11-2016

3. Select Supriya Traders from the **List of Ledger Accounts** to **debit**

4. Enter the amount as **Rs. 5600**

5. Select Computer Sales from the **List of Ledger Accounts** to **credit**

6. In the **Inventory Allocations** screen, select Smart Watch as the item and press **Enter**

7. In the **Item Allocations** screen, select **Godown** as Onsite, Quantity as 2, Rate as Rs. 2,800 and the Amount will be calculated automatically

8. Accept the **Item Allocations** screen

9. Accept the **Inventory Allocations** screen

11. Enter **Narration** if required

The completed Sales Voucher appears as shown below (Figure 6.34):

Figure 6.34: Sales Voucher

12. Press **Y** or **Enter** to accept

6.6.4.3 Debit Note

Illustration-18

On 09-11-2016, Surya Traders returned 3 Nos. of Keyboard as they were found to be defective, to New Computers Ltd.

To record the transaction:

1. Go to the **Gateway of Tally > Accounting Vouchers > F9: Debit Note**
2. Press **F2** and change the date to 09-11-2016
3. Mention the original invoice number and original invoice date i.e. Mention the date and invoice number of purchase voucher which is returned.
4. Select New Computers Ltd. from the List of Ledger

Accounts to debit

5. Enter the amount as **Rs. 1350**
6. Create Computer Purchases Return Ledger under Purchase Accounts (Press Alt+C for ledger creation and activate Inventory Value)
7. In the **Inventory Allocations** screen, select Keyboard as the item and press **Enter**
8. In the **Item Allocations** screen, select **Godown** as Onsite, Quantity as 3, Rate as Rs. 450 and the Amount will be calculated automatically
9. Accept the **Item Allocations** screen
10. Accept the **Inventory Allocations** screen

The completed Debit Note appears as shown below (Figure 6.35):

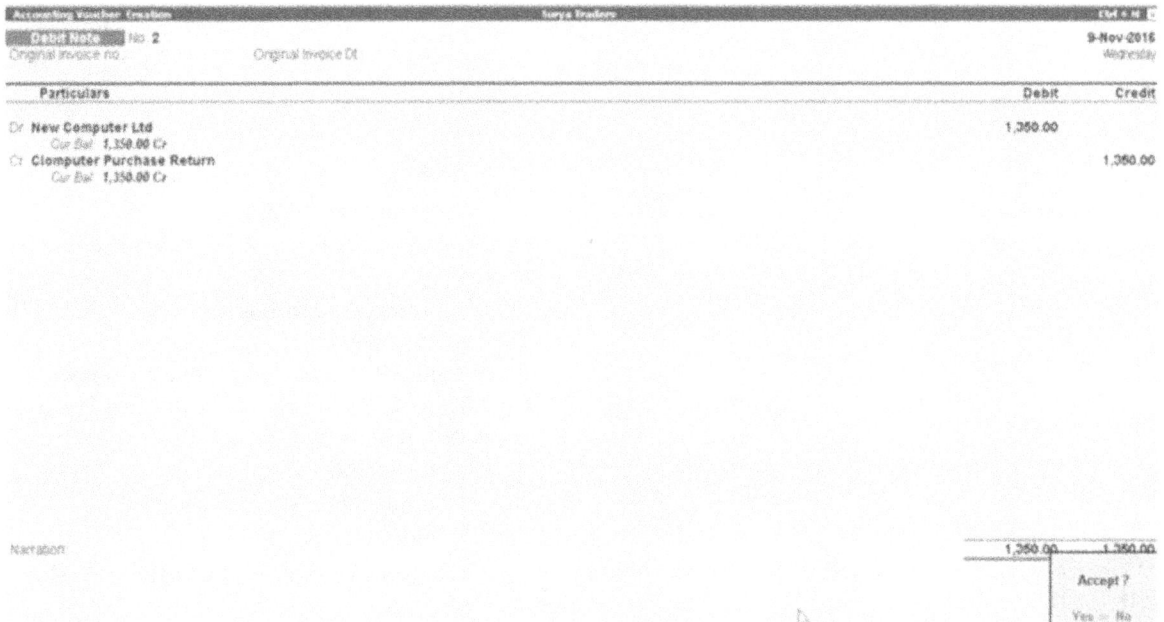

Figure 6.35: Debit Note

11. Press **Y** or **Enter** to accept

6.6.4.4 Credit Note

Illustration-19

On 10-11-2016, Surya Traders received 1 Samsung Smart Watch from Supriya & Co., as they were found to be defective.

To record the transaction:

1. Go to the **Gateway of Tally > Accounting Vouchers > F8: Credit Note**
2. Press **F2** and change the date to 10-11-2016
3. Select Supriya & Co. from the List of Ledger Accounts to credit
4. Enter the amount as **Rs. 2,800**

5. Create Computer Sales Return under Sales Accounts (Press Alt+C for ledger creation and activate Inventory Value)
6. from the **List of Ledger Accounts** to **debit**
7. In the **Inventory Allocations** screen, select Samsung Smart Watch as the item and press **Enter**
8. In the **Item Allocations** screen, select **Godown** as Onsite, Quantity as 1, Rate as Rs. 2,800 and the Amount will be calculated automatically
9. Accept the **Item Allocations** screen
10. Accept the **Inventory Allocations** screen
11. Press **Enter** to get back to the voucher entry screen

The completed Credit Note appears as shown in (Figure 6.36):

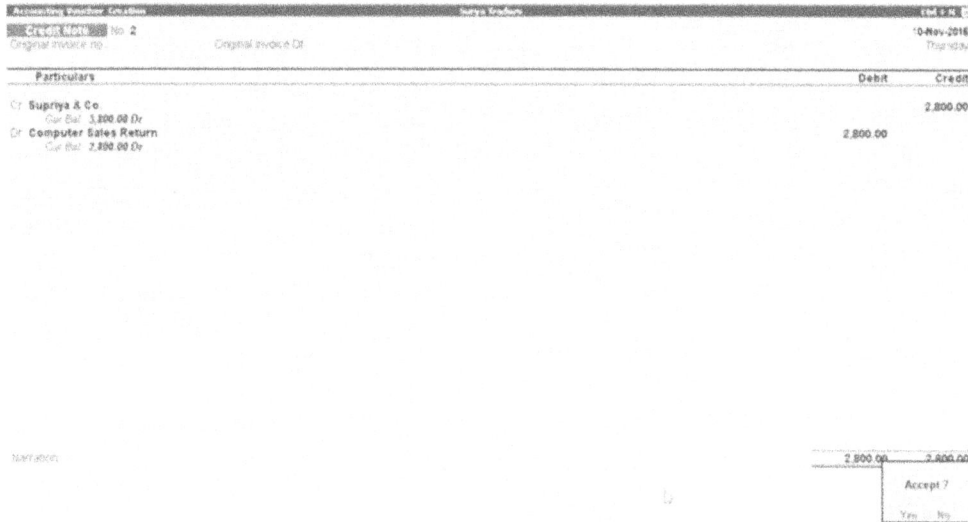

Figure 6.36: Credit Note

12. Press **Y** or **Enter** to accept

6.6.5 Item Invoice and Account Invoice

Tally.ERP 9 gives you an option called Account Invoice where you can select the ledgers instead of the stock items. An Item Invoice, on the other hand, allows you to select stock items instead of ledgers.

Businesses that require an invoice raised with the item details, can select the Item Invoice option. Businesses that want to raise invoices for services rendered, can do so by selecting the Account Invoice.

6.6.6 Creating an Item Invoice

Tally.ERP 9 has an in-built system to create and print sales invoices. You will now record sales and purchase invoice details, adjust accounting and inventory balances (Figure 6.37).

To enable the option of invoicing:

1. Set '**Yes**' to the following options in **F11: Features**

(Accounting Features/Inventory Features).

o   Allow Invoicing,

o   Enter Purchases in Invoice Format

Illustration-20

As on 10-11-2016, Surya Traders sold 2 Nos. of Samsung Galaxy Tablet @ Rs. 6,500 to Sunny Electronics. Recording sales invoice:

1. Go to the **Gateway of Tally > Accounting Vouchers > F8: Sales**

2. Ensure that the button above the Post-Dated option reads As Voucher. This button enables you to toggle between the voucher and invoice format for data entry. The button visible is the format not in use

3. Ensure that Use Common Ledger A/c for Item Allocation is set to Yes in Sales Invoice Configurations screen (F12: Configure)

4. Press **F2** and change the date to 10-11-2016

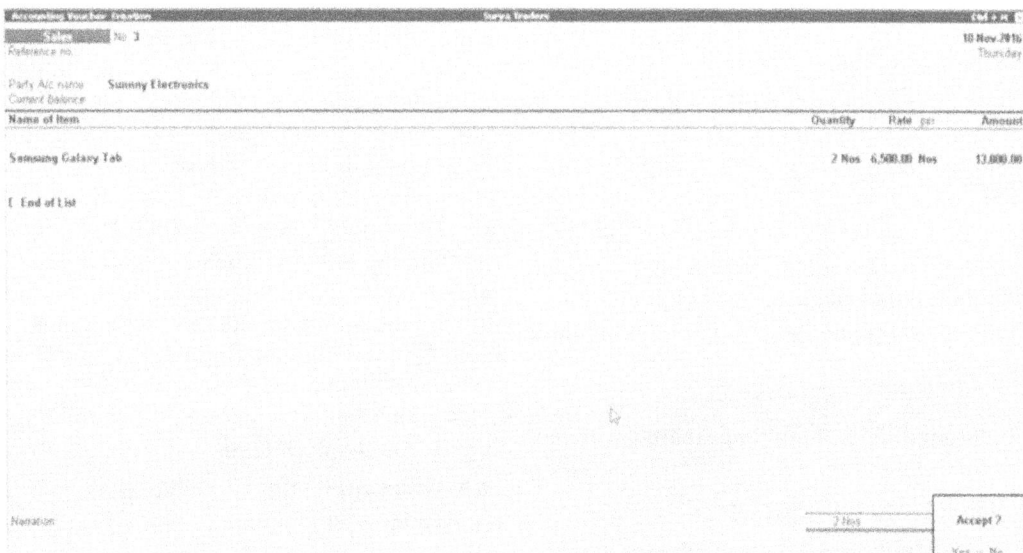

Figure 6.37: Sales Transaction in Invoice Mode

5. Select **Sunny Electronics** in the **Party's A/c Name field**
6. Accept the **Party Details** screen
7. Select Computer Sales in the **Sales Ledger field**
8. Select the item being sold, that is Samsung Galaxy tablet
9. In the **Item Allocations** screen,
    o   Select Onsite as the **Godown**
    o   Enter Quantity being sold. Here, it is 2 Nos. The Rate and Amount will be filled automatically
10. Press **Enter** to get back to the voucher entry screen
11. Enter **Narration** if required

    The completed Sales Invoice will appear as shown below (Figure 6.38):

13. Press **Y** or **Enter** to accept

6.6.7   Creating an Account Invoice
Go to the **Gateway of Tally > Accounting Vouchers > F8: Sales**

1. The invoice screen must display the following columns: Name of Item, Quantity, Rate and Amount
2. Click on the Acct Invoice button. You will notice that Tally.ERP 9 now displays the columns as Particulars, Rate and Amount
3. Select the **Party's A/c Name as Customer One**
4. Press **Enter** till you reach the **Particulars** field. Press **Space bar** and Tally.ERP 9 displays the **List of Ledgers**

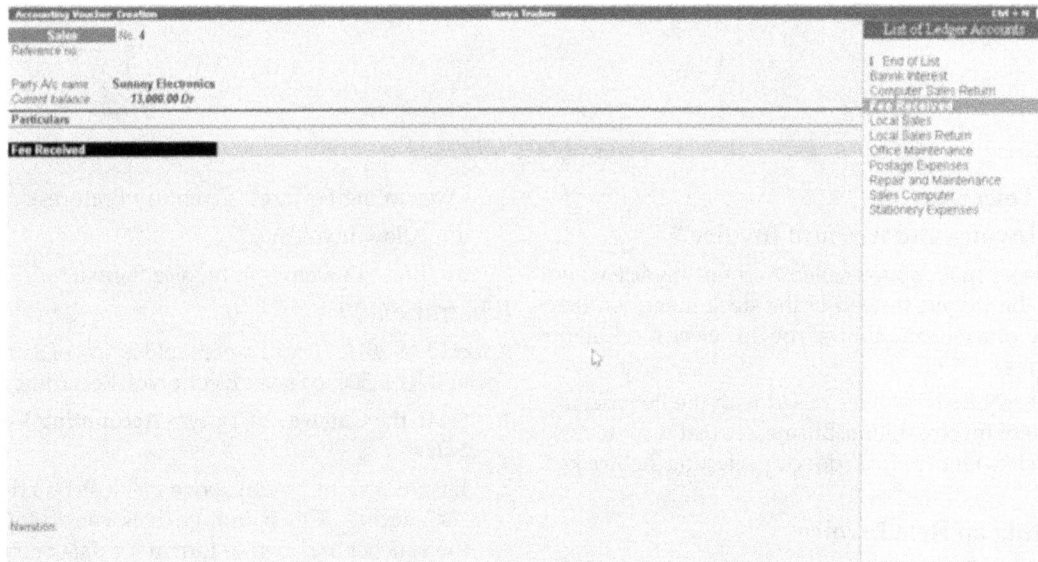

Figure 6.38: Sales Voucher in Accounting Invoice Mode

5. Select the **Fees Received** (create one if it is not displayed under Direct Income)
6. Specify the amount as Rs. 2,000 and press **Enter**

Activity
Transaction from the books of Surya Traders

02-05-2016	Purchase 10 Nos. Keyboard @Rs. 400/- from Raxson Ltd
03-05-2016	Sold 5Nos. of Keyboard to Supriya & Co. @ Rs. 650
04-05-2016	Received 5 Nos of Mouse from Jakson Ltd.
05-05-2016	Delivered 2 Nos Samsung Smart Watch from Onsite to Sunny Electronics.
11-05-2016	Stock check reveals physical stock of Keyboard is 6Nos.
12-05-2016	Supriya & Co. returned 1Nos. keyboard
13-05-2016	Transferred 4 Nos of Samsung Smartwatch from onsite to Shop.

6.7   ACCOUNTING REPORTS

Tally's display of information is designed to allow a user to get the maximum benefit out of the data of the transactions and dealings of a company. A user gets a holistic picture of the data and is also able to present information using different options. The purpose of compiling data is to present it in comprehensible accounting, inventory and Management Information System reports. On entering the vouchers, Tally.ERP 9 uses the data and provides the user with various reports in addition to all books and statements.

The display screens of Tally.ERP 9 are dynamic and interactive. Whatever a user sees on the screen can also be printed, depending on the printer's capabilities and settings.

The **Gateway of Tally** displays a few reports directly, i.e. the **Balance Sheet, Profit & Loss Account, Stock Summary** and **Ratio Analysis** as these statements are extremely critical for day-to-day business analysis. The **List of Accounts** report, a display of the Chart of Accounts of the company, is available in the Display Menu, along with all other Tally.ERP 9 report.

To view the Display Menu:

Go to **Gateway of Tally > Display**

The **Display Menu** appears as shown in Figure 6.39:

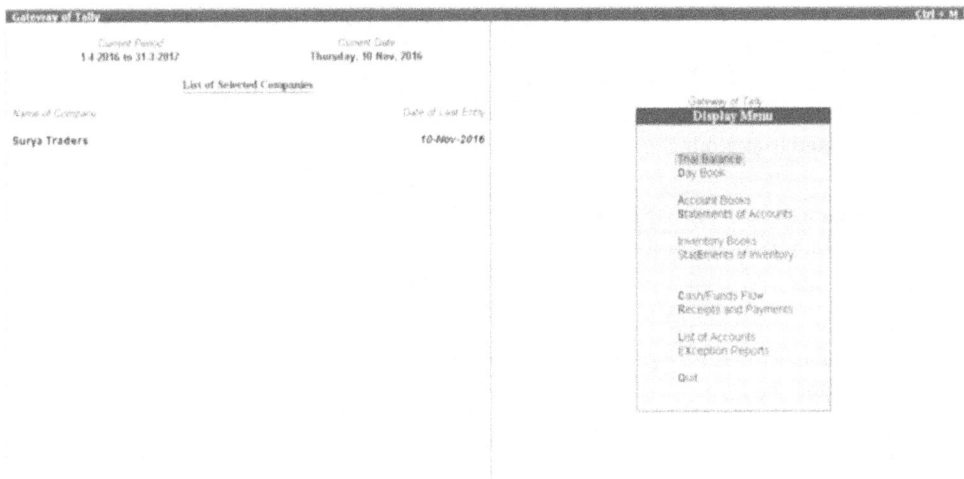

Figure 6.39: Display Menu

In this chapter, we will see the accounting reports which are available by default in Tally.ERP 9. However, based on the modules enabled, for example Payroll, the relevant reports for that module will also be available in the Display menu.

6.7.1 Basic Features of Displaying Reports

Tally.ERP 9 creates the books of accounts and the financial statements based on the vouchers entered till date. The appearance of reports can be customised as required.

For example, the user can compare different companies, periods of the financial year, groups and ledgers.

The user can also drill down to the transaction level from any report. For this, select an item in the report and press '**Enter**' to navigate to the next level. Following this process will make the user drill down, till they reach an individual voucher. To navigate back to previous levels, press '**Esc**'. The special features available for a displayed report are indicated on the button bar, which can be operated by a single-click of the mouse.

6.7.2 Financial Statements

Financial statements summarize the individual transactions to show totals, ratios and statistics required by users to analyse the company's financial data in a wide variety of ways. Broadly, financial statements are classified into the following major statements, which form a part of the statutory requirements in most countries:

* Balance Sheet
* Profit & Loss A/c

6.7.2.1 Balance Sheet

A Balance Sheet is a financial statement that reports a business' financial position as on a specific date. The term balance sheet implies that the report shows the balance between two figures. It shows a balance between the assets and liabilities of a business. The fundamental accounting equation is, **Assets = Liabilities + Owner's Equity**

To view the Balance Sheet:

Go to **Gateway of Tally > Balance Sheet**

The **Balance Sheet** appears as shown below (Figure 6.40):

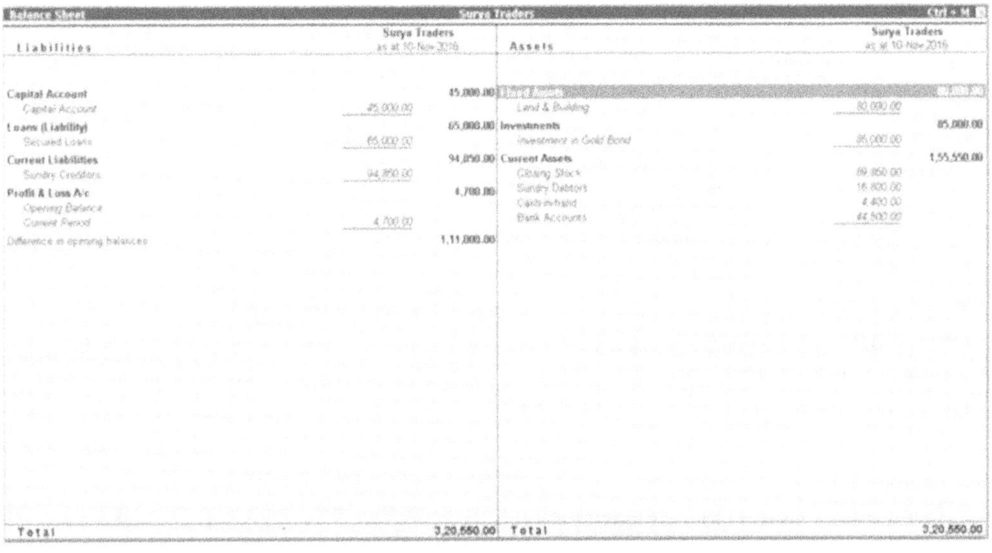

Figure 6.40: Balance Sheet

Balance Sheet gets updated instantly with every transaction that is recorded. The Button Bar can be used to view additional information or toggle to another report. From the options available in the **Button Bar,** a user can:

◆ Select **F1:Detailed/Condensed** to explode the summarized information

◆ Change the date of the Balance Sheet using **F2: Period**

◆ See the effect of different **Stock Valuations** on the Balance Sheet

◆ Add new columns to:

    o   Display the Balance Sheet for a different date and compare with the current one

    o   Display the Balance Sheet of another company when more than one company is open

    o   Display the Balance Sheet in a different currency

    o   Display the budget figures, if any, and analyse the variances

◆ Press **F12: Configure** and set the required parameters

6.7.2.2 *Profit and Loss Account*

Profit and Loss Account or Income Statement is a periodic statement, which shows the net result of a business' operations for a specified period. All the expenses incurred and incomes earned during the reporting period are recorded in the Profit and Loss account or Income and **Expenditure** account.

The profit and loss account in Tally.ERP 9 displays the information based on the default primary groups. It is updated instantly with every transaction/voucher that is entered and saved. No special processing is required to produce a profit and loss account in Tally.ERP 9.

To view the Profit & Loss Account:

1. Go to **Gateway of Tally > Profit & Loss A/c**

2. Click **F1: Detailed,** to view the Profit & Loss Account in detailed format

The **Profit & Loss Account** appears as shown (Figure 6.41):

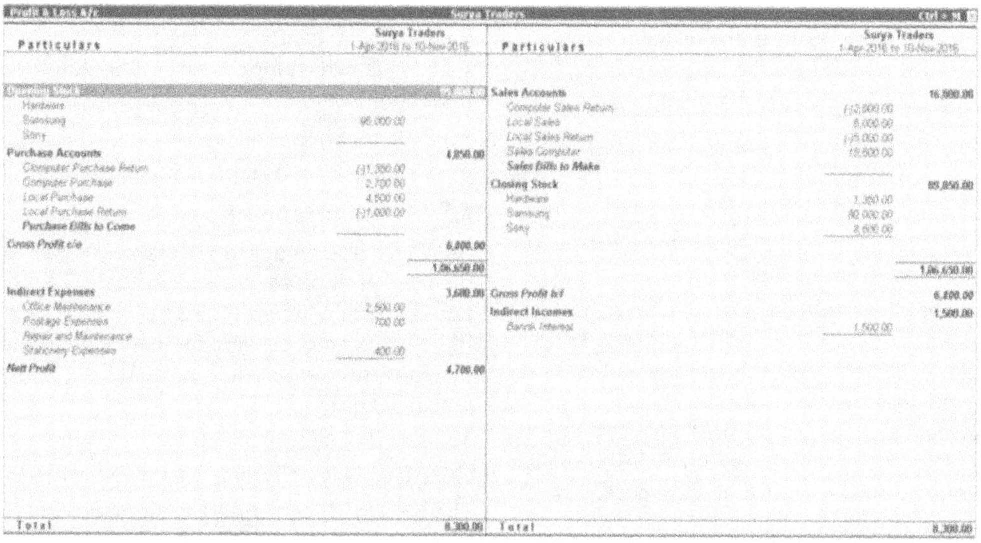

Figure 6.41: Profit & Loss Account

The Profit & Loss account is generated and updated immediately from the date of opening of books till the date of last entry. It is displayed according to the configurations set in the F12: Configure menu.

Horizontal and vertical form of Profit & Loss Account

The Profit & Loss A/c, by default is in horizontal form. However, this can be configured to display the Profit & Loss A/c in Vertical form by selecting the option in **F12: Configure.**

Some of the **Button Bar** options are:

◆ Select **F1: Detailed/Condensed** to display more information or see the summarized format

◆ Change the date of the Profit & Loss Account using **F2: Period**

◆ Add new columns to:

    o   Display the Profit & Loss Account for a different period to compare with the current one

    o   Display the Profit & Loss Account in a different currency

    o   Display a column with Budget figures, if any and analyse variances

    o   See the effect of different Stock Valuations on the Profit/Loss account

    o   Select and compare Profit & Loss of different companies

6.7.2.3 *Trial Balance*

A Trial Balance is a summary report of all ledger balances to check whether the figures are correct and balanced. Considering that the journal entries are error-free and posted correctly to the general ledger, the total of all debit balances should be equal to the total credit balances.

To view the Trial Balance, go to **Gateway of Tally > Display > Trial Balance.**

The **Trial Balance** appears as shown (Figure 6.42):

Figure 6.42: Trial Balance

6.7.2.4 Analysis

The Ratio Analysis report provides a critical overview of the company's performance in the form of ratios. Not only does this report provide an instant understanding of the Working Capital, the Operating Cost percentage and the Nett and Gross Profit percentage, but also gives information about the payment performance of debtors. The return on investment percentage and the return on working capital percentage are other critical ratios available in this report.

To view the Ratio Analysis report, go to **Gateway of Tally > Ratio Analysis**

The **Ratio Analysis report** appears as shown below (Figure 6.43):

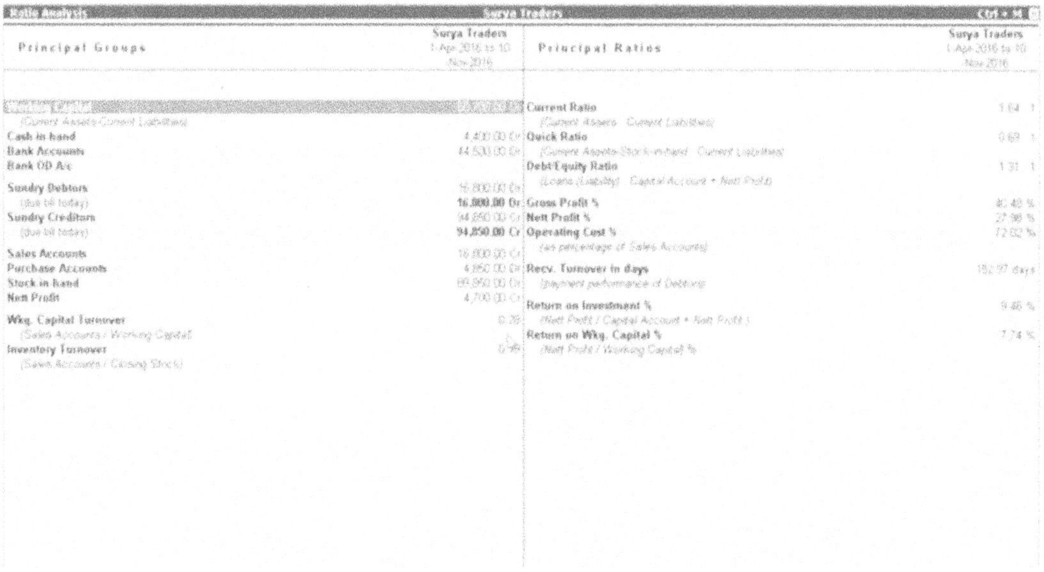

Figure 6.43: Ratio Analysis

6.7.2.5 Books and Registers

In Tally.ERP 9, as soon as transactions are entered they are immediately posted to the respective ledgers, books and registers, thereby facilitating instant reporting and faster decision making.

Books of Account is a record of the commercial accounts of a company and consolidates the transaction details as they are entered. Although the elements of a transaction are posted to many different ledgers simultaneously, Tally.ERP 9 brings all the transactions of a particular type together into relevant books of account for viewing and printing. For example, Cash Book records all the transactions affecting cash and the Sales Book records all sales transactions.

6.7.2.6 Day Book

The Day Book contains all the transactions made by a business, irrespective of the type of transaction. By default the display is set to the date of the last voucher entry made, but this can be set to list all the transactions made over a certain period. Transactions include all financial vouchers, reversing and memorandum journals as well as inventory vouchers.

To view the Day Book:

1. Go to **Gateway of Tally > Display > Day Book**
2. Click **F2: Period** on the button bar
3. Specify the required period

The **Day Book** for a specified period appears as shown below (Figure 6.44):

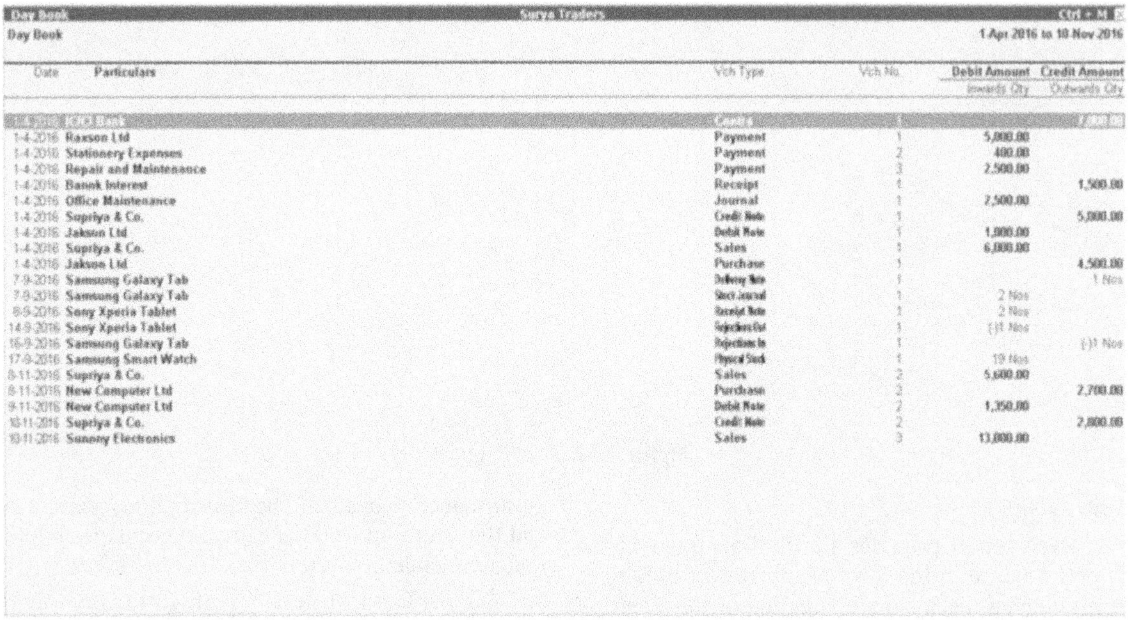

Figure 6.44: Day Book

Purchase and Sales Registers

6.7.2.7 Purchase Register

A Purchase Register displays the information about all the purchases made by a business concern. Purchase register also helps in analysing the details of movement of purchased goods to various godowns, on the basis of which the stock movement at each godown can be determined.

To view the Purchase Register:

Go to **Gateway of Tally > Display > Account Books > Purchase Register**

The **Purchase Register** for the selected period appears as shown below (Figure 6.45):

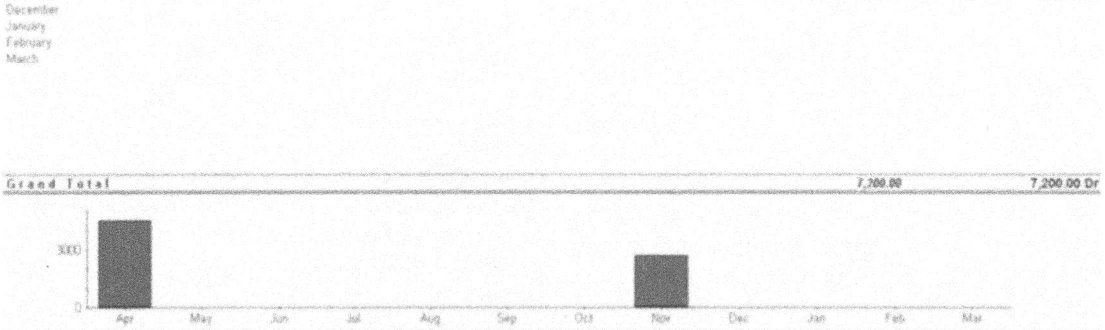

Figure 6.45: Purchase Register

6.7.2.8 Sales Register

Sales Register displays the monthly summary of all sales transactions and the closing balances at the end of each month, for the selected period. The list of transactions pertaining to any month can be viewed by selecting that month and pressing 'Enter' to view its details. Tally.ERP 9 enables change of display according to the information required.

To view the Sales Register:

Go to **Gateway of Tally > Display > Account Books > Sales Register**

The **Sales Register** for the selected period appears as shown below (Figure 6.46):

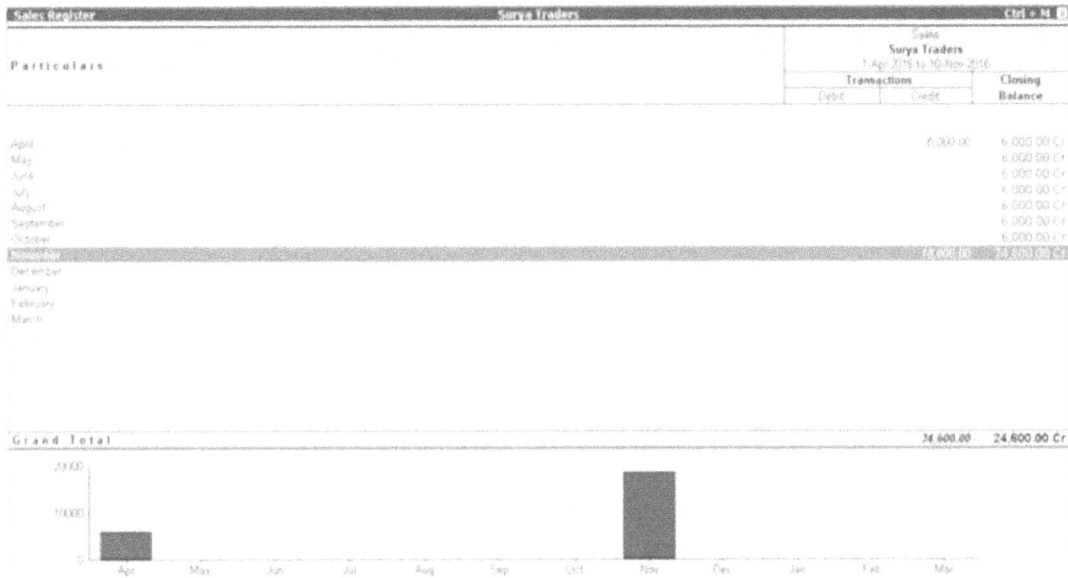

Figure 6.46: Sales Register

The benefits of a sales register are as follows:

- The periodic turnover can be analysed using the F2: Period button
- The periodic taxes on such turnovers can be easily computed
- Errors made while recording transactions can be easily traced
- Sales returns during the year can be analysed and timely action can be taken to remove the undesirable causes.

6.7.2.9 Statement of Accounts

Statistics

The Statistics report displays the masters created for that company and the number of vouchers entered for each type of transaction. You can drill down to the transaction level from this report.

To view the Statistics report:

Go to **Gateway of Tally > Display > Statement of Accounts > Statistics**

The **Statistics** report appears as shown below (Figure 6.47):

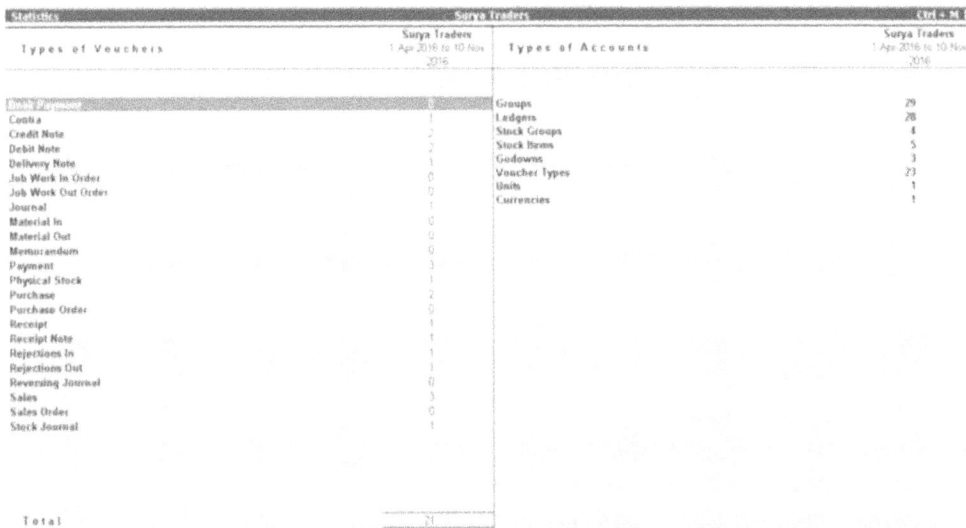

Figure 6.47: Statistics

6.8   BANKING

The Banking module focuses on managing and streamlining banking transactions and activities i.e., Transactional Banking, Analytical Banking & Deposit Management. The banking feature in Tally.ERP 9 supports the requisite recording and processes essentials for effective bank accounting and recording of accounting transactions.

The features of Banking in Tally.ERP 9 are as follows:

*   Cheque Printing
*   Cheque Register
*   Bank Reconciliation
*   Deposit Slip
*   Payment Advice

6.8.1   Cheque Printing

A cheque is a written order to the bank to pay the stated sum of money. Cheques are usually handwritten. In order to automate the entire cheque printing process, Tally.ERP 9 allows cheques to be printed directly. Cheques can be printed while printing a payment voucher. Since the cheque formats differ from bank to bank, Tally.ERP 9 facilitates a sample format and formats of various banks besides user-defined cheque dimensions.

Activity

Open Radhika Enterprises and follow the below mentioned instructions

The following illustration will demonstrate how to activate and configure Cheque Printing for a specific bank (here Axis Bank) in Tally.ERP 9. We will be creating the Bank Ledger master to configure the cheque printing.

Step 1: Activation of Cheque printing

1. **Press** F11: Company features > F1: Accounting Features
2. Set **Enable Cheque Printing** to **Yes**

Step 2: Create the Bank Account Ledger

1. Go to **Gateway of Tally > Accounts Info. > Ledger > Create**
2. Mention the ledger name as Axis Bank.
3. Enable the option Set/Alter Bank Details to **Yes** and press Enter to view the Banking Configuration screen
4. In the Banking Configuration screen, Select Axis Bank in the Select Your Bank field (Figure 6.48)

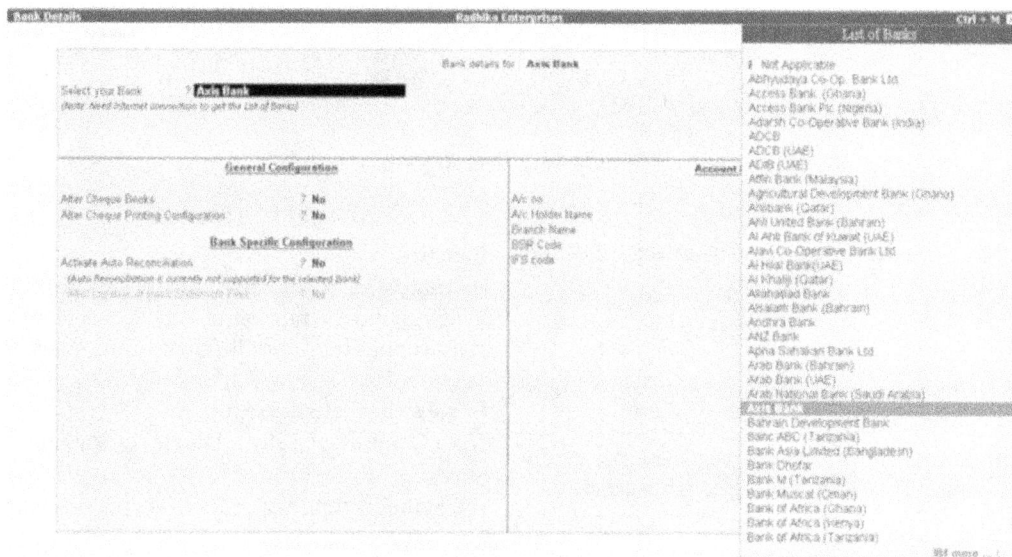

Figure 6.48: Selecting the Bank

5. Enable the option Set Cheque Books and press Enter to view the Cheque Book Management screen.
6.   Enter the From Number and To Number
7. The Number of Cheques will be filled automatically
8. Enter the Cheque Book Name.
9. Ensure that the Cheque Book Management screen is as shown in Figure 6.49:
10. Press **Enter** and accept the screen

    Enable **Set Cheque Printing Configuration**

11. On enabling this option, various formats of cheque of Axis Bank are displayed in the **Cheque Format Selection** screen
12. The **Cheque Format Selection** screen appears as shown in Figure 6.50:

13. Select the required format and press **Enter**

    The Cheque dimension will be auto-filled and will appear as shown in Figure 6.51:

    o   To preview the setting, press ALT+P
    o   Press Enter to view the preview and press Esc to go out of preview screen.
    o   Mention the necessary details in the Bank Details screen.
    o   Press Enter to accept the Bank Details Screen and you will come back to Ledger creation screen.
    o   Mention the Mailing details if required.
    o   Press Enter and bring the cursor on Opening balance field and provide the opening balance of Rs. 2,50,000 (Figure 6.52)

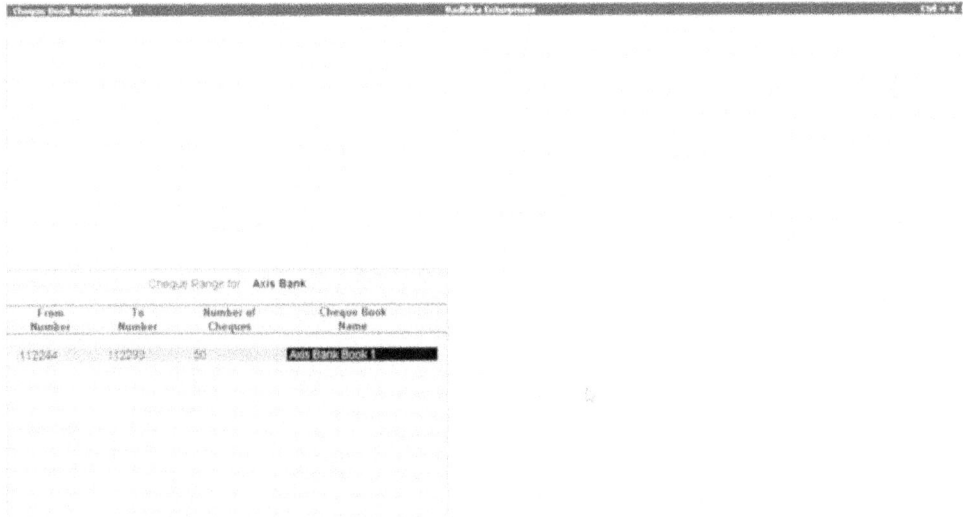

Figure 6.49: Cheque Range screen

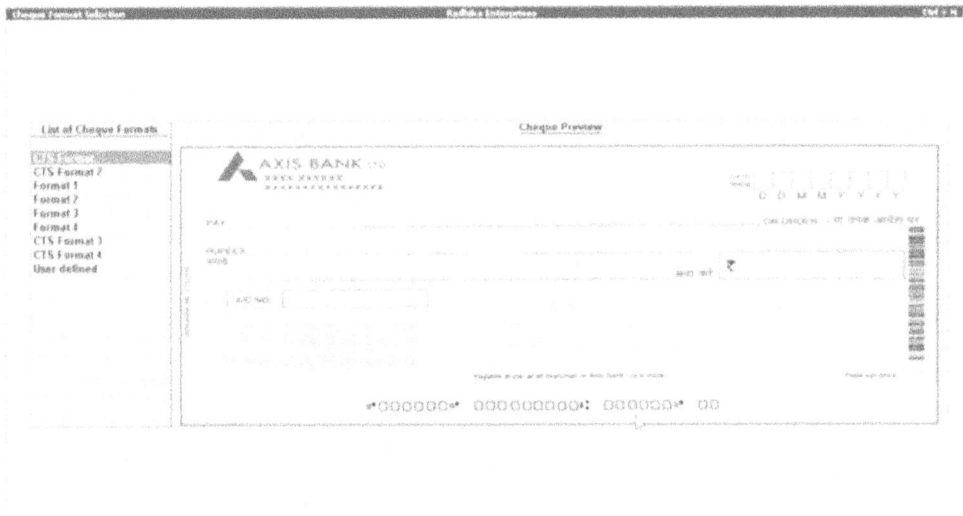

Figure 6.50: Cheque Format Selection screen

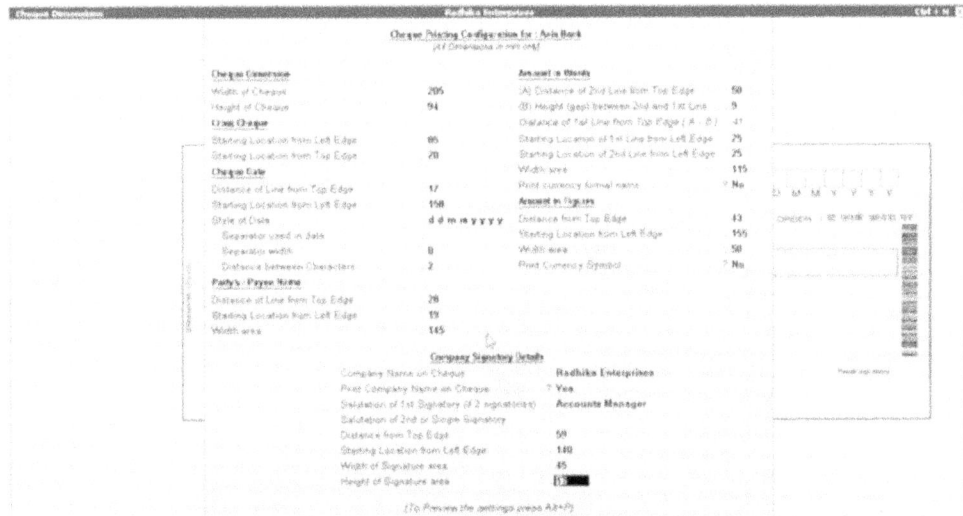

Figure 6.51: Cheque Dimensions Pre-Filled

Tip

You can compare the cheque dimensions (sample) with the actual cheque and modify accordingly to suit your requirement. Take the bank's cheque book and measure the dimensions of a cheque carefully in millimetres and fill the form. You may need to correct it after trying out a couple of cheques so that the positioning is accurate. The placing of the cheque in the printer also determines the printing. Trials could be made on photocopies of a cheque before using an actual cheque leaf.

In case of a cheque with two signatories, both can be specified (Both could be the same salutation or different, e.g., the first one as Director and the second one as Secretary).

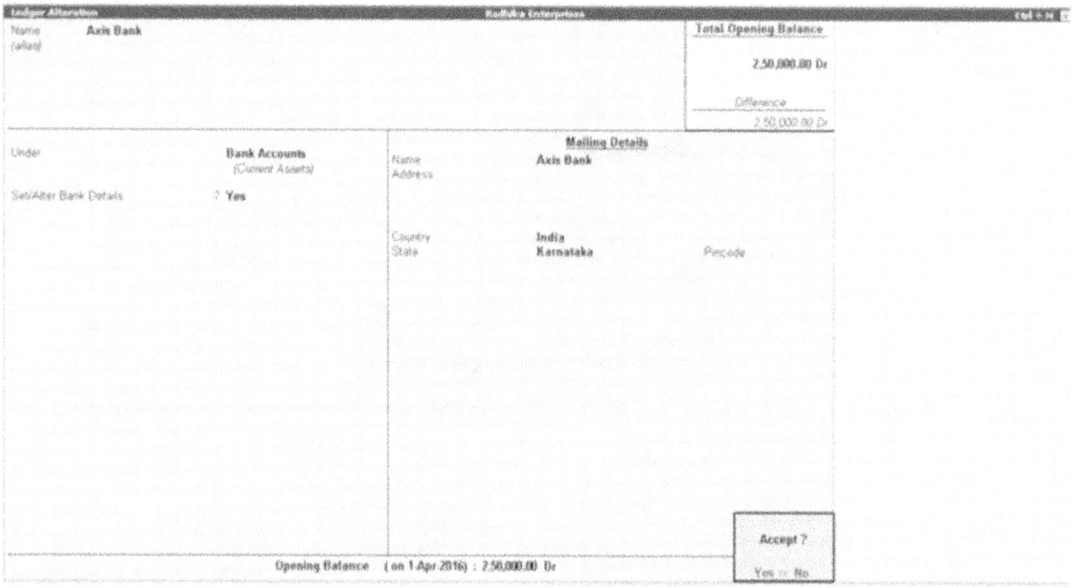

Figure 6.52: Ledger Creation screen

Activity

Create Sudhir Enterprises Ledger account under Sundry creditors

Recording transaction of Related to Bank .

The illustration below will help you understand how these cheque ranges can be selected during voucher entry.

1. **Go to** Gateway of Tally > Accounting Voucher > F5: Payment > Select Payment Vouchers.
2. Press F12:Payment standard configuration and disable the option "Use Single entry mode for Pymt/rcpt/contra.
3. Press **F2** and change the date to 15-04-2016
4. In the **Debit** Field, select Sudhir Enterprises ledger and enter the **Amount** as Rs. **25000**
5. Enter the amount as **Rs. 25,000**
6. In the **Credit** field, select **Axis Bank** and accept the **Amount**
7. Press **Enter** to view the **Bank Allocations** screen
8. The **Bank Allocations** screen appears as shown below (Figure 6.53):

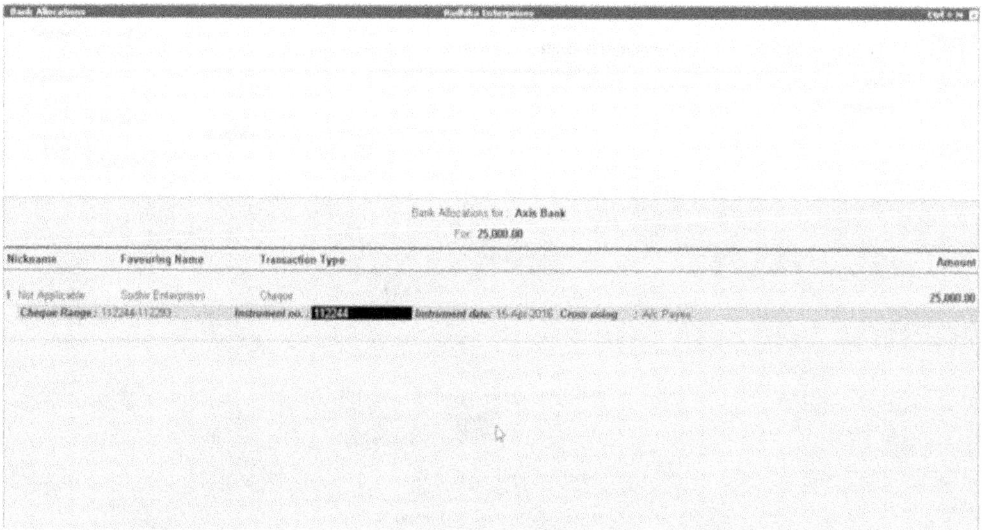

Figure 6.53: Bank Allocations screen

In the Bank Allocations screen, the Cheque Range and the Instrument Number are auto filled as the cheque numbers were configured earlier

9. Accept the Bank Allocations screen
    The completed Payment Voucher appears as shown below (Figure 6.54):

Figure 6.54: Completed Payment Voucher

10. Enter the **Narration** if required and accept the voucher

11. On accepting the screen, the **Cheque Printing** configuration

    screen appears (Figure 6.55)

12. Press **Enter** to print the cheque (Figure 6.56)

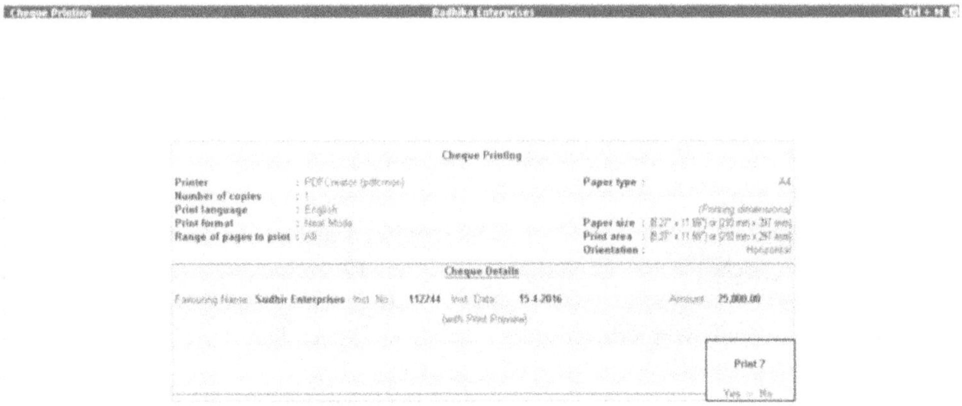

Figure 6.55: Cheque Printing Configuration screen

Figure 6.56: Cheque Printing screen

The illustration below will help you understand how to pass cash purchase entry with bank details: On 24-4-2016 Cash paid for Purchas product worth of Rs. 10,000

Required Ledgers Local Purchase

Go to **Gateway of Tally > Accounts Info > Ledgers > Create Purchase Account Under Purchase Account Group and activate Inventroy Values**

Let us account the entries to print cheque.

1. **Go to** Gateway of Tally > Accounting Vouchers > F9: Purchase

2. Click on **As voucher** on vertical menu bar or you can press **CTRL+V**

3. Enter the details in the purchase invoice as per the transaction details

4. **Cr Axis Bank** Rs. 10,000

5. **Enter** to get **Bank allocation** screen

6. Select the Transaction type as Cheque

7. Dr the **Purchase Account**

8. Enter **and** accept

9. Immediately you get the screen as:

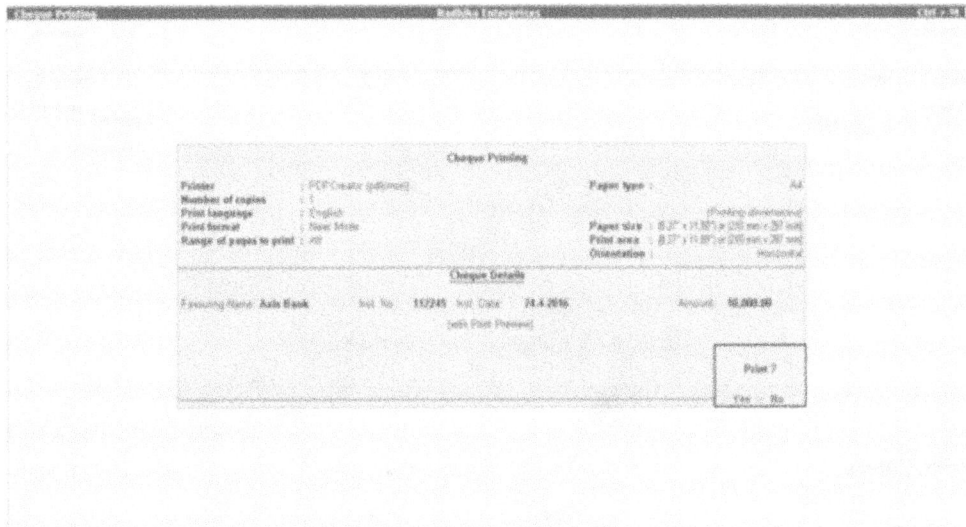

Figure 6.57: Cheque printing screen

10. **Say** Print **to** Yes and get a printout of the cheque (Figure 6.57).

6.8.2   Single Cheque Printing

Tally.ERP 9 allows you to print a single cheque and/or multiple cheques at the same time.

The following illustration will show you how to print cheques for transactions (payment or Purchase) which are done using **Bank Account.**

Single Cheque Printing

To print a single cheque:

1. **Go to** Gateway of Tally > Banking > Cheque Printing

2. Select **Axis Bank** in the **Name of Bank field**

3. Click **F2: Period** and enter the period in which the cheque is dated. Enter **1-04-2016** to **30-04-2016**

4. Press **Space Bar** to select the transaction for which the cheque has to be printed

5. The **Cheque Printing** screen is displayed as shown (Figure 6.58):

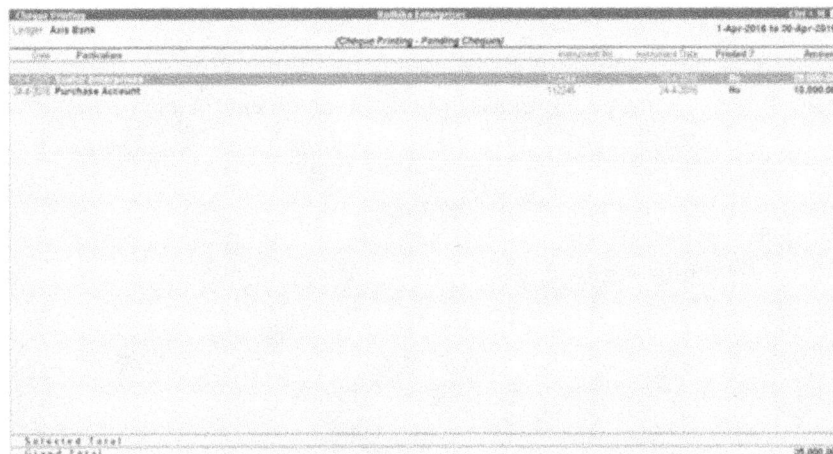

Figure 6.58: Cheque Printing screen

Select pressing space bar and press ALT+P

The printed cheque appears as shown below (Figure 6.59):

Figure 6.59: Printed Cheque

Note: ◆ The **Cheque Printing** facility is also available directly from the **Payment** voucher when the concerned Bank account is credited.

◆ After crediting the Bank account, Tally.ERP 9 asks for details of the Name on Cheque, Cheque No.,

and Cross Cheques explained below:

o **Name on the Cheque:** On selection of the Party Account, the Name on the cheque is filled with the Party's account name

o **Cross Cheque using:** This is filled in by the most common words used - Account payee. However, you can change it.

The following illustration will help you understand how to pass a cash deposit entry with bank details:

On 29-4-2016 deposited Rs. 10,000 cash in Axis Bank account

1. **Go to** Gateway of Tally > Accounting Voucher > F4: Contra > Select Bank Payment

2. Press **F2** and change the date to **29-04-2016**

3. In the Credit Field, select Cash ledger and enter the Amount asRs. 10,000 (Figure 6.60)

4. In the Debit field, select Axis Bank and accept the Amount

5. Press **Enter** to view the **Bank Allocations** screen

6. Press **Y** or **Enter** to accept (Figure 6.61)

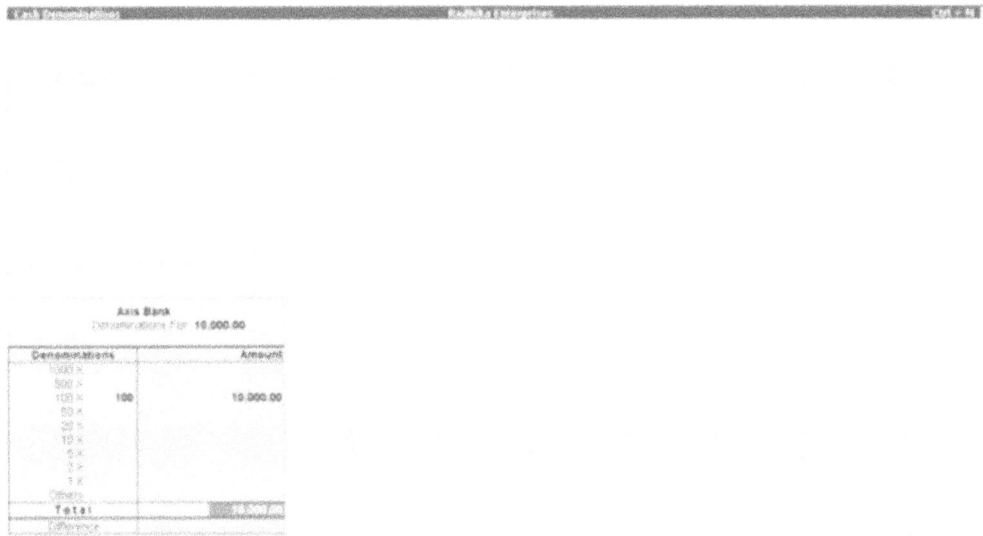

Figure 6.60: Cash Denominations

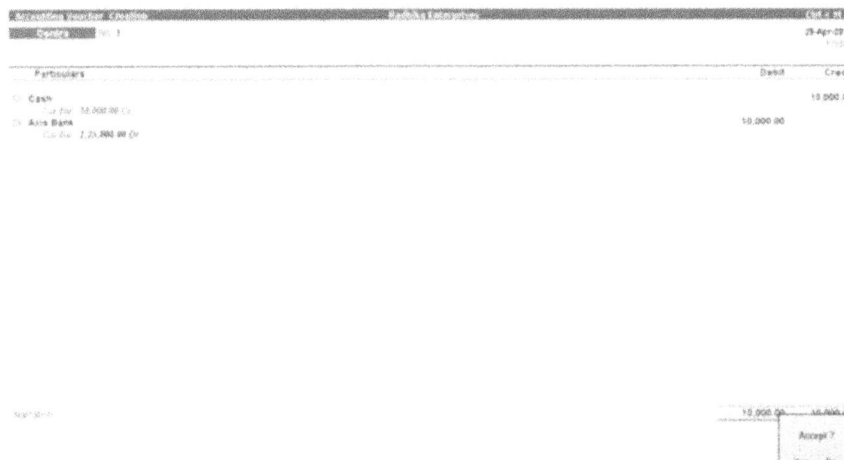

Figure 6.61: Accounting Voucher Creation

6.8.3   Cancellation of a Cheque

Tally.ERP 9 provides its users with the facility to cancel cheques. The status of an available cheque can be changed to cancelled either by cancelling a particular voucher or by cancelling a new cheque for reasons like torn cheque, lost in transit and so on.

The following illustration will demonstrate how to cancel a cheque. Radhika Enterprises cancelled the cheque numbered 112244 as it was torn. To cancel the cheque,

1. Go to Gateway of Tally > Banking > Cheque Register

2. Press Enter on Bank Account to view the Cheque Range Register screen

3. Press Enter on the range of cheque 112244-112293

4. Open the transaction which you want to cancel then press ALT+X for Cancel voucher.

6. Select Cancel Voucher and press Enter

7. After cancel the voucher cheque will automatically cancel. The Voucher Cancel screen appear as shown below (Figure 6.62):

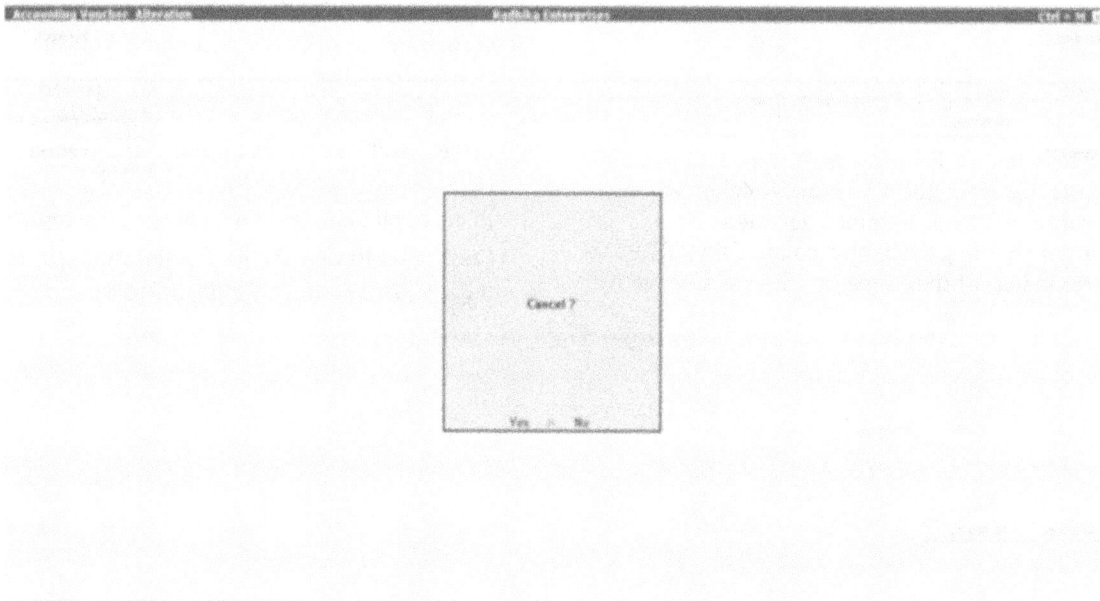

Figure 6.62: Voucher Cancel Screen

8. Press Y or Enter for Cancel

The completed Cancellation of Cheque Numbers screen appears as shown below (Figure 6.63):

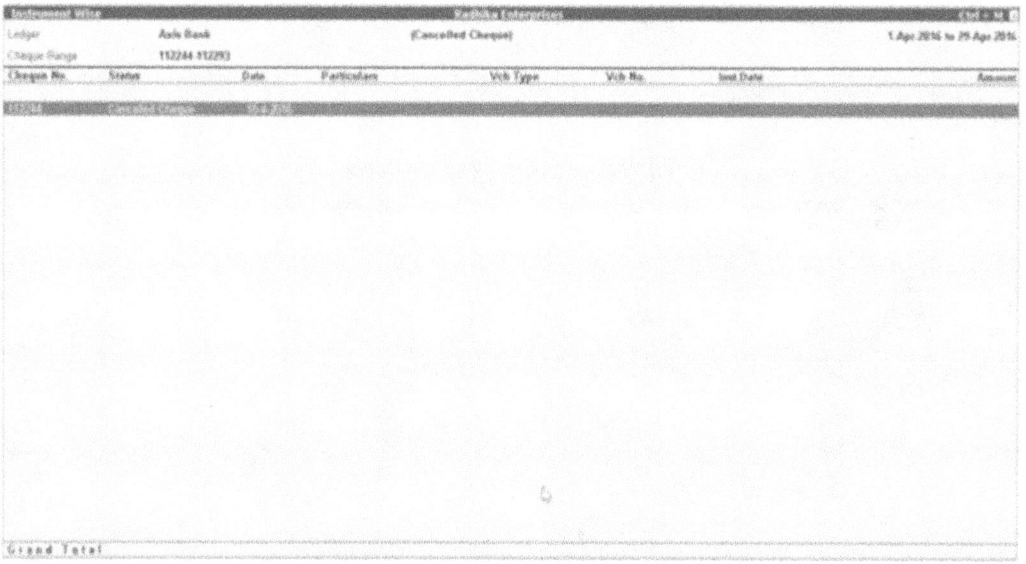

Figure 6.63: Cancellation of Cheque Numbers screen

To view the Cheque Register:

1. Go to Gateway of Tally > Banking > Cheque Register

2. Press ALT+F1 to obtain a detailed view

The **Cheque Register** screen appears as shown in Figure 6.64:

Figure 6.64: Cheque Register screen

6.8.4 Deposit Slip

The Deposit Slip option in Banking enables you to generate deposit slips for cheque(s)/DD/cash that are deposited into the bank for any particular date.

To view Deposit Slip menu:

Go to Gateway of Tally > Banking > Deposit Slip (Figure 6.65)

6.8.5 Cash Deposit Slip

The Cash Deposit Slip option allows

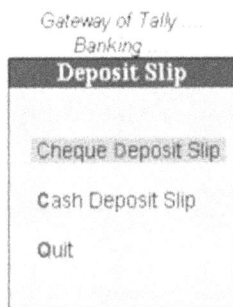

Figure 6.65: Deposit Slip menu

the user to generate the deposit slip for payments which need to be deposited into the bank for any particular date.

To create a Cash Deposit slip for this:

1. **Go to** Gateway of Tally > Banking > Deposit Slip > Cash Deposit Slip

2. Select **Axis Bnak** from the **List of Bank**

   The Cash Deposit Slip screen appears as shown below (Figure 6.66):

3. Press **ALT+P** to print the deposit slip. The **Print Report** screen appears as shown below (Figure 6.67):

Figure 6.66: Cash Deposit Slip

Figure 6.67: Printing Cash Deposit Slip

Two Copies will be generated:

(Banker's Copy)
Cash Deposit Slip/Pay-in-Slip

Bank name	: Axis Bank		Date	: 29-Apr-2016
Branch name	:			
Account no	:			
Account holder name	: Radhika Enterprises			

Denominations		Amount
1000 X		
500 X		
100 X	100	10,000.00
50 X		
20 X		
10 X		
5 X		
2 X		
1 X		
Others		
Total		₹ 10,000.00

Amount (in words) : INR Ten Thousand Only

Deposited by   Received by

Signature   Signature

(Customer's Copy)
Cash Deposit Slip/Pay-in-Slip

Bank name	: Axis Bank		Date	: 29-Apr-2016
Branch name	:			
Account no	:			
Account holder name	: Radhika Enterprises			

Denominations		Amount
1000 X		
500 X		
100 X	100	10,000.00
50 X		
20 X		
10 X		
5 X		
2 X		
1 X		
Others		
Total		₹ 10,000.00

Amount (in words) : INR Ten Thousand Only

Deposited by   Received by

Signature   Signature

Figure 6.68: Printed Cash Deposit Slip

Similarly you can generate the Cheque Deposit Slip from Banking Report (Figure 6.68)

6.8.6 Payment Advice

The **Payment Advice** option enables the user to generate payment advice for the cheques that are issued to the suppliers and other parties.

The following illustration will demonstrate how to generate a payment advice.

Let us generate a payment advice for Payments made to Ramesh & Sons Rs. 15,000 on 10-04-2016 by Bank Account. To print **Payment Advice**,

- Create Ledger by name of Ramesh & Sons under Sundry Creditor.

- Pass Payment entry Debited Ramesh & Sons & Credited Axis Bank

- **Go to** Gateway of Tally > Banking > Payment Advice

- Select the ledger to which the payment is made, from the list of ledgers. (Select **Ramesh & Sons** from the list of ledgers)

- Press **Space Bar** to select the payment vouchers recorded on **10-04-2016**.

The **Payment Advice** screen appears as shown below (Figure 6.69):

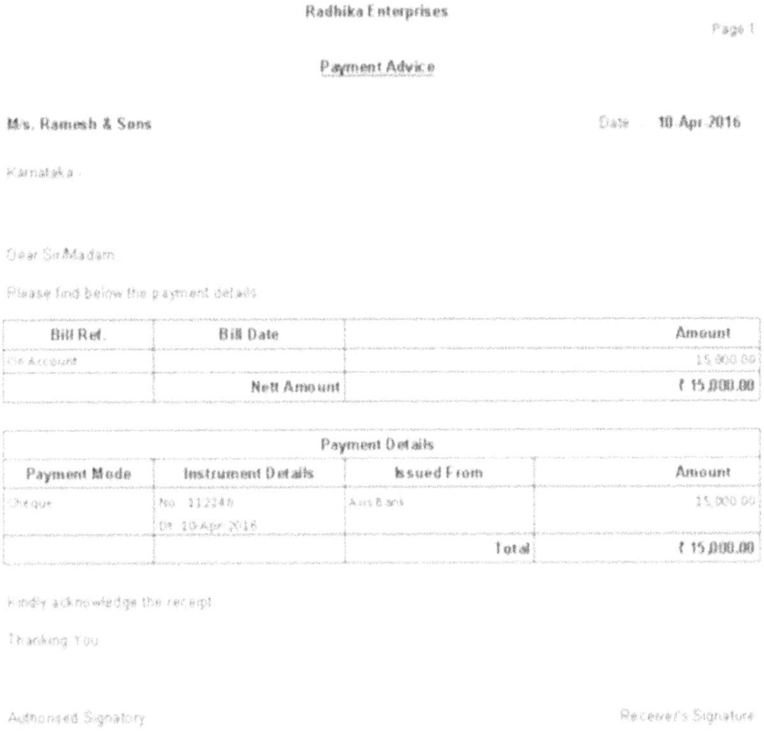

Radhika Enterprises

Page 1

Payment Advice

M/s. Ramesh & Sons   Date : 10-Apr-2016

Karnataka -

Dear Sir/Madam

Please find below the payment details

Bill Ref.	Bill Date		Amount
On Account			15,000.00
	Nett Amount		₹ 15,000.00

Payment Details			
Payment Mode	Instrument Details	Issued From	Amount
Cheque	No: 112348	Axis Bank	15,000.00
	Dt: 10-Apr-2016		
		Total	₹ 15,000.00

Kindly acknowledge the receipt

Thanking You

Authorised Signatory   Receiver's Signature

Figure 6.69: Payment Advice screen

6.8.7 Bank Reconciliation

Reconciling the Company's Bank Accounts with the Bank Statement is a fundamental and regular task of accounting. This process is referred to as Bank Reconciliation.

The following illustration will demonstrate how you can reconcile bank transactions.

To view and reconcile the transactions relating to Bank Account for Radhika Enterprises:

1. **Go to** Gateway of Tally > Banking > Bank Reconciliation

2. Select **Axis Bank** as the Bank from the **List of Bank**

3. Set the Period as **01-04-20615** to **30-04-2016**

4. The **Bank Reconciliation** screen displays Balance as per Company Books, Amounts not reflected in Bank and Balance as per bank at the bottom of the screen

You can see there is a difference in the Balance as per Bank and the Balance as per Company Books.

The **Bank Reconciliation** screen appears as shown below (Figure 6.70):

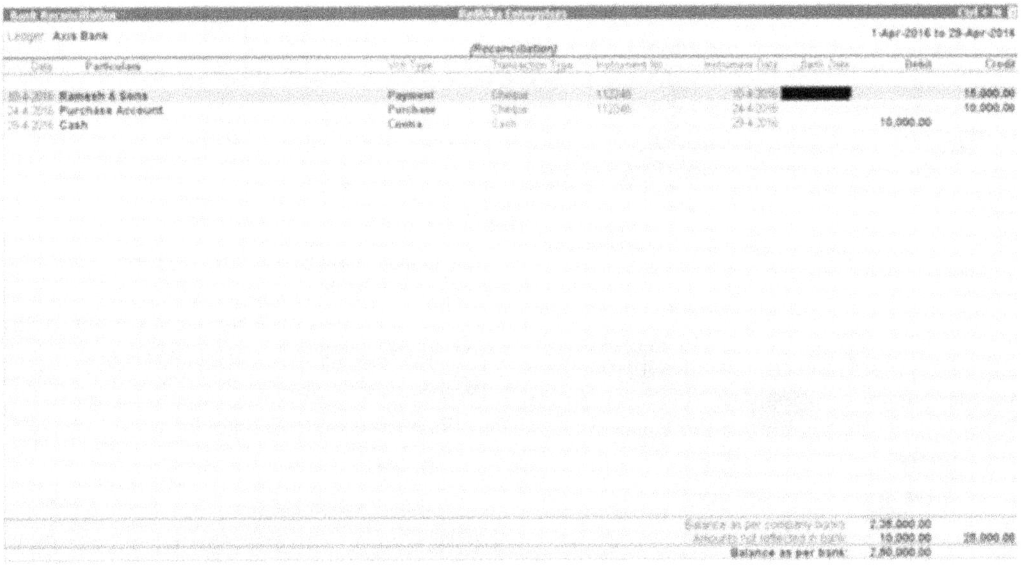

Figure 6.70: Bank Reconciliation screen

5. Enter the **Bank dates** as **15-04-2016** (Once the dates are entered, you will find the **Bank Balance as per Company books** is impacted i.e., decreases/increases accordingly)

The **Bank Reconciliation** screen appears as shown below (Figure 6.71):

Figure 6.71: Bank Reconciliation screen

You can observe that the balances in the books of the company are balanced and the field **Amounts not Reflected in Bank** is blank.

This means the accounts are reconciled.

Note:	◆	The Bank Reconciliation screen can also be accessed from Gateway of Tally > Display > Accounts Books > Cash/ Bank Books > Select Bank Ledger > Select a month > F5: Reconcile.
	◆	The Bank Date has be to be provided based on the Instrument Date and not on the Voucher Date

Tip

◆   Press **CTRL+Enter** on the required transaction row to open the voucher in alteration mode.

◆   In **F12: Configuration** or in **Print Configuration**, set the option **Show Payment Favouring/Received From** to **Yes** to display the **Payment Favouring/Received From** details in the report. The **Favouring Name** column displays only those names which are different from the **Party/Ledger** account names.

◆   Press **C: Create Voucher** to create vouchers from the reconciliation screen itself.

◆   In case, if you have opening bank transactions (transactions pertaining to the last year) which are not yet credited/ debited into Bank Account, you can provide Opening BRS for such transactions by pressing **ALT+U** (**U: Opening BRS**) and provide the information in the **Unreconciled Details** for sub-screen.

6.9   COST CENTRE AND COST CATEGORIES

A **Cost Centre** is any unit of an organisation to which

transactions (generally, revenue) can be allocated. When only costs or expenses are allocated to these units, they are referred to as Cost Centres. When profits are also allocated to these units, they become Profit Centres.

Cost Centre: "Tally.ERP 9's cost centres allow a dimensional analysis of financial information. Tally.ERP 9 gives you the cost centre break-up of each transaction as well as details of transactions for each cost centre."

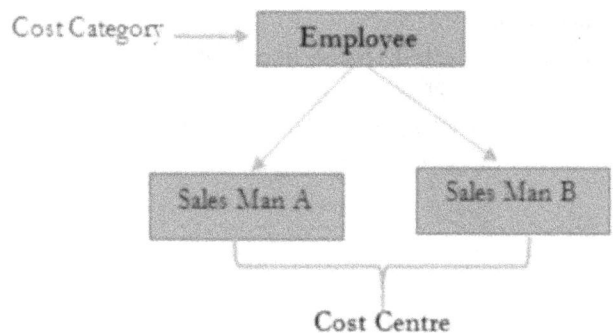

6.9.1   Cost Categories

Cost Categories are useful for organisations that require allocation of Revenue and Non-Revenue Items to parallel sets of Cost Centres. Cost categories facilitate third dimensional reporting of Expenditure and Revenue.

Some of the examples are:

◆   Region-wise or Geography-wise

◆   Employee-wise

◆   Department-wise

Let us take an example of Cost Centres and Cost Categories given above. To understand the above examples in combination of cost centre and categories given below:

Scenario:

Sultan Traders started a company as on 1-4-2016. They sell **Software**. In these process they have a different departments and many employees in the organization. In this activity business generates some expenses and income for different levels.

The objective of an organization to activate Cost Centre and Cost Category is to generate and view the reports of sources of income and expenses department-wise and employees-wise, which helps to develop and control the finance.

Let us create the Company Company Name: **Sultan Traders**

Financial year: 01-04-2016

6.9.2 Using Cost Category and Cost Centre in Transactions

Let us, illustrate the above Employee scenario:

As on 01-04-2016, Sultan Traders paid Rs. 60,000 towards Advertisement, out of which Rs. 30,000 was paid towards Mumbai Office and Rs. 30,000 towards Kolkata office (Use Cost Centre).

On 02-04-2016, the sales team of Sultan Traders began customer visits for giving a demo of its Software. The company provided Rs. 25,000 towards their transportation and food expenses, out of which, Rs. 15,000 is allocated for Ram (Salesman) and Rs. 10,000 to Hari (Salesman) (Use Cost Center and Cost Category).

Step 1: Activation

To activate Cost Centre and Cost Categories:

Enable the following options from **Gateway of Tally>F11:Company feature>F1:Accounting Feature** (Figure 6.72).

* Maintain Cost Centre set to **Yes**
* More than one Payroll/cost category set to **Yes**

Step 2: Cost Centre Creation

Go to Gateway of Tally > Accounts Info > Cost Centres > Create

Cost centre Name: Mumbai Office, Kolkata Office
Category Name: Primary
Under: Primary
Bangalore Office

Step: 3 Create Cost Categories and Cost Centre

Create Cost Categories

Go to Gateway of Tally > Accounts Info > Cost Category > Create

Cost category Name — Employee
Allocate Revenue Item: Yes
Allocate Non Revenue Item: No

Create Cost Centres

Go to **Gateway of Tally > Accounts Info > Cost Centres >**

Cost Centre Name: Ram, Hari
Category Name: Employee
Under: Primary

Create Ledger Master Kotak Bank

Go to **Gateway of Tally > Accounts Info > Ledger > Create ICICI Bank under Bank Accounts give opening balance Rs. 2,50,000**

Go to **Gateway of Tally > Accounts Info > Ledger > Create Advertisement Expenses under Indirect Expenses.**

Step 3: Record Rent Payment Voucher

1. Go to **Gateway of Tally > Accounting voucher > F5: Payment**
2. To pass the entry in double entry mode **Disable the option F12 > Use single entry mode pymt/rcpt/contra= No**
3. Enter date as **01-04-2016**
4. Dr Advertisement Expenses **Rs. 60,000** next you will get the option **Cost Allocation for Screen**.

   Select Primary cost category. Then, Select Cost centre as Mumbai office Rs. 30,000 and Kolkata Office Rs. 30,000

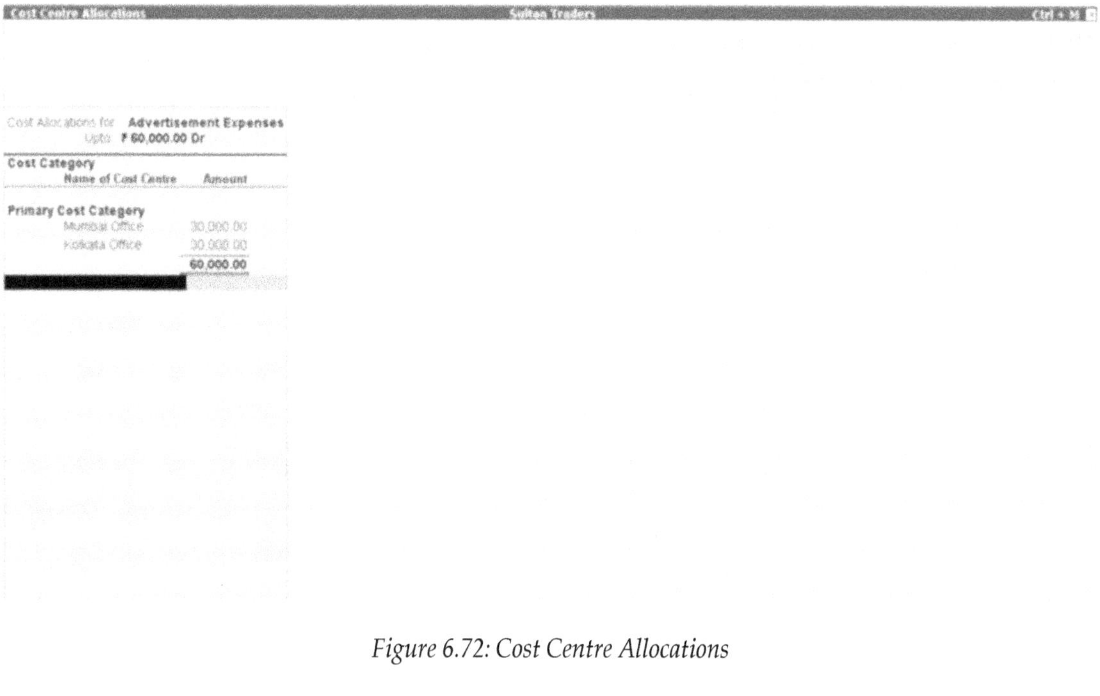

Figure 6.72: Cost Centre Allocations

5. Cr ICICI Bank Account and accept the Payment.

Step 4: Record Payment Voucher

1. Create Office Expenses Ledger under Indirect Expenses

2. Go to **Gateway of Tally > Accounting voucher > F5: Payment**

3. To pass the entry in double entry mode, Disable the option **F12 > Use single entry mode pymt/rcpt/contra= No**

4. Enter date as **02-04-2016**

5. Dr **Office Expenses Rs. 25,000** next you get the option Cost of Allocation (Figure 6.73)

    o Select cost category as Employees

    o Then, Select Cost centre as Ram Rs. 15000

    o Hari Rs. 10000

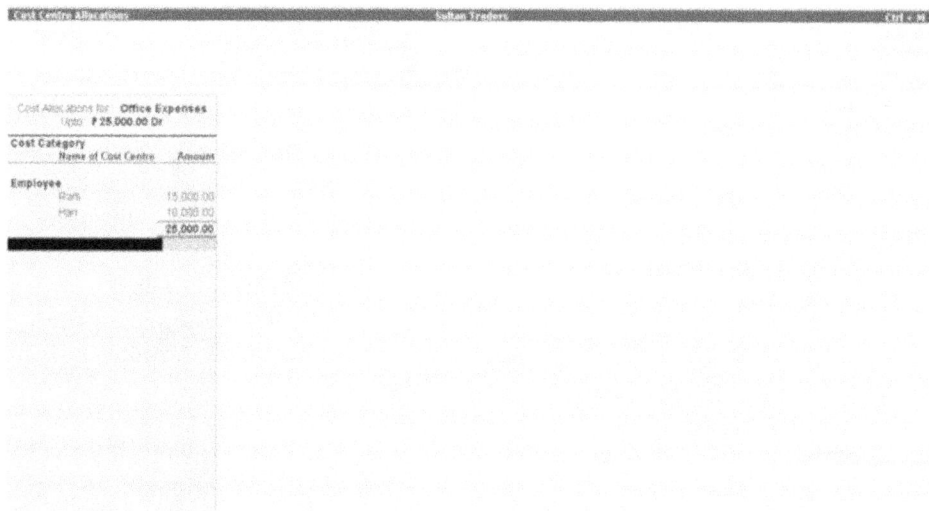

Figure 6.73: Cost centre allocation screen

6. **Cr ICIC Bank Account** and accept the **Payment**

6.9.3 Cost Centre Classes

Cost Centre Classes are used to automate cost centre allocations in transactions. On creating a cost centre class, you need to select it in the voucher screen before making the entry. You can also use cost centre classes when Voucher Classes are being used.

This illustration helps us understand the application of cost centre classes in Item invoice mode.

On 20-4-2016, the company has pre-allocated the Training Expenses to Employee-wise (45% to Ram and 55% to Hari.)

Company paid Rs. 10,000 for training expenses.

Step 1: Activate the Cost centre Class

1. Go to **Gateway of Tally > F11: Features > F1: Accounting Features**

2. Press **Enter** from the option **Use Pre-defined Cost Centre Allocations** during Entry to view the **Auto Cost Allocation** screen (Figure 6.74)

3. Type **Class Name** in the **Cost Centre Class**

4. Press **Enter** and specify the details

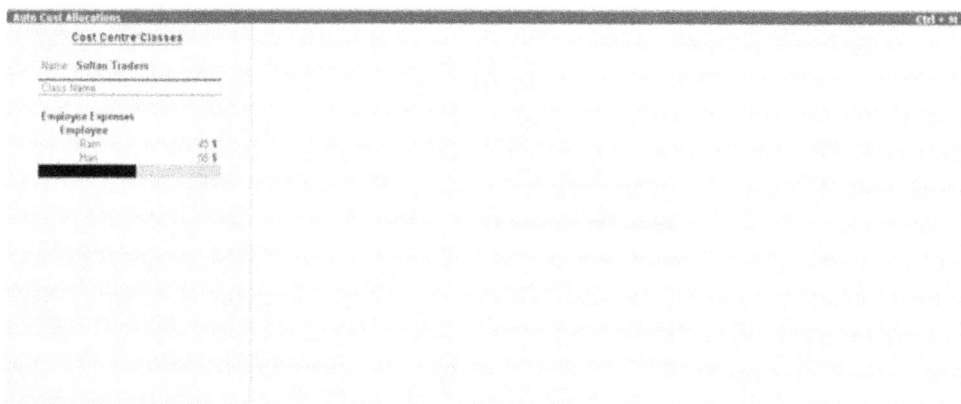

Figure 6.74: Auto Cost Allocations screen

5. Select **Cost Category** as **Employees**
6. Select the **Cost centres** and enter the **percentage of allocation** as follows:
   - o   Ram 45%
   - o   Hari 55%
7. Press Enter to accept the Auto cost allocation screen and

you will come back to Accounting feature screen.

8. Press Enter and save the Accounting feature screen.

Step 2: Create the Required Ledger

Go to **Gateway of Tally > Accounts Info > Ledger**

Create Training Expenses under Indirect Expenses

1. Select the **Cost Centre/Classes**

Figure 6.75: Accounting Voucher Creation

2. Select Training Expenses as Debit side
3. Select ICICI Bank under credit side (Figure 6.75)

6.9.4   Cost Centre Reports

Cost centre reports are primarily performance reports. To access Cost Centre reports,

Go to **Gateway of Tally > Display > Statements of Accounts > Cost Centres**

The Cost Centres Menu comprises of the following sub menus:

Category Summary

Cost Centre Break-up

Ledger Break-up

Group Break-up

Let us discuss each report in detail.

6.9.4.1 Category Summary

This report lists out all cost categories for which transactions have been allocated. Below each cost category, all the cost centres under the cost category are also listed, with the sub-cost centres, if any.

The **Cost Category Summary** report for the period 1-4-2016 to 20-04-2016 appears as shown below (Figure 6.76):

Figure 6.76: Cost Category Summary report

It is possible to drill down to the transaction level from this report.

Cost Centre Vouchers Report

All transactions pertaining to a cost centre will be displayed in this report.

Press Enter on the required option and you will get the Cost Centre Vouchers report

6.9.4.2 Cost Centre Break-up

We noticed that transactions were allocated to cost centres. A list of all ledger accounts used in these transactions, with details of the transaction values and balance are displayed here.

Select **Cost Centre Break-up** from the **Cost Centres** menu to open it.

Select **Ram**, from the **List of Cost Centres**

Press **F2** and change the period 1-04-2016 to 20-04-2016. The **Breakup of Cost Centres** screen appears as shown below (Figure 6.77):

Figure 6.77: Breakup of Cost Centres screen

6.9.4.3 Ledger Break-up

One ledger can be allocated to different cost centres. For example, the ledger Cost of expenses is allocated to Junior and senior. We can view a comparative report of conveyance expenditures incurred by the two cost centres using the **Ledger Break-up** report.

1. From the **Cost Centres** menu, select **Ledger Break-up**
2. Select **Cost of Expenses**

The **Cost Breakup of Ledger** screen appears as shown below (Figure 6.78):

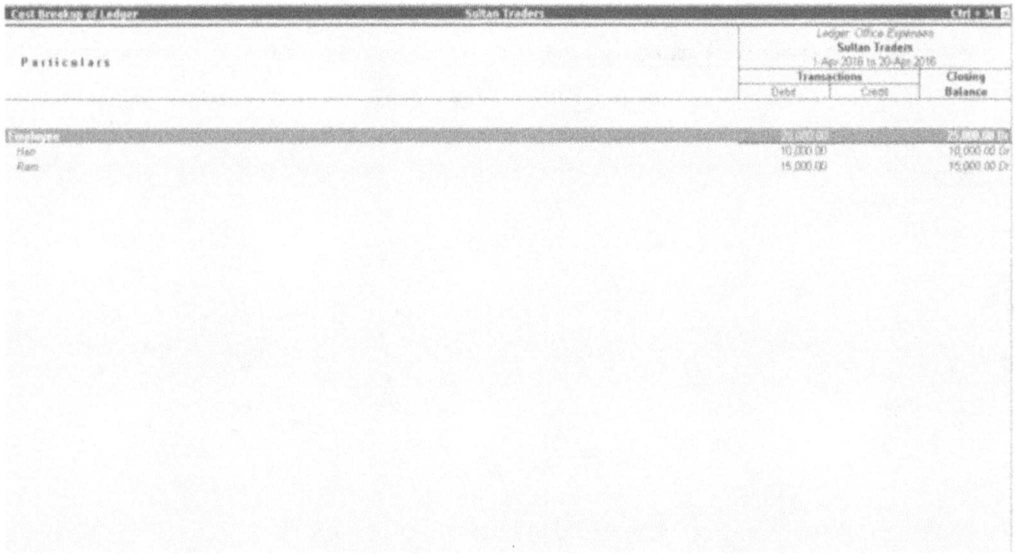

Figure 6.78: Cost Breakup of Ledger screen

6.9.4.4 Group Break-up

This report displays the summarised information of all Cost Centres for the selected Group. You can drill down to the list of

voucher

Similar to the method that applies to Ledger Break-up, explore the Group Break-up of Cost Centres (Figure 6.79).

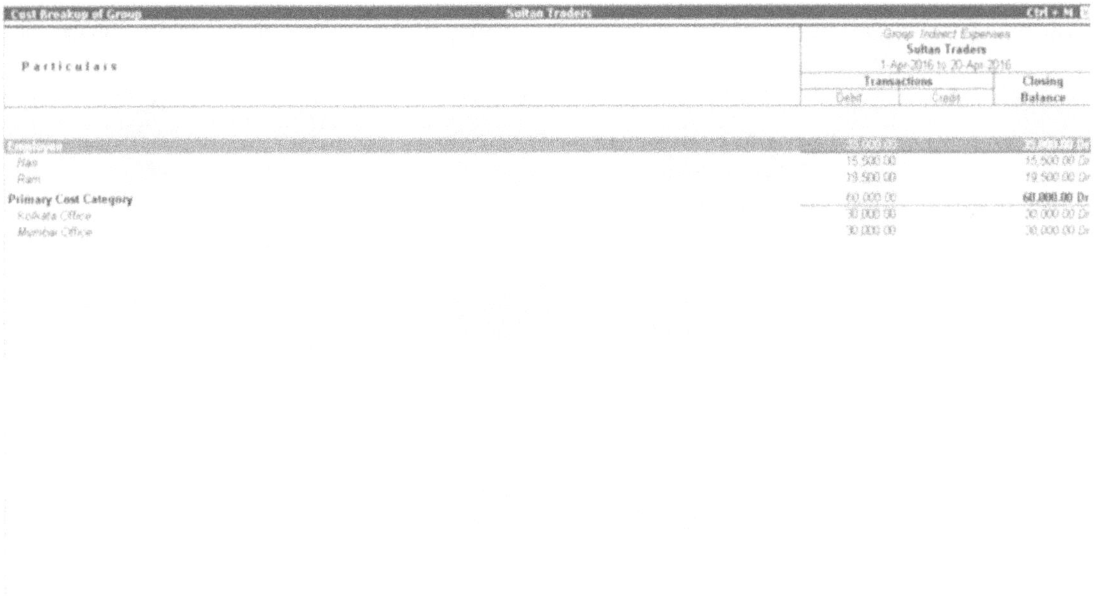

Figure 6.79: Cost Breakup of Group screen

Activity

Create a company with the name of Raghuraj Pvt. Ltd. Financial year and book beginning is 01-04-2016

1. On 01-04-2016 Company paid Commission through cheque of Kotak Bank, Rs. 15,000 to his Agent Dinesh Rs. 5,500 and Mahesh Rs. 9,500 (Hint: Create Kotak Bank with opening balance Rs. 1,50,000).

2. On 02-04-2016 Paid electricity bill of Rs. 8,000 to his Bangaluru Branch Rs. 3,500 and rest of amount for Delhi Branch through Kotak Bank.

3. Paid incentive Rs. 20,000 to Employee Raghu 20%, Nidhi 30% and Suresh 50% through Kotak Bank.

6.10   ORDER PROCESSING

Order Processing refers to:

◆ placing purchase orders with suppliers/receiving order from customers for sale

◆ tracking the receipt of the goods/tracking the delivery of the goods

◆ paying for the goods purchased/receiving the payment for the goods sold.

Using Order processing you can:

◆ track the order position of a stock item

◆ know whether the goods ordered have been received or not

◆ know whether the orders have been delivered on time and the reasons for the delay, if any

Scenario

To understand Order Processing in Tally.ERP 9, let us consider

that Surya Traders placed an order for DELL Latitude Laptop from Jivan Ram & Sons and then sold it to Ridhi technologies after they received the order.

6.10.1   Purchase Order Processing

Let us use the same company: Surya Traders created previously. To activate Order Processing, enable the following options in the **F11: Features (Inventory Features):** Allow Purchase Order Processing Allow Sales Order Processing Use Tracking Numbers (Delivery / Receipt Notes)

The illustration below will help you understand how to record a Purchase Order.

Illustration

On 05-12-2016, raise a purchase order on Jivan Ram & Sons for 10 Nos of Dell Latitude Laptop at Rs. 25,000 each. The Laptops are due on 06-12-2065 and are to be stored in Onsite (godown).

Step 1: Create Required Masters Party

Party Ledger:	Jivan Ram & Sons
Under:	Sundry Debtros
Maintain Balance Bill-by-bill:	Yes
Inventory Values are affected:	No
Stock Item:	Dell Latitude Laptop
Under:	Dell
Unit:	Nos

Step 2: Configure Purchase Order

1. Go to **Gateway of Tally > Order Vouchers > F4: Purc. Order**

2. Click **F12: Configure:**

    o Set **Complete Accounting Allocations in Order/ Delivery Note** to **Yes.** Enabling this option will allow you to select accounting masters (Purchase ledgers) in the order voucher

o   Set **Use Common Ledger A/c for Item Allocation** to **No**

Step 3: Create Purchase Order

In the Purchase Order Voucher,

1.   Enter date as 05-12-2016
2.   Select Jivan Ram & Sons in the Party's A/c Name field
3.   The voucher number will be displayed in the Order No. field by default. This field can be changed as per requirement.

Enter ORD-001 in this field

4.   Under Name of the item, select Dell Latitude Laptop and press Enter. The Item Allocations screen appears
5.   Enter 06-12-2016 in the Due on field. This is the due date for the delivery of the item. This will enable the monitoring of outstanding deliveries. The order can be split for delivery on different dates
6.   Select Onsite in the Location field. (Only when the multiple Godown feature is enabled, this field will be displayed)
7.   Enter 10 in the Quantity field and Rs. 25,000 in the Rate field. The Amount will be calculated automatically

The completed Item Allocations screen appears as shown below (Figure 6.80):

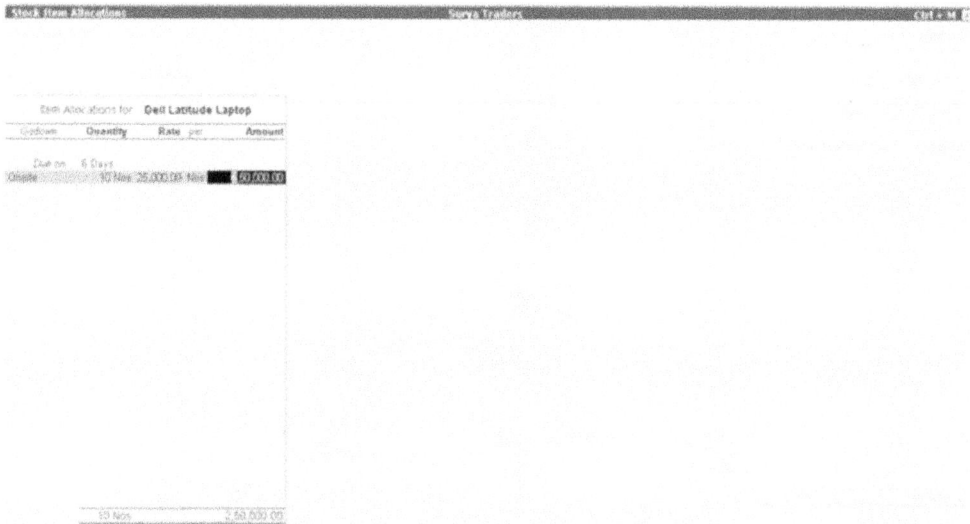

Figure 6.80: Item Allocation for Dell Latitude Laptop

8.   Accept the **Item Allocation** screen to return to the **Purchase Order** screen
9.   Press **Enter** from the **Amount** field to view the **Accounting Details** screen
10. Allocate the amount to **Purchases ledger** and return to the **Purchase Order** screen
11. Press **Enter** on the blank field
12. **Narration** can be entered, if required

The completed Purchase Order screen appears as shown below (Figure 6.81):

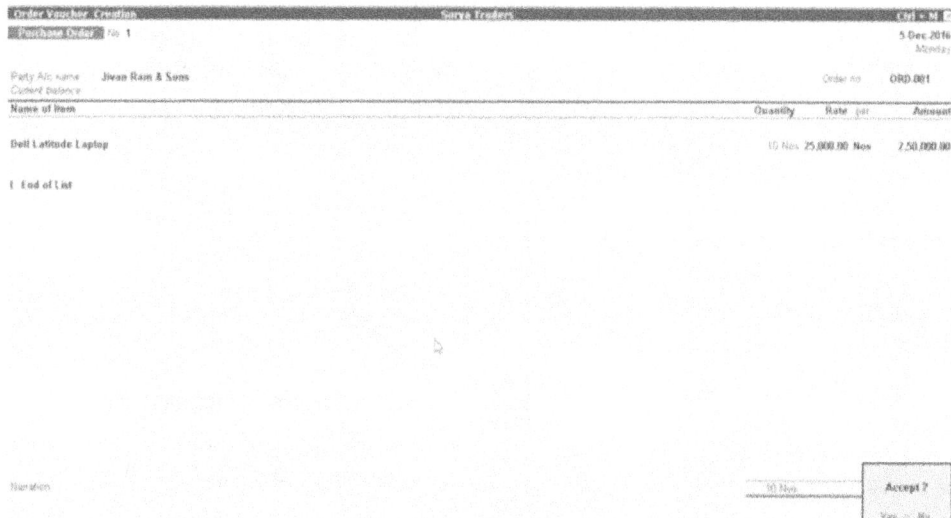

Figure 6.81: Purchase Order

14. **Accept** the Purchase Order

6.10.1.1 Altering a Purchase Order

To alter a Purchase Order:

Go to **Gateway of Tally > Display > Day Book > F4: Chg Vch** and select Purchase Orders or **Go to Gateway of Tally > Display > Inventory Books > Purchase Order Book** and select the required Purchase Order to open the Order Voucher Alteration screen.

Raising Purchase Invoices (or Delivery Notes) against Purchase Orders

Purchase Invoice or Delivery Notes can be raised against previously recorded purchase orders.

The illustration below will help you understand how to record a purchase invoice against the order placed when the goods are received.

Illustration

On 07-12-2016, raise a purchase invoice on Jivan Ram & Sons for 10 Nos of Laptops at Rs. 25,000. The goods are to be stored in Onsite (godown). This purchase invoice will be linked to the purchase order – ORD-001 that was recorded on 07-12-2016.

Step 1: Configure Purchase Invoice

1. Go to **Gateway of Tally > Accounting Vouchers > F9: Purchase**

2. Make sure that the **Voucher Creation screen** is in **Item Invoice mode**

3. Click **F12: Configure** button and set the following option to **Yes:**

Accept Supplementary Details. Enabling this option will allow you to select the order number against which the purchase invoice is being raised

Step 2: Record Purchase Invoice

1. In the Supplier Invoice No. field enter JR-001/022. This will be the number on the invoice that the supplier raises on the Purchase Order

2. Enter date as 07-12-2016

3. Select Jivan Ram & Sons in the Party's A/c Name field and press Enter. The Party Details screen will appear

4. Select ORD-001 in the Order No(s) field under Party Details as shown below (Figure 6.82):

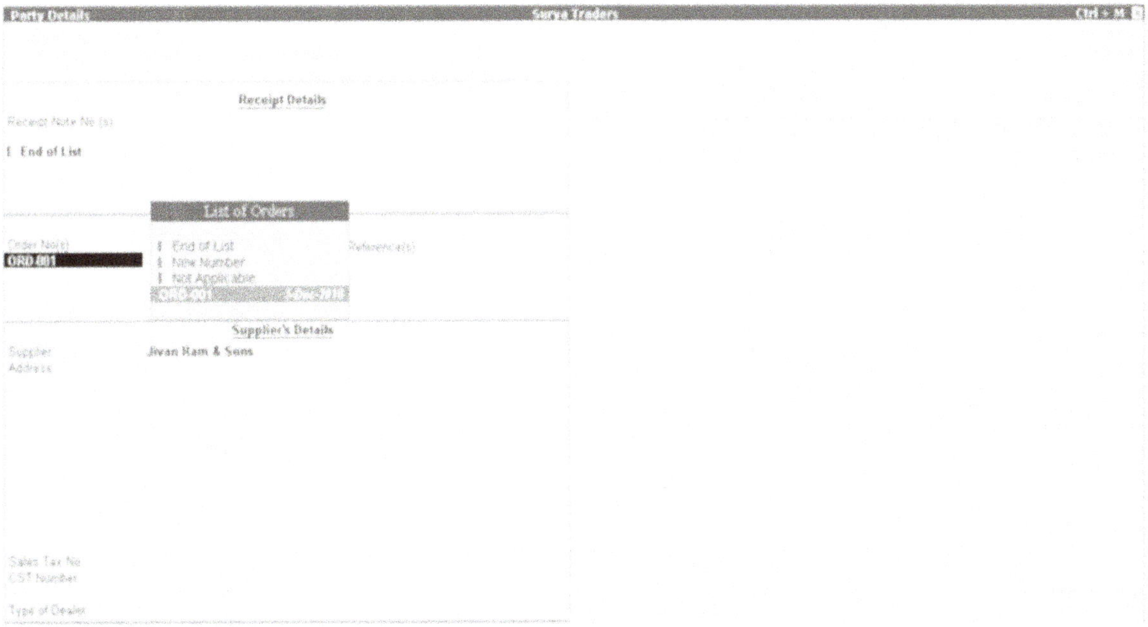

Figure 6.82: Party Details screen

5. **Accept** the screen to return to the voucher creation screen

6. The stock item Dell Latitude Laptop will appear automatically. Press **Enter** and the **Item Allocations screen** will appear with the quantity details

7. Select **Not Applicable** in the **Tracking number field** as goods are accompanying the bill

8. Select ORD-001 again in the **Order Number field** and **accept** the **Item Allocations screen**

9. Freight charges details will be automatically captured

   The completed Purchase Invoice appears as shown in Figure 6.83

10. **Accept** the Purchase Invoice

    To activate Order Processing in Tally.ERP 9, enable the following options in the F11: Features (Inventory Features):

    o   Allow Purchase Order Processing

    o   Allow Sales Order Processing

    o   Use Tracking Numbers (Delivery / Receipt Notes)

Note: Use the same company- Surya Traders that was created earlier

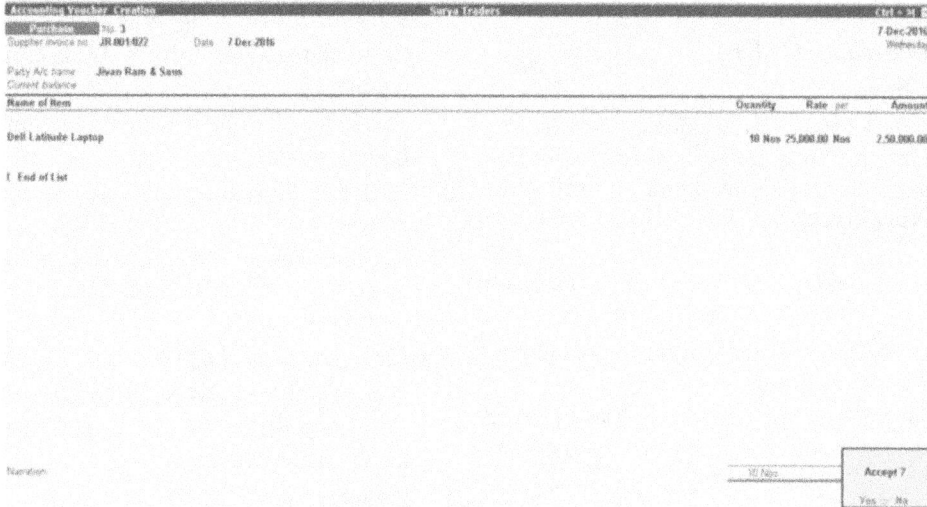

Figure 6.83: Purchase Invoice

6.10.2 Sales Order Processing

The illustration given below will help you understand how to record an order received for a sale. These orders are recorded in a Sales Order Voucher.

Illustration

On 10-12-2016, record a sales order for the order received from Ridhi Technologies (vide Order No. SL-004) for 5 Nos of Dell Latitude Laptop at Rs. 28,000 each. The due date for delivering the Laptop is 15-12-2016.

Step 1: Create Required Masters

Party Ledger:	Ridhi Technologies
Under:	Sundry Debtors
Maintain Balance bill-by-bill:	Yes
Inventory value:	No

Step 2: Create Sales Order

1. Go to **Gateway of Tally > Order Vouchers > F5: Sales Order**
2. Enter the date as 10-12-2016

3. Select Ridhi Technologies in the Party's A/c Name field
4. Enter SL-004 in the Order No field. The voucher number will be displayed here by default. This field is editable as this Order No. refers to the customer's order number which is different from the voucher number
5. Under Name of the Item, select Dell Latitude Laptop and press Enter. The Item Allocations screen will appear
6. Enter 15-12-2015 in the Due on field. This is the due date for the delivering the item to the customer
7. Select Onsite in the Location field. (Only when the Multiple Godown feature is enabled, this field will be displayed)
8. Enter 5 in the Quantity field, and Rs. 28,000 in the Rate field. The Amount will be calculated automatically
9. Allocate the amount to Sales ledger and return to the Sales Order screen
10. Press Enter on the blank field
11. Type the narration if required

    The completed Sales Order appears as shown below (Figure 6.84):

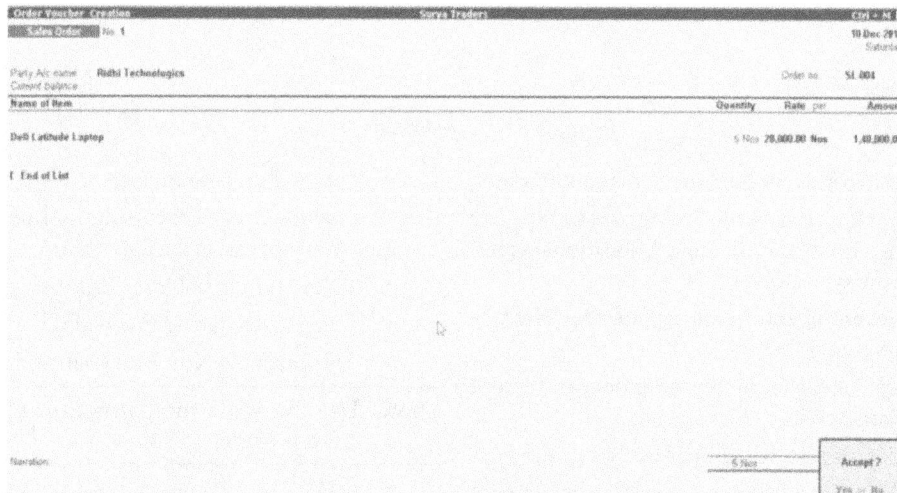

Figure 6.84: Sales Order

13. **Accept** the Sales Order

6.10.2.1 Altering a Sales Order

To alter a Sales Order:

Go to **Gateway of Tally > Display > Day Book > F4: Chg Vch** and select Sales Orders or **Go to Gateway of Tally > Display > Inventory Books > Sales Order Book** select the required Sales Order to open the Order Voucher Alteration screen

Raising Sales Invoices (or Receipt Notes) against Sales Orders

Sales invoice or Receipt Notes can be raised against previously recorded sales orders.

6.10.3 Viewing Order Details

After recording purchase and sales orders, you can view the details of the orders to know the amount of stock that needs to be processed for the order, (before recording invoices for the order) both inward and outward.

To view Order Details:

1. Go to **Gateway of Tally > Stock Summary**
2. Press the **button ALT + F7**
3. Select **Sales Orders Outstanding**, and set **Use Due orders only** to **No**
4. Select Dell and drill down to the **Order Details** screen (Figure 6.85)
5. In the **Sales Order Outstanding** screen, press **ALT+F1** to view the report in detailed format

The Order Details screen appears as shown below (Figure 6.86):

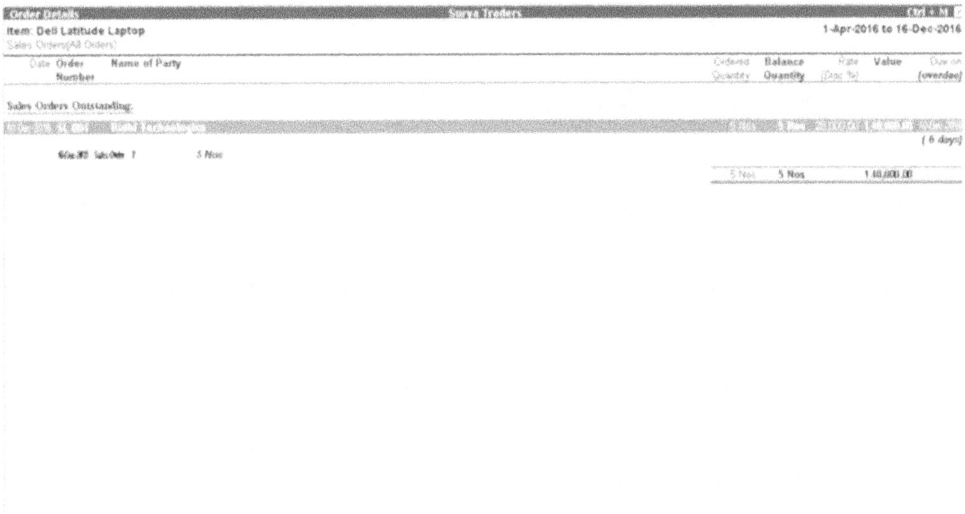

Figure 6.85: Order Details screen

The Order Details report is generated as on 16th December, 2016. Based on the period of the report and the due date of the order, the report will display the outstanding status of the order.

Note: The Sales Order Outstanding screen, by default will show the report as on last date of the voucher entry. Hence, change the period to view the report of the desired period.

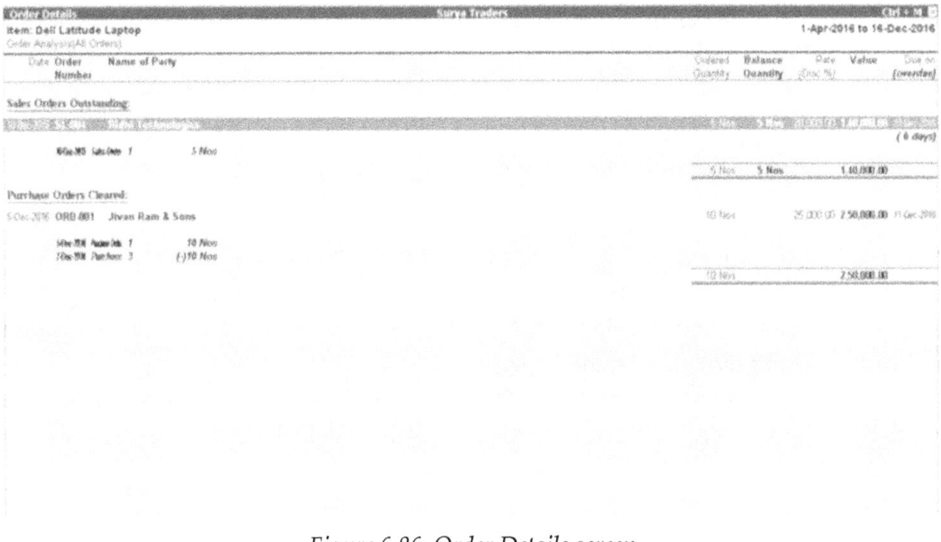

Figure 6.86: Order Details screen

6. Now, press **F2** or click F2: Period and change the period till 16-12-2016

7. Click **F12: Configure** button and set the following to Yes:

   o   Show Cleared Purchase Orders

The report now shows the Outstanding positions of the Sales and Purchase Orders for the stock item Dell Latitude Laptop.

Note: The information changes instantly depending on the date filter you use. This is Tally.ERP 9's power of real time report generation

---

6.10.4 Display Columnar Orders & Stock Details

To view Columnar Order details, return to the Stock Summary screen:

♦ Click **F1: Detailed and view** the report as on 31-12-2015

♦ Press **ALT + N** or click Auto-Column Button, select Orders & Stock Details

♦ Remove Rate and Value from display, by configuring it in **F12: Configuration** (This will enable all the columns to fit in one screen)

The Sales Order Outstandings (Stock group wise) screen appears as shown below (Figure 6.87):

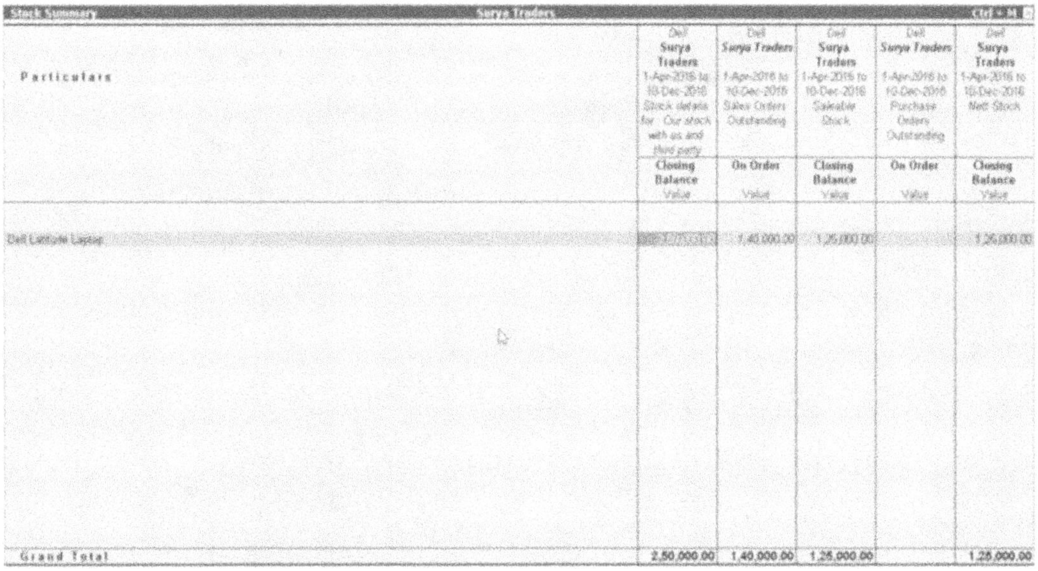

Figure 6.87: Stock Summary

Tip

♦ You may further drill down each column to view it in detail.

♦ In the Stock Summary screen, you can even bring up a new column using the New Column button and get more options for more details.

♦ Experiment with the different Types of Values to get familiar with them and return to the Gateway of Tally.

Activity

Perform the following actions:

1. View Orders details after recording the Sales Invoice against the Order recorded on 10-12-2016.

2. Record a Purchase Order for Dell Latitude Laptop on 20-12-2016 on Jivvan Ram & Sons Dell Latitude Laptop with the Order Number – PO02. Give the Due date as 24-12-2016 and Quantity as 5 Nos (godown - Shop) at Rs. 25,000.

3. Record another Purchase Order for Dell Latitude Laptop on 24-12-2016 on Jivvan Ram & Sons Dell Latitude Laptop with the Order Number as PO03, Due date as 28-12-2016

and Quantity as 4 Nos (godown - Onsite) at Rs. 25,000.

4. On 25-12-2016, raise Sales Order on Ridhi Technologies with Order No. as RD/007 for 5 Nosof Dell Latitude Laptop (godown - Shop) at Rs. 28,000. Give the Due date as 30-12-2016.

6.11 DATA BACKUP AND RESTORE

Data on the computer is vulnerable to different types of threats and any data lost will be disastrous for the organisation. Hence, there is a need to store data at a different location by taking a backup.

6.11.1 Backup

Tally.ERP 9 helps users to take back up of one or more companies in a single directory.

To take a single or multiple company data backup,

1. Go to **Gateway of Tally > Company Info. > Backup** (Figure 6.88)

2. Enter Source and Destination of the backup as shown below (Figure 6.89):

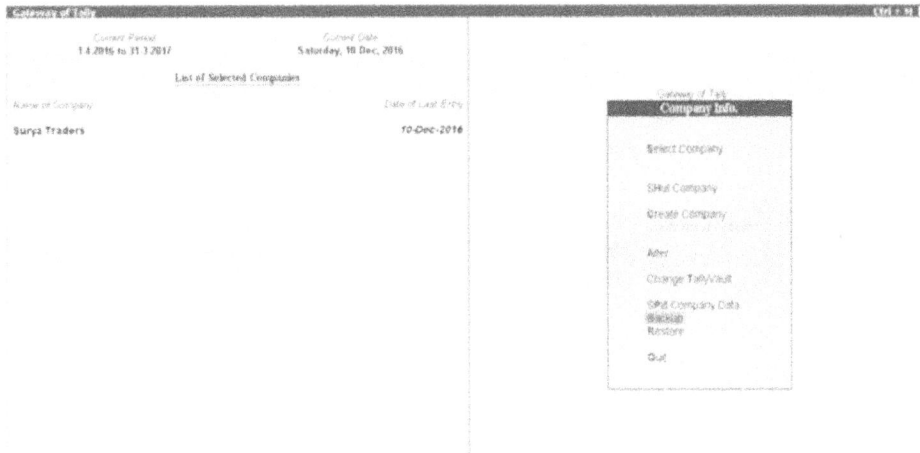

Figure 6.88: Company Info. screen

Figure 6.89: Selecting Source and Destination for Backup

3. Press Enter and the List of Companies available for backup will appear. Select the required companies for which data backup needs to be created, as shown below (Figure 6.90):

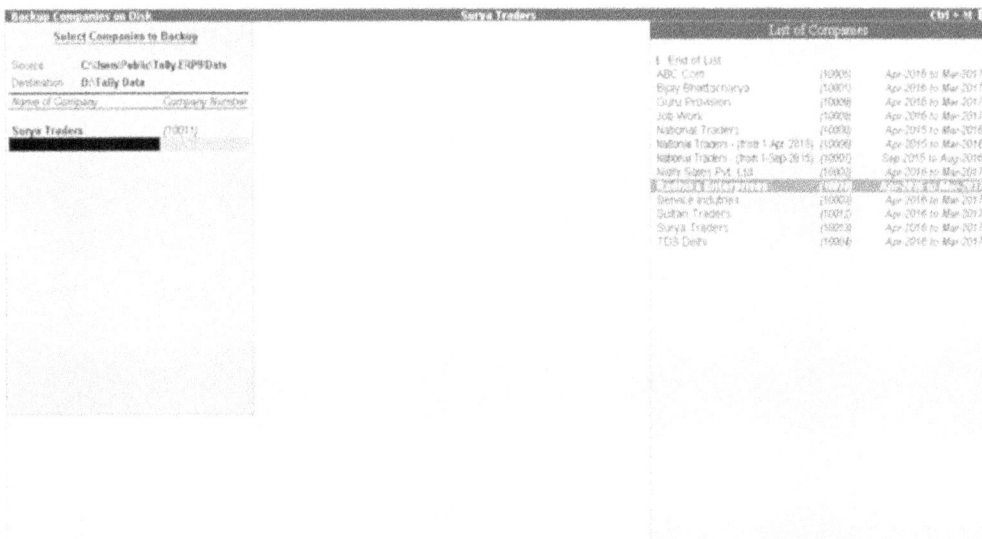

Figure 6.90: Selecting Companies to Backup

4. Once the required companies are selected, select End of List and accept the screen. The backup file is stored with the name TBK900.001.

6.11.2 Restoring Data from a Backup File

The Restore functionality allows you to restore the data backup taken earlier.

While restoring the auto-back up data of multiple companies, the system displays the time of the last backup taken along with the auto-backup version. This helps in identifying the latest

backup version to restore it.

1. Go to **Gateway of Tally > Company Info. > Restore**

2. Enter **Source and Destination** of the backup that needs to be restored

3. Select the required companies from the list of companies and then restore

4   Select **End of List** to complete the selection and accept the screen (Figure 6.91).

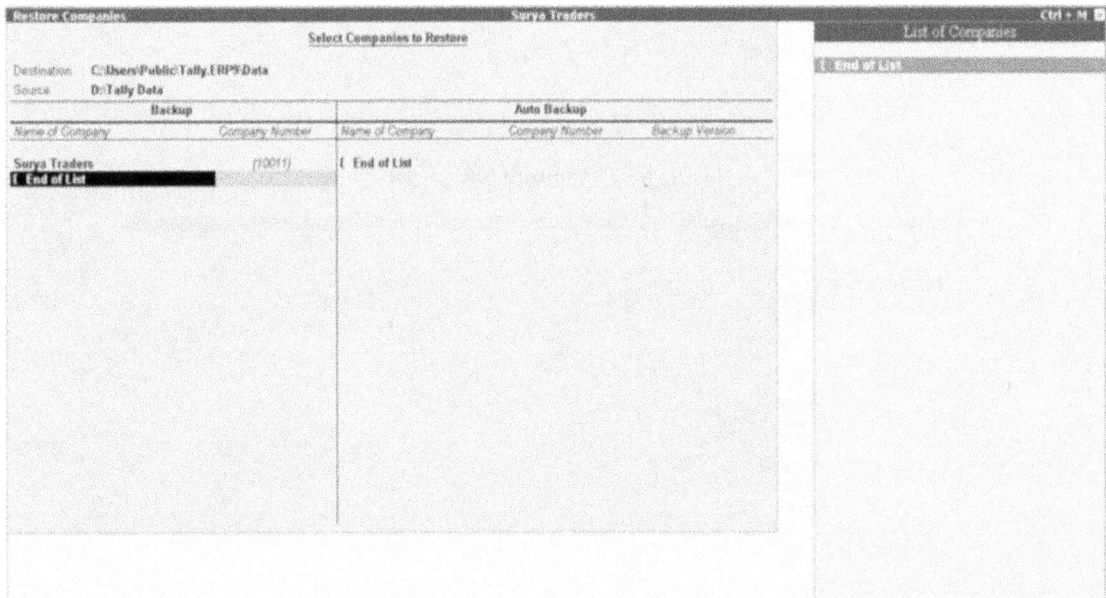

Figure 6.91: Restores Companies on Disk

PART B – STATUTORY FEATURES & ADVANCED FEATURES

VALUE ADDED TAX (VAT)

OBJECTIVES

After studying this section, you will be able to understand how to:

- Use the Regular VAT features in Tally.ERP 9
- Create Masters for VAT
- Configure Voucher Types
- Record Different Types of Transactions Related to VAT
- View VAT Reports in Tally.ERP 9
- View and Generate Returns
- e-File VAT Return

6.12 INTRODUCTION

The Value Added Tax (VAT) system is a popular system of taxation that emerged in the European countries. The VAT system is adopted by most of the countries to bring about convenience and transparency in the entire system of taxation. The working system of VAT is simple to follow, implement and administer.

In this system, the tax is levied on the value of the good at every level of value addition i.e., on the value added portion of goods at each level. At the same time, the tax paid for acquiring this product will be allowed as "input tax credit" and can be used for payment of VAT at the time of selling the product to the immediate dealer. The net effect of tax will be only on the portion of value added by the seller.

The tax paid on purchases is termed as **Input Tax** and VAT payable on the goods after value addition is called **Output Tax**. The input tax paid can be taken as **Input Tax Credit**. The VAT liability of the dealer will be arrived at, as given below:

VAT Payable = Output Tax – Input Tax

If the tax paid on purchases (input tax), is more than the tax payable (output tax), the same can be either carried forward to next return period or claimed as refund. The tax amount carried forward will be accounted as input tax credit for the next return period. In the subsequent periods, this credit can be utilised for payment of any liability to the department like output tax, interest, penalty etc., subject to the provisions or restrictions specified in VAT Rules.

6.12.1 VAT in India

The Value Added Tax (VAT) is a type of indirect tax and is one of major sources of revenue to the state. The VAT system was introduced in India by replacing the General Sales Tax laws of each state. All the states have implemented VAT. The States/ Union territories which are yet to implement the VAT system are Andaman and Nicobar Islands and Lakshadweep.

The VAT system of taxation was adopted by Indian States and Union Territories in the Year 2005 by replacing the General Sales Tax Laws with New Value Added Tax Acts and the supporting Value Added Tax Rules for proper administration and collection of Tax. Each state or union territory has its own methods to assess the tax liability and collection methods from the dealers who fall under the purview of VAT.

The Administration of VAT system was undertaken by the Commercial Taxes Department of each state along with the Excise and other indirect taxes. For easy and quick assessment of taxation and prevention of tax evasion, the department has introduced the Registration System. This Registration system of VAT helps in identifying the assessees who come under purview of VAT and are liable to collect and pay VAT. For encouraging the Registration process some benefits or concessions are given to the dealer.

The Registered dealers are allowed to collect VAT payable by them from the immediate buyer. They can claim the VAT paid on purchases made only from a registered dealer. The unregistered dealer cannot charge VAT on the invoices, so the buying dealer cannot claim the VAT amount paid as Input Tax Credit. Also, the unregistered dealers are not eligible for availing concessions, for e.g., exemptions, which are given by the government.

The commercial tax department introduced a new method of levying tax called the Composition Scheme especially after considering the small dealers whose turnover was low and were unable to maintain the records as per the requirements of VAT Act. These dealers have to pay a lump sum as VAT on the sale value of goods. The VAT paid will not be shown in the invoices. They can account for the total turnover and pay VAT on the same at the end of the return period.

For Assessing the VAT liability of dealers, each state has introduced the system of Filing Returns for different tax periods. The tax periods could be Monthly, Quarterly, Half-yearly and Annual. Each dealer has to file the Return by specifying the total turnover which is exempted as well as liable for VAT along with the purchases made and tax paid on it with the amount of VAT payable or Input tax credit carried forward within the stipulated period.

Term	Description
Input Tax	This is the tax paid on purchases
Output Tax	This is the tax charged on sales
Input Credit	The excess amount of Input tax over output tax for the current period which is permitted to be set off against OutputTax of subsequent periods is termed as Input Credit.
TIN	Tax Identification Number (TIN) is the Registration Number given by the department to the dealer at the time of Registration. This needs to be quoted at all required places where the registration details are to be provided.
Tax Invoice	This is the Sales invoice format issued by one Registered Dealer to another. Based on this Invoice, the Input Tax Credit can be claimed by the purchasing dealer.
Retail Invoice	The Sales invoice format used for invoicing the Exempted Sales and the Sales made to Unregistered dealers is termed asRetail Invoice.
Registered Dealer	This term is used to identify a dealer who is registered either under Voluntary Registration or Compulsory Registration under the VAT Act. Such dealer can issue tax invoice and also claim the tax paid on purchases made from other registered dealers as Input tax credit.
Unregistered Dealer	Dealers who are not registered under the VAT Act are called Unregistered Dealers (URD). Such dealers cannot issue tax invoice. They can neither Charge Tax nor Claim Input TaxCredit.
Purchase Tax	The Tax paid on goods purchased from unregistered dealers is liable to Purchase Tax. The Purchase Tax is treated as Output VAT payable by the dealer as it is a liability. It has to be paid while making the payment towards VAT liability. Based on the Rules and Regulations, the Input Tax Credit can be claimed on the payment made towards Purchase Tax.

6.12.2   Cyclic view of VAT Computation

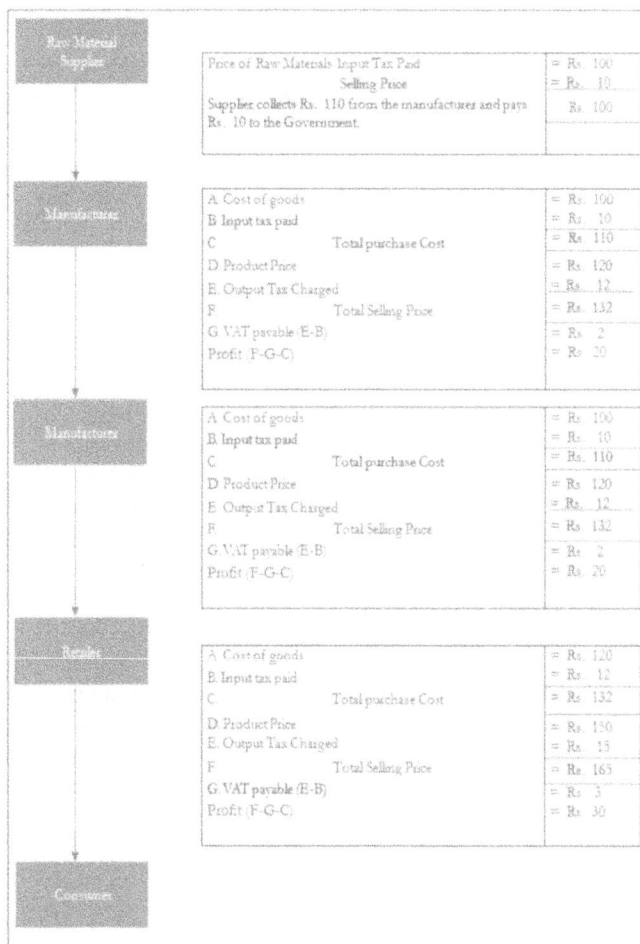

Figure 6.92: Cyclic view of VAT Computation

The above diagram depicts computation of (10%) VAT at each stage of business. Hence, it is not the manufacturers and retailers but only the consumer who has paid 10% VAT to the government. The profits for manufacturers and retailers thus remain unaffected.

Tally.ERP 9 facilitates defining VAT details at different levels. This provides the convenience of applying tax rules at the highest level, which is the company level, as well as the flexibility to modify, override or define details at the lower levels, based on one's business requirement.

6.12.3   Maintaining Stock Items with Same VAT Rate

Scenario: 1

Aruna Traders Company is a registered dealer, dealing with only two kinds of product namely Stainless Steel and SteelPan, both the stock items have the same VAT rate that is VAT at 5%.

The following illustration will help you understand how to record a taxable purchase and sales transaction in Tally.ERP 9. You will also see how to define the same VAT rate in the company. Rates once defined, will be automatically applied to all the stock items.

As on 1-4-2016, Aruna traders Company purchased from Vikas Ltd. Bengaluru., 100 strainless steel at Rs. 200 each and 100 steel pan at Rs. 300 each at VAT rate 5% each.

Activity

Create a Company by name Aruna Traders Company with the financial year 1-4-2016

Step 1: Define VAT rates at the company level

1. Go to **Gateway of Tally > F11: Features > Statutory & Taxation**
2. Set the option **Enable Value Added Tax (VAT)** to **Yes**
3. Enable the option **Set/Alter VAT Details**
4. Enter **VAT Details**
   - o   Select the state **Karnataka**
   - o   TIN: **29123456789**
   - o   Enable **Set/alter tax/rate details**
   - o   Press **F12** and Set **Enable Commodity Details** to **Yes**
   - o   Enter **Tax Rate** as **5%** and Tax Type as Taxable
5. **Other info.**
   - o   Commodity Name: **Steel utensils**
   - o   Commodity Code: **2A007001**
   - o   Sub commodity code: **2016**
   - o   The complete Tax
6. Press **Enter** to save (Figure 6.93)

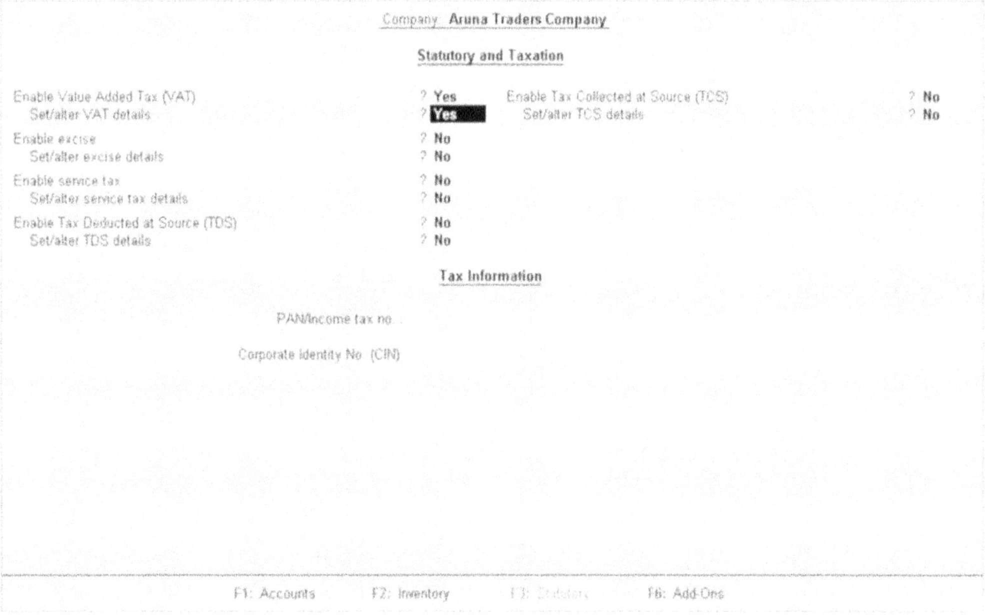

Figure 6.93: Activating VAT in Company

Step 2: Required Ledgers

Accounting Masters

Go to **Gateway of Tally > Accounts Info > Create**

1. Create Party ledger – Vikas Ltd
   - o   Group under **Sundry Creditors**
   - o   Maintain balances bill by bill, select as **YES**

- o   Default credit period as **Blank**
- o   Check for credit days during voucher entry, select as **No**
- o   Inventory values are affected, select as **No**
- o   Set/Alter VAT Details, select as **YES**
- o   VAT TIN no **29987654321**

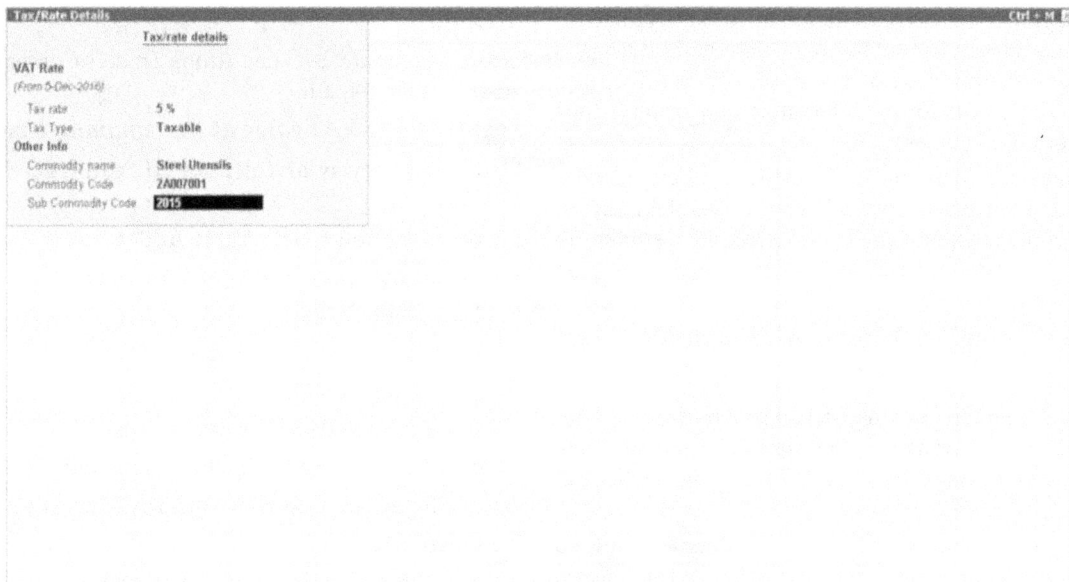

Figure 6.94: Setting Tax Rate in Company Level

2. Create purchase ledger as **Purchase Ledger @5%**
   o Group under **Purchase Account**
   o Maintain balances bill by bill select as **No**
   o Inventory values are affected select as **YES**
   o Is VAT/CST Applicable, Select as **Applicable**
   o Set/Alter VAT details, select as **No**
3. Create Tax/Duty Ledger as Input Vat@5%
   o Group under **Duties and Taxes**
   o Type of Duty/Tax, select as **VAT**
   o Use for purchase tax, select as **NO**
   o Inventory values are affected, select as **No**
   o Percentage of calculation (eg. 5), provide **5%**
   o Rounding method select as **Not Applicable** (Figure 6.94)

Inventory Masters

Go to **Gateway of Tally > Inventory Info > Create**

1. Create **Units of Measure – Nos**
   o Type as **Simple**
   o Symbol as **Nos**
   o Formal name as **Numbers**
   o Number of decimal places as **0**
   o Enter and accept to screen
2. Create **Stock Items** of **Stainless Steel and Steel Pan**
   o Stock item name as **Stainless Steel**
   o Group under **Primary**
   o Units select **Nos**
   o VAT applicable, select as **Applicable**
   o Set/Alter VAT details, select as **No**
   o Enter to accept the screen

Activity: Similarly create Steel Pan stock item referring to Stainless Steel

---

Note: While creating the Accounting and inventory masters, VAT rates are not defined because they are defined at the company level. Hence it is not required to mention the same at the master level.

Step 3: Recording Purchase Transactions

1. Go to **Gateway of Tally > Accounting Vouchers > F9: Purchase**
2. Ensure that it is in **Item Invoice** mode. If it is in **Accounting Invoice** mode click **I: Item Invoice**
3. Click **F12: Configure** and set the option **Use Common Ledger Account for Item Allocation** to **Yes** and **save**.
4. Enter **01-04-2016** as the date
5. Enter **Supplier Invoice No.** as **S/01**. The **Date** field will be automatically filled with the voucher date
6. Select **Vikas Ltd.** in the **Party's A/c Name** field
7. Select the purchase ledger which needs to be used for accounting the purchase. Here, it is **Purchases @ 5%**
8. Select **Stainless Steel** in the **Name of Item** field
9. Enter the **Quantity** as **100** and the **Rate as Rs. 400**. The **Amount** will be calculated automatically
10. Select **Steel Pan** in the second line under **Name of the item** Field
11. Enter the **Quantity** as **100** and the **Rate as Rs. 500**. The **Amount** will be calculated automatically
12. Select the **VAT Ledger**. Here, it is **Input VAT @ 5%.** Once the ledger is selected, the **Amount** of input VAT will be filled in automatically
13. Set the option **Provide VAT details?** to **No**
14. Press **Alt+A** and enable the option to view the **Tax Analysis details** or **Tax Calculation details** (Figure 6.95).

The completed **Purchase Invoice** appears as shown below:

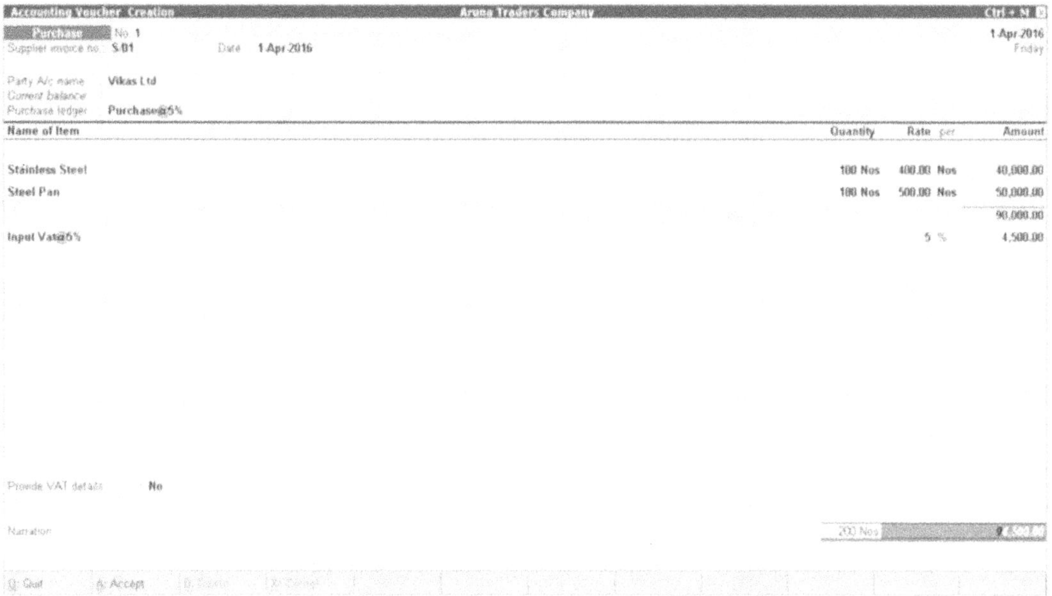

Figure 6.95: Purchase Invoice

15. Press **Enter** to accept

Note: The Commercial Taxes Department of Karnataka has introduced e-Sugam to upload the transportation details of notified goods before the movement of such goods. The option Is e-Sugam Applicable needs to be set to Yes on purchase of Notified Goods.

As on 2-4-2016, Aruna Traders Company sold 100nos of Stainless steel at Rs. 500 and 100nos of Steel Pan at 500 each to Jagadish Ltd with the same VAT rate of 5%

Recording Sales Transactions:

Step 1: Required Masters

1. Create voucher type as **Sales Tax Invoice**

The **Sales** voucher type can be created to use as a **Tax Invoice** or **Retail Invoice** and the default print title can also be specified here.

To configure **Sales Tax Invoice**

1. Go to **Gateway of Tally > Accounts Info > Voucher type > Create**
2. Enter the **Name of Voucher Type** as **Tax invoice**
3. In the **Type of Voucher** field select **Sales**
4. Select **Automatic** in **Method of Voucher Numbering**
5. Enter **Tax Invoice** as Default **Print Title**
6. Set **Is Tax Invoice** to **Yes**

The **Voucher Type Setup** screen appears as shown below (Figure 6.96):

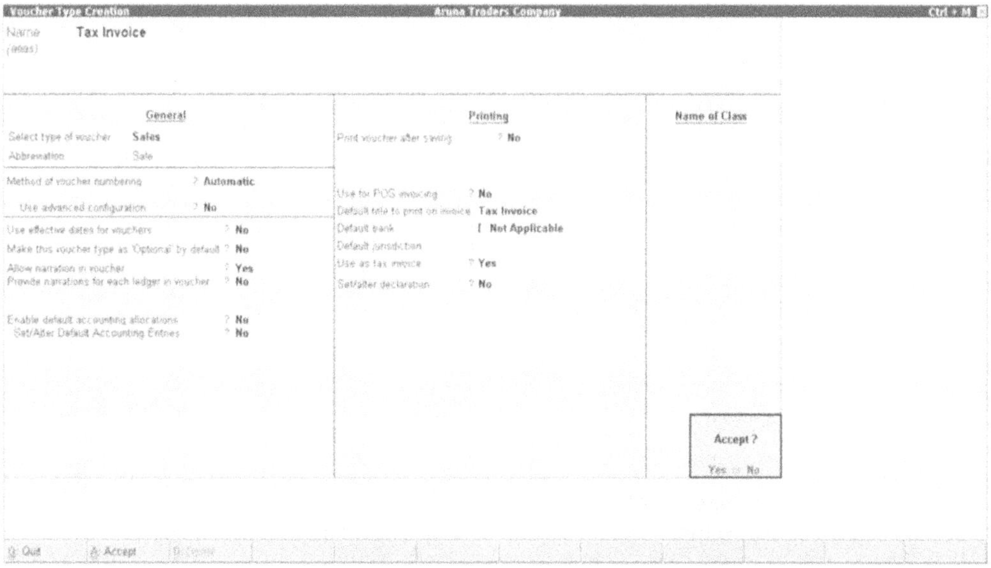

Figure 6.96: Voucher Type Creation

7. Accept the screen

Step 2:

2. Create the Accounting Masters Party Ledger – Jagadish Ltd.
    o   Group under **Sundry Debtors**
    o   Maintain balances bill by bill, select as **YES**
    o   Default credit period as **Blank**
    o   Check for credit days during voucher entry, select as **No**
    o   Inventory values are affected, select as **No**
    o   Set/Alter VAT Details, select as **YES**
    o   VAT TIN no **29543216789**

3. **Create sales ledger as Sales@5%**
    o   Group under **Sales Account**
    o   Maintain balances bill by bill select as **No**
    o   Inventory values are affected select as **YES**
    o   Is VAT/CST Applicable, Select as **Applicable**
    o   Set/Alter VAT details, select as **No**

4. Create Tax/Duty Ledger as Output Vat@5%
    o   Group under **Duties and Taxes**
    o   Type of Duty/Tax, select as **VAT**
    o   Use for purchase tax, select as **NO**
    o   Inventory values are affected, select as **No**
    o   Percentage of calculation (eg. 5), provide **5%**
    o   Rounding method select as **Not Applicable** (Figure 6.97)

VAT Duty Ledger

Output VAT @5%	
Field	**Action to be Performed**
Under	**Duties and Taxes**
Type of Duty/Tax	**VAT**
Use for purchase tax	**No**
Maintain balances bill by bill	**No**
Inventory values are affected	**No**
Percentage of calculation (eg. 5)	**5%**

Note: Common VAT duty ledger can also be used to record sales and purchase transactions. However, to avoid confusion, we have created two separate ledgers here.

Step 3: Recording of Sales Transactions:

1. Go to **Gateway of Tally > Accounting Vouchers > F8: Sales**
2. Select the Voucher Type **Tax Invoice**
3. Enter **2-04-2016** as the date
4. Enter **Reference No.** as **SAL/01**
5. Select **Jagadish Ltd** in the **Party's A/c Name** field
6. Select **Sales @ 5%** as the **sales** ledger. The VAT/Tax class gets captured automatically
7. Select Stainless Steel as the item
8. Enter the **Quantity** as **50** and the **Rate** as **Rs. 400**. The **Amount** will be calculated automatically
9. Select Steel Pan as the second stock item

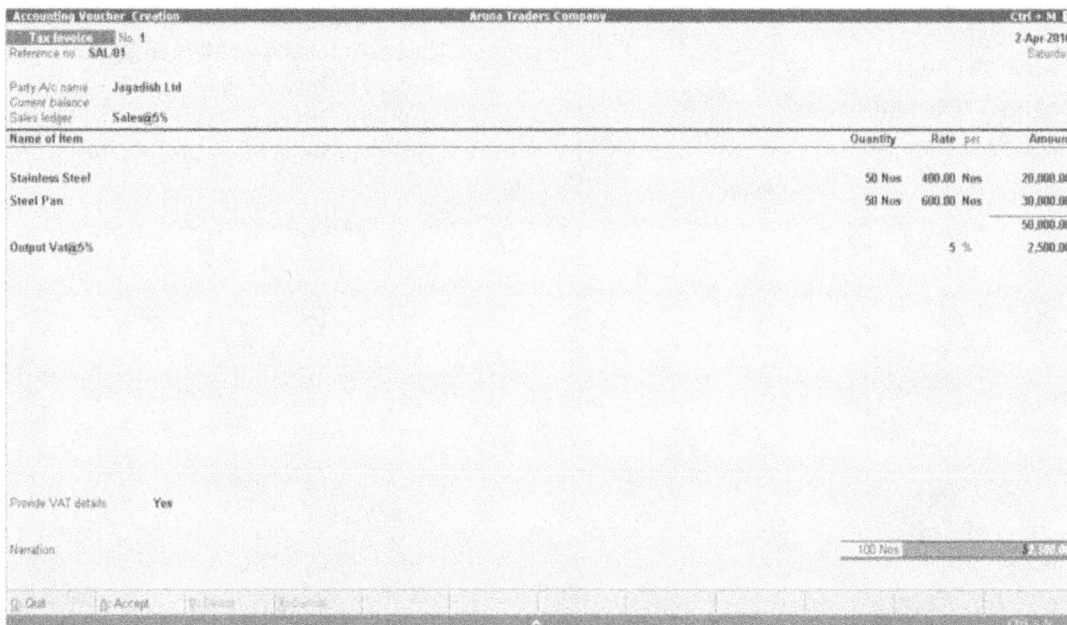

Figure 6.97: The completed Tax Invoice

10. Enter the **Quantity** as **50** and the **Rate** as **Rs. 600**. The **Amount** will be calculated automatically

11. Select the relevant **VAT Ledger**. Here, it is **Output VAT @**

5%. Once the ledger is selected, the **Amount** of Output VAT will be filled in automatically

12. Set the option **Is e-Sugam Applicable?** to **No**

13. Press **Alt + A** or click **A:Tax Analysis** to view the assessable value and VAT amount. Press **ALT+F1** for a detailed view of the same

The completed Tax Invoice appears as shown below:

6.12.4 Dealing with Different Stock Items with Multiple VAT Rate

Scenario 2:

Aruna Traders Company has expanded its business and entered in dealing of two new products i.e., PCC pipes and PVC pipes, both the stock items attract different VAT rate i.e., 14.5% and 12.5%.

The following illustration will help you understand how to record a taxable purchase and sales transaction where the stock items attract different VAT rates.

As on 1-5-2016, Aruna Traders Company purchased the following items attracting different VAT rates from SRP Ltd.

Name of the stock item	Quantity	Rate	VAT %
PCC pipes	100	50	12.5%
PVC pipes	100	100	14.5%

As on 2-5-2014, Aruna Traders Company sold the following stock items attracting different VAT Rate to Mahesh tradeRs.

Name of the stock item	Quantity	Rate	VAT %
PCC pipes	100	100	12.5%
PVC pipes	100	150	14.5%

Step 1: *Required Masters*
Accounting Masters

1. Create Party Ledger – **SRP Ltd**
   o Group under **Sundry Creditors**
   o Maintain balances bill by bill, select as **YES**
   o Default credit period as **Blank**
   o Check for credit days during voucher entry, select as **No**
   o Inventory values are affected, select as **No**
   o Set/Alter VAT Details, select as **YES**
   o VAT TIN no **29918273645**

2. Create purchase ledger as **Common Purchase Ledger**
   o Group under **Purchase Account**
   o Maintain balances bill by bill select as **No**
   o Inventory values are affected select as **YES**
   o Is VAT/CST Applicable, Select as **Applicable**
   o Set/Alter VAT details, select as **No**

3. Create Tax/Duty Ledger as **Input Vat@12.5%**
   o Group under **Duties and Taxes**
   o Type of Duty/Tax, select as **VAT**
   o Use for purchase tax, select as **NO**
   o Inventory values are affected, select as **No**
   o Percentage of calculation (eg. 5), provide**12. 5%**
   o Rounding method select as **Not Applicable**

4. Create Tax/Duty Ledger as **Input Vat@14.5%**
   o Group under **Duties and Taxes**
   o Type of Duty/Tax, select as **VAT**
   o Use for purchase tax, select as **NO**
   o Inventory values are affected, select as **No**

   o Percentage of calculation (eg. 5), provide **14.5%**
   o Rounding method select as **Not Applicable**

Activity

Similarly create Mahesh traders ledger account, common sales ledger account and Output vat of 12.5% and 14.5% ledgers for accounting sales invoice.

Inventory Masters

1. Create **Stock Items** of PCC pipes **and PVC pipes**
   o Stock item name as **PCC pipes**
   o Group under **Primary**
   o Units select **Nos**
   o VAT applicable, select as **Applicable**
   o Set/Alter VAT details, select as **Yes**
      Tax/Rate details screen
   o Commodity name as **Pipes**
   o Commodity Code as **2B007001**
   o Sub commodity code as **2016**
   o Tax rate as **12.5%**
   o Enter to accept the screen

Activity

Similarly create the stock item by name PVC pipes and mention the VAT rate as 14.5% (with same commodity details).

Step 2: *Recording Purchase Transaction:*

1. Go to **Gateway of Tally > Accounting Vouchers > F9: Purchase**

2. Ensure that it is in **Item Invoice** mode. If it is in **Accounting Invoice** mode click **I:Item Invoice**

3. Click **F12: Configure** and set the option **Use Common Ledger Account for Item Allocation** to **Yes** and **save**

4. Enter **01-05-2016** as the date

5. Enter **Supplier Invoice** No. as **S/02**. The **Date** field will be automatically filled with the voucher date

6. Select **SRP Ltd.** in the **Party's A/c Name** field

7. Select the purchase ledger which needs to be used for accounting the purchase. Here, it is **Common Purchase**

8. Select **PCC pipes** in the **Name of Item** field

9. Enter the **Quantity** as **100** and the **Rate** as **Rs. 50**. The **Amount** will be calculated automatically

10. Select **PVC pipes** in the second line under **Name of the item** Field

11. Enter the **Quantity** as **100** and the **Rate** as **Rs. 100**. The **Amount** will be calculated automatically

12. Select the **VAT Ledger**. Here, it is **Input VAT @ 12.5%** and **14.5%**. Once the ledger is selected, the **Rate** and **Amount** of Input VAT will be filled in automatically

13. Set the option **Provide VAT details?** to **No**

14. Press **Alt+A** and enable the option to view the **Tax Analysis details** or **Tax Calculation details**.

The completed Purchase Invoice appears as shown below (Figure 6.98):

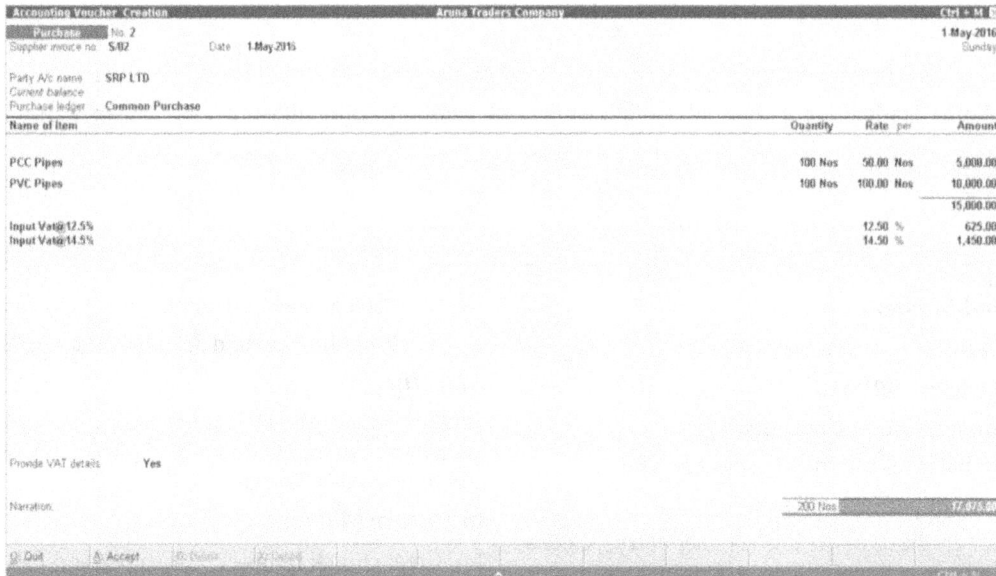

Figure 6.98: Completed Purchase Invoice

15. Press enter to accept the invoice

Activity

Similarly record the sales transactions with different VAT rates for dated 2-5-2016 .

6.12.5 Defining VAT Rate Stock Group wise

Scenario 3:

Aruna Traders has expanded its business and entered into the dealing of electric products and pipe products. All the leather products attract 12.5% of VAT rate and all the pipes attract 5% of VAT rate.

The following illustration will help you understand how a company dealing with multiple stock items with multiple tax rates classify the groups such that each group has a common VAT rate.

145

As on 1-6-2016, Aruna Traders Company purchased the following electric goods and pipes from KP Ltd.

Stock Group-Electric Goods			
Name of the stock item	Quantity	Rate	VAT percentage
Switches	5	200	12.5%
Electric wires	10	100	12.5%
Switch board	5	500	12.5%

Stock Group-Pipes			
Name of the stock item	Quantity	Rate	VAT Percentage
T shape pipes	50	500	5%
Shoe pipes	50	200	5%
L shape pipes	50	50	5%

In the above given illustration we see two Stock groups with different VAT rates, let us record the above given transactions in Tally.ERP 9

Step 1: Required Masters
Accounting Masters

Create Party Ledger – **KP Ltd**

* Group under **Sundry Creditors**
* Maintain balances bill by bill, select as **YES**
* Default credit period as **Blank**
* Check for credit days during voucher entry, select as **No**
* Inventory values are affected, select as **No**
* Set/Alter VAT Details, select as **YES**
* VAT TIN no **29918273645**

Duty Ledgers Creation: Use the same common purchase ledger, duty ledgers which were used in the earlier scenarios 1 and 2 that is VAT at 5% and VAT at 12.5% duty ledgeRs.

Inventory Masters

1. Create Stock Group

   Go to **Gateway of Tally > Inventory Info. > Stock Group > Create**

   o Group name as **Electric Goods**
   o Under **Primary**
   o Should quantities of items be added, set to **YES**
   o Set/alter VAT details, set to **YES**

   Press F12-Enable commodity details option

   o Commodity name as **Electric**
   o Commodity code is **3A007001**
   o Sub commodity code is **2016**
   o Tax Rate is **12.5%**
   o Tax Type will **By default the field will capture taxable.**
   o **Save the screen**

Note: Once the VAT rate is defined in the stock group then the same does not require to be configured in the corresponding stock items or any other master for those items.

Activity

Create the stock group Pipes and define the VAT rate as 5%

2. Create the **Stock item**

   Go to **Gateway of Tally > Inventory Info. > Stock Item > Create**

   o Name as **Switches**
   o Group under **Electric Goods**
   o Units select **Nos**
   o VAT applicable, select as **Applicable**
   o Set/Alter VAT details, select as **No**

Activity

Similarly create the other stock items which belongs to both the groups.

Step 2: Record the Purchase Transaction:

1. Go to **Gateway of Tally > Accounting Vouchers > F9: Purchase**
2. Ensure that it is in **Item Invoice** mode. If it is in **Accounting Invoice** mode click **I:Item Invoice**
3. Click **F12: Configure** and set the option **Use Common Ledger Account for Item Allocation** to **Yes** and **save**
4. Enter **01-06-2016** as the date
5. Enter **Supplier Invoice** No. as **S/03**. The **Date** field will be automatically filled with the voucher date
6. Select **KP Ltd.** in the **Party's A/c Name** field
7. Select the purchase ledger which needs to be used for accounting the purchase. Here, it is Common **Purchase**
8. **Select** all the stock items which belong to two stock groups
9. Enter the **Quantity, Rate** and The **Amount** will be calculated automatically
10. Select the Common **VAT Ledger**. Here, it is **Input VAT @ 12.5%** and **5%.** Once the ledger is selected, the **Rate** and **Amount** of Input VAT will be filled in automatically
11. Set the option **Provide VAT details?** to **Yes** to mention the e-sugam details (Figure 6.99)

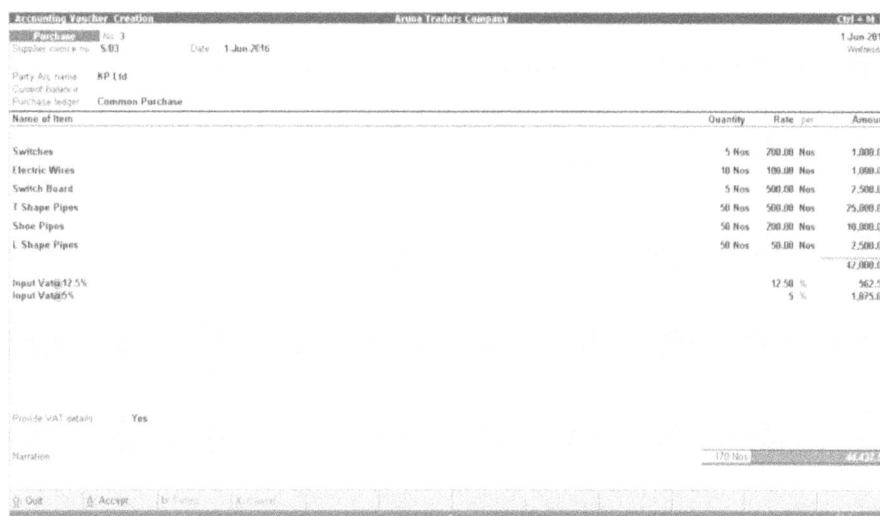

Figure 6.99: The Purchase Voucher Creation screen

Press Enter to accept the screen.

Activity

Similarly record a sales transaction and check how the output tax is computed. As on 3-6-2016 Aruna traders sold 5 quantity of Electric Goods @ 500 each to Mishra Electric Company (registered dealer 29112233445) with 12.5% VAT.

6.12.6 Adjustment against Tax Payable

At the end of every tax period, it is advisable to set off the Output

VAT amount with Input VAT amount. On 30-4-2016.

Follow the steps given below to record the adjustment entry in the journal voucher.

- **Go to** Gateway of Tally > Accounting Voucher > Press F7: Journal Voucher
- Press F2 and mention the date as **30-4-2016**.
- Debit the Output vat 5%,and credit Input vat 5%
- The completed journal voucher is given below (Figure 6.100):

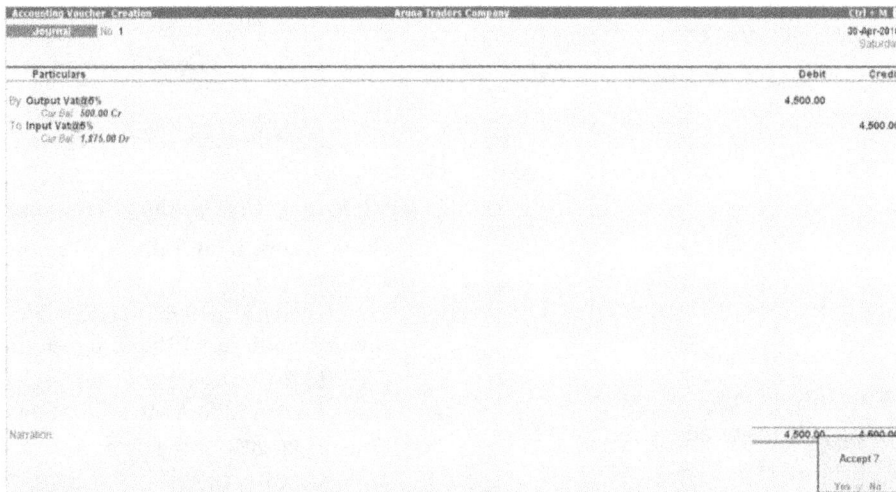

Figure 6.100: The Journal Voucher Creation scree

Press enter to accept the journal voucher

Activity

Check the VAT computation report and find out whether VAT is payable or refundable, if the VAT is payable then need to record a payment voucher, if it is refundable then there is no need of recording any payment entry

6.12.7 Making VAT Payment to the Government

Once after adjusting the output VAT against Input VAT, if the output VAT is remaining then we have to make a stat payment to the government.

Follow the below given steps to record the stat payment entry in Tally.ERP 9

1. Gateway of Tally->Accounting Voucher->Press F5: Payment
2. Press F2 and mention the period as 30-4-2016
3. Press Alt+S
4. Select Type of Tax
5. Mention the Period from 1-4-2016 to 30-4-2016
6. Select the payment type as Regular
7. Press Enter, you will come to payment voucher screen
8. Select Kotak bank in the Account field
9. Debit any one output duty ledger and mention the amount payable
10. The complete payment voucher screen is given below (Figure 6.101):

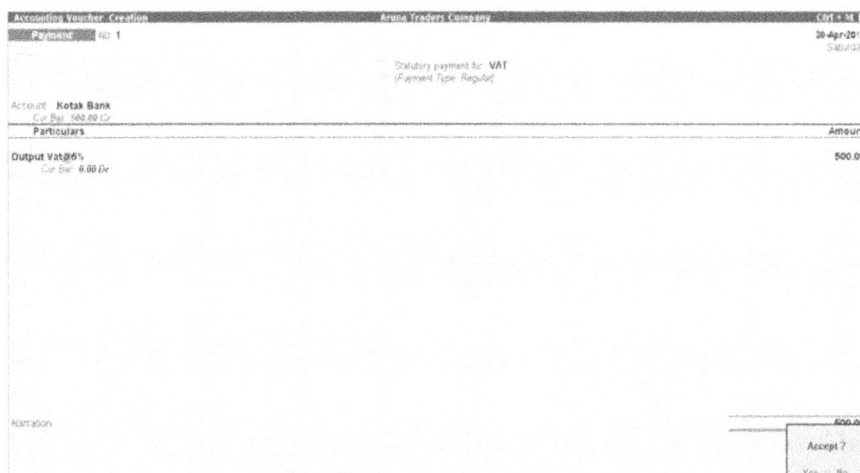

Figure 6.101: The Payment Voucher Creation screen

11. Press Enter to accept the screen.

Note: We can make a payment even from the VAT computation screen by pressing Alt+S from the report scree

---

5 .12.8 VAT Reports

Statutory forms for VAT can be generated in Tally.ERP 9. The forms shown below pertain to the State of Karnataka. VAT Forms available in Tally.ERP 9 vary as per the State selected.

6.12.8.1 VAT Form 100

The **Form VAT 100** report is designed to provide an overview of the statistics of transactions pertaining to a period. It displays the assessable value and tax amount on purchases and sales, payments made, and the amount of VAT payable/refundable.

To view the Form VAT 100

*   Go to **Gateway of Tally > Display > Statutory Reports > VAT > Form VAT 100** (Figure 6.102).

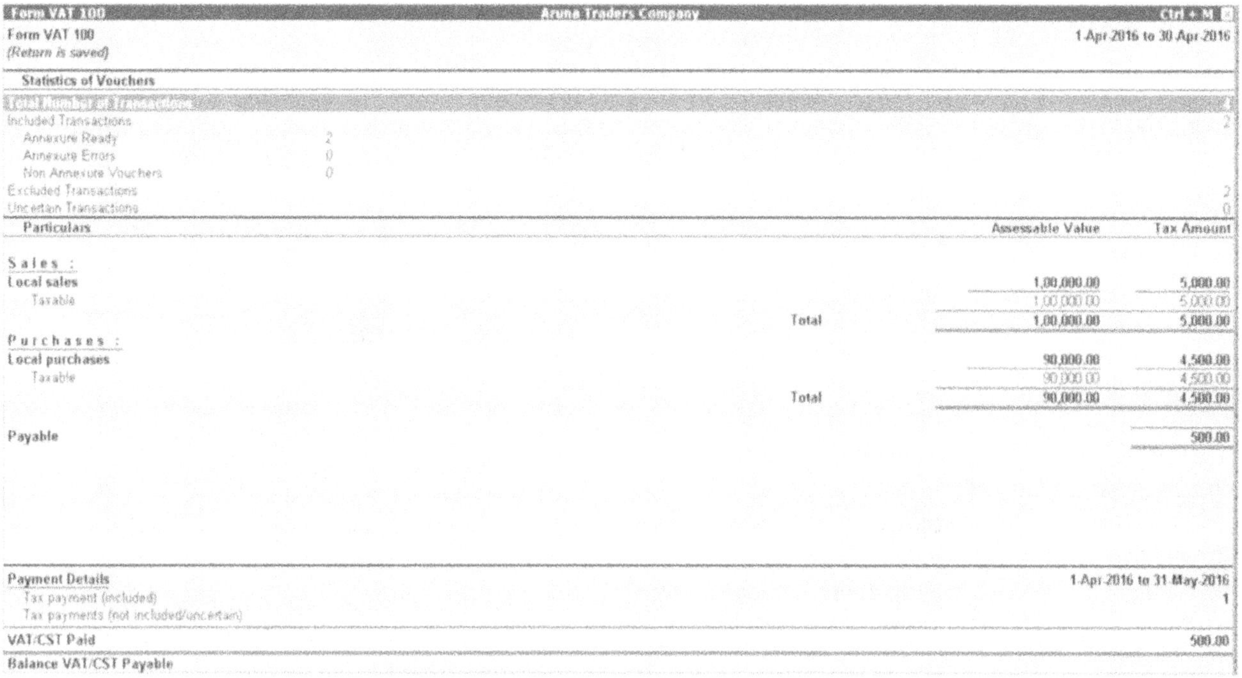

Figure 6.102: VAT Form 100

Note: To generate and print the VAT Form 100 Press Ctrl+P from the Form VAT 100 report.

VAT Form 100 contains three main sections:

1. **Statistics of Vouchers:** It contains the detailed Summary of Included, Excluded transactions and the exception summary.

2. **Computation:** It contains details of the values used in the returns and annexures along with the amount of liability, input credit, adjustments, and VAT/CST payable or refundable.

3. **Payment Details:** It contains the detailed statistics of all VAT/CST payment vouchers for the current period.

Key Combination	Functionality
ALT+F1	To view the detailed report
ALT+S	To make a Statutory Payment

GETTING STARTED WITH SERVICE TAX

OBJECTIVES

After studying of this section, you will be able to understand how to:

- Enable Service Tax for different types of business requirements
- Create the masters necessary for Service Tax transactions
- Record Service Tax transactions
- Generate Service Tax reports

6.13 INTRODUCTION

Service Tax is an indirect tax levied on services rendered. For example, an advertising agency renders its advertising services to a client, the tax is levied on the Service amount. The person who renders the service is liable to pay the service tax. Service tax was imposed for the first time in 1994 and its scope is increasing every year.

6.13.1 Features of Service Tax

- Service tax is payable on the gross amount charged for the service provided or to be provided excluding material cost. Tax is also payable on reimbursement of expenses which form part of service
- In cases where the value of the service provided is not ascertainable, the valuation is done on the basis of another similar service or on the basis of cost
- Gross amount charged is considered as inclusive of service tax and then tax is back-calculated
- Service tax is payable only when the bill amount is received from the service receiver. However, in case of service provided to associated enterprises, service tax is payable on booking such entry

6.13.2 Basic Terminology

Let us understand the following definitions and terminologies used in Service Tax:

Service Provider

As defined u/s 65(105), a service provider is one who provides taxable service.

Taxable Service

Service tax is payable on **taxable service**. The definition of taxable service is different for each class of services, e.g. in case of an advertising agency, any service provided to a client in relation to the advertisement in any manner will be **taxable service**.

Value of Taxable Service

Service tax is payable on the **value of services**. The value of service shall be the gross amount charged by the service provider for such service rendered by the provider.

Person Liable to Pay Service Tax

Every person providing taxable service to any person has to pay service tax at the prescribed rates. In a few cases, tax is payable by a service receiver under reverse charge method.

Exemption from Service Tax

- Small service providers whose total value of services provided (including exempt and non-taxable services) is less than Rs. 10 lakhs in the previous year, are not required to pay service tax in the current financial year till they reach a turnover of Rs. 10 lakhs
- Services provided to SEZ units or developer for consumption within SEZ are exempt
- Refund is eligible for specified services utilised for export
- Services provided by the RBI are exempt but service provided to the RBI are not exempt

Rate of Service Tax

The service tax rate has been increased from 12.36% to flat 14%, Swachh Bharat Cess 0.50% and Krishi Kalyan Cess 0.50%,. The new rate of Service Tax @ 14% is applicable from 1st June 2015 and education cess and secondary education cess are not required to be disclosed/charged separately. Thus the total service tax will be collected by the service tax provider and paid to the government. From 1-june-2016 Swachh Bharat Cess 0.50% and Krishi Kalyan Cess 0.50%

Let us consider the following example to understand how Service Tax is calculated:

Particulars	Rs.
Charge on service (i.e., Bill amount)	10,000
Service Tax @ 14%	1,400
Swachh Bharat Cess 0.50%	50
Krishi Kalyan Cess 0.50%	50
Total invoice amount	11,500

Abatements

Abatement refers to the percentage of amount exempted from tax provided by the government on the value to be considered for calculation of service tax. It is either a percentage of the service charges or a lump sum amount.

Particulars	Rs.
(a) Charge on service	10,000
(b) An abatement of 30% amounts to	3,000
Here, the assessable value is (a-b)	7,000
Therefore, Service Tax @ 14% on Rs. 7,000.	980
Swachh Bharat Cess 0.50% on 7,000	35
Krishi Kalyan Cess 0.50% on 7,000	35

CENVAT Credit

The service provider can avail CENVAT credit of service tax paid on services received (input services) and excise duty paid on inputs and capital goods. The credit can be utilized for payment of service tax on services provided (output services). However, in cases where the assessee is providing both taxable and exempt services and if input services are common, CENVAT credit can either be taken on proportionate basis or 8% 'amount' is required to be paid on exempted services.

Payment of Service Tax

When the assessee is a corporate, service tax is payable on a monthly basis by the 5th of the following month. For example, service tax has to be paid by 5th January for the month of December. If the service tax payer opts for online payment, then he is given a grace period of 1 day i.e., the due date will be 6th of the following Quarter.

Non-corporate bodies such as individuals, proprietary firms and partnership firms pay service tax for the fiscal quarter. The payment is to be made by the 5th day of the month, following the quarter. For example, service tax for the quarter ending 30th June is to be paid by 5th July. If the service tax payer opts for online payment, then he is given a grace period of 1 day, i.e, the due date will be 6th of the following Quarter. For the month of March though, corporate and non-corporate bodies have to pay the service tax by 31st March.

The service tax assessee must use a GAR 7 Challan to pay tax in the bank nominated by the commissioner ate. The payment must

be rounded off to the nearest rupee. It is advisable to use separate GAR 7 Challans for different categories of service.

6.13.3 Setup

6.13.3.1 Company Creation

Create a company with the following details:

Name: Gayi Digital Pvt. Ltd.

Fin year beginning from: 01-04-2016

6.13.4 Configuration of service tax in the company level.

Scenario 1:

Gayi Digital Pvt Ltd is a registered service provider which renders the Advertising services to their clients but doesn't receive any services.

The following illustration will help you understand how to record the transaction where a company renders the service but doesn't receive any services.

As on 15-6-2016 Gayi Digital Pvt Ltd rendered advertising service of worth Rs. 3,00,000 to Purvika Pvt Ltd with 15% service tax rate.

Let as record the above transaction in Tally ERP 9.

Step 1: Defining Service Tax Details.

To Define Service Tax Details for M & M Company

1. Go to **Gateway of Tally > F11: Features > Statutory and Taxation** (Figure 6.103)
2. Enable the option **Set/alter service tax details**

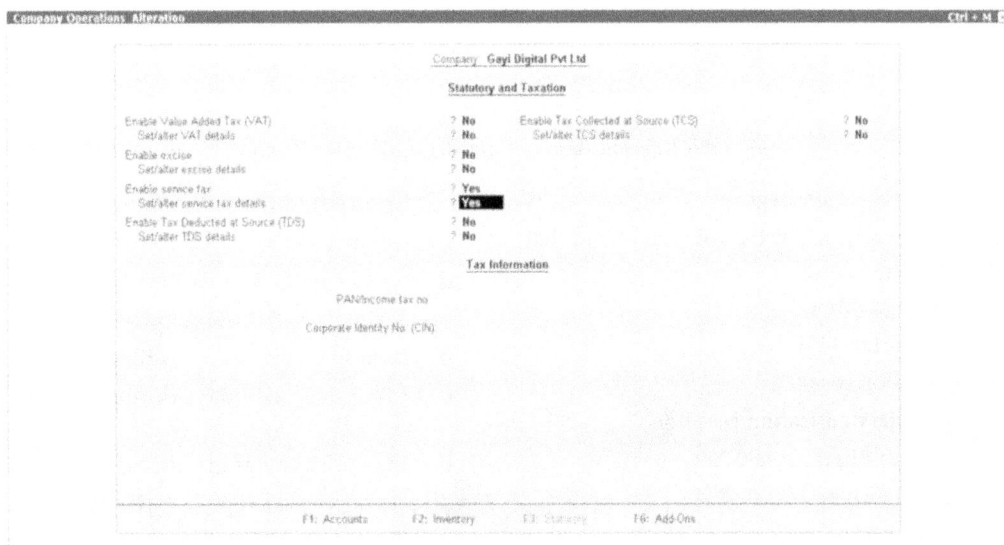

Figure 6.103: The Company Operations Alteration screen

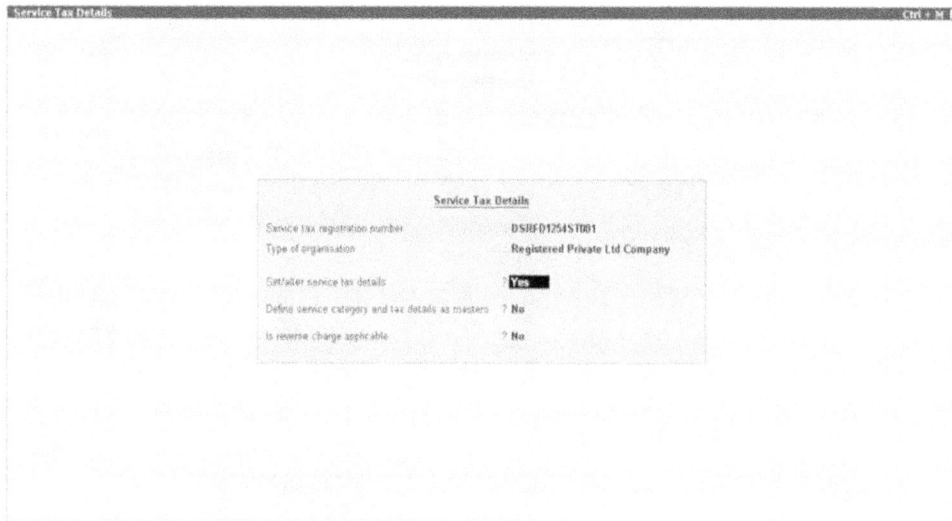

Figure 6.104: Service Tax Details

3. In the service tax details screen, mention the service tax registration number

4. Mention the Type of organization, select it "Registered Private Ltd Company"

5. Enable the option "Set/Alter service tax details"

6. Press F12 from the screen and enable the option "Show service code and sub clause number".

7. Service tax details screen will appear (Figure 6.104).

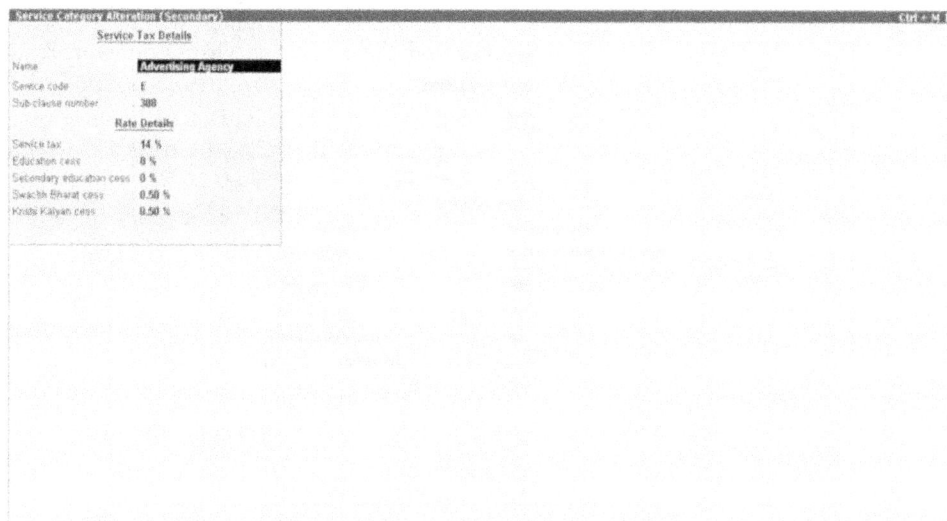

Figure 6.105: The Service Category Alteration screen

8. Enter the **name of the service category**

9. Enter the **service code** provided by the government for that particular service category

10. Enter the **Sub-Clause number**

11. Set the rate for **Service tax-14%**

12. Set the rate for **education cess-0%**

13. Set the rate for **secondary education cess-0%**

14. Set the rate for **Swachh Bharat cess-0.50%**

15. Set the rate for **Krishi Kalyan cess-0.50%**

16. Press **Enter** (Figure 6.105)

17. Press **Enter** to save the details

Step 2: Create Required Masters

1. Create party ledger as – Purvika Pvt Ltd
   o Group under **Sundry Debtors**
   o Maintain balances bill by bill, select as **YES**
   o Default credit period as **Blank**
   o Check for credit days during voucher entry, select as **No**
   o Inventory values are affected, select as **No**

2. Create purchase ledger as **Sales of Advertising agency**
   o Group under **Sales**
   o Maintain balances bill by bill select as **No**

- o Inventory values are affected select as **YES**
- o Is Service Tax Applicable, Select as **Applicable**
- o Set/Alter Service Tax details, select as **No**
3. Create Tax/Duty Ledger as **Service Tax@14%**

- o Group under **Duties and Taxes**
- o Type of Duty/Tax, select as **Service Tax**
- o Tax Head as **Service Tax**
- o Inventory values are affected, select as **No**
- o Rounding method select as **Not Applicable**

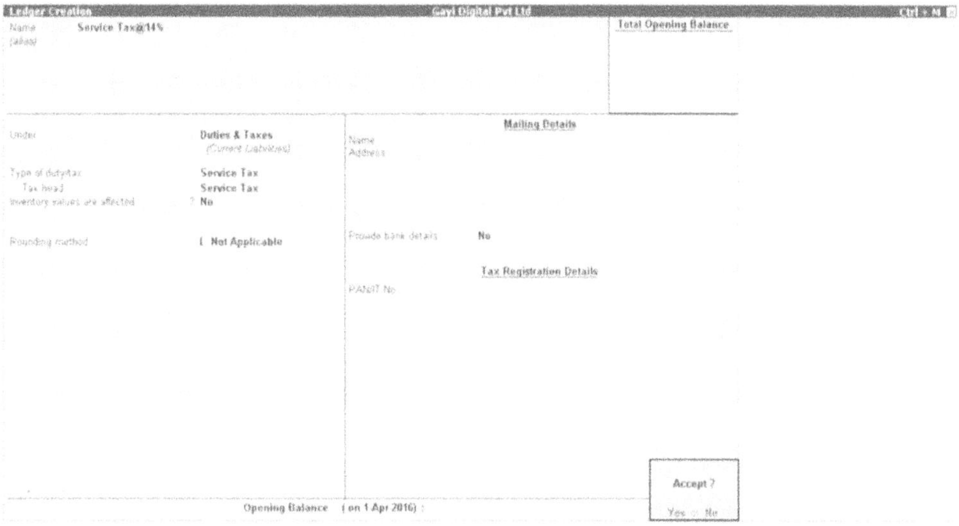

Figure 6.106: Tax Ledger Creation

4. Create Tax/Duty Ledger as **Swachh Bharat Cess@0.50%**
   - o Group under **Duties and Taxes**
   - o Type of Duty/Tax, select as **Swachh Bharat Cess**
   - o Inventory values are affected, select as **No**
   - o Rounding method select as **Not Applicable**
5. Create Tax/Duty Ledger as **Krishi Kalyan Cess@0.50%**
   - o Group under **Duties and Taxes**
   - o Type of Duty/Tax, select as **Krishi Kalyan Cess**
   - o Inventory values are affected, select as **No**
   - o Rounding method select as **Not Applicable** (Figure 6.106)

Step 3: Recording the Sale of Service Transaction.

1. Go to **Gateway of Tally > Accounting voucher > Press F8: Sales**
2. Sales voucher should be in Accounting invoice mode->Press Alt+I from the item invoice screen to come to Accounting invoice screen
3. Mention the reference number as **SAL/001**
4. Select the party ledger name
5. Under particulars, select the ledger **sale of advertising service**
6. Select the **Service tax** duty ledger
7. On selecting the service tax ledger in the transaction, the service tax amount is calculated as shown in the screen below (Figure 6.107):

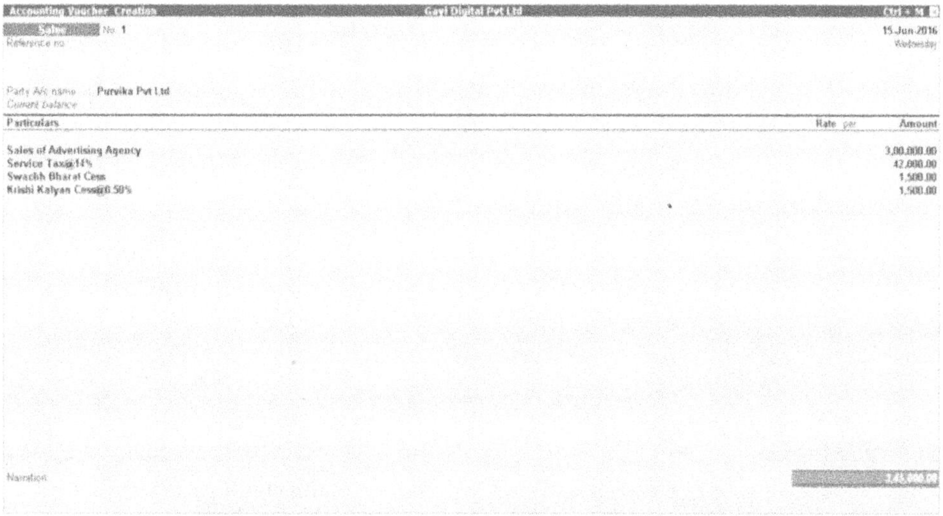

Figure 6.107: Sales Invoice

8. Press Enter to accept the sales invoice

6.13.5 Configuration of Service Tax in the Ledger Level

Scenario 2:

Gayi Digital Pvt Ltd now started receiving the Courier service from Blue dart Express Ltd and providing the Advertising services to its customer

The following illustration will help you understand how to record the transaction where a company renders and receives service.

As on 1-7-2016 Gayi Digital Pvt Ltd received courier services for worth Rs. 50,000 from Green Dart Express Ltd and the service is subjected to a service tax of 15%.

Recording of service received transaction in purchase invoice:

Step 1: Defining Service Tax Details.

1. Go to **Gateway of Tally > F11: Features > Statutory and Compliance** (Figure 6.108)
2. Enable the option **Set/alter service tax details**

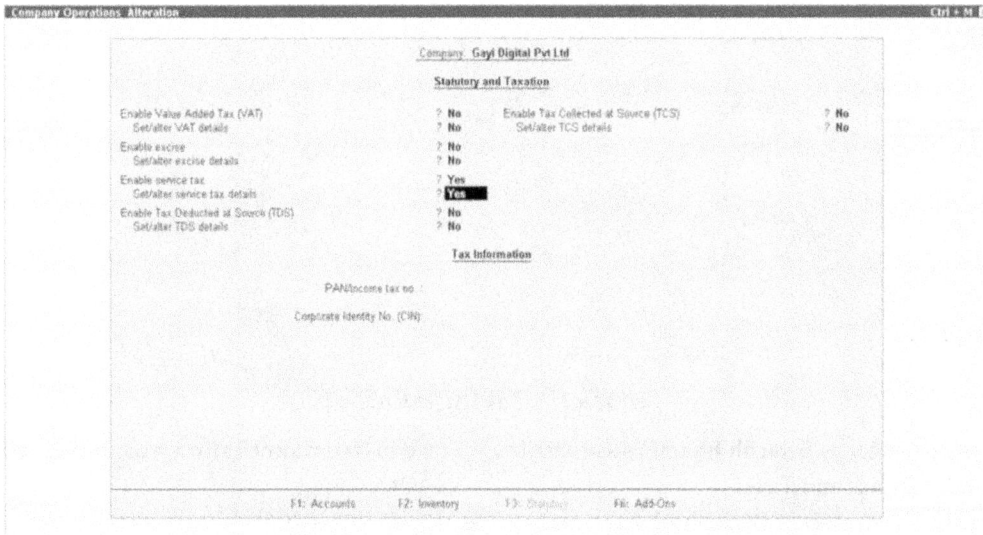

Figure 6.108: Company Operations Alteration Screen

3. Set the option **Define service category and tax details as Masters** to **Yes**, by enabling this option you can define the service classification while creating the ledger and group

4. Press **Enter** (Figure 6.109)
5. Press **Ctrl + A** to save the details

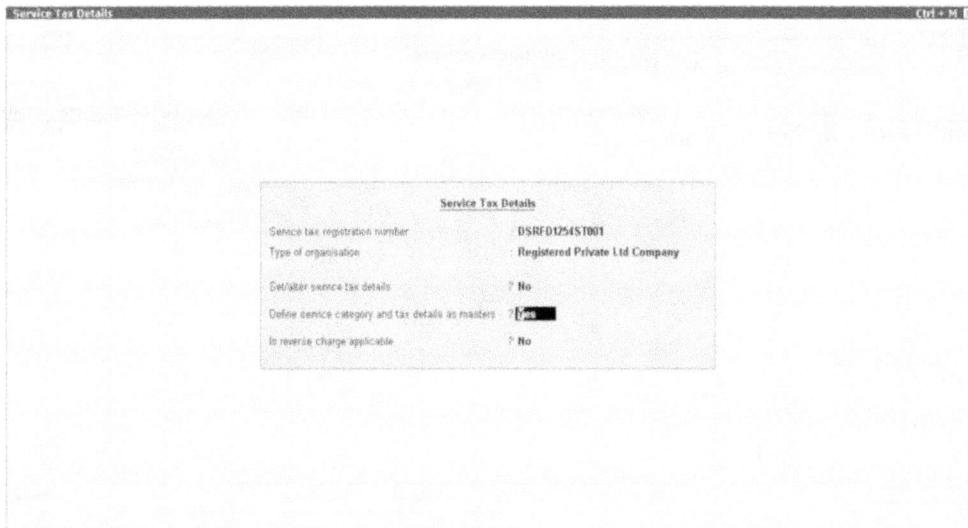

Figure 6.109: Service Tax Details

Step 2: Create Required Masters

1. Create party ledger as – Green Dart Express
   o Group under **Sundry Creditors**

   o Maintain balances bill by bill, select as **YES**
   o Default credit period as **Blank**
   o Check for credit days during voucher entry, select as **No**

 o Inventory values are affected, select as **No**

2. Create purchase ledger as **Purchases on courier services**

 o Group under **Purchase Account**

 o Maintain balances bill by bill select as **No**

 o Inventory values are affected select as **YES**

 o Is Service Tax Applicable, Select as **Applicable**

 o Set/Alter Service Tax details, select as **Yes**

  Service Tax Details screen

 o Service Category - **Place the cursor in this field and press Alt+C**

 o **Name as Courier service**

 o **Service code as 392**

 o **Sub-Clause number – F**

  Service Tax Rate details

 o Service **Tax @ 14%**

 o Swachh Bharat Cess @0.50%

 o Krishi Kalyan Cess @0.50%

 o Save the ledger screen by entering screen and sub-screens

Note: Service category can be created from Gateway of Tally > Accounts Info. > Statutory Info. > Service Categories > Create

---

Service Tax Ledger: Use the same service tax ledger which was created earlier.

Step 3: Recording of Purchase of Service Transaction.

1. Go to **Gateway of Tally > Accounting voucher > Press F9: Purchase**

2. Date as 1-7-2016

3. Purchase voucher should be in Accounting invoice mode->Press Alt+I from the item invoice screen to come to Accounting invoice screen

4. Mention the reference number as **PUR/001**

5. Select the party ledger name

6. Under particulars, select the ledger **Purchase of courier service** and mention the amount as **Rs. 50,000,** press Enter

7. Select the **Service tax, Swachh bharat cess and Krishi Kalyan cess** duty ledger

8. On selecting the service tax ledger in the transaction, the service tax rate 14%,0.50% and 0.50% is calculated automatically, as shown in the screen below (Figure 6.110):

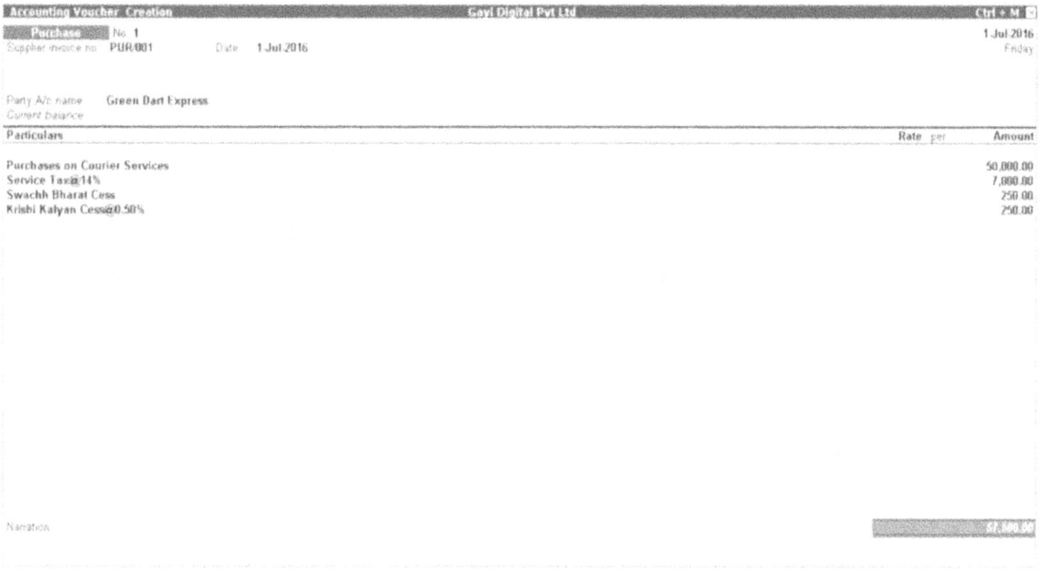

Figure 6.110: Purchase Invoice

9. Press Enter to accept the Purchase Invoice

6.13.6 Configuration of Service Tax in the Group Level

Scenario 3:

Gayi Digital Pvt Ltd, has decided to arrange a formal party to its clients and employees and the whole event will be arranged and managed by the A to Z Company on a chargeable basis.

Gayi Digital Pvt Ltd is receiving the event management and convention service from Alpha Company.

Let's see how service tax details can be defined in a scenario, where a company receives more than one service and also provides more than one service.

Illustration:

As on 1-8-2016 Gayi Digital Pvt Ltd received the event management service worth Rs. 10,000 and Convention service worth Rs. 5,000 from Alpha Company, both the services are subjected to service tax of 15%.

Step 1: Defining Service Tax Details

1. Go to **Gateway of Tally > F11: Features > Statutory and Compliance**

2. Enable the option **Set/alter service tax details**

3. Set the option **Define service category and tax details as**

Masters to **yes**, by enabling this option you can define

The service classification while creating the ledger and group (Figure 6.111)

4. Press **Enter**

5. Press **Ctrl + A** to save the details

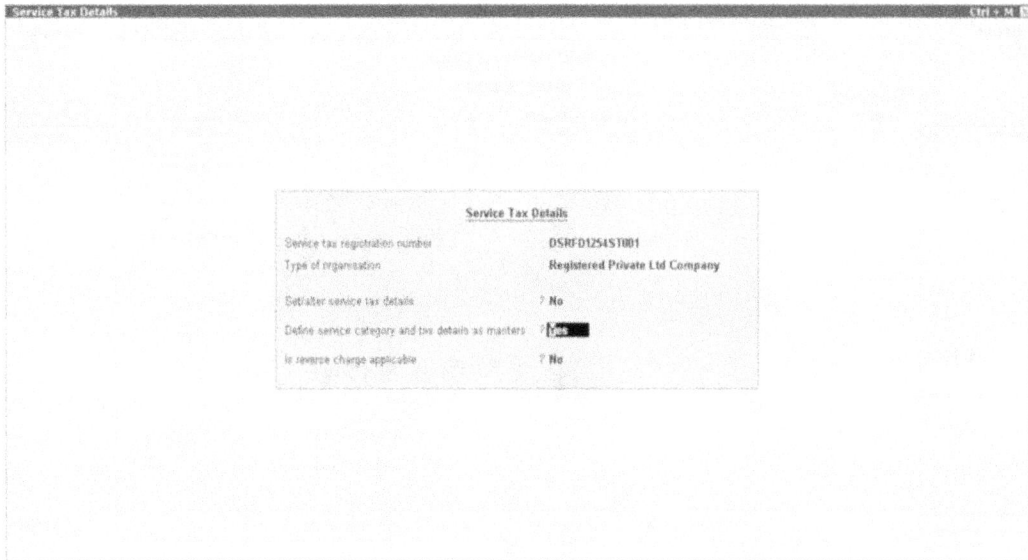

Figure 6.111: Service Tax Details

Note: No need of repeating the above steps, because it is already done in the scenario 2.

Step 2: Creation of service category.

1. Gateway of Tally->Accounts info->Statutory Info->Service Categories->Create.

2. Mention the **service category name**, **Service code** and **Sub-clause number**, if **service code** and **clause number**

    Is not appearing then press **F12 configuration** and enable the option "**Show service code and clause number**".

3. Mention the **service tax rate**.

4. The complete **Service category Creation** screen is given below (Figure 6.112).

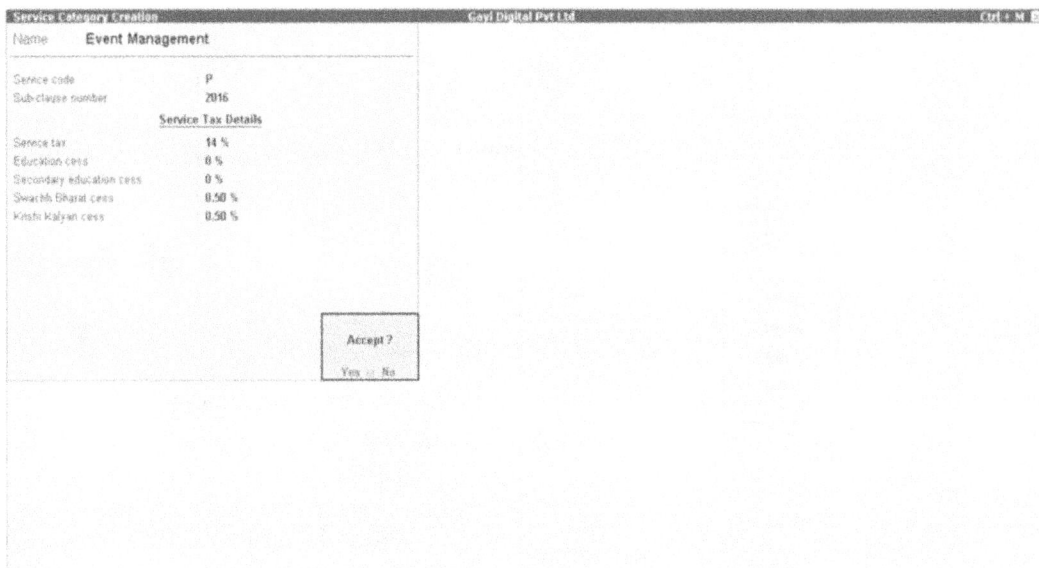

Figure 6.112: Service Category Creation

5. Press **Enter** to accept the screen

Activity: Similarly create the Service category for Convention service.

Step 3: Accounting Ledgers/Groups

1. Create party ledger as – **Alpha Company**
    o   Group under **Sundry Creditors**

o   Maintain balances bill by bill, select as **YES**

o   Default credit period as **Blank**

o   Check for credit days during voucher entry, select as **No**

o   Inventory values are affected, select as **No**

2.   Create Purchase Group – Purchase on Event Management Services

Go to **Gateway of Tally > Accounts info > Groups > Create > Mention the name as Purchase of event management service > Under Purchase Account** (Figure 6.113)

o   Group under **Purchase Account**

o   Keep other option as default

o   Set/Alter Service Tax details, select as **Yes**

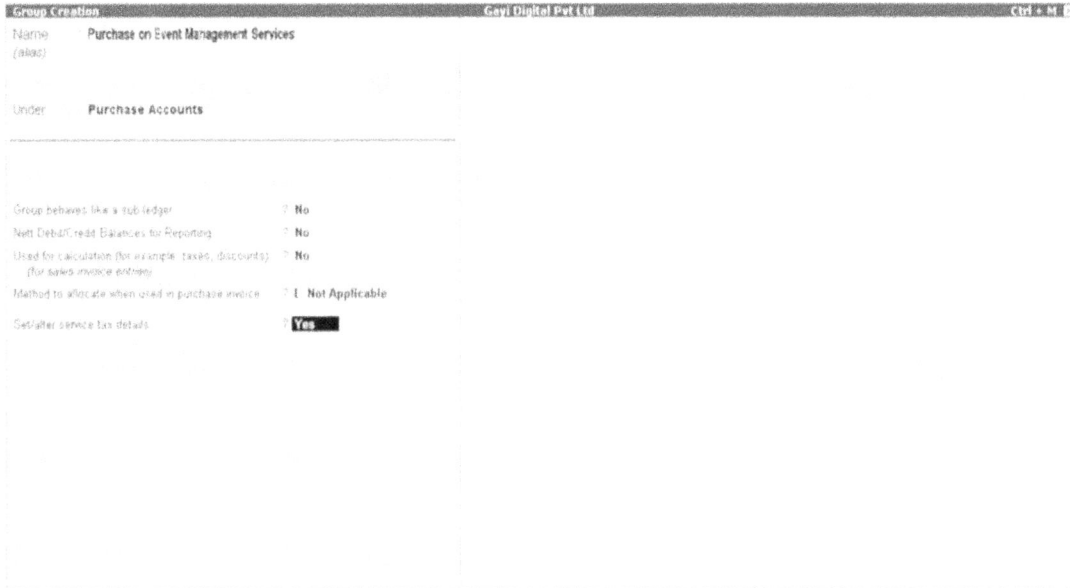

Figure 6.113: Group Creation

Service Tax Details screen

o   Enable the option **Set/Alter Service tax details**

o   Place the cursor in the **Service category** field and press

Spacebar button.

o   From the **list of Service category,** select the category which is required (Figure 6.114).

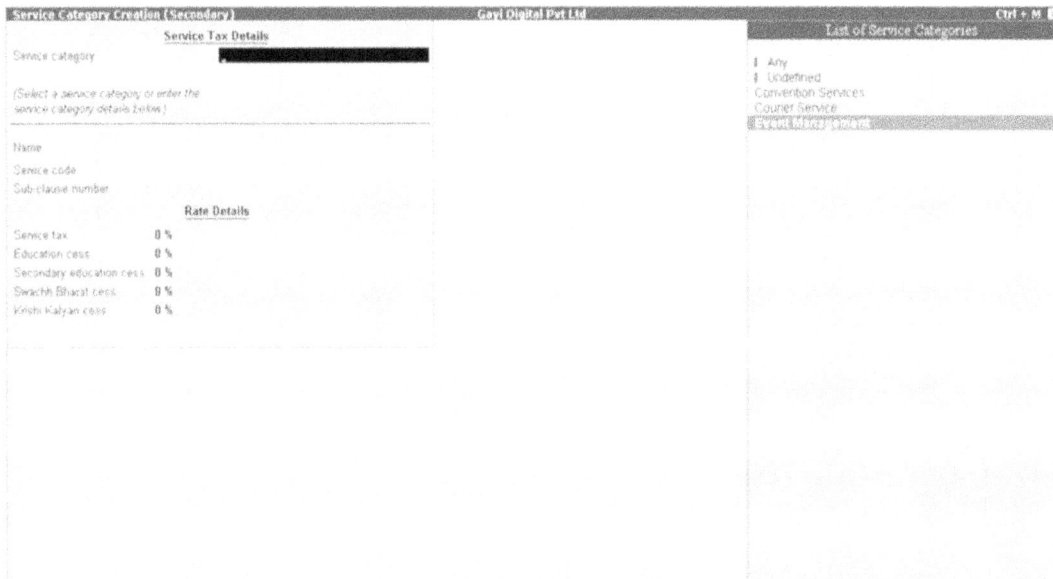

Figure 6.114: Selection of Service Category

Enter and accept the scree

Activity: Create the Accounting Group by name Purchase of convention service, in the same way

3. Create purchase ledger as **Purchases of Event Service**

   o   Group under **Purchase on Event management services**

   o   Maintain balances bill by bill select as **No**

   o   Inventory values are affected select as **YES**

   o   Is Service Tax Applicable, Select as **Applicable**

   o   Set/Alter Service Tax details, select as **No**

4. Create purchase ledger as **Purchases of Convention**

   o   Group under **Purchase on Event Convention services**

   o   Maintain balances bill by bill select as **No**

   o   Inventory values are affected select as **YES**

   o   Is Service Tax Applicable, Select as **Applicable**

   o   Set/Alter Service Tax details, select as **No**

Note: We have selected service tax applicable as undefined because the service tax is defined at the group level.

Step 4: Recording purchase of Service Transaction in Tally ERP 9.

1. Go to **Gateway of Tally > Accounting voucher > Press F9: Purchase**

2. Press F2 and mention the date as 1-8-2016

3. Purchase voucher should be in Accounting invoice mode > Press Alt+I from the item invoice screen to come to Accounting invoice screen

4. Mention the reference number as **PUR/002**

5. Select the party ledger name

6. Under particulars select the ledger **Purchase of Event Service** and mention the amount as Rs. **10,000** and press Enter.

7. Select **Purchase of Convention** and mention the amount as Rs. **5,000**

8. Select the **Service tax** duty ledger

9. On selecting the service tax ledger in the transaction, the service tax at 14% is calculated automatically, as shown in the screen below (Figure 6.115):

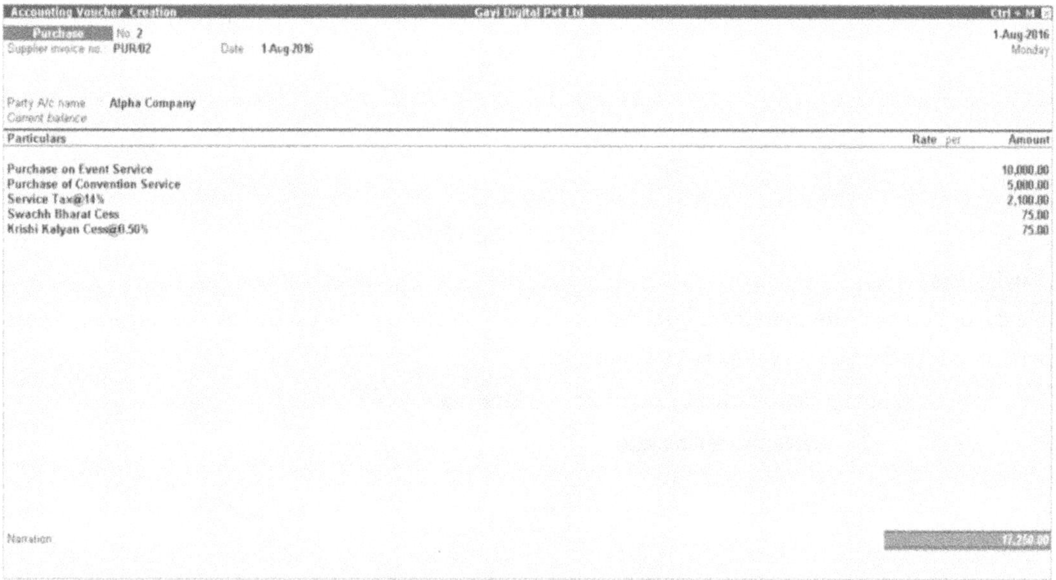

Figure 6.115: Purchase Invoice

10. Press **Enter** to accept the Purchase Invoice.

Activity: Similarly record the Sale of service by defining the service tax in the Group level.

6.13.7 Input Credit Adjustment

Scenario 4:

Gayi Digital Pvt ltd Company wants to make a payment of Service tax duty after adjusting the Service tax input credit.

Illustration:

As on 31-8-2016 Gayi Digital Pvt Ltd Company utilized the total available credit against the service tax payable.

Before recording the entry, let use check the Computation report and find out the Available credit and total service tax payable

To the Government.

To check the Service Tax Computation report, follow the path given below:

Go to **Gateway of Tally > Display > Statutory Info > Form ST3 > Press F2** and mention the period as **1-4-2016 to 31-8-2016**

The Above report is displaying the Service Tax computation.

Service tax Liability: It is the amount payable to the government, for example in the computation screen it is shown as Rs. 45,000 (Tax Value).

Service tax credit availed: It displays the Service tax value calculated at the time of receiving the service i.e., at the time of recording the purchase transaction.

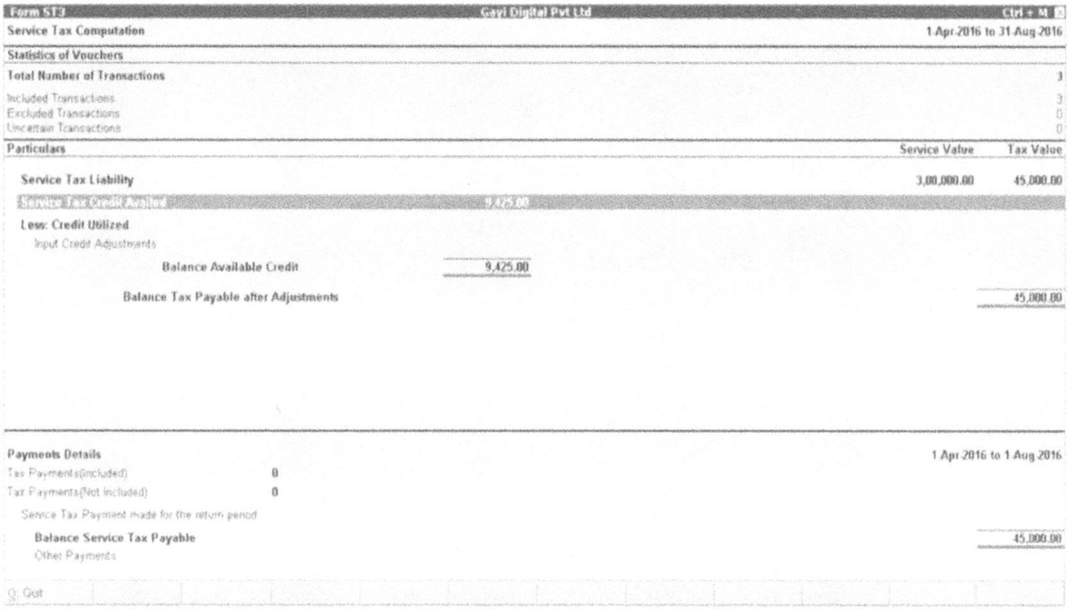

Figure 6.116: Form ST 3 screen

We can adjust the value displayed over here with output service tax (Figure 6.116).

Less Credit utilized: It displays the Input service tax credit adjusted against output service tax. But you cannot adjust Swachh Bharat cess it is consider as expenses.

Payment details: It displays the details of payment like total service tax payable to the government.

As per the report we will come to know that the service tax payable to the government is Rs. 45,000 and the available Service

tax credit is Rs. 9,425.

Before making a payment to the government, we need to adjust the Service tax payable amount against Available Service tax credit.

Recording of Service tax Adjustment entry

1. Go to **Gateway of Tally > Accounting Voucher > Press F7**
2. Press **F2** and mention the date as **31-8-2016**
3. Press **Alt+J** (Figure 6.117)

Figure 6.117: The Journal Voucher Creation screen

4. Select the **Type of service** as **Service Tax**
5. Nature of Adjustment as **Input credit Adjustment**
6. Debit the **Service tax duty ledger** mention the amount to be adjusted that is Rs. **9100 and Krishi Kalyan cess is Rs.**

325 and credit the Service tax duty ledger and mention the same amount. You will get the **Tax payment detail** screen

7. Mention the amount as **Rs. 9100** in the **service tax field** and **Krishi Kalyan cess is Rs. 325** and **accept the screen** (Figure 6.118)

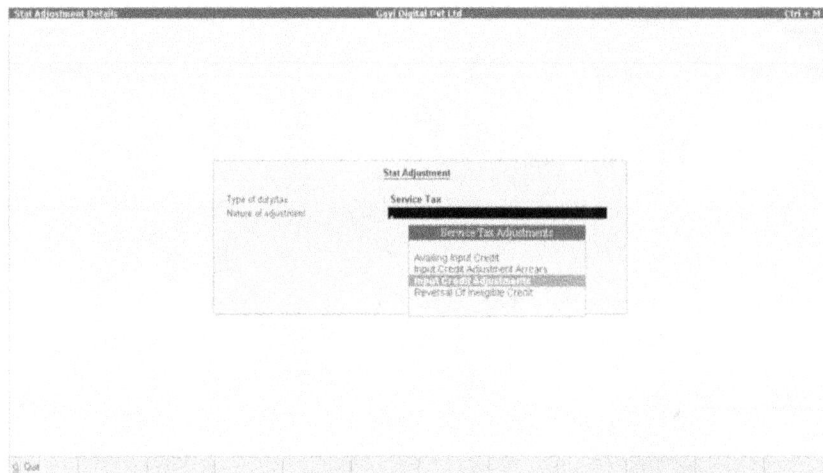

Figure 6.118: Input Credit Adjustment in Journal Voucher

8. The completed Journal voucher screen is given below (Figure 6.119):

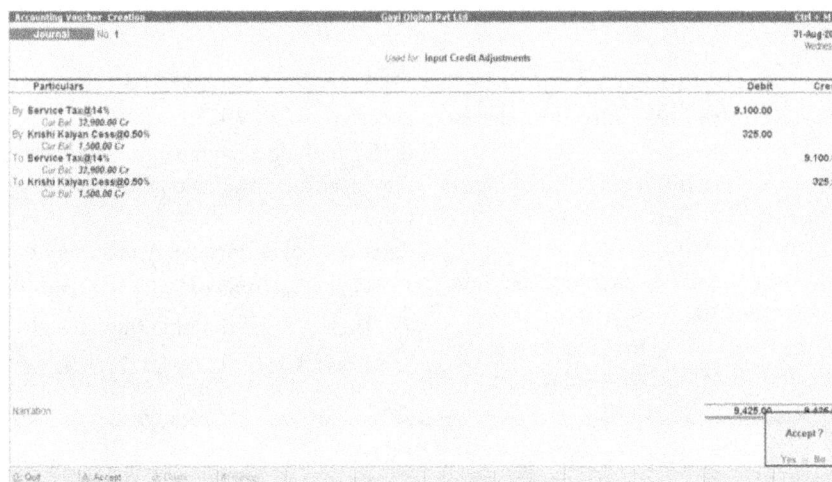

Figure 6.119: The Journal Voucher Creation screen

9. Press **Enter** to accept the screen.

Note: ◆ Adjustment entry can also be recorded from the service Tax computation report by pressing Alt+J from the Computation report.
◆ Check the Service tax Computation report: adjusted amount Rs. 9100 is reflected under the field Credit Utilized and Service tax payable is showing as Rs. 35,575.00

6.13.8 Payment of Service Tax to the Government

Illustration:

After adjusting the Service tax credit, Gayi Digital Pvt Ltd wants to make a payment of Service tax 35,575 to the government on 1-9-2016.

Recording of the payment of Service Tax to the government:

1. Go to **Gateway of Tally > Accounting Voucher > Press F5: Payment**
2. Press **Alt+S: Stat Payment**
3. Select the **Tax Type as Service tax**

4. Mention the **period** for which you are making the payment as ex:1-4-2016 to 31-9-2016
5. Select the **Payment Type as regular** and press Enter
6. Select the Bank Account. Create a bank ledger with the name Kotak Bank by pressing ALT+C if it is not available
7. Under **Particulars,** select **service tax duty** ledger and **mention the payable** amount and press enter, you will get the **tax payment details** screen to **allocate the tax amount**
8. Mention **Service tax** as Rs. **32900, Swachh bharat cess Rs. 1175 and Krishi Kalyan Cess as Rs. 1175.**
9. Mention the **bank details** in the **bank allocation screen**.
10. The complete Stat payment voucher is given below:
11. Press **Enter** and accept the screen.

Reconcile the Challan from **Gateway of Tally > Display > Statutory Report > Challan reconciliation > Select the line by pressing F5 > Mention the details,** like bank name, BSR code, Challan number, date and save (Figure 6.110).

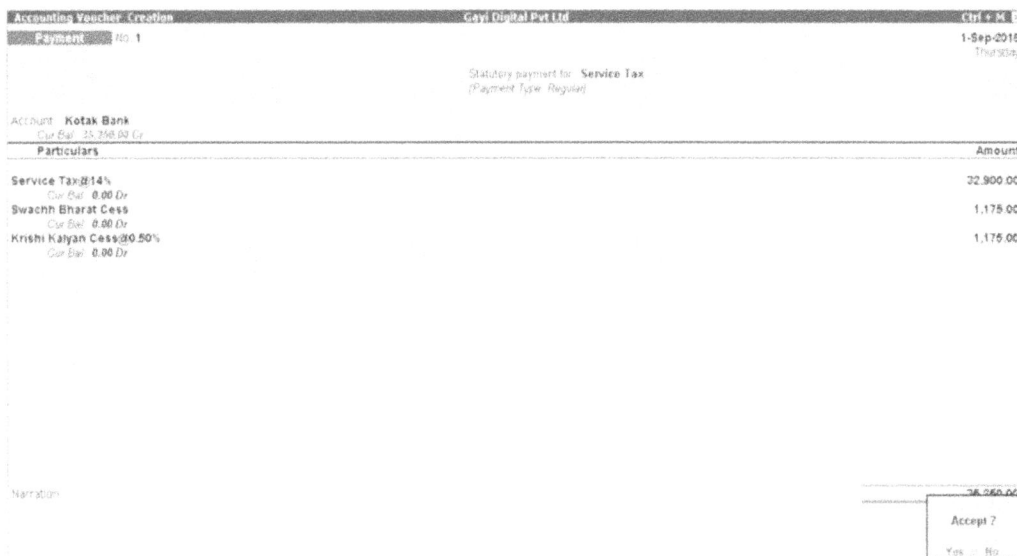

Figure 6.110: The Payment Voucher Creation screen

Note: Check the Service Tax Computation report, the service tax paid amount will be reflected in the field "Service tax payment made for the return period. And the service tax payable report will be nil.

6.13.9 Service Tax Report

According to Service Tax rules, every registered service provider is required to maintain proper books of accounts and record for all input services consumed and output services provided by them during the specified period.

In Tally.ERP 9, the following service tax reports are available:
1. Form ST3
2. Form A-3
3. Return Transaction Book
4. Challan Reconciliation

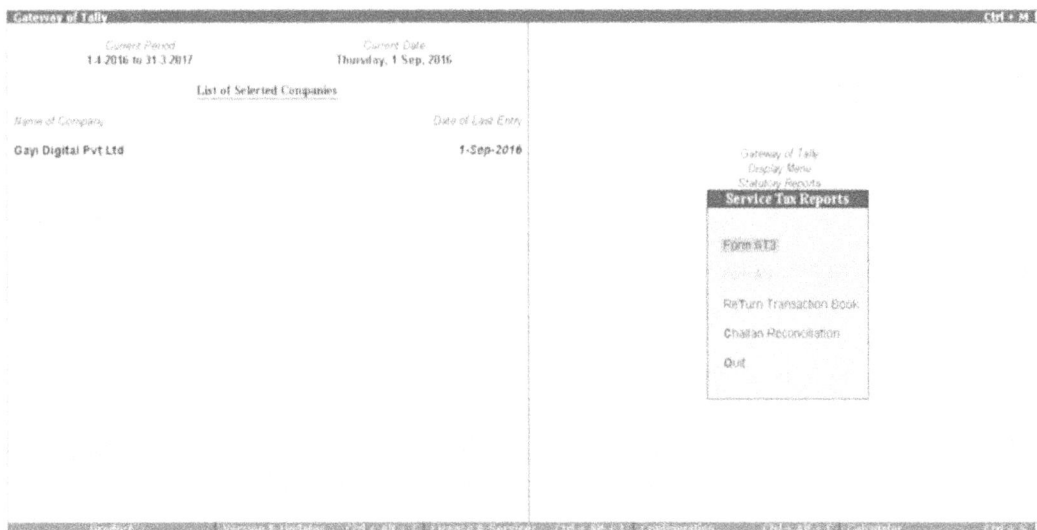

Figure 6.111 Service Tax Reports Menu

1. **Form ST3:** ST-3 form is used to file half-yearly service tax returns to the Commissioner ate of Service Tax. The Form ST3 report in Tally.ERP 9 assists you in generating accurate returns to be filed

2. **Form A-3:** It is a quarterly return to be furnished by SEZ (Special Economic Zones) Unit, it contains the details of the service procured without payment of the Service tax.

Form A-3 is not highlighted because the company doesn't fall under SEZ unit

3. **Return Transaction Book:** It contains the details of the saved returns

4. **Challan Reconciliation:** It contains the details of statutory payment vouchers, from this report we can reconcile the voucher by pressing F5 (Figure 6.111)

GETTING STARTED WITH TAX DEDUCTED AT SOURCE (TDS)

OBJECTIVES

After studying this section, you will be able to understand how to:

* Configure Tax Deducted at Source in Tally.ERP 9
* Record simple TDS transactions
* View TDS reports

6.14   INTRODUCTION

TDS stands for **Tax Deducted at Source**. The concept of TDS was introduced in the Income Tax Act, 1961, with the objective of deducting the tax on an income, at the source of the income. It is one of the methods of collecting Income Tax, which ensures regular flow of revenue to the Government.

6.14.1   Basic concepts of TDS

It is important to understand some of the terminologies & concepts of TDS:

Scope and Applicability

At present, incomes from several sources are subjected to TDS. Some of the incomes which are subject to TDS are:

* Salary
* Interest on securities, debentures
* Deemed Dividend
* Interest other than interest on securities
* Winnings from lottery or crossword puzzles
* Winnings from horse races
* Payment to contractors (Advertisement contractors)
* Payment to contractors (Other than advertisement)
* Payment to sub-contractors
* Payment to non-residents
* Payment to non-resident sportsmen or sports association
* Payment in respect of deposit under NSS
* Payment on account of re-purchase of units by Mutual Fund or UTI
* Payment in respect of units to an offshore fund
* Payment of compensation on acquisition of immovable property
* Insurance commission
* Commission etc., on sale of lottery tickets
* Commission, brokerage etc.
* Rent of land, building or furniture
* Rent of plant, machinery or equipment
* Royalty agreement made on or after June 1, 2005
* Short-term capital gains U/s 111A
* Fees for professional or technical services
* Fees for tech. services agreement made on or after June 1, 2005
* Income in respect of units of non-residents
* Income from foreign currency bonds or shares of Indian company
* Income of foreign institutional investors from securities
* Income from foreign exchange assets payable to an Indian citizen
* Income by way of long term capital gains referred to in Section 115E
* Any other interest on securities
* Interest on 8% Savings (Taxable) Bonds, 2003

What is TAN?

TAN is the Tax deduction Account Number issued by the Income Tax Department to all persons deducting tax at source. TAN has to be quoted in all relevant challans, tax deduction certificates, TDS returns and other notified documents. To obtain TAN, the person or organisation is required to apply in Form 49B to the TAN Facilitation Centres of NSDL.

Who has to deduct the tax?

Any person making the payments to third parties as specified in the scope and applicability section mentioned above are required

To deduct tax at source.

Who is a Deductee?

A Deductee is a third party that provides services and bills to the buyer (deductor) and the buyer will then deduct the tax at source at a prescribed rate, before paying the bill amount.

Deductees may belong to any of the following categories:

* Individual
* Hindu undivided Family (HUF)
* Body of Individual (BOI)
* Association of persons (AOP)
* Co-Operative society
* Local Authority
* Partnership firm
* Domestic Company (Indian company)
* Foreign Company
* Artificial Judicial Person

6.14.2   TDS in Tally.ERP 9

The TDS module in Tally.ERP 9 is integrated with financial accounts and takes care of all the TDS and e-TDS requirements of your business, right from voucher entry to report generation. Tally.ERP 9 completely automates your TDS management - accurately computes tax to be deducted at source & TDS payable amount, and generates TDS payment challans, TDS Certificates, Statutory Returns and other related MIS reports.

Its e-TDS features further assist you to file your mandatory tax returns in electronic format as specified by the Income Tax Department. It helps in minimizing error-prone entry of information, incorrect remittances and also provides accounting for interest & penalties (if any) for smooth and effective functioning of your business.

Features of TDS compliant Tally.ERP 9

Tally.ERP 9 comprises of comprehensive features to ensure accurate and automatic computation of Tax Deductible at Source for non-salaried deductees according to the provisions stipulated in the Income Tax Act.

The TDS functionality in Tally.ERP 9 encompasses the following salient features:

- Simple & user friendly
- Easy & quick to set up and implement
- Maintains complete tracking of each transaction from booking deduction till payment
- Allows deduction of TDS at the time of booking expenses in the same voucher or separately at a later date
- Allows deduction of TDS at lower/zero rate
- Allows deduction of TDS on multiple expenses of single nature of payment type in a single voucher.
- Allows computation of TDS on expenses partly subject to tax
- Allows TDS calculation on advance payments
- Provides facility to compute TDS with/without considering Surcharge Exemption Limits for parties

- Provides retrospective surcharge calculations for prior/current period
- Allows partial/full payment of TDS
- Provides automatic computation of TDS amount for each nature of payment
- Generates TDS payment Challan ITNS 283 (for Corporate & Non-Corporate)
- Generates TDS Certificates, TDS Outstanding report and various other TDS related MIS Reports
- Facilitates automatic generation of quarterly as well as annual e-TDS returns in both physi- cal and eReturns formats
- Provides challan reconciliation facility to keep track of issue of TDS certificates and remit- tance through challans
- Comprises of all required provisions for TDS as specified by Income Tax Department
- Also generates consolidated TDS Certificates, Challan and Annual Returns for statutory and tax audit purpose

6.14.3 Setup

Scenario:

Prathap Trading Co started a business of customer care service center in different locations and different products for which it has to pay the Rent. Since the rent amount crosses the exemption limit, Prathap Trading co as to pay TDS duty on Rent to Government.

Let us create a company for Prathap Trading Co.

The completed Company Creation screen appears as shown below (Figure 6.112):

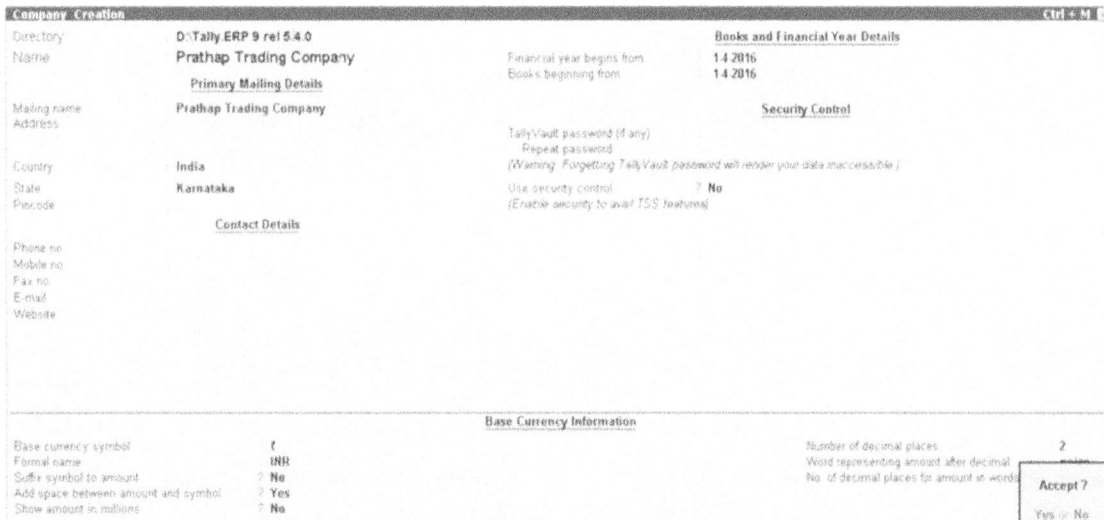

Figure 6.112: Completed Company Creation screen

6.14.3.1 Activation

1. Go to **Gateway of Tally > F11: Features > Statutory and Taxation**
2. In the **Company Operations Alteration** screen, set **Enable Tax Deducted at Source (TDS)** to **Yes**
3. Enable the option **Set/alter TDS details**

The Company Operations Alteration screen appears as shown below (Figure 6.113):

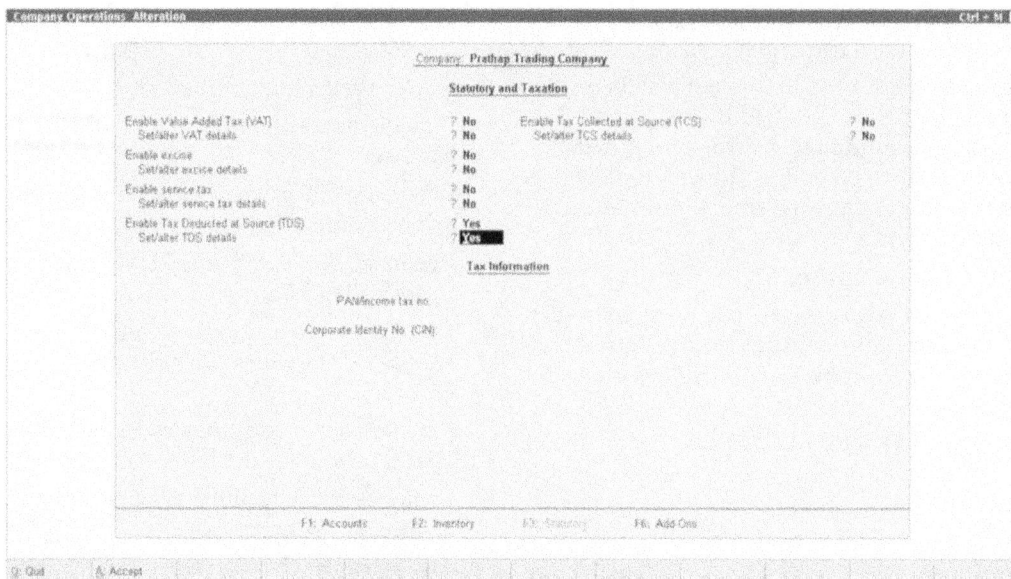

Figure 6.113: Company Operations Alteration screen

- Press Enter.
- Enter the Rate of TDS if PAN not available.
- Enable the option Ignore IT Exemption Limit for TDS

Deduction, if required.

- Enable the option Activate TDS for stock items, if required. The TDS Deductor Details screen appears as shown below (Figure 6.114):

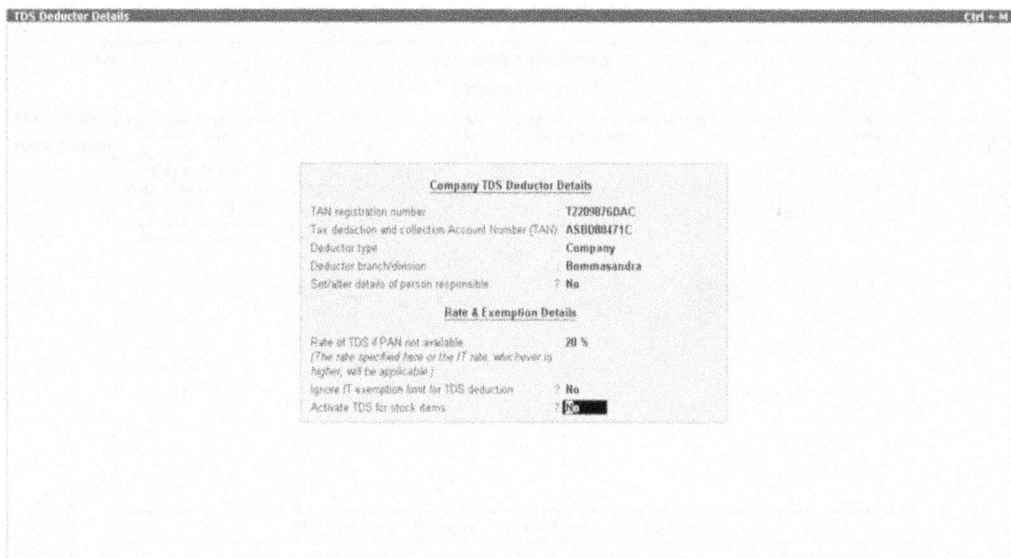

Figure 6.114: TDS Deductor Details screen

- Press **Enter**
- Press **Ctrl + A** to save the details

6.14.4 TDS Statutory Masters

The statutory masters contain details in respect of TDS nature of payments, Deductee Types, rate of TDS for each nature of payment and period of applicability. These TDS nature of payment masters have to be created in Tally.ERP9.

Create TDS Nature of Payment

1. Go to **Gateway of Tally > Accounts Info. > Statutory Info.**

> **TDS Nature of Pymts > Create**
2. Enter the **Name**
3. Enter the **Section number**
4. Enter the **Payment Code**
5. Enter the **Rate of TDS**
6. Enter the **Threshold/exemption limit**

The TDS Nature of Payment Creation screen appears as shown below (Figure 6.115):

Figure 6.115: TDS Nature of Payment Creation screen

Note: To view all the natures of payment and section codes press Ctrl+C

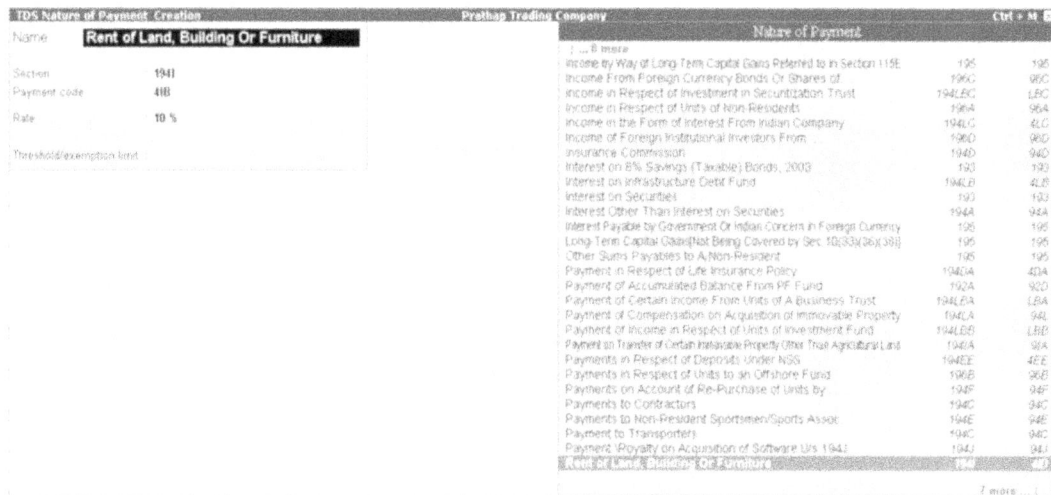

Figure 6.116: displaying complete list of Nature of Payment

4. Press **Enter** to save the details (Figure 6.116)

6.14.5 Illustration: Configuring TDS at Group Level

The illustration below will demonstrate how to account various expenses (rent) of same nature of payment. Prathap Trading Co has various expenses on rent like Rent on Building, Rent on machinery.

On 30-4-2016, Prathap Trading generated the liability for Rent on Building of Rs. 2,00,000. Since the liable amount is exceeding the exemption limit, Prathap Trading company has decided to deduct the TDS on the same bill and pay the remaining to Guru Agencies. Let us account the same in Tally.ERP 9.

Step: I Create Required Accounting Masters Group Ledger

Go to **Gateway of Tally > Accounts Info > Group > Create**

1. Create party ledger – **Guru Agencies**

o   Group under **Sundry Creditors**

o   Maintain balances bill by bill, select as **YES**

o   Default credit period as **Blank**

o   Check for credit days during voucher entry, select as **No**

o   Inventory values are affected, select as **No**

o   Is TDS Deductable, select as **YES**

o   Deductee Type select **Company-Resident**

o   Deduct TDS in Same Voucher, Set to **Yes**

o   Provide PAN Set to YES and

o   Select Available

o   Accept the screen

2. Create Group Rent Expense as **Rent Expenses**

o   Group under **Indirect Expenses**

o   Keep all the option as it is and follow next steps

o   Set/Alter TDS Details, Set to **Yes**

o   Nature of Payment, Select **Rent of Land, building or Furniture** (Figure 6.117)

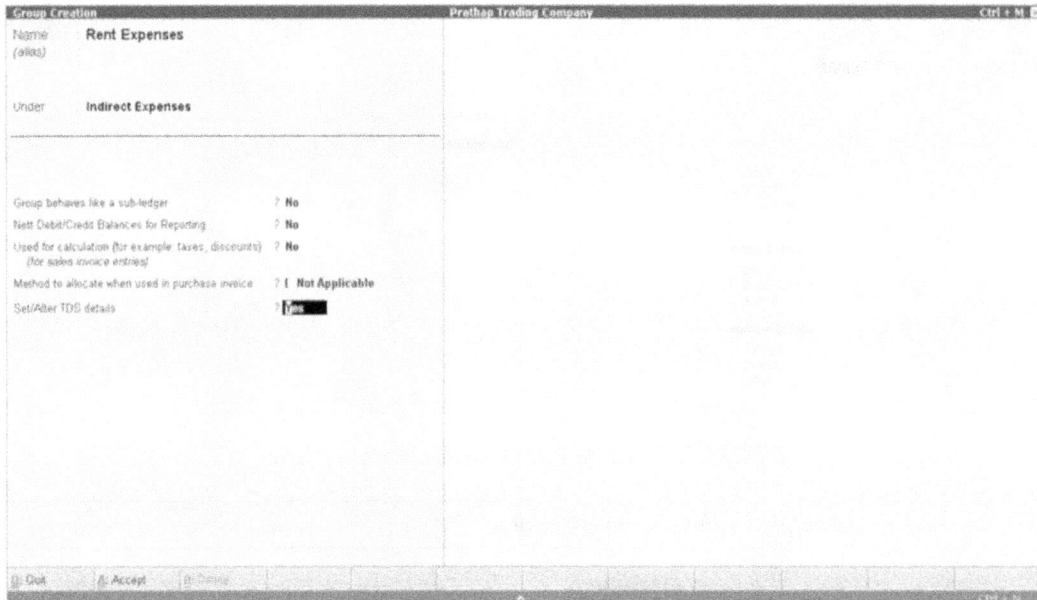

Figure 6.117: Group Creation

3.   Create Ledger as **Rent on Building**

o   Group under **Rent Expenses**

o   Inventory values are affected, select as **No**

o   Is TDS is Applicable, Select **Applicable**

o   Nature of Payment as **Undefined** (Figure 6.118)

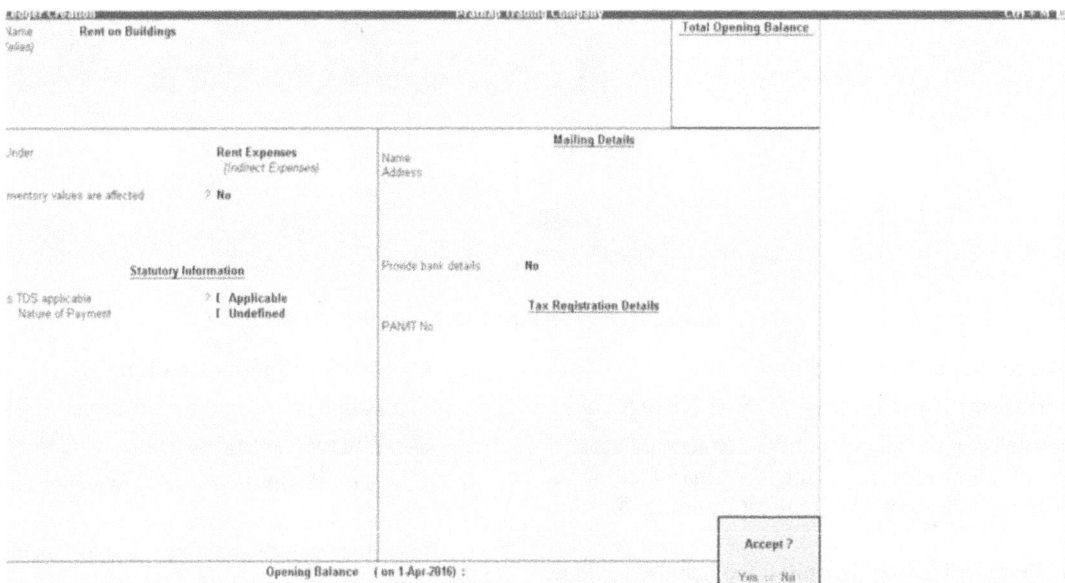

Figure 6.118: Completed Ledger Creation screen

Activity:

Create Rent on Machinery following Rent on Machinery

Create Tax/Duty Ledger as **TDS Duty on Rent**

1.   Go to **Gateway of Tally > Accounts Info. > Ledgers > Create**

2.   Type **TDS duty on Rent** in the **Name** field

3.   Select **Duties & Taxes** group in the **Under** field

4.   Select **TDS** from the list in the **Type of Duty/Tax** field

5.   Select **Rent of Land, Building Or Furniture** from the list, in the **Nature of Payment** Field as shown below (Figure 6.119):

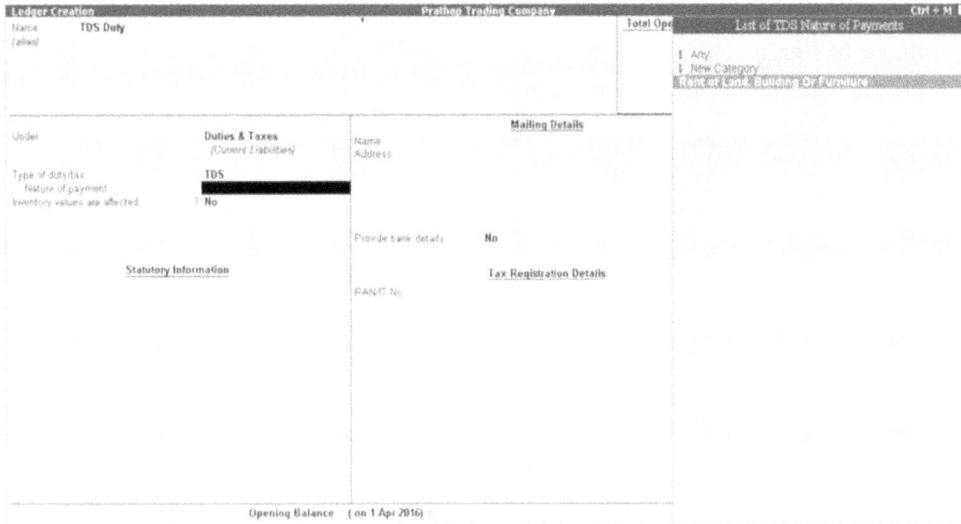

Figure 6.119: Ledger Alteration screen

6. Set **No** in the **Inventory values are affected** field

7. Press **Enter** to accept

6.14.5.1 Recording Transactions

As discussed earlier, tax deducted at source on incomes specified by Income Tax department is affected at source when income arises/accrues or paid whichever is earlier.

The applicable income tax rates for payment of **'Rent of Land Building Or Furniture'** to **'Company Resident Deductee'** Type is given below:

Particulars	Rate
TDS	10%
Surcharge	-
Education Cess	-
Secondary Education Cess	-

Step 1: Create Journal Voucher to book the expenses and deduct TDS

1. Go to **Gateway of Tally > Accounting Voucher > F7: Journal**

2. Click **F2: Date** to change the date to **30-4-2016**

3. Debit the **Rent on Building** expense ledger

4. Enter Rs. **2,00,000** in the amount field

5. Credit **Guru agencies**. The amount after TDS deduction will appear in the **Amount** field automatically

6. Press **Enter**

7. Enter the **Bill-wise Details**, as required

8. Press **Enter**

9. Credit the TDS tax ledger. The TDS amount will automatically get filled in the **Amount** field

10. Press **Enter**

11. Enter **Narration**, if required

The **Journal** voucher appears as shown below (Figure 6.120):

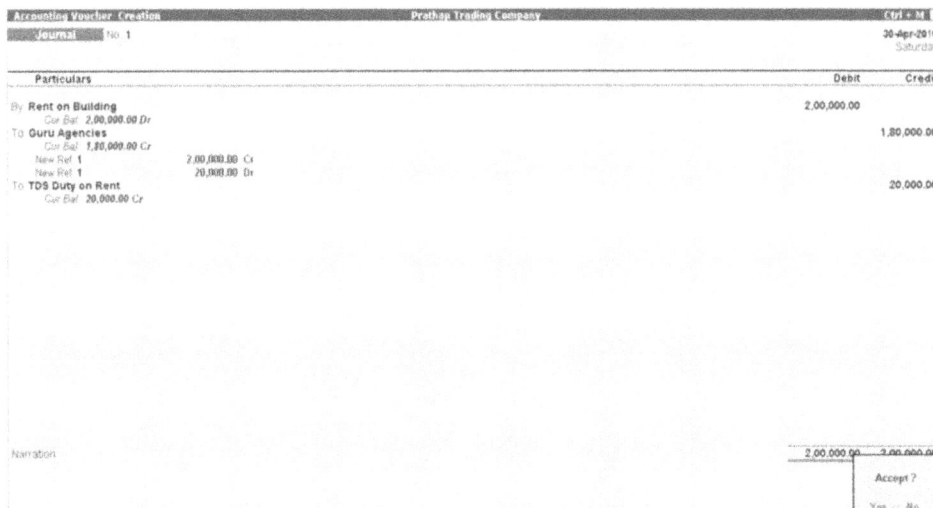

Figure 6.120: Journal Voucher screen

12. Press **Ctrl + A** to save the voucher

Step 2: Making Payment to Party

1. Create a bank ledger as Kotak Bank under Bank Accounts.

2. Go to **Gateway of Tally > Accounting Voucher > F5: Payment**

3. Make the payment entry as per the screen shown below (Figure 6.121):

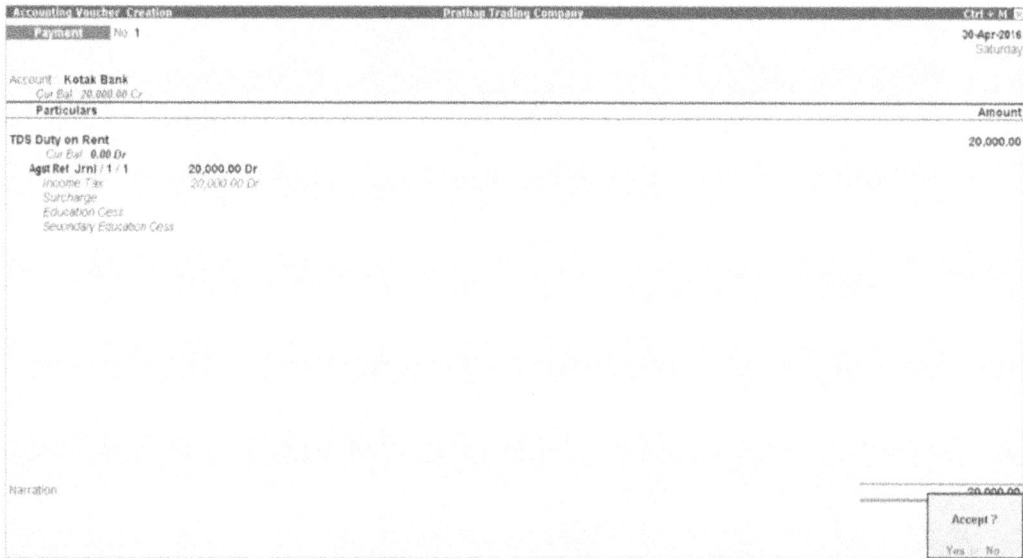

Figure 6.121: Payment Voucher screen

Activity

On 30-4-2016, PrathapTrading Co has booked rent expenses on Machinery. Since the **Rent on Machinery** expenses is of Rs. 190000 it has to deduct the TDS and needs to make the payment to Guru **Agencies**. Account the same in Tally.ERP 9.

6.14.6 Illustration: Configuring TDS at Ledger level

If there is a single expense pertaining to any particular Nature of Payment, e.g. Commission expenses, it is advisable to maintain the TDS detail at the ledger level itself.

The illustration below will demonstrate how to configure TDS in the ledger for a single expense pertaining to a particular Nature of Payment.

On 30-04-2016, **Prathap Trading Co** has incurred a commission expenses of Rs. 1,20,000 for the service taken from **Ravi Consultancy**.

Step 1: To Create TDS Nature of Payment

1. Go to **Gateway of Tally > Accounts Info. > Statutory Info. > TDS Nature of Pymts > Create**

2. Enter the **Name**

3. Enter the **Section** number

4. Enter the **Payment Code**

5. Enter the **Rate** of TDS

6. Enter the **Threshold/exemption limit**.

The **TDS Nature of Payment Creation** screen appears as shown below (Figure 6.122):

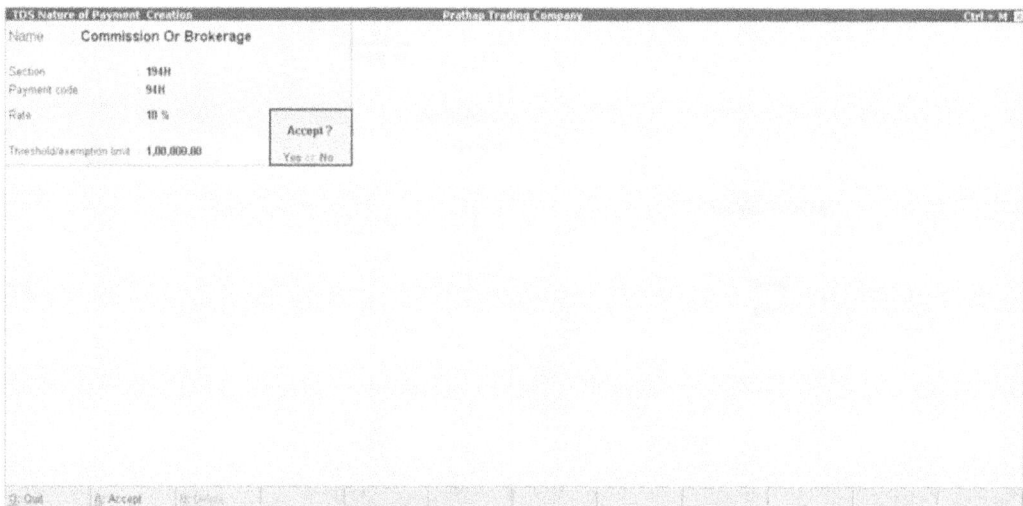

Figure 6.122: TDS Nature of Payment Creation screen

7. Press **Enter** to save the details

Step 2: Create Required Masters Expense Ledger

1. Go to **Gateway of Tally > Accounts Info. > Ledgers > Create**
2. Enter the Name **Commission**
3. Select **Indirect Expenses** as the group name in the **Under** field

4. Set **Inventory values are affected** to **No**
5. Set the option **Is TDS Applicable** to **Applicable**
6. Select the **Nature of Payment** from the **List of Nature of Payments**

The **Ledger Creation** screen appears as shown below (Figure 6.123):

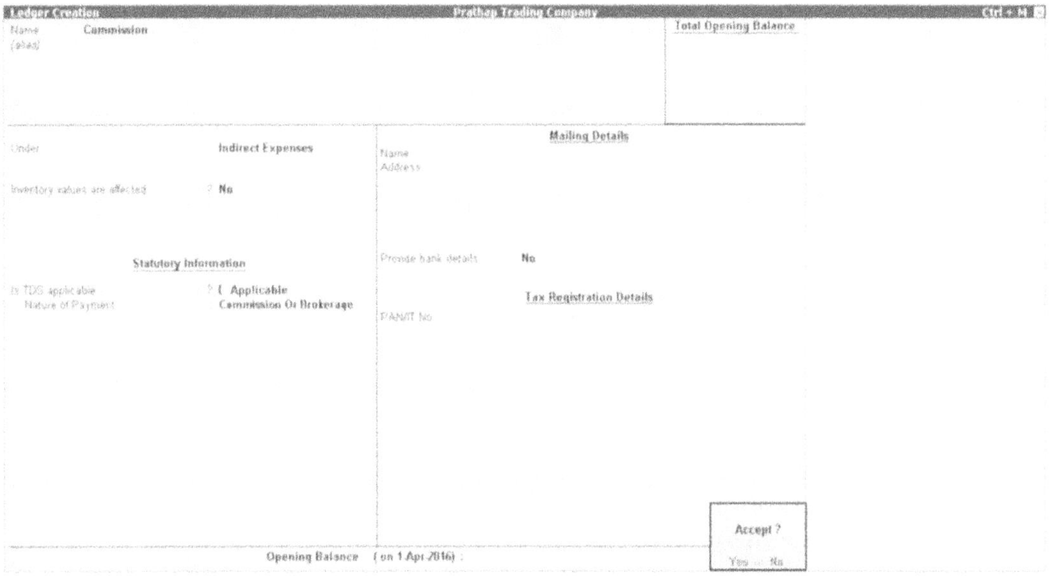

Figure 6.123: Ledger creation screen (Expense Ledger)

Party Ledger

Go to **Gateway of Tally > Accounts Info > Ledgers > Create**

1. Create party ledger –**Ravi Consultancy**
   - Group under **Sundry Creditors**
   - Maintain balances bill by bill, select as **YES**
   - Default credit period as **Blank**
   - Inventory values are affected, select as **No**
   - Is TDS Deductable, select as **YES**
   - Deductee Type select **Company-Resident**
   - Deduct TDS in Same Voucher, Set to **Yes**
   - Provide PAN Set to YES and
   - Update the PAN no as XYZPQ1234K
   - Accept the screen (Figure 6.124)

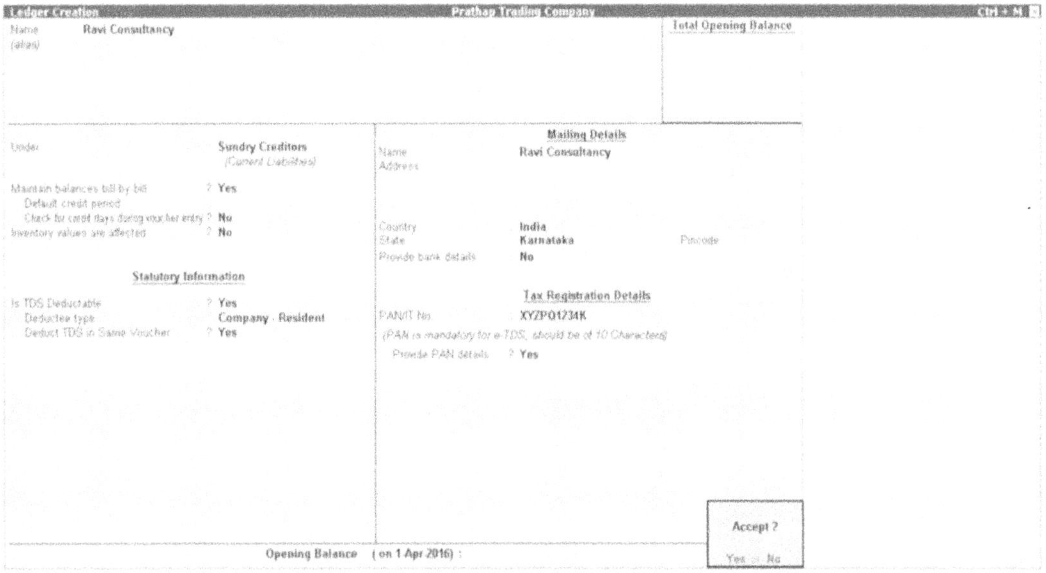

Figure 6.124: Ledger creation screen (Party Ledger)

TDS Ledger

1. Go to **Gateway of Tally > Accounts Info. > Ledgers > Create**
2. Type **TDS duty on Commission** in the **Name** field

3. Select **Duties & Taxes** group in the **Under** field
4. Select **TDS** from the list in the **Type of Duty/Tax** field
5. Select **Commission & Brokerage** from the list, in the **Nature of Payment** Field, as shown below (Figure 6.125):

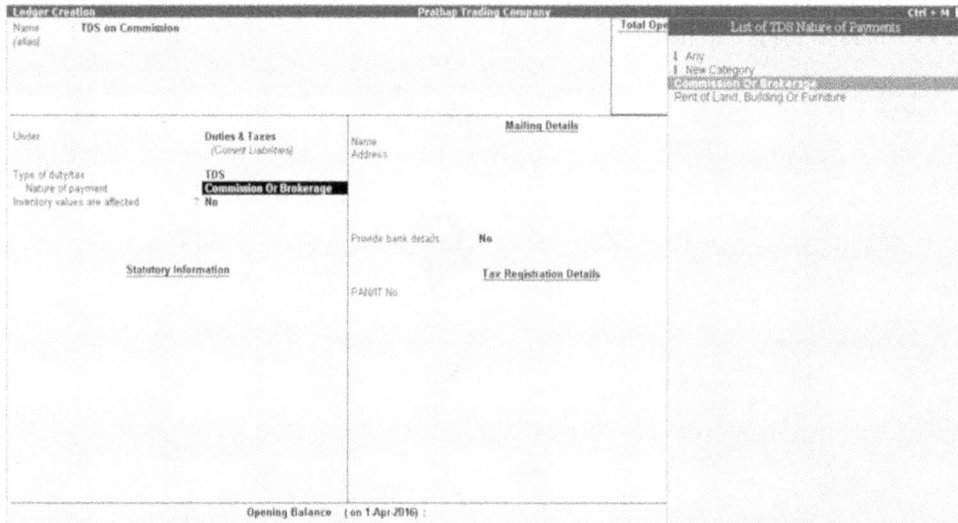

Figure 6.125: Ledger Creation screen

6. Set **No** in the **Inventory values are affected** field
7. Press **Enter** to accept

The applicable income tax rates for payment of 'Commission & Brokerage to 'Company Resident Deductee' Type is given below:

Particulars	Rate
TDS	10%
Surcharge	-
Education Cess	-
Secondary Education Cess	-

Step 2: Create Journal Voucher to book the expenses and deduct TDS

1. Go to **Gateway of Tally > Accounting Voucher > F7: Journal**

2. Click **F2: Date** to change the date to **30-4-2016**
3. Debit the **Commission** expense ledger
4. Enter Rs. 1,**20,000** in the amount field
5. Credit **Ravi Consultancy**. The amount after TDS deduction will appear in the **Amount** field automatically
6. Press **Enter**
7. Enter the **Bill-wise Details**, as required
8. Press **Enter**
9. Credit the TDS tax ledger. The TDS amount will get filled automatically in the **Amount** field
10. Press **Enter**
11. Enter **Narration**, if required

The **Journal** voucher appears as shown below (Figure 6.126):

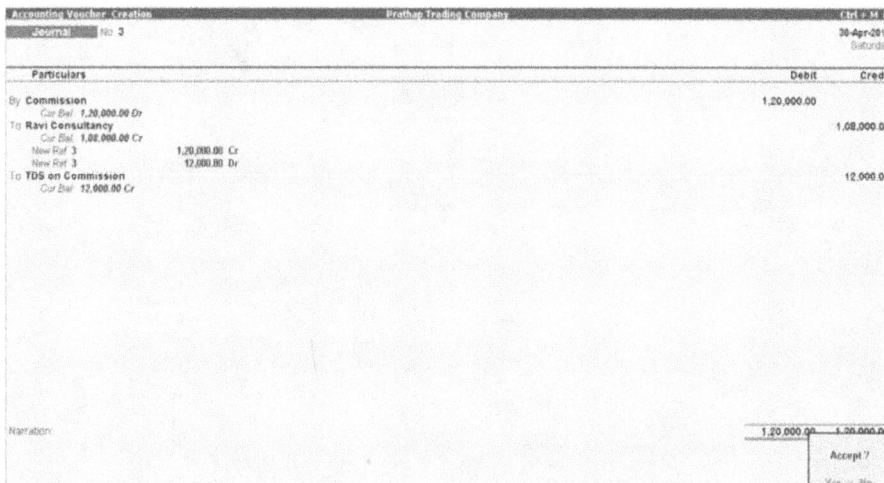

Figure 6.126: Journal Voucher Creation screen

Press **Ctrl + A** to save the voucher.

6.14.7 Making Payment to Government

On 10-5-2016, Global Trading Co paid the deducted TDS amount in the month of May. i.e., of Rent of Land, Building or Furniture and Commission & Brokerage.

Record a payment transaction for Rent of Land, Building or Furniture:

1. Go to **Gateway of Tally > Accounting Vouchers > F5: Payment**

2. Click **S: Stat Payment** button

3. Select **TDS** as the **Tax Type**

4. Enter the **Period From** and **To** dates

5. Enter the **Deducted Till Date**

6. Select the **Section** from the **List of Section**

7. Select the required **Nature of Payment**

8. Select the **Deductee Status**

9. Select the **Residential Status**

10. Select either bank or cash ledger in the **Cash/Bank** field. The payment voucher will be automatically filled with the Relevant values

The **Statutory Payment** Details screen appears as shown below (Figure 6.127):

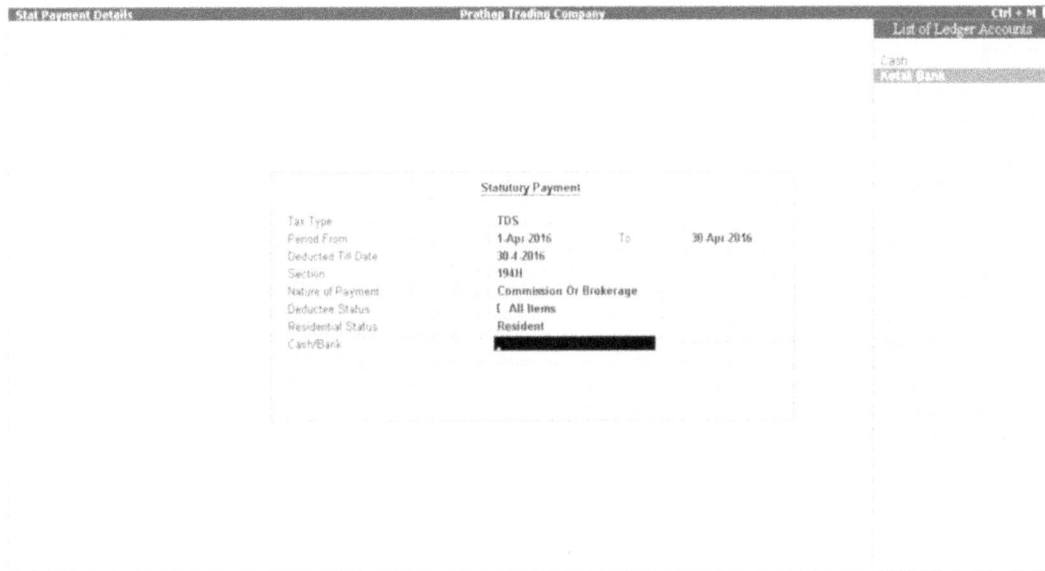

Figure 6.127: Statutory Payment Details

11. Press **Enter**

12. Enter the **Bank Allocation details** as required

13. Enter **Narration**, if required

The Payment voucher appears as shown below (Figure 6.128):

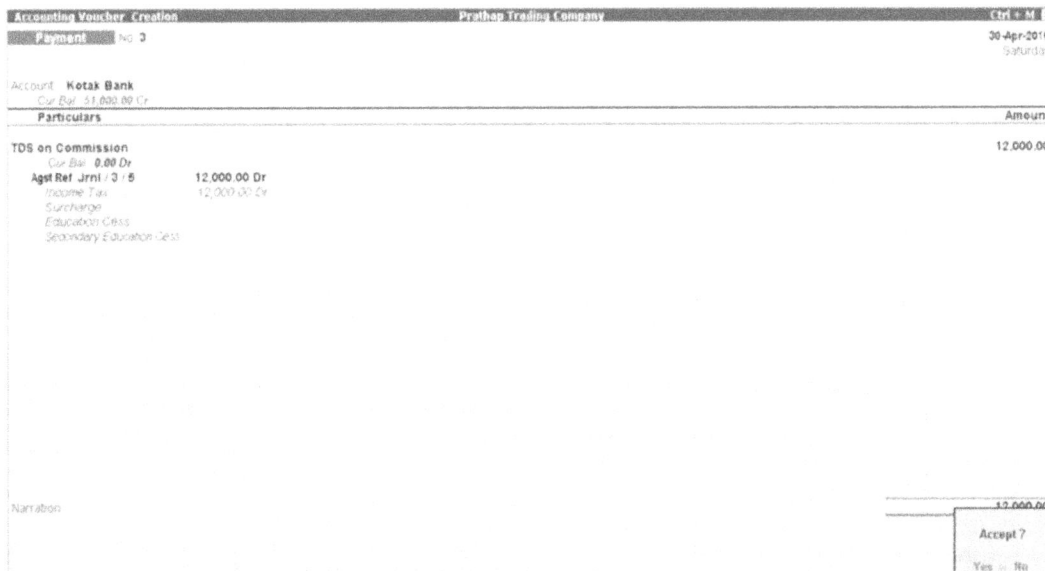

Figure 6.128: Payment Voucher Creation screen

14. Press **Ctrl + A** to save the voucher

To take the ITNS 281 Challan printout (Figure 6.129):

Open the Payment made to Government > Press Alt+P > Enter (Figure 6.130).

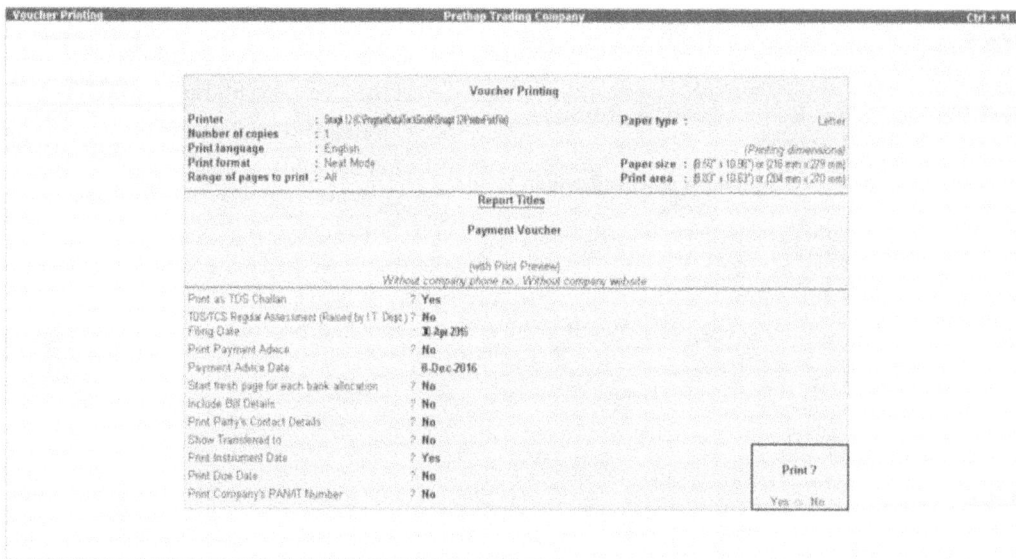

Figure 6.129: Printing ITNS Challan

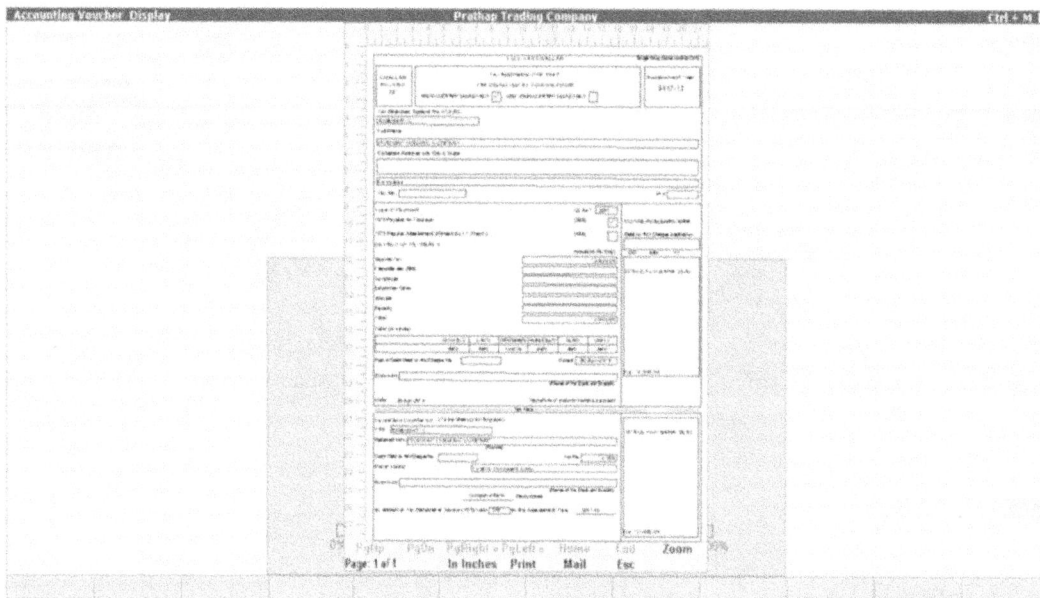

Figure 6.130: Print Preview of ITNS challan

Note: Since the nature of payment is configured in Group level, it is not required to configure in the ledger level.

Activity: Record a payment transaction for Commission and Brokerage and generate the Challan.

6.14.8 TDS Reports

As per the Income Tax Act, 1961, every corporate and government entity responsible for deduction of tax at source should furnish TDS returns containing details of deductee(s) and challan details relating to deposit of tax with the Income Tax Department. Form 26Q is the Quarterly return of TDS in respect of all payments other than salaries. This is applicable for Resident and the due date for Government entities is July 31st, October 31st, January 31st and May 15th; for non-government entities the due dates for filing returns are July 15th, October 15th, January 15th and May 15th.

The Form 26Q report in Tally.ERP 9 assists you in generating accurate the returns to be filed.

To Generate Form 26Q:

1. Go to **Gateway of Tally > Display > Reports > Statutory Reports > TDS Reports > Form 26Q**

2. Click **F1: Condensed** (Figure 6.131)

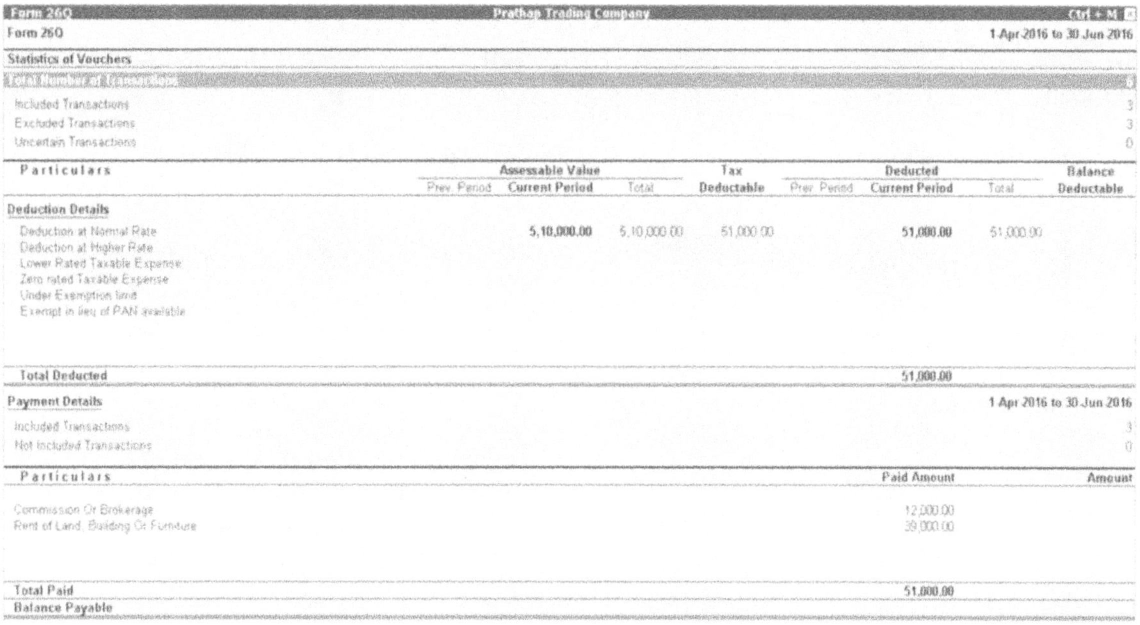

Figure 6.131: Form 26Q

The Form 26Q report has the following sections:

Statistics of Vouchers

All transactions, whether recorded correctly, incorrectly, or inadequately will be captured and categorized in the Form 26Q report as follows:

Included

These are transactions that will be a part of Form 26Q. Transactions that will be considered as Included for generating Form 26Q are:

* Booking entries, with or without TDS deduction
* TDS deduction entries
* Advance payments made to parties
* TDS adjustment entries (in the case of government entities)
* Entries accounting for TDS reversals and TDS deduction with respect to escalations and de-escalations

Excluded

These are transactions that do not carry the TDS details that are requisite to generate Form 26Q, and hence will be excluded while generating the form. Transactions that will be considered as Excluded for generating Form 26Q:

* All entries where TDS is not applied
* Entries recorded using any of the following Voucher Types:
  o Payment
  o Contra
  o Inventory Vouchers
  o Sales Order
  o Purchase Order
  o Debit Note (recorded for purchases with no TDS implications)
  o Credit Note (entries with no TDS implications)
  o Vouchers marked as Optional
  o Payroll Vouchers

Uncertain Vouchers

These are transactions that do not fulfill the criteria of the Included and Excluded categories. A voucher will be listed as Uncertain when there is insufficient information entered in:

* Masters
* Transactions

Deduction Details

This section denotes the type of deduction under which each of the Included transaction is grouped.

* Deduction details are classified into:
* Deduction at Normal Rate
* Deduction at Higher Rate
* Lower Rated Taxable Expense
* Zero Rated Taxable Expense
* Under Exemption Limit
* Exempt in lieu of PAN Available

The assessable value, tax deductible, and the tax deducted for transactions grouped in the above categories are displayed here.

Payment Details

This will contain the statistics of all TDS payments (deemed or actual) that exist in the data till date. This will not contain any of the payment entries that are not related to the current period. Any payment entries other that TDS payment entry will not appear here.

The section will display the payments against two fields:

* Included Transactions
* Not Included Transactions

ADVANCED FEATURES OF TALLY.ERP 9

OBJECTIVES

After studying this section, you will understand:

♦ E-mailing capabilities in Tally.ERP 9

♦ How to send reports, invoices etc., by e-mail in Tally.ERP 9

♦ How to Export and import data in Tally.ERP 9

6.15 E-MAILING IN TALLY.ERP 9

Using the e-mail facility provided in Tally.ERP 9, you can e-mail reports like outstanding statements and documents such as invoices, purchase orders, reminder letters to customers.

6.15.1 E-mailing a Report

To e-mail a report,

1. Go to **Gateway of Tally > Display > Statement of Accounts > Outstanding > Ledger** (or any report)

2. Select the required ledger

3. Click **M: E-Mail** or press **ALT+M**

4. Specify the required configurations and details such as the e-mail IDs of the sender and the recipient. Tally.ERP 9 also allows sending it to multiple email addresses

   To specify only one e-mail address in the **To** field, select one of the e-mail addresses that appears by default (e-mail addresses specified in the ledger master) or select **New Address** option and specify the new e-mail address

   To specify more than one e-mail address in the **To** field, select the option **Multiple Address** (Figure 6.132)

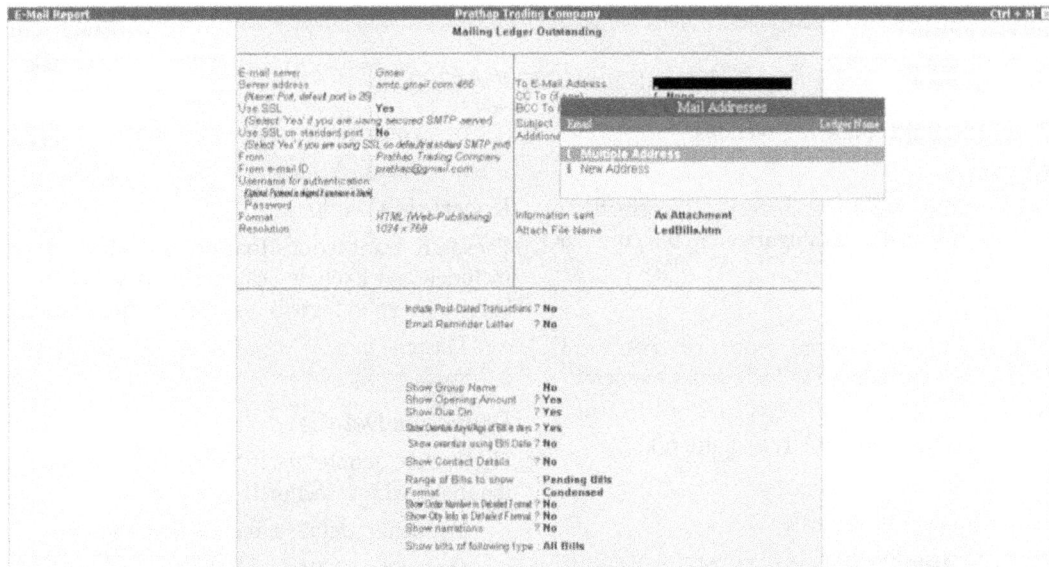

Figure 6.132: E-mail Report

5. On selecting **Multiple Address**, the **Multiple E-mail Ids Selection** screen appears

   In the **Multiple E-mail Ids Selection** screen,

   o Select **New Address** to add an e-mail address that is not displayed in the list or select other e-mail addresses that are displayed by default

   o The completed **Multiple E-mail Ids Selection** screen appears as shown below:

   o Press **Enter** to accept and navigate back to the **E-Mail Report** screen

6. Specify an e-mail address or multiple e-mail addresses in the **CC or BCC To (if Any)** field to send a copy of the same mail to other recipients

7. By default, the **Subject** line is pre-filled with the respective line for each report. Alter the message, if required. In the

   Additional Text (if any) field, type a message to the recipient which will precede the report in the mail, if required

8. In the **Information Sent** field, select the required **Mail Sending** type i.e., as an attachment or direct view in mail (Applicable only for HTML format)

9. In the **Attach File Name** field, the report name is displayed by default. Alter the attachment name, if required

10. Set **Include Post-Dated Transactions?** to **Yes** to include post-dated transactions

11. Set **E-mail reminder letter to?** to **Yes** to e-mail reminder letter to the customers

12. By default, **Show Group Name** is set to **No**. Enable this option to mail the parent group name of the respective ledger (Figure 6.133)

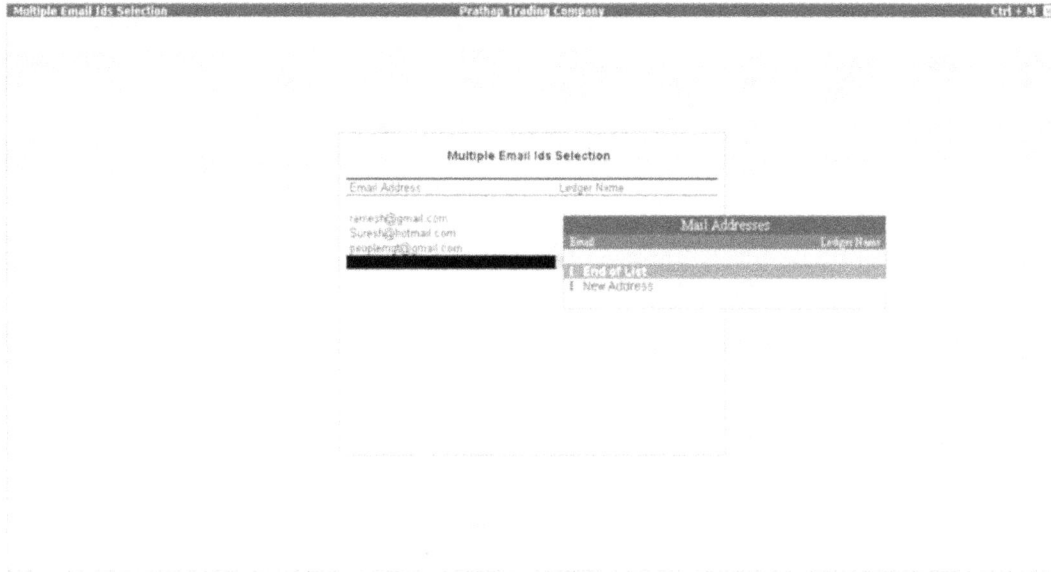

Figure 6.133: Multiple Email Ids Selection screen

13. Set **Show Opening amount?** to **Yes** in order to give the details of opening amount of the ledger

14. Set **Show Due on** to **yes** to mail the details of due on date

15. Set **Show overdue using Bill Date?** option to **Yes** to mail the ageing days based on bill date

    For example: If the **Bill date** is **01-04-2013** and **Due date** is on **01-05-2013**, and the option **'Show overdue using Bill Date'** is set to **Yes**, then the **'Age of Bill in Days'** will be calculated from the **Bill date** and not from the **Due date**

16. Set the option **Show Contact Details** to **Yes** to mail the ledger contact details as mentioned in the ledger master

17. In the **Range of Bills to show** field, select **All Bills** or **Overdue Bills** or **Pending Bills** to mail only those bills

18. In the **Format** field, select the required option to mail the report in **Condensed** or **Detailed format**.

19. Set **Show order number in detail format? To yes** in order to get the details of order number.

20. Set **Show Qty Info in Detailed Format?** to **Yes** or **No** based on requirement. If it is set to **Yes**, a complete break-up of quantity details will be sent in the mail. This option can be set to **Yes** only if the **Format** is set to **Detailed mode**

21. In the **Show bills of the following type** field, select the required **Types of Bills** to be mailed i.e. Credit, Debit or both

    The **Mailing Ledger Outstanding** screen appears as shown below (Figure 6.134):

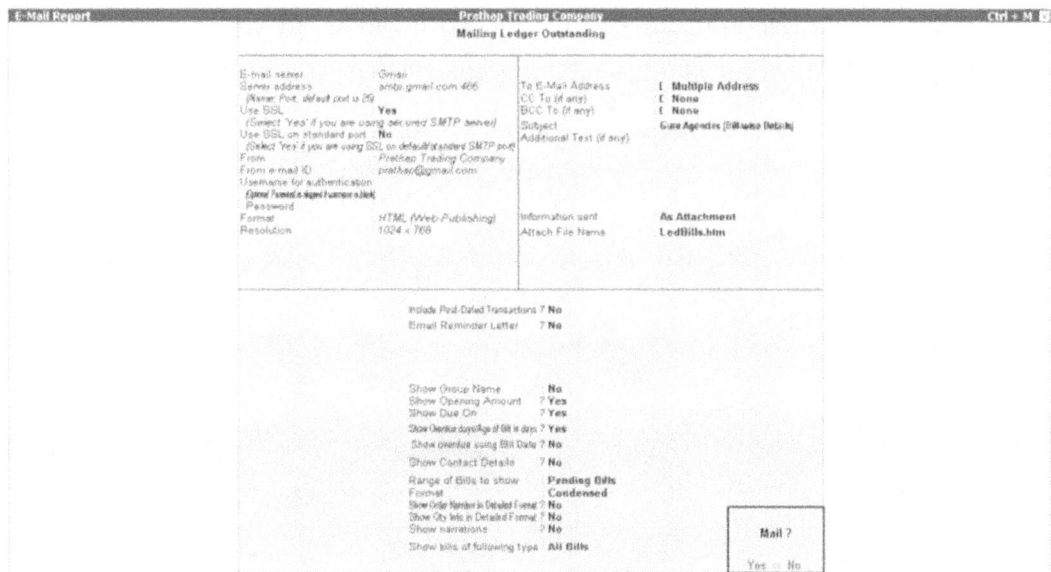

Figure 6.134: Mailing Ledger Outstanding

22. Accept the screen to mail the ledger account details to the client

Note: Tally.ERP 9 contains pre-defined server address for 3 email servers namely. Gmail, Yahoo and Hotmail. Select user defined to enter the same for any other service provider

The options shown in the bottom part of e-mailing screen belong to the report being e-mailed and hence vary accordingly.

6.15.2 Benefits

* The need for an external e-mailing software for mailing reports generated using Tally.ERP 9, is eliminated
* A convenient and time saving option to disburse information and reportsTM

6.15.3 Export and Import of Data

Tally.ERP 9 allows import and export of data in different formats for e.g., ASCII, Excel, HTML, JPEG, PDF, and XML.

Exporting the data in XML format:

XML Format is used to export and import the data from one company to another which is maintained in Tally.

6.15.4 Exporting Data

To understand exporting of reports, consider the example of List of Ledgers

1. Go to **Gateway of Tally > Display > List of Accounts**
2. Press **ALT+E** or click **E: Export**
3. Select the **Language**, **Format**, and **Export** Location as shown below (Figure 6.135):

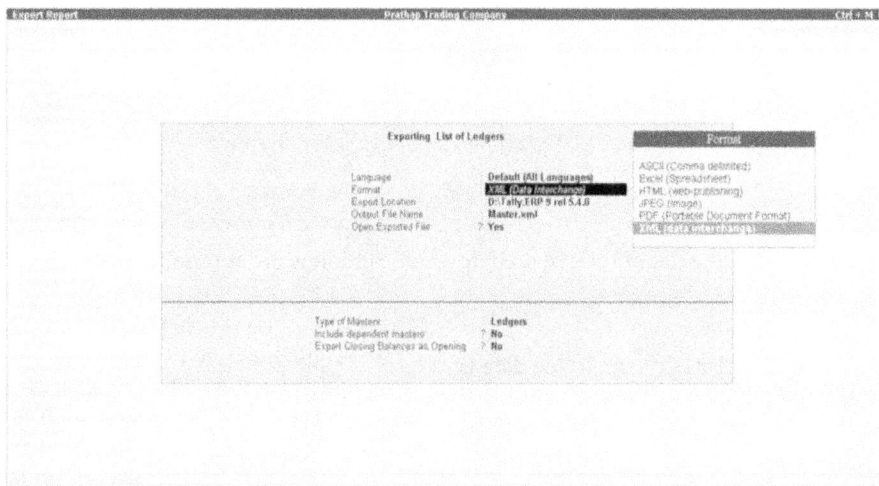

Figure 6.135: Export Report screen

4. Based on the Format selected, the file name will be created. For example, Master.xml
5. Select the **Type of Masters** as **Ledgers** to export
6. Set the option **Export Closing Balances as Opening** to **Yes** if it is required to take closing balances of all theledgers as

opening balances for the next financial year. Otherwise, set it to **No**

The **Export Report** screen appears as shown below:

7. Accept the screen (Figure 6.136)

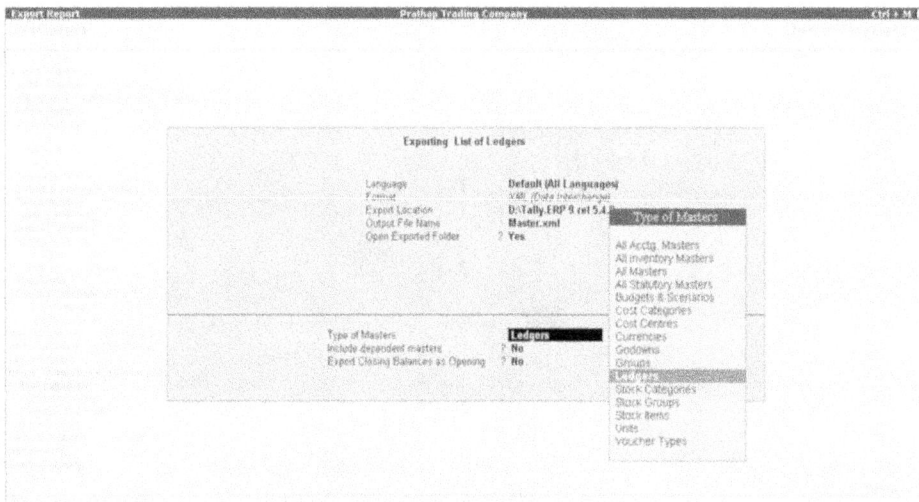

Figure 6.136: Exporting List of Ledgers

6.15.5 Importing Data

8. Go to **Gateway of Tally > Import of Data > Select Masters** (Figure 6.137)

9. Enter the path of the file with its name and extension in

Import File Name (XML)

10. Select the required **Behaviour** for the **Treatment of entries already existing**

The **Import of Data** screen appears as shown below (Figure 6.138):

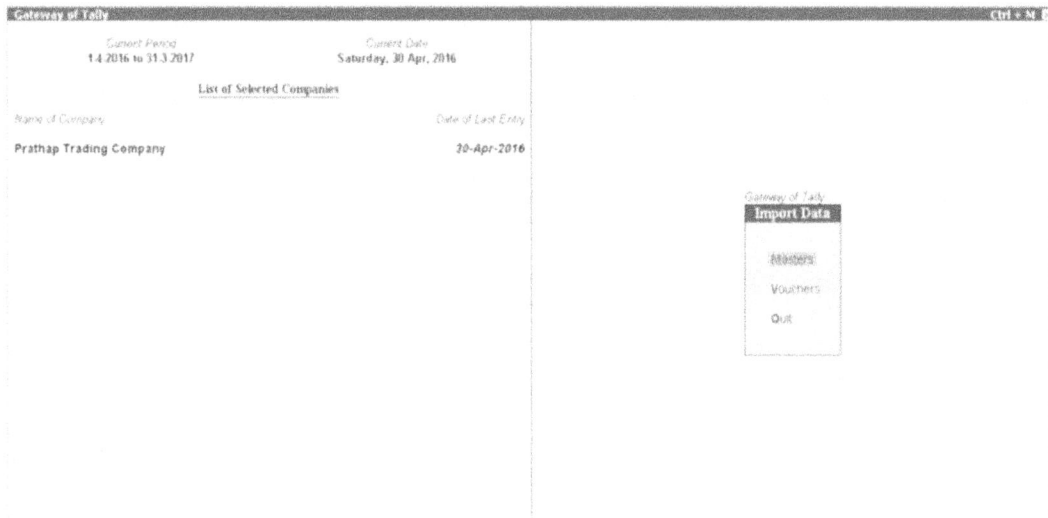

Figure 6.137: Import of Data Menu

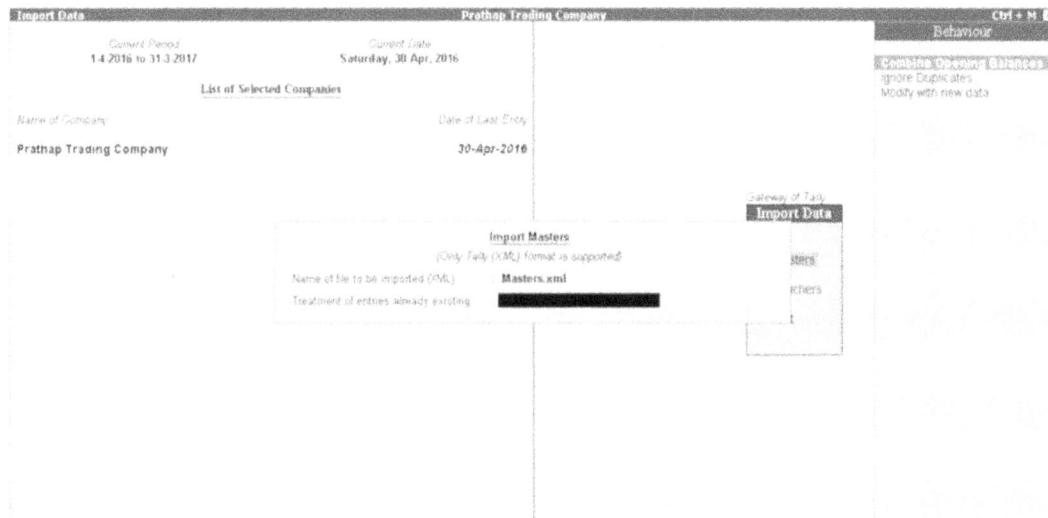

Figure 6.138: Import of Data

6.15.6 Benefits

♦ Exporting company data helps in transfer of data to another location in a secure manner

♦ Data can be transferred to other applications

♦ No additional steps are required when migrating data from an older version of Tally to a newer one

Activity: Export the transactions from one company to another.

6.16 E-FILING RETURNS

6.16.1 VAT Returns

E-VAT Annexures

Tally.ERP 9 facilitates the generation of files for the online submission of VAT Annexures. To obtain the E-VAT Annexures, Load any company.

Go to **Gateway of Tally > Display > Statutory Reports > VAT > VAT Form 100** (Figure 6.139)

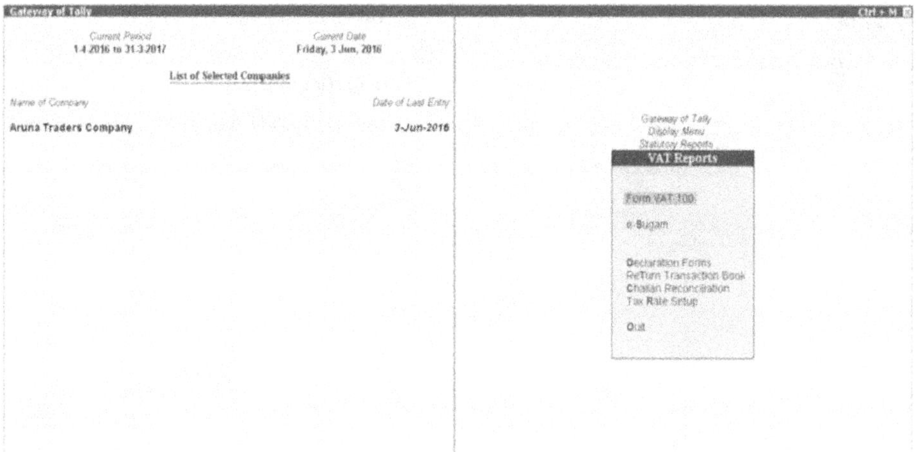

Figure 6.139 Vat Report Menu

Then enter on VAT Form 100 (Figure 6.140)

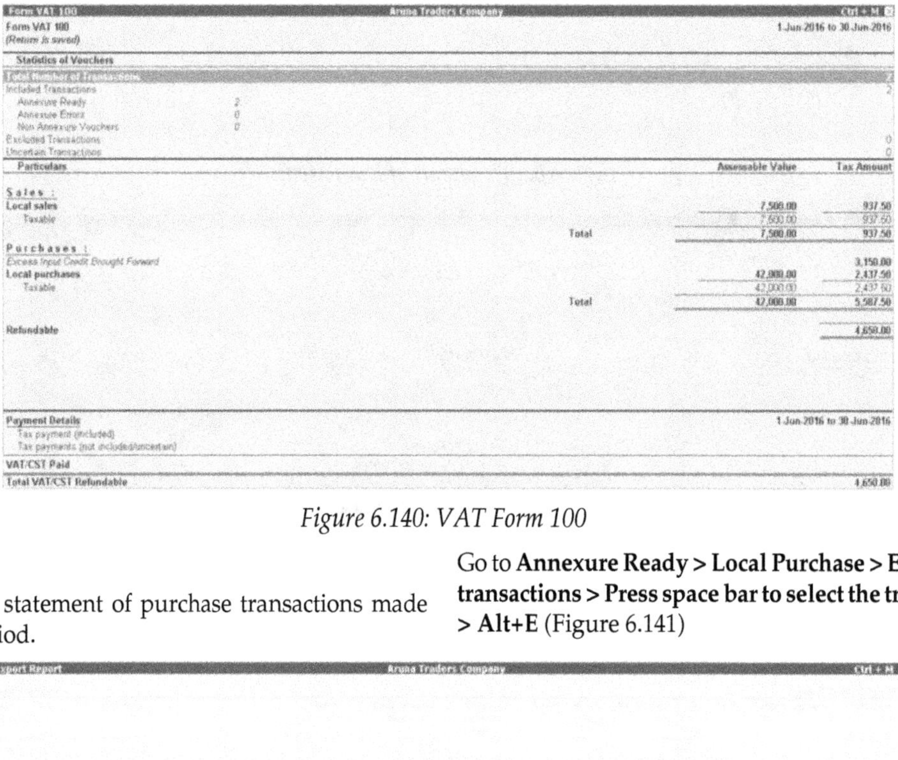

Figure 6.140: VAT Form 100

E-VAT Purchase

This is essentially a statement of purchase transactions made for the specified period.

Go to **Annexure Ready > Local Purchase > Enter to get purchase transactions > Press space bar to select the transaction to upload > Alt+E** (Figure 6.141)

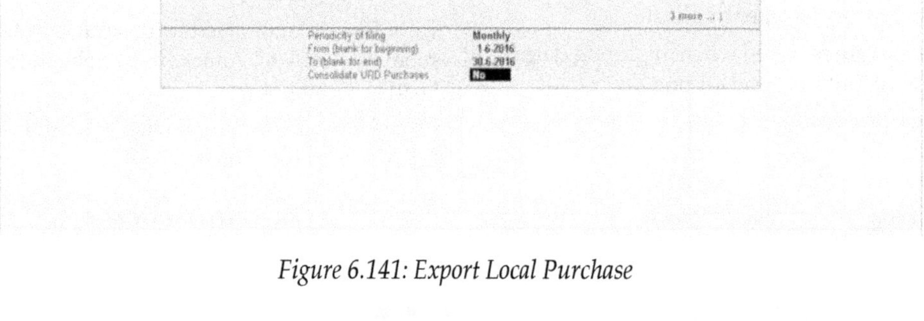

Figure 6.141: Export Local Purchase

E-VAT Sales

This is essentially a statement of sales transactions made for the specified period

Go to **Annexure Ready > Local Sales > Enter to get sales transactions > Press space bar to select the transaction to upload > Alt+E** (Figure 6.142)

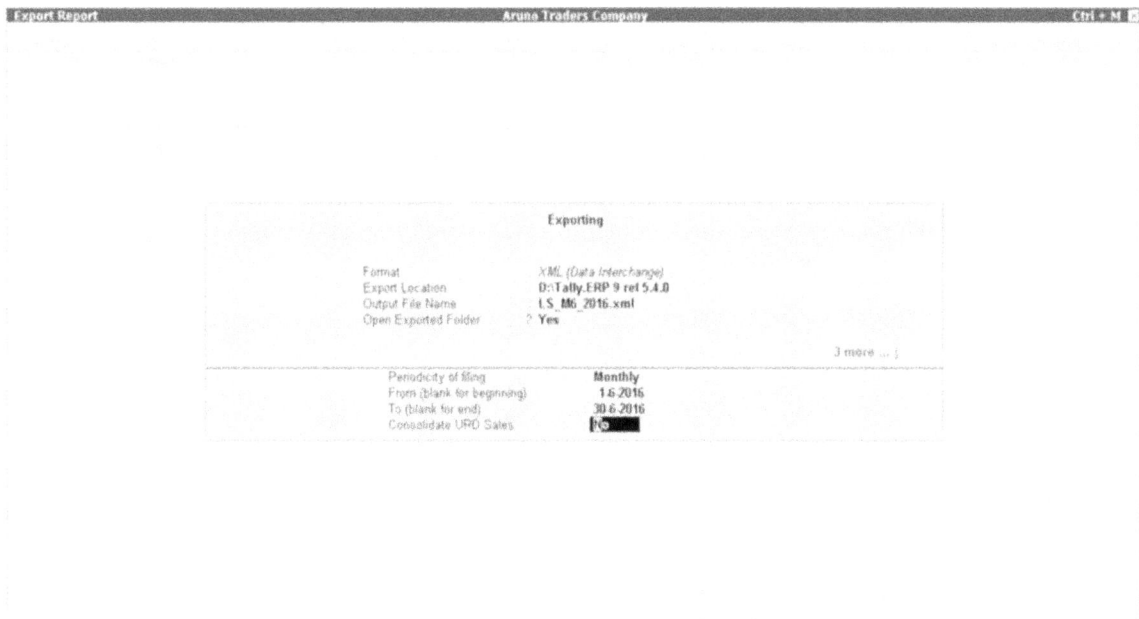

Figure 6.142: Export Local Sales

6.16.2 Service Tax Returns

How to generate Form ST3 from Tally.ERP 9 and e-File the Return

Starting 1st October 2011, government had made it mandatory to file ST3 electronically. So, every service tax assessee needs to electronically file their half yearly return regardless of the Service Tax paid.

A template in MS Excel format is provided by CBEC (Central Board of Excise and Customs) and using this, assessee can manually enter the required values and generate XML format. This XML format can be uploaded in ACES website.

Tally.ERP 9 has provided an easy-to-use option to enable users to fill the details in the Excel file using ST3 E-filing option.

Step 1: Rectify the Uncertain transactions.

* Go to **Gateway of Tally > Display > Statutory Report > Service tax reports > Form ST3 Report** ? Mention the period

* Check for any uncertain transactions

* In the screen given below (Figure 6.143):

Figure 6.143: Form ST3

- The completed Form ST3 screen is given below after accepting the Vouchers

- Uncertain transactions are zero (Figure 6.144)

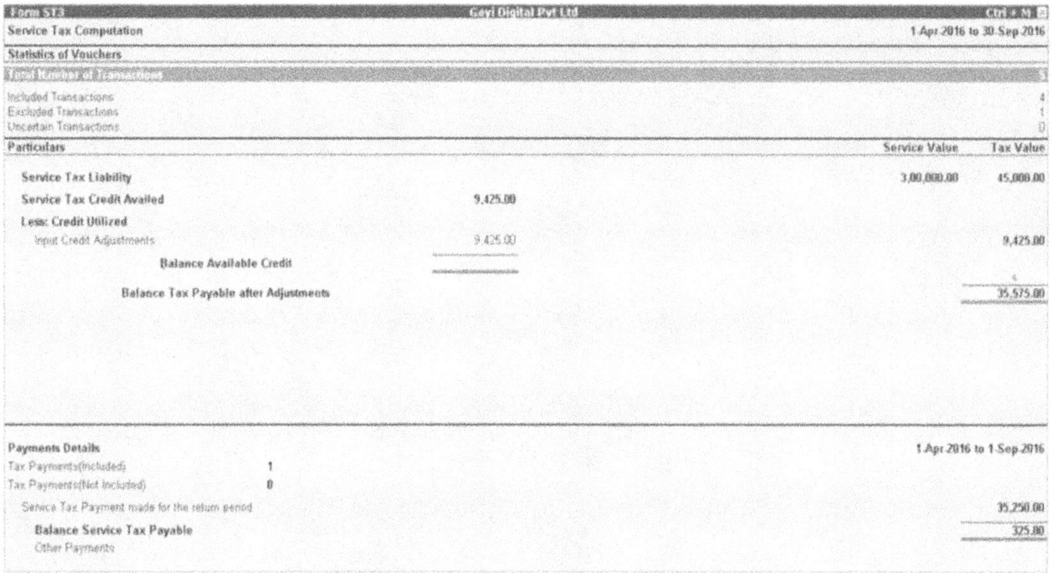

Figure 6.144: Final ST3 Report

Note: After making the uncertain voucher as zero, you will get the accurate payable and input credit amount report you can adjust the same and make a payment to the government and then save the return.

Step 2: Save the Return.

- Go to **Gateway of Tally > Display > Statutory Info > Service tax report > Form ST3** ? Press F6 to save the return (Figure 6.145)

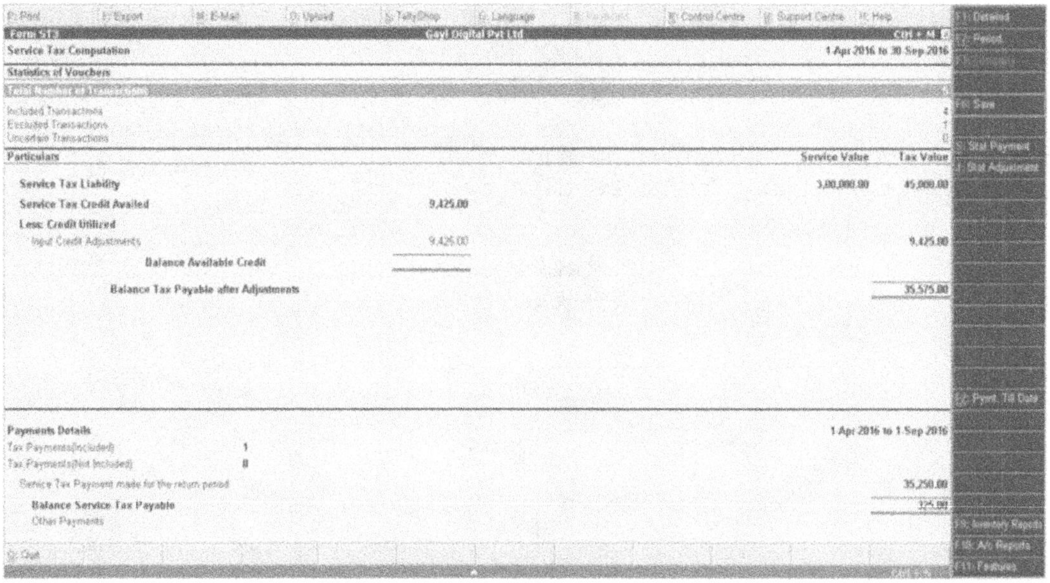

Figure 6.145: Saving the ST3 Return

- Press Ctrl+E and export the Form ST3 File in XLS or XML.

6.16.3 TDS Returns

E- Return

With the automation of collection, compilation and processing of TDS returns, the ITD notified Electronic Filing of Returns of Tax Deducted at Source in the Scheme 2003.

Under this scheme,

- It is mandatory (w.e.f. June 1st, 2003) for corporate deductors to furnish their TDS returns in electronic form (e-TDS return)

- From F.Y. 2004-2005 onwards furnishing TDS returns in electronic form is also mandatory for government deductors in addition to corporate deductoRs.

- Deductors (other than government and corporates) may file TDS return in

- National Securities Depository Ltd. (NSDL) is the e-TDS Intermediary body (appointed by ITD) to receive the e-TDS returns from the deductors, on behalf of ITD

How to generate Form 26Q and file the E-Return.

Form 26Q is a quarterly return for deduction of tax in respect of payments (other than salary) made to residents.

Step 1: Resolve the exceptions or uncertain transactions

- Go to **Gateway of Tally > Display > Statutory Report > TDS Report > Select Form 26Q** ? Bring the Cursor under uncertain transaction and press enter (Figure 6.146).

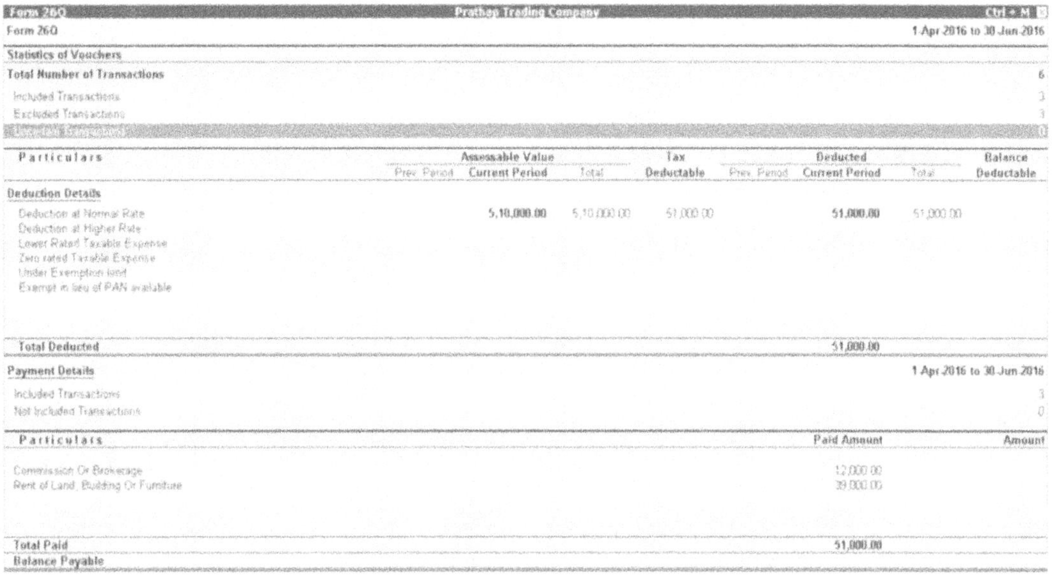

Figure 6.146: Resolving Uncertain Transactions in Form 26Q

Note: In the above given screen we don't have the uncertain transactions. Hence no need to rectify the transactions.

Step 2: Saving Form 26Q

After resolving the required exceptions, the changes made can be saved.

To save the Form 26Q

1. Click F6: Save button from the Form 26Q Report

   If all the exceptions are resolved, and the count of uncertain transactions is zero, then a message prompt appears as shown below (Figure 6.147):

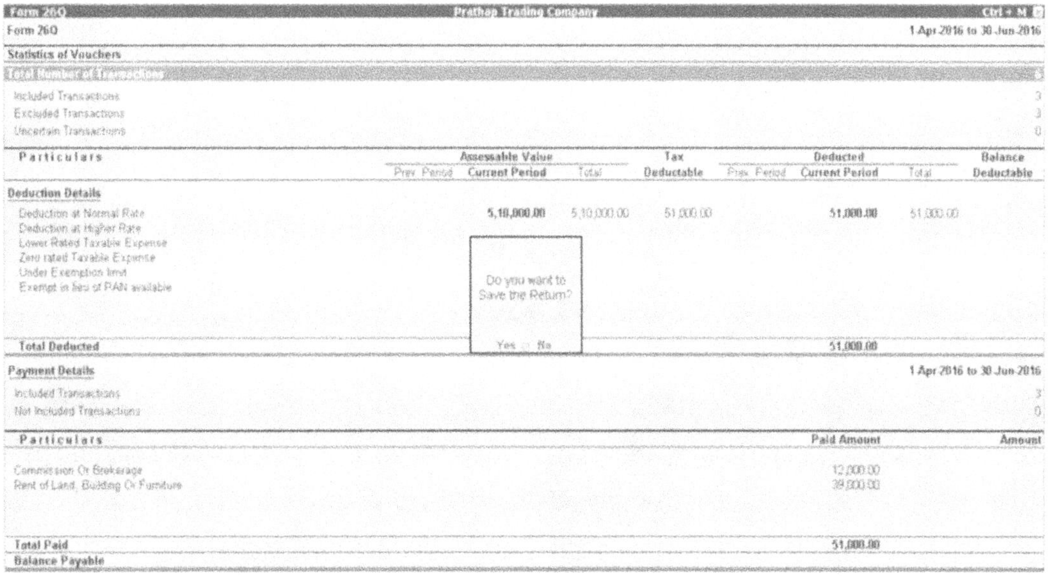

Figure 6.147: Saving Form 26Q

2. Set as **Yes** and save the Return
3. The saved return will be available in the Return Transaction book

The complete screen of Return transaction book is given below (Figure 6.148):

Note: Once after saving the return, if you make any changes in the TDS voucher then the return will come for reconciliation can either overwrite the previous return with the existing one or save a revised one.

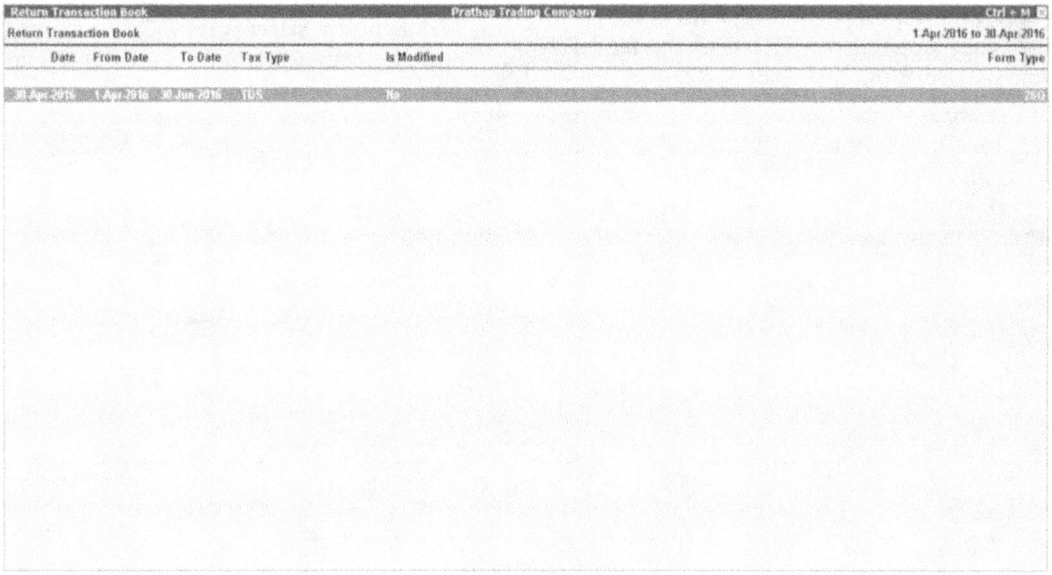

Figure 6.148: Return Transaction Book

The saved return will be available in the return transaction book where you will get the details of return along modification details.

Step 3 Exporting the Form

On saving the modifications, e-filing of the returns can be done from Form 26Q.

To export Form 26Q:

1. Go to **Gateway of Tally > Display > Statutory Report > TDS Report > Select Form 26Q** (Figure 6.149)

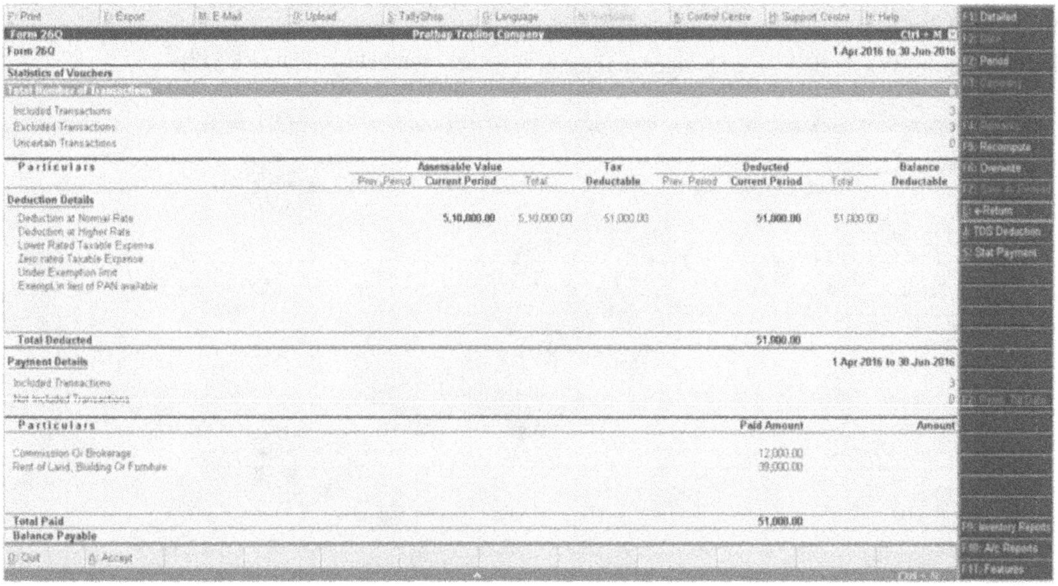

Figure 6.149: Form 26Q

Note: From the Form 26Q/27Q, you can record the Journal voucher to deduct the TDS and also you can make a payment of TDS to the government

2. Press **Ctrl+E**, you will get the following screen
3. Press **Enter** to export the data in the selected format (Figure 6.150)

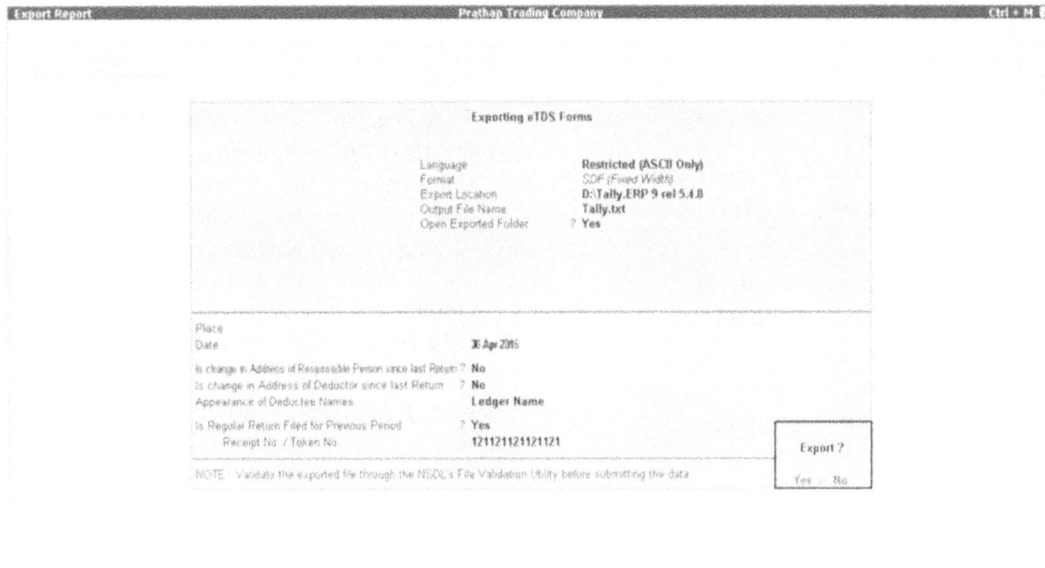

Figure 6.150: Exporting eTDS Forms

The exported file is placed in the Tally.ERP 9 Directory with the specified file name as shown below:

The exported file (Form 26Q) is required to be validated with the File Validation Utility (a freely downloadable utility from NSDL website) and after validation, the returns should be submitted to the department in a CD along with the Form 27A in physical format (Figure 6.151).

Figure 6.151: Exported Form 26Q in Tally.ERP 9 Directory

Note: It is mandatory to validate the TDS returns with File Validation Utility to conform to the requirements as by the Income Tax department. In case of any errors in exported file(returns), the FVU prompts an error with an error code. The assesse may correct the same and revalidate the returns (The File Validation Utility for Quarterly and Annual returns separately)

Form 27 Q

Form 27Q is a Quarterly return for deduction of tax in respect of payments made (other than salary) to non-residents.

To print Form 27Q:

1. Go to **Gateway of Tally > Display > Statutory Reports > TDS Reports > Form 27Q**

2. Save the return by pressing F6

3. Press Ctrl+E and export the file

4. It is mandatory to validate the TDS returns with File Validation Utility to conform to the requirements as prescribed by the Income tax department. In case of any errors in exported file (Returns), the FVU prompts an error message with an error code. The assessee may correct the same and revalidate the returns (The File Validation Utility is available for Quarterly and Annual returns separately)

After Validating upload the return to the government website along with Annexure to 27Q

PRACTICE EXERCISES

Section A: Review Questions

1. Define VAT.
2. Explain the following terms.
3. Input Credit, Tax Invoice, TIN, Registered Dealer.
4. Distinguish between Retail Invoice & Tax Invoice.
5. Discuss VAT Challan.
6. Create a company with the following details:
7. Company Name   -   National Distributors
   State   -   Karnataka
8. Year   -   2016-17
9. Enable Vat   -   Yes (Regular Dealer)
10. TIN   -   29098819221
11. On 01-04-2016 Company Purchased 20 Nos Samsung Glaxy Mobile from Mobile world @ Rs. 4500 with VAT
12. @5% Pur/VAT/001)
13. Generate Tax Invoice on 02-04-2016 for 10 Nos mobile @ Rs. 5800 to Ajay Telecom with VAT@5%
14. On 03-04-2016 Purchase 10 Nos. pen drive (8 GB) @ Rs. 200 from Scandisk Co. paid VAT @5% (Bill. PUR/ PD/001)
15. Sold 8 Pcs Pen drive @ Rs. 400 & 5 Pcs Mobile @ Rs. 5800 to Ajay Telecom with VAT @5% dated 04-04-2016. (Bill SL/VAT/001)
16. On 01-05-2016 pass Adjustment entry & VAT Pyment entry.
17. Display various reports including VAT challan.
18. Explain Service tax.
19. What is abatement? Explain.
20. Define the following terms:
    ST-3, A-3
21. Create a company with the following details:
    Company Name - National Educator Pvt. Ltd. Date   -   2016-17
    ST Reg. No.   - ASDCE1231Q
    Date of Reg.   - 01-04-2016
22. On 10-06-2016, Company received advertising services of Rs. 75,000 plus ST. and paid all the amount on the same day by Kotak Bank (Op. Balance- Rs. 5,00,000) CH. 112233.
23. On 12-06-2016, paid Rs. 5000 including ST to BSNL for telephone uses through Kotak Bank ch. No. 112234.
24. Company received Rs. 80,000 plus ST from Mr. Amit as a course fee on 15-06-2016.
25. On 16-06-2016, company received Rs. 50,000 including ST from Ajay Kumar as a consultancy fee.
26. Adjust & pay ST to govt. on 02-07-2016, through Kotak Bank Ch. No. 112235.
27. Define TDS.
28. What is TAN? Explain.
29. Explain the following terms. Form 26Q, ITNS 281
30. Write down the various return forms with dates.
31. Create a company with the following details.

Company Name   -   National Supplier
Date   -   2016-17
32. TAN   -   TABN11221W
    TAN Reg. No.   -   T2240455ASD
33. On 01-04-2016 commission charged by ABC of Rs. 75,000. Company paid all the amount after deducting TDS through Che. of Axis Bank. 112233.
34. A. Rajgopal and associates (PAN- ASDCA1122Q) charged Rs. 1,25,000 as an audit fee on 03-04-2016. Paid all the amount on 04-04-2016 after TDS deduction ch. No. 112234.
35. Paid TDS amount to govt. on 06-05-2016. Che. No. 112235. Generate challan.

Section B: Multiple Choice Questions

Select the most appropriate answer from the choices given below:

1. If the tax paid on purchases (input tax), is more than the tax payable (output tax), the same cannot be either carried forward to the next return period or claimed as refund.
   a.   True   b.   False
2. The Sales invoice format used for invoicing the Exempted Sales and the Sales made to Unregistered dealers is termed as _____ .
   a.   Retail Invoice   b.   Tax Invoice
3. The tax paid on purchases is termed as _____ .
   a.   Input Tax   b.   Output Tax
4. The Value Added Tax (VAT) is a type of _____ .
   a.   Direct Tax   b.   Indirect Tax
5. Service Tax is _____ .
   a.   an indirect tax   b.   a direct tax
6. Service tax is payable on the gross amount charged for the service provided or to be provided _____ the material cost.
   c.   Excluding   d.   Including
7. Service tax is payable on the value of services. The value of service shall be the _____ amount charged by the service provider for such service rendered by the provider.
   a.   Gross   b.   Nett
8. The service provider can avail CENVAT credit of _____ paid on services received (input services) and _____ paid on inputs and capital goods.
   c.   Service Tax, Sales Tax
   c.   Excise duty, Service Tax
   d.   Service Tax, Excise Duty
   d.   Service Tax, VAT
9. When the assesse is a corporate, service tax is payable on a monthly basis by the 5th of the following month. Non-corporate bodies such as individuals, proprietary firms and partnership firms pay service tax for the fiscal:
   a.   Year   b.   Month
   c.   Half-year   d.   Quarter
10. The concept of TDS was introduced in the _____ .
    a.   Income Tax Act, 1951   b.   Income Tax Act, 1961
    c.   Income Tax Act, 1971   d.   Income Tax Act, 1968

Chapter 7

Depreciation

LEARNING OBJECTIVES

After studying this chapter, you will be able to:

- You will learn about depreciation
- How deprecation is charged on fixed assets
- Disposal of fixed assets

7.1 INTRODUCTION

Every fixed asset has useful life, which is utilized over a period of time, this cause loss of its productivity hence when the productivity of the asset gets declined its value gets lower by lower, this reduction in the value of asset is called depreciation. Finally when the asset becomes useless it is disposed after charging depreciation.

Factors to remember

Cost – This is the total value of asset which includes purchase price of asset, transportation, installation, maintenance and any other additional expenses.

Estimated life of Asset – This is the expected life during the course of business.

Residue – This is the value of an unproductive asset which remains after charging depreciation to the cost of asset.

Disposal of Asset – The unproductive asset is sold as scrap is called as disposal of asset

---
Note: The land is the only fixed asset which is not depreciated.

7.2 DEPRECIATION METHODS

There are various methods to compute depreciation on fixed asset out of which we would understand the most important methods used for accounting.

7.2.1 Straight line method

In this method a fixed rate is charged on the original cost of the asset as depreciation every year. It is a very easy and simple to calculate.

$$\text{Depreciation} = \frac{\text{Original Cost value of Fixed Asset} - \text{Residual Value}}{\text{Estimated life of the Asset}}$$

7.2.1.1 Illustration

In the books of **Bismill Traders** - Financial Year 16-17, On 1-4-2012, The company purchased Machinery worth Rs. 4,00,000, payment made through bank and company estimates to use that asset is for 5 years, which means the effective rate of depreciation will be @ 20% and 5 Years later machinery can be disposed after recovering Rs. 25000 by selling it as scrap. Company sold the machinery for Rs. 63750/- on 31-08-2016 after charging the deprecation which was credited in the bank account.

- Let's make **Working Note**
- Pass the necessary **Journal Entries**
- Prepare **Deprecation A/c**

Depreciation = (400000-25000) = 375000 X 10%
= 37500 fixed for each year.

Working Note

Date	Particulars	Periods	Depr	Amount
01-04-12	Original Cost of Machinery			400000
31-03-13	Depreciation for the effective financial period	12 months	75000	
31-03-14	Depreciation for the effective financial period	12 months	75000	
31-03-15	Depreciation for the effective financial period	12 months	75000	
31-03-16	Depreciation for the effective financial period	12 months	75000	
31-08-16	Depreciation for the effective financial period 37500 X 5 / 12	5 months	31250	
31-08-16	Total Deprecation		331250	
31-08-16	Value of asset after Depreciation Original Cost of Machinery – Total Deprecation			68750
31-08-16	Sale of Machinery			63750
31-08-16	Loss on Sale of Machinery			5000

Journal Entries in the book of Bismill Traders

Date	Particulars		Debit	Credit
01-04-12	Machinery A/c	Dr	400000	
	To Bank A/c	Cr		400000
31-03-13	Depreciation A/c	Dr	75000	
	To Machinery A/c	Cr		75000
31-03-14	Depreciation A/c	Dr	75000	
	To Machinery A/c	Cr		75000
31-03-15	Depreciation A/c	Dr	75000	
	To Machinery A/c	Cr		75000
31-03-16	Depreciation A/c	Dr	75000	
	To Machinery A/c	Cr		75000
31-08-16	Depreciation A/c	Dr	31250	
	To Machinery A/c	Cr		31250
31-08-16	Bank A/c	Dr	63750	
	Loss on Sale A/c	Dr	5000	
	To Sale of Machinery A/c	Cr		68750

In the books of Bismill Traders

Depreciation A/c					
Date	Particulars	Amount	Date	Particulars	Amount
31-03-13	To Machinery A/c	75000	31-03-13	By Profit & Loss A/c	75000
31-03-14	To Machinery A/c	75000	31-03-14	By Profit & Loss A/c	75000
31-03-15	To Machinery A/c	75000	31-03-15	By Profit & Loss A/c	75000
31-03-16	To Machinery A/c	75000	31-03-16	By Profit & Loss A/c	75000
31-08-16	To Machinery A/c	31250	31-08-16	By Profit & Loss A/c	31250
		331250			**331250**

7.2.2   Diminishing balance method

Under this method, a fixed rate of depreciation is charged on asset instead of fixed amount of deprecation. Which means if the value of fixed assets get changed the rate of depreciation charged on fixed asset will be constant. Hence, when the value of fixed asset get reduced, the following deprecation will be charged on written down value of the fixed asset. Thus amount of depreciation is high at initial period and lowers in later periods

Deprecation = Fixed Rate is charged on cost value for the first year and further on declining book value of the asset.

Under this method the book value remaining at the closing of the year of the asset is considered as salvage value of the asset.

Computation of Depreciation

Years	Book value at beginning of year	Rate	Depreciation for the Year	Declined book value of asset
1st				
2nd				

7.2.2.1 *Illustration*

In the books of **Bhugan Enterprises** - Financial Year 16-17, On 1-4-2010, The company purchased Machinery worth Rs. 5,00,000, payment made through bank and company estimates to use that asset is for 7 years, company decided to charge depreciation @ 20% and later machinery can be disposed as scrap.

Company sold the machinery for Rs. 115000/- on 31-08-2016 after charging the deprecation which was credited in the bank account.

- Let's make **Working Note**
- Pass the necessary **Journal Entries**
- Prepare **Deprecation A/c and Machinery (Asset) A/c**

Depreciation Computation

Year	Book value at beginning of year	Rate	Depreciation for the Year	(Written Down) Book value of asset after Depreciation
1	500000	20%	100000	400000
2	400000	20%	80000	320000
3	320000	20%	64000	256000
4	256000	20%	51200	204800
5	204800	20%	40960	163840
6	163840	20%	32768	131072
7	131072	20%	(For 5months) 10923	120149

Note: The deprecation of asset, in the year which is sold would also be taken into consideration

Written Down/ Book value after deprecation (–) **Scrap sales** value Here it is the 7th year, hence the calculation is
120149 – 1150000 = **5149**

Calculations are as follows

Working Note

Date	Particulars	Periods	Depr	Amount
01-04-10	Original Cost of Machinery			500000
31-03-11	Depreciation for the effective financial period	12 months	100000	
31-03-12	Depreciation for the effective financial period	12 months	80000	
31-03-13	Depreciation for the effective financial period	12 months	64000	
31-03-14	Depreciation for the effective financial period	12 months	51200	
31-03-15	Depreciation for the effective financial period	12 months	40960	
31-03-16	Depreciation for the effective financial period	12 months	32768	
31-08-16	Depreciation for the effective financial period (difference in scrap value and last diminished book value is considered)	5 months	10923	
	Total Deprecation			379851
31-08-16	Value of asset after Depreciation (Original Cost of Machinery – Total Deprecation)			120149
31-08-16	Sale of Machinery			115000
31-08-16	Loss on sale of Machinery			5149

Journal Entries in the book of Bhugan Enterprises

Date	Particulars		Debit	Credit
01-04-10	Machinery A/c	Dr	500000	
	To Bank A/c	Cr		500000
31-03-11	Depreciation A/c	Dr	100000	
	To Machinery A/c	Cr		100000
31-03-12	Depreciation A/c	Dr	80000	
	To Machinery A/c	Cr		80000
31-03-13	Depreciation A/c	Dr	64000	
	To Machinery A/c	Cr		64000
31-03-14	Depreciation A/c	Dr	51200	
	To Machinery A/c	Cr		51200
31-03-15	Depreciation A/c	Dr	40960	
	To Machinery A/c	Cr		40960
31-03-16	Depreciation A/c	Dr	32768	
	To Machinery A/c	Cr		32768
31-08-16	Depreciation A/c	Dr	10923	
	To Machinery A/c	Cr		10923
31-08-16	Bank A/c	Dr	115000	
	Loss on Sale of Machinery A/c	Dr	5149	
	To Sale of Machinery A/c	Cr		120149

In the books of Bhugan Enterprises

Depreciation A/c					
Date	Particulars	Amount	Date	Particulars	Amount
31-03-11	To Machinery A/c	100000	31-03-11	By Profit & Loss A/c	100000
31-03-12	To Machinery A/c	80000	31-03-12	By Profit & Loss A/c	80000
31-03-13	To Machinery A/c	64000	31-03-13	By Profit & Loss A/c	64000
31-03-14	To Machinery A/c	51200	31-03-14	By Profit & Loss A/c	51200
31-03-15	To Machinery A/c	40960	31-03-15	By Profit & Loss A/c	40960
31-03-16	To Machinery A/c	32768	31-03-16	By Profit & Loss A/c	32768
31-08-16	To Machinery A/c	10923	31-08-16	By Profit & Loss A/c	10923
		379851			379851

In the books of Bhugan Enterprises

Machinery A/c					
Date	Particulars	Amount	Date	Particulars	Amount
31-03-11	To Bank A/c	500000	31-03-11	By Depreciation A/c	100000
			31-03-12	By Depreciation A/c	80000
			31-03-13	By Depreciation A/c	64000
			31-03-14	By Depreciation A/c	51200
			31-03-15	By Depreciation A/c	40960
			31-03-16	By Depreciation A/c	32768
			31-08-16	By Depreciation A/c	10923
			31-08-16	By Bank A/c	115000
			31-08-16	By Loss on Sales	5149
		500000			500000

PRACTICE EXERCISE

1. In the books of **Long-Life Enterprises** - Financial Year 16-17, On 1-4-2013, The company purchased Machinery worth Rs. 10,00,000, payment made through bank and company estimates to use that asset is for 5 years, which means the effective rate of deprecation will be @ 20% and 5 Years later machinery can be disposed after recovering Rs. 50000 by selling it as scrap. Company sold the machinery for Rs. 3,33,900/- on 30-09-2016 after charging the deprecation which was credited in the bank account.

    *   Prepare **Working Note**
    *   Pass the necessary **Journal Entries**
    *   Prepare **Deprecation A/c and Machinery (Asset) A/c**

    Solve the above question using Straight Line Method

2. In the books of **Sampro Tech** - Financial Year 16-17, On 1-4-2012, The company purchased Machinery worth Rs. 4,00,000, payment made through bank and company estimates to use that asset is for 20 years, company decided to charge depreciation @ 45% and later machinery can be disposed as scrap.

    Company sold the machinery for Rs. 28,000/- on 30-09-2016 after charging the deprecation which was credited in the bank account.

    Depreciation for the 5th year by 30th September 2016 is – Rs. 8236/-

    Loss on sale of machinery – Rs. 367/-

    *   Prepare **Working Note**
    *   Pass the necessary **Journal Entries**
    *   Prepare **Deprecation A/c and Machinery (Asset) A/c**

    Solve the above question using Diminishing Balance Method

Chapter 8

Accounting for Joint Venture

LEARNING OBJECTIVES

After studying this chapter, you will understand:

- The Meaning of Joint Venture
- The Difference Between Joint Venture and Consignment
- The Different Methods of Maintaining Joint Venture

Accounting Records

- The Preparation of Different Accounts Relating to Joint Venture

8.1   JOINT VENTURE

Joint Venture is a business activity in which two parties combine their resources to complete a specific business project or task and once the project is completed the parties share the profit and loss equally or share the same as per the agreement.

For Example: Shyam and Ram decided to combine their resources for completion of specific project i.e., Construction of Commercial Building for ₹ 5, 00,000 and the profit and loss will be shared equally between the parties. Once the project/ transaction is completed the venture will be over between two parties.

When two parties joint to complete a specific job (It can be construction, purchase of property or any other business activity), it is termed as Joint Venture and both the parties will be termed co-venturer.

8.2   IMPORTANT FEATURES OF JOINT VENTURE

1. **Agreement between the parties:** Agreement is made between two or more parties who are joining together to complete a Venture.

2. **Agreement for Execution of Venture:** Agreement is prepared for the completion of the Venture.

3. **Sharing of Profit and Loss:** If the agreement is not available then the profit and loss will shared equally, if the agreement is available, then the profit and loss will be shared as per the agreed ratio.

4. **Closure of Venture:** Once the Business project or any activity undertaken by the parties is completed, then the venture is closed automatically.

8.3   DIFFERENCE BETWEEN JOINT VENTURE AND CONSIGNMENT

The Difference between the Joint Venture and Consignment is given below:

	Joint Venture	Consignment
Meaning	Joint Venture is a business activity in which two parties combine their resources to complete a specific business project or task and once the project is completed the parties share the profit and loss equally and the project is closed on its completion.	In Consignment the goods are sent to another party/consignee for further sale.
Fund Contribution	In case of Joint Venture the fund is provided by the co-venturers.	In case of Consignment the funds is provided by the consignor not consignee.
Profit Sharing	Profit is shared by the joint venture equally or it is shared based on the agreed ration.	Profit is not shared between consignor and consignee, but the commission is provided to consignee for the sales made by him.
Loss/Risk Sharing	Risk factor will be on all co-venturers	Risk factor will be on consignor.
Rights	Co-Venturers have equal rights to make payments, sell, and buy on account of joint venture.	Here, consignee need to work based on the instructions given by the consignor/principal.

8.4   ACCOUNTING TREATMENT

In Joint Venture accounting records can be maintained in the following ways:

1. **Maintenance of Separate Accounting Book:** This method is followed when the size of the venture is huge.

2. **Maintenance of Accounting Book by One Venturer:** In this method books of account are maintained by one

venturer and the other venturers will contribute their part of share.

3. **Maintenance of Accounting Book by all Venturers:** This method is followed when the size of the venture is small and in this methods all the venturers will keep the accounting of transactions related to them.

8.4.1   Maintenance of Separate Accounting Book

As explained earlier, this method is followed when the size of the venture is huge. In this method first the contribution of fund is made by all the venturers to joint funds in the joint bank account and any payments will be made from Joint Bank Account and then Joint Venture Account is maintained and the nature of this account is same as Trading and Profit & Loss Account and it is debited for purchases made and for expenses incurred. Personal Accounts of all the venturers are opened and it is credited when funds are contributed towards joint venture and it is debited with loss. The following accounts are maintained under this method:

a. Joint Venture Account

b. Joint Bank Account

c. Personal Accounts of all Venturers

Following are the list of Journal Entries recorded in case of Maintenance of Separate Accounting Books:

		Journal Entries			
S. N o.	Transactions	Particulars		Debi t (₹)	Credi t (₹)
1.	Contribution of cash by joint venturers to joint funds	Joint Bank A/c	Dr	xxx	
		(Enter the total amount of all venturers)			
		To Venturer's A/c			xxx
		(Enter the individual contribution amount)			
2.	Expenses incurred or purchases made for venture	Joint Venture A/c	Dr	xxx	
		To Joint Bank A/c			xxx
3.	Expenses paid by any venturers	Joint Venture A/c	Dr	xxx	
		To Venturer's A/c			xxx
4.	Cash Sales	Joint Bank A/c	Dr	xxx	
		To Joint Venture A/c			xxx
5.	Credit Sales	Sundry Debtor's A/c	Dr	xxx	
		To Joint Venture A/c			xxx
6.	Stock lying unsold	Joint Venture Stock A/c	Dr	xxx	
		To Joint Venture A/c			xxx
7.	Stock taken by a venturer	Venturer's A/c	Dr	xxx	
		To Joint Venture A/c			xxx
8.	Balance of joint venture account showing profit	Joint Venture A/c	Dr	xxx	
		To Venturer's A/c			xxx
9.	Balance of joint venture account showing loss	Venturer's A/c	Dr	xxx	
		To Joint Venture A/c			xxx

The following illustration will demonstrate about the maintenance of separate accounting book for a venture.

Illustration 1: Pratap Enterprises and Mohan Enterprises agreed to import machineries from Japan to India on 1st August 2016, both the parties opened a joint bank account with ₹ 1, 00,000 out of which Pratap Enterprises contributed 50,000 and remaining amount was contributed by Mohan Enterprises, both the parties agreed to share profit and loss

based on their cash contribution. They remitted ₹92,000 to their agent to pay for the machinery purchased and later remitted ₹5,000 and settled his account. Dock charges, Fright Charges and insurance charges amounted to ₹5,000. On 1st December, 2016, the sales amounted to ₹ 1, 10,000 and the venture was closed and Mohan Enterprises decided to take over the unsold machinery for ₹ 2,000. Prepare the joint venture account showing profit and loss and prepare the accounts of Pratap Enterprises and Mohan Enterprises.*

Solution:

Joint Venture Account				
Particulars	₹	Particulars	₹
To Joint Bank A/c	1,00,000	By Joint Bank A/c	1,10,000
To Joint Bank A/c (Commission paid to agent)	5,000	By Mohan A/c	10,000
To Joint Bank Account (Freight insurance)	5,000		
To Profit transferred to:			
Pratap Enterprises 50% of profit (10,000*50%)	5,000		
Mohan Enterprise 50% of profit (10,000*50%)	5,000		
	1,20,000		1,20,000

Joint Bank Account				
To Pratap Enterprises A/c	50,000	By Joint Venture A/c	92,000
To Mohan Enterprises A/c	50,000	By Joint Venture A/c	5,000
To Joint Venture A/c	1,10,000	By Joint Venture A/c	5,000
		By Pratap Enterprises A/c (contribution amount + Profit share i.e., 50,000 + 5,000)	55,000
		By Mohan Enterprises A/c (50,000 + 3000), 3000 is the amount got after removing the unsold stock value of 2000 from profit	53,000
	2,10,000		2,10,000

Pratap Enterprises				
To Joint Bank A/c	55,000	By Joint Bank A/c	50,000
		By Joint Venture A/c	5,000
	55,000		55,000

Mohan Enterprises				
To Joint Bank A/c	53,000	By Joint Bank A/c	50,000
To Joint Venture A/c	2,000	By Joint Venture A/c	5,000
	55,000		55,000

8.4.2 Maintenance of Accounting Books by One Venturer

In this method of accounting the books of accounts are maintained by one of the co-venturers and he will be paid extra for the services rendered from profit earned. Following are the accounts maintained by the co-venturer.

a. **Joint Venturer Account:** This account is will show the profit and loss earned on the venture.

b. **Personal Account:** This account will record the accounting details of all the co-venturers.

Following are the list of Journal Entries recorded in case of Maintenance of Separate Accounting Book by One Venturer:

		Journal Entries			
S. No.	Transactions	Particulars		Debit (₹)	Credit (₹)
1.	Receiving of share of investment by the working partner from other co-venturers.	Cash/Bank A/c	Dr.	xxx	
		To Venture's A/c			xxx
2.	Purchase of goods	Joint Venture A/c	Dr.	xxx	
		To Cash/Creditors A/c			xxx
3.	Expenses incurred for venture	Joint Venture A/c	Dr.	xxx	
		To Cash A/c			xxx
4.	Goods are sold on cash.	Cash A/c	Dr.	xxx	
		To Joint Venture A/c			xxx
5.	Goods are sold on credit.	Sundry Debtor's A/c	Dr.	xxx	
		To Joint Venture A/c			xxx
6.	Working partner is allowed an extra commission for the services rendered by him	Joint Venture A/c	Dr.	xxx	
		To Commission A/c (Later the same is transferred to working partner P&L A/c)			xxx
7.	Distribution of profit or loss earned on the venture				
	i. Working partner profit will be transferred his P&L A/c	Joint Venture A/c	Dr.	xxx	
		To P&L A/c			xxx
	ii. Profit of all others co-venturers will be transferred to their accounts. iii. Then the venturers account will show the due amount in respect of profit or loss and their investment.	Joint Venture A/c	Dr.	xxx	
		To Individual A/c (Accounts of co-venturers)			xxx

The following illustration will demonstrate about the maintenance of accounting books by one venturer.

Illustration 2: Shakti Traders and Mukta Traders entered into a joint venture and agreed to share the profit and losses in the ratio of 2:1. Shakti Traders sent the goods to Mukta Traders for ₹ 70,000 and incurred expenses of ₹ 3,000 for packing, freight and insurance charges. While transferring the goods, few goods of ₹ 6,000 were damaged for which insurance was claimed for ₹ 3,000. As reported by Mukta Traders that 90% of the remaining goods were sold at a profit of 35% of their original cost. At the closure of venture due to fire remaining goods were damaged and the damaged goods were not insured and Mukta Traders agreed to compensate Shakti Traders by paying the cash 80% of aggregate of the original cost of such goods with proportionate expenses incurred by Shakti Traders. Apart from joint venture profit Mukta Traders is also entitled of 5% commission on net profit of joint venture and after charging commission total selling Expenses incurred by Mukta Traders is ₹ 2,000. Mukta Traders earlier remitted an advance of ₹11,000, he duly paid the balance due to Shakti Traders by draft. Prepare the Joint Venture Account and Mukta Traders Account in the books of Shakti Traders.

Solution:

Accounting Books of Shakti Traders Joint Venture Account			
Particulars	₹	Particulars	₹
To Purchases (Cost of goods sent)	70,000	By Bank (Insurance Claim)	3,000
To Bank (Expenses)	3,000	By Sales (Mukta Traders) (Refer Calculation 2)	77,760
To Mukta Traders Expenses	2,000	By Mukta Traders (agreed value for damaged goods) (Refer Calculation 3)	5,339
To Mukta Traders Commission (5% on 11,099)	555		
To Profit Transferred to.			
P&L A/c (10,544 * 2/3)	7,030		
Mukta Traders (10,544 * 1/3)	3,514		
	86,099		86,099

Mukta Traders Account			
To Joint Venture A/c (sales)	77,790	By Bank (Advance)	11,000
To Joint Venture A/c (claim portion)	5,339	By Joint Venture A/c (Expenses incurred by Mukta)	2,000
		By Joint Venture A/c (Commission)	555
		By Joint Venture A/c (Profit share of Mukta)	3,514
		By Bank (Balance received)	66,060
	83,129		83,129

Calculations:

2. Calculation of Sales	
Cost of goods sent	70,000
Less: Cost of damaged goods	6,000
	64,000
Cost of unsold stock (64,000*10%)	6,400
Cost of goods sold (64,000* 90%)	57,600
Profit of 35%	20,160
Sales	77,760

3. Claim calculation for loss of goods by fire admitted by Mukta Traders	
Cost of Goods	6,400
*Add: Proportionate Expenses (3,000 * 6,400)/70,000*	274
	6,674
Less:20%	1,335
Amount to be claimed	5,339

1. Assume that the goods damaged during transit have no residual value.

8.4.3 Maintenance of Accounting Book by all Venturers:

Under this method all the venturers will keep the accounting records. Under this method they are two ways to keep the books of accounts as given below:

1. When co-ventures inform each other regarding the transactions made by them on account of joint venture on regular interval of time.

2. When co-venturers furnish the information on the completion of the venture. This is also known as Memorandum Method.

8.4.3.1 Each venturer gets the complete information from other venture on regular interval

In the above method following accounts are maintained by all the co-venturers.

a. **Joint Venture Account:** This account is similar to profit and loss account and this account is debited with Purchases and expenses, it is credited with sales account and stock in hand amount. The balanced amount will profit or loss.

b. **Personal Account:** In this we will maintain co-venturers account, this account is written as Joint Venture with ....Account. This is done to distinguish it from other personal accounts of main business. This account is closed after settlement of the balance.

Following are the list of Journal Entries recorded in case of Maintenance of Accounting Book by all Venturers:

S. No.	Transactions	Particulars	Debit ₹ (₹)	Credit ₹ (₹)
1	When goods are purchased or Money is paid on joint venture by him	Joint Venture A/c Dr.	xxx	
		To Seller's / Bank A/c		xxx
2	When he receives a report that his co-venture has purchases the goods and paid money on the joint venture	Joint Venture A/c Dr.	xxx	xxx
		To Co-Venturers Personal A/c		
3	When goods are sold by him on joint venture	Cash/Purchasers A/c Dr.	xxx	
		To Joint Venture A/c		xxx
4	When he receives a report that his co-venture has sold the goods on Joint Venture A/c	Co-Venturers A/c Dr.	xxx	
		To Joint Venture A/c		xxx
5	Distribution of profit or loss earned on the venture			
	i. Share of profit to be taken by him	Joint Venture A/c Dr.	xxx	
		To P&L A/c		xxx
	ii. Share of profit to his co-venturers (**In case of loss entries will be reversed**) iii. When co-venturers accounts are balanced, it will show the amount due to him or amount due from him	Joint Venture A/c Dr.	xxx	
		To Individual A/c (Accounts of co-venturers)		xxx

The following illustration will demonstrate about the maintenance of accounting books by all venturer, if venturer gets accounting information on regular basis.

Illustration 3: Akash Traders and Biswas Traders entered into an agreement of joint venture and decided to share the profit and losses in the ratio of 60 per cent and 40 per cent. Akash Traders purchased goods for ₹ 4,00,000 and the goods were sent to Biswas Traders. Akash Traders paid ₹ 30,000 in the process and Biswas reported stating that he had sold the goods for ₹ 4,20,000 and few goods were left unsold. Akash and Biswas Traders decided to send the goods on consignment basis to KK & Co., he agreed to sell the goods on commission basis, all expenses incurred by him on consignment and 5% commission need to be paid to him. KK sent the details of sales made by him along with the cheque of ₹ 40,000 to Biswas Traders (KK & Co., deducted expenses of ₹ 5,000 and 5% commission) and the unsold stock were sent to Biswas Traders and he purchased the goods for ₹ 25,000 and prepared a statement of account to Akash Traders and reported that he spent ₹ 15,000 on this joint venture and both of then agreed to settle their account on completion of venture. Prepare the required ledger accounts in the books of Akash Traders and Biswas Traders and show the final settlement of accounts.

Solution:

Books of Akash Joint Venture Account

Particulars	₹	Particulars	₹
To Bank A/c (Purchase of goods)	4,00,000	By Biswas Traders	4,20,000
To Bank A/c (Expenses)	30,000	By Biswas Traders (through consignment)	40,000
To Biswas Traders (Expenses)	15,000	By Biswas Traders (Stock)	25,000
To Profit and Loss A/c ((Profit = 40,000) 40,000 * 60/100 = 24,000)	24,000		
To Biswas Traders (40,000 * 40/100 = 16,000)	16,000		
	4,85,000		4,85,000

Biswas Account

Particulars	₹	Particulars	₹
To Joint Venture A/c (Sales made)	4,20,000	By Joint Venture A/c (Expenses)	15,000
To Joint Venture A/c (Consignment sales)	40,000	By Joint Venture A/c (Profit)	16,000
To Joint Venture A/c (Stock purchased)	25,000	By Bank A/c	4,54,000
	4,85,000		4,85,000

Books of Biswas Joint Venture Account

Particulars	₹	Particulars	₹
To Akash A/c (Goods sent)	4,00,000	By Cash (Sales)	4,20,000
To Akash (Expenses)	30,000	By Cash (Consignment sales)	40,000
To Cash (Expenses)	15,000	By Purchases (Stock)	25,000
To Profit & Loss A/c ((Profit = 40,000) 40,000 * 40/100 = 16,000)	16,000		
To Akash Traders (40,000 * 40/100 = 16,000)	24,000		
	4,85,000		4,85,000

Akash Account				
Particulars	₹	Particulars		₹
To Bank A/c	4,54,000	By Joint Venture A/c (Goods)		4,00,000
		By Joint Venture A/c (Expenses)		30,000
		By Joint Venture (Profit)		24,000
	4,54,000			4,54,000

8.4.3.2 Memorandum Joint Venture Method of Accounting

In this method the all the accounting information is reported on completion of the venture, following are the important features of Memorandum Joint Venture Method.

1. **Maintenance of Only One Personal Account:** Under Memorandum Method only one personal account needs to be maintained by every venturer. For example XYZ enter into Joint venture, and X will maintain only one personal joint account for Y and Z, similarly Y will maintain only one personal joint account for X and Z.

2. **Recording of Transactions by Co-Venturer:** Each venturer will account only those transactions recorded by him on joint venture. For example suppose X is purchasing some goods, then this entry will be accounted in the books of X not in the books of Y and Z.

3. **Opening of Memorandum Account:** To find the profit and loss made on the venture memorandum account is prepared. All the personal accounts are combined and presented in memorandum account i.e., all the debit side balance of personal accounts are debited in the memorandum account and the credit side balances are credited in the account. Any transaction which will not affect the profit and loss, then the same is not accounted.

The following illustration will demonstrate about the maintenance of accounting books by all venturer under memorandum joint venture method.

Illustration 4: Arun and Bikram came together for dealing in land and started the venture from 1st August 2016, Arun purchased plot of land measuring 10,000 square yard on the advanced money for ₹1,00,000. Both the venturer decided to sell the land in smaller plots and prepared a plan at a cost of ₹1,000, which was paid by Bikram. Plot was planned in such a way that 1/3 of the total area of land was left for roads and the remaining land were divided into 5 plots of equal size. On 1st November 2016, 3 plots were sold at ₹40 per square yard, the buyer of the plot deducted ₹1,100 for stamp duty and he agreed to pay the registration expenses by himself. On 1st December 2016, remaining 2 plots were sold at net price of ₹30 per square yard. Arun received all the sales money. After charging interest at 5% p.a. on the investment of A and allowing 1% on the net sale value of plots as commission to Bikram, then the net profit or loss made on venture needs to be shared in proportion of 3/4 and 1/4 to Bikram. Prepare the memorandum joint venture account and personal accounts of venturer and show the balance payable to one another and Joint venture was completed on 1st December 2016,

Solutions:

Akash Books Joint Venture with Bikram				
Particulars	₹	Particulars		₹
To Bank A/c (Advance)	1,00,000	By Bank (Sales) (3,999*40 = 1,59,960)	1,59,960	
To Interest (Refer below given calculation-2)	1,013	*Less: Stamp duty per plot i.e., 1,100 per plot(1,100 * 3 = 3,300)*	3,300	1,56,660
To P & L A/c (Profit share of Arun) (Refer below given calculation- 3)	99,196	By Bank (Sales) 2,666*30		79,980
To Bank (Final Settlement) (Refer below given calculation-4)	36,431			
	2,36,640			2,36,640

Bikram Books Joint Venture with Arun			
Particulars	₹	Particulars	₹
To Bank (Expense)	1,000	By Bank (Final Settlement)	36,431
To Commission	2,366		
To P & L A/c (Share of profit)	33,065		
	36,431		36,431

Memorandum Joint Venture Account			
Particulars	₹	Particulars	₹
To Purchases (Arun)	1,00,000	By Sales	2,36,640
To Interest (Arun)	1,013		
To Expenses (Bikram)	1,000		
To Commission (Bikram)	2,366		
To Profit			
Akash 99,196			
Bikram 33,065	1,32,261		
	2,36,640		2,36,640

Calculations:

1. **Area used for roads =** 1/3 of total plot i.e., (1/3 * 10,000 = 3,334)

   Remaining area of land = Total Plot – Area used for road i.e. (10,000 – 3,334 = 6,666)

   Distribution of remaining area of land in 5 equal plots i.e. (6,666/5 = 1,333), hence per plot = 1,333 square yards.

2. Interest Receivable by Arun = Advance amount * Interest rate * Period (1st August 2016 to 1st December 2016)

   = 1,00,000 * 5/100*4/12

   = 1,666

   Interest Payable by Arun = Sales amount * Interest rate * Period (1st November 2016 to 1st December 2016)

   = 1,56,660 * 5/100*1/12

   = 653

   Net Interest Receivable by Arun = Interest Receivable – Interest Payable

   = 1,666 – 653

   = 1,013

3. **Profit share of Arun** = Profit – Expenses incurred by Bikram – Commission payable to Bikram*3/4

   = (Profit = 2,36,640 – 1,01,013) – (1000) – (1% on 2,36,640)* (3/4)

   = (1,35,627) – (1,000) – (2,366) * (0.75)

= 1, 32,261*0.75

= 99,196

4. **Profit share of Bikram** = (1,32,261 * 1/4) + 1,000 + 2,366

= (33,065) + 1,000 + 2,366

= 36,431

KEY TAKEAWAYS

♦ Joint Venture is a business activity in which two parties combine their resources to complete a specific business project

♦ Person who will join the joint venture will be termed as Venturer

PRACTISE EXERCISES

Section A: Review Questions

1. What is Joint Venture?

2. Who is a Venturer?

Section B: Multiple Choice Questions

Select the most appropriate answer from the choices given below:

1. The person who will join a joint venture is termed as?
   a. Joint Venturer   b. Consignee
   c. Bank   d. Consignor

2. In joint venture fund is contributed by _____.
   a. Consignee   b. Joint Venturer
   c. Consignor   d. Bank

Section C: Practical Questions

1. Akash Enterprises and Suresh Enterprises agreed to import machineries from Japan to India on 1st May 2016, both the parties opened a joint bank account with ₹ 2, 00,000 out of which Akash Enterprises contributed 1, 00,000 and remaining amount was contributed by Suresh Enterprises, both the parties agreed to share profit and loss based on their cash contribution. They remitted ₹ 1, 00,000 to their agent to pay for the machinery purchased and later remitted ₹ 10,000 and settled his account. Dock charges, Fright Charges and insurance charges amounted to ₹ 15,000. On 1st August, 2016, the sales amounted to ₹ 2, 50,000 and the venture was closed and Suresh Enterprises decided to take over the unsold machinery for ₹ 5,000. Prepare the joint venture account showing profit and loss and prepare the accounts of Akash Enterprises and Suresh Enterprises.

2. Surya Traders and Mukhi Traders entered into a joint venture and agreed to share the profit and losses in the ratio of 2:1. Surya Traders sent the goods to Mukhi Traders for ₹ 1, 00,000 and incurred expenses of ₹ 4,000 for packing, freight and insurance charges. While transferring the goods, few goods of ₹ 7,000 were damaged for which insurance was claimed for ₹ 4,000. As reported by Mukhi Traders that 90% of the remaining goods were sold at a profit of 30% of their original cost. At the closure of venture due to fire remaining goods were damaged and the damaged goods were not insured and Mukhi Traders agreed to compensate Surya Traders by paying the cash 80% of aggregate of the original cost of such goods with proportionate expenses incurred by Surya Traders. Apart from joint venture profit Mukhi Traders is also entitled of 5% commission on net profit of joint venture and after charging commission total selling Expenses incurred by Mukhi Traders is ₹ 3,000. Mukhi Traders earlier remitted an advance of ₹ 15,000, he duly paid the balance due to Surya Traders by draft. Prepare the Joint Venture Account and Mukhi Traders Account in the books of Surya Traders.

3. A & S Traders and B & C Traders entered into an agreement of joint venture and decided to share the profit and losses in the ratio of 70 per cent and 30 per cent. A & S Traders purchased goods for ₹ 5, 00,000 and the goods were sent to B & C Traders. A & S Traders paid ₹ 50,000 in the process and B & C reported stating that he had sold the goods for ₹ 5, 50,000 and few goods were left unsold. A & S and B & C Traders decided to send the goods on consignment basis to KK & Co., he agreed to sell the goods on commission basis, all expenses incurred by him on consignment and 5% commission need to be paid to him. KK sent the details of sales made by him along with the cheque of ₹ 50,000 to B & C Traders (KK & Co., deducted expenses of ₹ 6,000 and 5% commission) and the unsold stock were sent to B & C Traders and he purchased the goods for ₹ 35,000 and prepared a statement of account to A & S Traders and reported that he spent ₹ 25,000 on this joint venture and both of then agreed to settle their account on completion of venture. Prepare the required ledger accounts in the books of A & S Traders and B & C Traders and show the final settlement of accounts.

Chapter 9

Accounting for Consignment

LEARNING OBJECTIVES

After studying this chapter, you will be able to:

◆ Explain the Concept of Consignment

◆ Prepare consignment Accounts

9.1 ACCOUNTING FOR CONSIGNMENT

In the present business environment, where success of a business is directly related to the ability of the manufacturers or dealers to quickly respond to market demand for goods, distance between suppliers and customers could prove to be a big challenge. It is this challenge that has given rise to the concept of consignment, wherein a dealer (or manufacturer) enters into a trading agreement with a reliable local trader to sell goods on his behalf (as an agent), at an agreed amount of commission. In such an arrangement, the dealer, called the Consigner remains the owner (title holder) of the goods until they are paid for in full and, after a certain period, takes back the unsold goods from the local trader called the Consignee. The goods sent by the consignor to the consignee are called 'Goods sent on Consignment'.

For example, if Ram of Tamil Nadu sends 500 television sets to Shyam in Bihar, to sell the television on his behalf and risk (Ram's risk), the transaction between the two will be a consignment transaction with Ram being the 'consignor', Shyam being the 'consignee' and the cell phones being the 'goods on consignment'. Under the arrangement, Ram will be liable to pay Shyam only as and when the goods (televisions) are sold; the payment will include the reimbursement of expenses incurred by Shyam for obtaining, storing and selling the goods, in addition to the commission as agreed upon. At the end of the consignment period, Shyam will have to return the unsold televisions back to Ram.

Note: Originally, the term consignment was associated with despatch or shipping of goods to an agent in a foreign country for sale on commission basis. However, over time, the term came to be used for despatch of goods to an agent in different parts of the same country.

9.1.1 Features of Consignment

The key features of a consignment transaction are:

Principal and Agent: The relationship between the consignor and consignee is that of a Principal and Agent (not seller and buyer).

Transfer of Possession: A consignment arrangement involves the transfer of possession of goods (not title of goods like in a sale).

Consignor's Risk: The risk of goods sent on consignment is borne by the consigner. Therefore, in case of any loss or destruction of goods, the loss will be borne by the consignor

and not the consignee.

Remuneration for Consignee: The consignee will be eligible to receive remuneration that includes the reimbursement of expenses incurred in obtaining, storing and selling the goods, in addition to the commission as agreed upon. The sale proceeds belong to the consignor.

9.1.2 Differences between a Sale and a Consignment

The main differences between a consignment and sales are as shown in the following table:

Terms of Agreement	Sale	Consignment
Nature of Relationship	Buyer and Seller, in case of credit sales, or a Debtor and a Creditor between the two persons	Consignor (Principal) and Consignee (Agent)
Transfer of Ownership	Ownership transferred from seller to buyer	Ownership remains with consignor till goods are sold by the consignee (only possession is transferred to consignee)
Risk	Transfer of risk from seller to buyer	Consignor bears risk till goods are sold by the consignee
Return of Goods	Goods sold cannot be returned, unless the seller agrees to take them back	Unsold goods are returned to the consignor
Expenses (freight, storage, insurance, etc.)	Borne by the purchaser unless specified in the agreement	Borne by the consignor

9.1.3 Important Terms in a Consignment Transaction

Some of the terms associated with consignment transactions accounting are explained below:

Proforma Invoice: A Proforma Invoice is a statement prepared by the consignor containing information regarding quantity, quality and price of the goods at which the consignee ought to sell the goods being despatched. It is sent to the consignee along with the goods despatched.

Note: Proforma Invoice and an Invoice are not the same. An invoice is prepared by a seller, and implies that a sale has taken place. It contains information regarding the goods sold and the amount due by the buyer to the seller.

Account Sales: An Account Sales is a periodic statement prepared and sent by the consignee to the consignor, stating the sales and expenses incurred, commission earned and the consequent net amount due from the consignee after deducting the advances, if any, to the consignor.

Account Sales - Specimen:

Account Sales of 50 cell phone sets sold by M/s A. Das & Co., Kolkata on account and risk of M/s Malabar & Co., Kerala, India.

M/s A. Das & Co., Kolkata			
Particulars	(₹)	(₹)	(₹)
80 cell phones @ 7,000		5,60,000	
20 cell phones @ 12,000		2,40,000	8,00,000
Less Charges			
Freight	6,000		
Warehouse Rent	5,000	11,000	
Commission @ 5%		40,000	51,000
			7,49,000
Less: Draft accepted			25,000
Balance due, Bank draft enclosed			7,24,000

E & O E

Kolkata, the 30th June, 2016

For M/s A. Das & Co.,
Kolkata
(Sd) Virat Kumar
Manager

Commission (Consignee's Remuneration): Commission is the remuneration payable to the consignee at a fixed rate on the proceeds of the goods sold by him, for his services. Apart from the commission, the consignee is reimbursed all expenses incurred by him in connection with the consignment sales. These expenses could be dock charges, custom duties, freight, storage rent, insurance of goods in possession, etc.

Commission can be classified into 3 types, namely, Simple, Overriding and Del-credere.

i. **Simple Commission:** The simple commission is usually calculated as a fixed percentage on total sales.

ii. **Over-riding Commission:** The arrangement wherein a consignee is given an additional commission over and above the smple commission when sales exceeds a certain limit is called the over-riding commission. It is also calculated as a percentage on total sales, and is usually used as an additional incentive to motivate the consignee to increase sales.

iii. **Del-credere Commission:** Under a consignment agreement, consignees are required to sell on cash-basis, as bad or doubtful debts resulting from credit sales are required to be borne by the consignor. However, at times an arrangement is made in a consignment agreement wherein the consignee guarantees payment and undertakes responsibility for bad debts (i.e, the consignee agrees to pay the consignor, even if does not receive payment from the purchaser/s). For taking on this risk, the consignee is given an additional commission on the total sales, called del-credere commission.

Illustration 9.1.1

Hero Appliances Private Ltd., Bangalore sent 1000 Flasks costing ₹ 80 each for sale on consignment basis to Griha Sukh, Mysore, on the following consignee remuneration terms:

i. Selling price per flask: ₹ 100

ii. Consignee's Commission:

a. Simple Commission: 5 percent on normal selling price;

b. Over-riding Commission: 2 percent if selling price is higher than normal selling price; and

c. Del-credere Commission: 1 percent on total sales for guaranteeing payment on credit sales.

The sales reported by Griha Sukh were:

Cash Sales:	₹
400 Flasks @ ₹ 100	40,000
100 Flasks @ ₹ 120	12,000
Credit Sales:	26,000
200 Flasks @ ₹ 130	
50 Flasks @ ₹ 140	7,000
Total	85,000

Ascertain the commission due to the consignee, Griha Sukh, Mysore.

Solution:

Statement of Commission due to Griha Sukh, Mysore

Statement of Commission due to Griha Sukh, Mysore	
Particulars	₹
Simple Commission: 400*100*5/100	2,000
Over-riding Commission: (12,000+26,000+7,000)*2/100	900
Del-credere Commission: 85,000*1/100	850
	3,750

Direct Expenses: All expenses incurred till the goods reach the consignee's godown, such as freight, carriage, loading and unloading charges, insurance, etc., are considered as part of direct expenses. These expenses are generally of a non-recurring nature.

Indirect Expenses: All expenses incurred after the goods reach the consignee's godown such as warehousing charges, advertising expense, salesmen's salaries, etc., form part of indirect expenses. These expenses are of a recurring nature.

Advance: The amount deposited by the consignee with the consignor as a security deposit for the goods being sent by the consignor to him is considered as an advance. The advance is usually a percentage of the value of goods sent as consignment. For example, if goods of ₹ 100,000 are goods, then the advance amount will be ₹ 10,000.

Pricing of Goods Sent on Consignment: The pricing of goods sent on consignment can either be (a) at Cost or (b) at Invoice Price

a. **At Cost Pricing:** As the name suggests, under this pricing method, the goods sent on consignment are charged at cost price to the consignor. So the Proforma invoice will also be prepared at the cost price of goods. For example, if Nirmal of

Delhi, purchases goods at a cost ₹ 50,000 and s a consignee, Rajesh in Mumbai, the proforma invoice will show the value of goods as ₹ 25,000. The consignee will be instructed to sell the goods at a certain price.

b. **At Invoice Price:** Under this pricing method, the goods are charged to the consignment at a price above the cost price. The proforma invoice is prepared accordingly, with goods being priced above the cost price. For example, if in the above case, the goods are consigned at a 25 percent on the cost price, the proforma invoice will be prepared for ₹ 31,250 (i.e, 25,000 + 6,250).

9.1.4 Accounting Treatment – Consignor's Books of Account

To maintain a proper record of transactions relating to each consignment, the consignor usually maintains three accounts, as discussed below:

i. **Consignment Account:** Considered a special Trading and Profit & Loss account, it is prepared to arrive at the profit or loss made on a particular consignment. A consignment account is a nominal account.

ii. **Consignee's Account:** It helps in evaluating the position of the consignee with regard to remittances on sales to the consignor. Since the consignee's account's is a personal account, if all payments are made in full to the consignor, he will be a debtor and if he has not paid all the balance due by him he will be a creditor.

iii. **Goods Sent on Consignment:** This real account is closed by transferring its balance to the Purchases account.

The following table gives details of the accounting entries to be passed in the books of a Consignor:

Sl. No.	Transaction	Debit	Credit
	Book of Consignor		
	Journal		
1	When goods are sent on consignment:		
(a)	at Cost price	Consignment A/c	Goods sent on Consignment A/c (cost price)
(b)	at Invoice Price	(i) Consignment A/c	Goods sent on Consignment A/c (invoice price)
	Adjustment entry to bring cost of goods sent on consignment to cost - with difference between invoice price and cost price)	(ii) Goods sent on Consignment A/c	Consignment A/c
2	Security deposit is sought	Bank or Cash A/c	Consignee's A/c
3	Expenses incurred (by consignor)	Consignment A/c	Cash A/c
4	On receipt of Account Sales from consignee:		
(a)	for sales made by consignee	Consignee's A/c	Consignment A/c
(b)	for expenses incurred by consignee	Consignment A/c	Consignee's A/c
(c)	for commission	Consignment A/c	Consignee's A/c
5	In case of bad debts (consignee is not del credere agent)	Consignment A/c	Consignee's A/c
6	For stock in hand with Consignee:		
(a)	Goods sent at cost price	Stock on Consignment A/c	Consignment A/c
(b)	Goods sent at invoice price	(i) Stock on Consignment A/c	Consignment A/c
	Adjustment entry to write-off unrealised profit on stock (with difference between invoice price and cost price)	(ii) Consignment A/c	Stock Reserve A/c
7	Settlement of Accounts with the Consignee:		
(a)	If the consignee pays the amount owed in cash or through bank to consignor	Bank or Cash A/c	Consignee's A/c
(b)	If the consignor pays the amount owed in cash or through bank to consignee	Consignee's A/c	Bank or Cash A/c
8	Transfer of profit or loss to Profit & Loss A/c		
(a)	Profit	Consignment A/c	Profit & Loss A/c
(b)	Loss	Profit & Loss A/c	Consignment A/c
9	Closure of Goods sent on Consignment A/c by transferring balance to Purchases or trading A/c	Goods sent on Consignment A/c	Purchases or Trading A/c

Illustration 9.1.2

On 1st June, 2016, Anirudh Textiles Private Limited, Mumbai, consigned 1000 pieces of dress material costing ₹ 20,000 to Vinayak Fabrics, Kerala. The consignee, Vinayak fabrics is entitled to a commission of 5% on total sales.

Anirudh Textiles incurred the following expenses: ₹

Insurance	200
Carriage	500
Freight	300

Anirudh Textiles issued a cheque of ₹ 5,000 in favour of Vinayak Fabrics, which was accepted by them.

On 31st July, 2016, Vinayak Fabrics sent the Account Sales with the following details: ₹

Goods sold	25,000
Expenses incurred	400
Stock in hand	5,000

Vinayak Textiles enclosed a demand draft for the net amount due to Anirudh Textiles, along with the Account Sales.

Pass the journal entries and ledger accounts in the books of the consignor.

Solution

Date 2016	Particulars	L.F	Dr.	Cr.
	Journal			
June	Consignment to Kerala A/c Dr.		20,000	
	To Goods sent on Consignment A/c			20,000
	(Being 1000 pieces of dress materials consigned to Vinayak Fabrics, Kerala)			
	Consignment to Mumbai A/c Dr.		1,000	
	To Cash A/c			1,000
	(Being expenses incurred: Insurance ₹200, Carriage ₹500 and Freight ₹300)			
	Bank A/c Dr.		5,000	
	To Vinayak Fabrics, Kerala A/c			50,00
	(Being cheque received from Vinayak Fabrics, Kerala)			
	Consignment to Kerala A/c Dr.		400	
	To Vinayak Fabrics, Kerala			400
	(Being expenses incurred by the consignee with respect to the consignment)			
	Consignment to Kerala A/c Dr.		1,250	
	Vinayak Fabrics, Kerala A/c			1,250
	(Being the 5% commission due to the consignee)			
	Vinayak Fabrics, Kerala A/c Dr.		25,000	
	To Consignment to Kerala A/c			25,000
	(Being sales made)			

Stock on Consignment A/c		Dr.		5,000	
To Consignment to Kerala A/c					5,000
(Being the remaining stock with the consignee)					
Jul-31	Goods sent on Consignment A/c	Dr.		20,000	
	To Trading A/c				20,000
	(Being transfer of goods sent on consignment to Trading A/c)				
	Bills Receivable A/c	Dr.		18,350	
	To Vinayak Fabrics A/c				18,350
	(Being B/R received as net amount due)				
	Consignment to Kerala A/c	Dr.		7,350	
	To Profit & Loss A/c				7,350
	(Being transfer of profit to P&L A/c)				

Ledger Accounts

Dr.   Consignment to Kerala A/c   Cr.

Date 2016	Particulars	₹	Date 2016	Particulars	₹
June 01	To Goods sent on Consignment	20,000	July 31	By Vinayak Fabrics, Kerala	25,000
	To Cash (expenses)	1,000		By Stock on Consignment	5,000
	To Vinayak Fabrics (expenses)	400			
July 31	To Vinayak Fabrics (commission)	1,250			
	To Profit & Loss A/c	7,350			
		30,000			30,000

Dr.   Good sent on Consignment A/c   Cr.

Date 2016	Particulars	₹	Date 2016	Particulars	₹
July 31	To Trading A/c (sales)	20,000	June 01	By Consignment to Kerala A/c	20,000

9.1.4.1 Valuation of Unsold Stock

If all stocks sent on consignment are not sold, the remaining unsold stocks have to be valued, like closing stock in case of a trading account. The valuation of unsold stock includes:

i. Proportionate cost price, and

ii. Proportionate direct expenses, i.e., expenses incurred by both the consignor and consignee till the goods reach the consignee's godown

Further, as is the practice with regard to valuation of stock, stock should be valued at cost or market price, whichever is lower.

Illustration 9.1.3

Chethan Enterprise, Goa, consigns 40 iron boxes of ₹ 1000 to Niranjan Electricals.

Chethan Enterprises bears the following expenses with regard to the consignment: ₹

Insurance	200
Carriage	300
Freight	500

Niranjan Electricals bears the following expenses till the goods reach his godown:

Customs Duty	1500

Dock Dues	400
Warehouse rent	300
Office rent	500

By the end of the year Niranjan Enterprise had managed to sell 30 transistors. The market value of the remaining iron boxes was ₹ 1,050 per piece.

Calculate the value of unsold stock with the consignee.

Solution:

Statement showing Value of Unsold Stock with Consignee		
Particulars	(₹)	(₹)
Cost of 10 iron boxes @ 1,000		10,000
Direct Expense (in proportion of 10/40)		
Insurance	50	
Carriage	75	
Freight	125	
Customs Duty	375	
Dock Dues	100	725
		10,725

Market value of unsold stock = 10 x 1,050 = 10,500

Market value being less than the cost, the 10 iron boxes should be valued at ₹ **10,500**

9.1.4.2 Loss of Stock

In a consignment transaction, loss of stock can occur due to several reasons; these could occur during transit or after the goods sent on consignment reaches the consignee's godown. The treatment of loss of stock depends on the type and place of loss of goods. Loss can be of two types, namely, normal loss or abnormal loss.

i. **Normal Loss:** Loss due to the inherent nature of goods, that leads to loss due to causes like evaporation, sublimation, leakage or drying up of goods is called normal loss. These losses are uncontrollable and unavoidable. Normal loss is not shown in a consignment account and there is no need to pass any entry in the books of account. It is used in arriving at the value of closing stock wherein the loss on account of normal loss is included in the value of good units. Thus,

Value of Closing Stock =

$$\frac{Total\ Value\ of\ Goods\ Sent \times Units\ of\ Closing\ Stock}{Units\ actually\ received\ by\ the\ Consignee}$$

ii. **Abnormal Loss:** Loss due to accidental causes is called an abnormal loss. Destruction of goods due to fire or floods, theft, etc., are examples of abnormal loss. It is unexpected loss and beyond human control. Abnormal loss is debited to Abnormal Loss Account and credited to Consignment Account. The Abnormal Loss Account may be closed after transferring the amount to the Profit & Loss Account.

The valuation of stock lost due to abnormal losses is on the same lines as the valuation of stock on consignment, viz., proportionate cost price in addition to proportionate direct expenses incurred up to the date of loss.

Value of Abnormal Loss =

$$\frac{Total\ Cost * Units\ of\ Abnormal\ Loss}{Total\ units\ to\ be\ received\ by\ the\ Consignee}$$

Note: The stage or phase of loss of goods is important in case of abnormal loss. i.e, if the loss is during transit to consignee or after reaching the consignee's godown, as illustrated below.

Illustration 9.1.4

Vivek of Chennai consigned 100 kgs of goods @ ₹ 60 per kg to Amit of Delhi. Freight and Cartage paid by the consignor was ₹ 3,000. Amit received only 95 kgs of goods. Heincurred unloading charges of ₹ 500. At the end of the consignment period, Amit was left with 20 kgs of unsold goods.

You are required to calculate:

(i)   Value of closing stock, considering the loss to be a normal loss due to leakage

(ii) Value of abnormal loss due to theft during transit from Chennai to Delhi; Value of closing stock in case of abnormal loss

(iii) Value of abnormal loss due to theft from the consignee's godown, instead of the theft durinh transit

Solution

(i) **Value of Closing Stock - Normal Loss**

Cost price of 100 kgs of goods @ ₹ 60 per kg	60,000
Freight and Cartage paid by the consignor	3,000
Unloading charges paid by consignee	500
Cost of 95 kgs =	63,500

Cost of Closing Stock = (Total Value of Goods Sent*Units of Closing Stock)/(Units actually received by the Consignee)

= (63,500 x 20)/95   **₹ 13,368**

(ii-a) **Value of Abnormal Loss:**

Cost price of 100 kgs of goods @ ₹ 60 per kg	60,000
Freight and Cartage paid by the consignor	3,000
Total Cost of Goods	63,000

Value of Abnormal Loss = (Total Cost*Units of Abnormal Loss)/Total Units to be received by the Consignee

= (63,000*5)/100=   **3,150**

(ii-b) **Value of Closing Stock - Abnormal Loss during Transit**

Cost price of 100 kgs of goods @ ₹ 60 per kg	60,000
Freight and Cartage paid by the consignor	3,000
Total Cost of Goods	63,000

Cost of 20 kgs of closing stock = (63,000/100)*20

= 12,600

Add: Proportionate expenses incurred by consignee = (500*20)/95= 105 **= 12,705**

(iii-a) **Value of Abnormal Loss at Consignee's Godown**

Cost price of 100 kgs of goods @ ₹ 60 per kg	60,000

Freight and Cartage paid by the consignor	3,000
Unloading expenses incurred by the consignee	500
Total Cost of Goods	63,500

Value of Abnormal Loss = (Total Cost*Units of Abnormal Loss)/Total Units to be received by the Consignee (63,500*5)/100= **3,175**

(iii-b) **Value of Closing Stock - Abnormal Loss from Consignee's Godown**

Cost price of 100 kgs of goods @ ₹ 60 per kg	60,000
Freight and Cartage paid by the consignor	3,000
Unloading expenses incurred by the consignee	500
Total Cost of Goods	63,500

Value of Closing Stock (20 units)=(63,500*20)/100 **12,700**

Often businessmen take an insurance policy in respect of the goods being sent or received on consignment. Such policies are available only in respect of abnormal losses. In such cases the amount of claim admitted by the insurer should be debited to the insurer and balance of the loss amount may be debited to the Profit and Loss Account.

9.2 ACCOUNTING TREATMENT – CONSIGNEE'S BOOKS OF ACCOUNT

In the consignee's books of account, only those transactions that affect him directly are entered.

	Book of Consignee	
	Journal	
Sl. No.	Transaction	Debit
1	On payment of advance (security deposit)	
	Consignor's A/c	Dr.
	To Bank or B/P	
	(amount of security deposit)	
2	On receipt of stock - No entry (entry in stock register)	
3	For expenses incurred for receipt of goods	
	Consignor's A/c	Dr.
	To Bank (or Creditor's) A/c	
	(amount of expenses incurred)	
4	On Sales made	
	Bank (or Debtor's) A/c	Dr.
	To Consignor's A/c	
	(sales amount)	
5	For Commission earned	
	Consignor's A/c	Dr.
	to Commission A/c	
	(commission amount)	
	Note: Del-credere commission has to be credited to Del-credere Commission A/c and bad debts debited from it. Balance has to be transferred to Profit & Loss A/c	

Illustration 9.2.1

Anand of Vijayawada sent a consignment of goods to Roop Kumar of Bihar at an invoice price of ₹ 15,000 and incurred the following expenses:

• Freight: ₹ 800

• Cartage: ₹ 300

• Insurance: ₹ 500

The consignee sold the goods at charges of

from the consignee in settlement of the dues.

was ₹ 22,000paid a ndsimple commission of 5 percent, storage The ₹ 150coansignordsellingreceivexpensesda3 ofmonths₹ 600 .bill of exchange

Pass the necessary journal entries and prepare the necessary accounts on the books of the consignee.

	Journal			
Sl. No.	Particulars		Dr ₹	Cr ₹
1	Anand, Vijayawada A/c	Dr.	750	
	To Bank A/c			750
	Being expenses incurred with receipt of goods on consignment - storage and selling expenses)			
2	Bank A/c	Dr.	22,000	
	To Anand, Vijayawada A/c			22,000
	Being credit of sale proceeds to Anand			
3	Anand, Vijayawada A/c	Dr.	1,100	
	To Commission A/c			1,100
	Being commission earned)			
4	Anand, Vijayawada A/c	Dr.	20,150	
	To Bills Payable A/c			20,150
	Being the bill of exchange accepted in settlement of account)			
5	Bills Payable A/c	Dr.	20,150	
	To Bank A/c			20,150
	Being payment made on maturity of B/E)			

KEY TAKEAWAYS

In a consignment transaction, a dealer (or manufacturer) enters into a trading agreement with a reliable local trader to sell goods on his behalf (as an agent), at an agreed amount of commission.

In a consignment transaction, ownership of goods remains with consignor till the goods are sold by the consignee.

The pricing of goods sent on consignment can either be (a) at Cost or (b) at Invoice Price.

The treatment of loss of stock depends on the type and place of loss of goods.

Loss in consignment can be of two types, namely, normal loss or abnormal loss.

PRACTICE EXERCISES

Section A: Review Questions

1. Explain the term 'consignment' in your own words.
2. Differentiate between the terms direct expenses and indirect expenses in connection with consignment transactions.
3. Discuss any three differences between a sale and a consignment transaction.

Section B: Multiple Choice Questions

1. Kiran Cements, Andhra Pradesh sent 50 tonnes of cement to Ravikanth Cements in Bihar, to sell the cement on their behalf. Kiran Cements has two partners in Telengana, Vishal Cements and Vishal Hardware. In the above consignment agreement, who is the consignee?
   a. Kiran Cements   b. Ravikanth Cements
   c. Vishal Cements   d. Vishal Hardware
2. Which of the following is an example of a normal loss of goods in a consignment transaction?
   a. Loss due to fire   b. Theft
   c. Evaporation   d. Mob violence

Section C: Practical Questions

1. Naveen Sports Private Ltd., Gurgaon consigned 200 carrom-boards costing ₹ 1,200 each for sale on consignment basis to Nita Sports Center, Odisha, on the following consignee remuneration terms:
   i. Selling price per carrom board: ` 1,500
   ii. Consignee's Commission:
      a. Simple Commission: 5 percent on normal selling price;
      b. Over-riding Commission: 1.5 percent if selling price is higher than normal selling price; and
      c. Del-credere Commission: 1 percent on total sales for guaranteeing payment on credit sales.

The sales reported by Griha Sukh were:

Cash Sales:

50 carrom boards @ ₹ 1,500

20 carrom boards @ ₹ 1,800

Credit Sales:

30 carrom boards @ ₹ 1,750

2. Visha, Delhi, consigns 100 goods of ₹ 20,000 to Arijit Electricals. The consignor bears the following expenses with regard to the consignment: ₹

Insurance	2,000
Carriage	900
Freight	10,00

The consignee bears the following expenses till the goods reach his godown:

Customs Duty	10,500
Dock Dues	600
Warehouse rent	600
Office rent	700

By the end of the year the consignee had managed to sell 80 goods. The market value of the remaining goods was [1] 22,000 per piece.

Calculate the value of unsold stock with the consignee.

Chapter 10

Hire Purchase and Instalment

LEARNING OBJECTIVES

- You will learn about hire purchase price
- How to calculate and preparing interest table
- How journal entries are recorded in both hire purchaser

- and seller
- How various ledger accounts are maintained

- **Instalment System begin with promise between two parties**
  - o Supplier is termed as **Seller**
  - o Purchaser is termed as **Buyer**
- **Cash Price** - The price at which the goods can be purchased from the market at full payment
- **Instalment** – The payment which is done in parts, at a definite interval instead paying it full, is called instalment. The instalment includes the principle amount with interest.
- **Down payment** – The sum of the amount demanded by the hire seller for commencement of the hire purchase is called down payment.

Note: The downpayment is not subjected to any interest.

10.3 AGREEMENT TERMS AND CONTENTS

It is a written statement which states that the goods are lent on hire and the hire purchaser can get the ownership of goods, only when the entire payments are made in definite periodic instalments by the hire purchaser.

The hire purchaser can obtain full possession of goods and use it as an when the agreement is applied.

10.3.1 Aspects

- **Hire Seller** delivers the goods to the buyer on **terms and conditions** of the agreement.
- **Hire purchaser** (buyer) can possesses the goods and can use it immediately but must keep the goods in **fine condition**.
- The hire purchaser have to make the payments to hire seller on fixed instalments and provide **down payment** if demanded, for commencement of the hire purchase activity.
- The instalment and the down payment paid by the hire purchaser is considered as hire charge for using the asset, hence it is not treated as the repayment price and the excess of total payment over the cash price is accounted as interest.
- If hire purchaser fails to make any of the instalments the seller reserves the right to **repossession** of the goods.
- Once the **last instalment** is paid by the hire purchaser the hire purchase activity becomes **complete purchase**.

Following points are emphasised

- Date of hire purchase agreement
- Value of goods on cash price
- Value of goods on hire purchase

10.1 INTRODUCTION

Hire Purchase System

It is a business activity, when a **buyer** obtain goods from the **seller** on an agreement, stating to repay the price of goods on instalment basis, which include the interest and does not allows the **ownership** of the goods until the last instalment is paid by the buyer.

In the activity of **hire purchase** the buyer gets the full possession of the goods immediately and can use the goods, the ownership of goods is transferred to the buyer once he pays all the instalments. But, if the buyer fails to makes the payment of instalments, the seller has the right to take back the possession of goods.

The seller may ask for a certain amount of money, from the buyer to commence the hire purchase activity as a down payment, and the remaining amount is collected by the seller with interest on instalment basis. The instalment are fixed and can be collected by seller on monthly, quarterly, half yearly or on yearly basis.

In this business activity the seller get the scope to increase the sales straightaway and collect the payments on instalments which includes **interest**. This system thus benefits both the parties and seller is assured and reserves the repossession of goods in case of any default in payment by the buyer.

Instalment System

In this system, when the buyer acquire goods from the seller, the ownership of the goods is transferred immediately by the seller regardless the payment procurement is on instalment basis. The buyer hold full possession and can start using the goods and the buyer promise to repay the price of goods on instalment basis. The buyer is not under any legal obligation and may evade the last instalment.

The instalment paid by the buyer is treated as repayment of principal with interest hence the relation between both the parties are similar to debtor and creditor.

If the buyer default to make payment, the seller cannot repossess the goods since the ownership of goods is already transferred to the buyer. The buyer is responsible for maintaining goods in fine condition and the buyer may also sell the goods to other party as he is the owner of the goods.

10.2 INSIGHTS

- **Hire purchase begin with an agreement between two parties**
  - o Supplier is termed as **Hire Seller**
  - o Purchaser is termed as **Hire Purchaser**

- Interest Column
- Instalment Amount
- Total Number of Instalments and date of Instalment
- Instalment payment method
- Details of property in goods and warranties
- Other Terms and Conditions

10.4 DEPRECIATION CHARGE ON ASSETS PURCHASED ON HIRE PURCHASE

In the hire purchase system, the assets in form of goods are also charged depreciation, in this business activity the deprecation to be charged on asset, is allowed to hire purchaser. The reason that the hire purchaser is allowed to charge deprecation on asset, is the hire purchaser possess and uses the asset for the business purposes. The hire purchaser is believed and deemed to be the owner of the asset once the entire instalments are paid therefore the hire seller is not allowed to charge deprecation.

10.5 COMPUTATION OF HIRE PURCHASE PRICE

It is very necessary to understand the exact hire purchase price, since it is the absolute payable amount by the hire purchaser, in order to complete the purchase or acquire the asset.

Hire Purchase Price		
If the case of downpayment	Down Payment + Total Instalments	Cash Price + Total Interest
If the case of no downpayment	Total Instalments	Not Applicable

10.6 INTEREST CALCULATION ON HIRE PURCHASE GOODS

The seller in the hire purchase or instalment system charge higher for goods beside the **cash price** of goods present at **market**. Hence, the excess of the cash price over the hire purchase price of the goods is the total amount of interest. Interest will be calculated on cash price if there is no downpayment and in the case of downpayment paid, then interest must be calculated on **net cash price** i.e. cash price less downpayment paid.

(Net Cash Price = Cash Price – Downpayment)

10.6.1 Computation of Interest and Closing Balance without knowing principal factor

A. **Interest Calculation based on Rate of Interest Only**

1. **If the case of downpayment**
   - First Period = Net Cash Price x Rate of Interest
   - Subsequently = Closing Balance x Rate of Interest

2. **If the case of no downpayment**
   - First Period = Cash Price x Rate of Interest
   - Subsequently = Closing Balance x Rate of Interest

B. Closing Balance
   - Closing Balance = Payable - Instalment

Interest Table Format

Hire Purchase Interest Calculation Method 1			
Periods	Effect	Particular	Amount
		Cash Price of Goods	
	Less	Down Payment	
		Net Cash Price	
	Add	Interest @ due	
		Payable	
	Less	1st Instalment	
		Closing Balance O/s	
	Add	Interest @ due	
		Payable	
	Less	Following or Last Instalment	

10.6.1.1 Illustration

A. **Interest Calculation based on Rate of Interest Only**

S Ltd purchased machinery from E Ltd on hire purchase based on the following details lets calculate the interest.

- Cash Price – Rs. 300000/-
- Down Payment – Rs. 100000/-
- Instalment – Rs. 56400 for 4 Years
- Rate of Interest Per annum – 5%
- Last Instalment Interest must be rounded off by Rs. 10.20/-

Interest Table

Hire Purchase Interest Calculation Method 1			
Periods	Effect	Particular	Amount
01/04/2011		Cash Price of Goods	300000
	Less	Down Payment	100000
		Closing Balance O/s	200000
	Add	Interest @ 10%	10000
		Payable	210000
	Less	1st Instalment	56400
		Closing Balance O/s	153600
	Add	Interest @ 10%	7680
		Payable	161280
	Less	2nd Instalment	56400
		Closing Balance O/s	104880
	Add	Interest @ 10%	5244
		Payable	110124
	Less	3rd Instalment	56400
		Closing Balance O/s	53724
	Add	Interest Rounded Off	2676
		Payable	56400
	Less	4th Instalment	56400

Note: Closing Balance = Payable - Instalment

10.6.2 Computation of Interest and Closing Balance with knowing principal factor

A. **Interest Calculation based on Rate of Interest with Principal Factor**

1. **If the case of downpayment**
   - First Period = Net Cash Price x Rate of Interest
   - Subsequently = Opening Balance x Rate of Interest

2. **If the case of no downpayment**
   - First Period = Cash Price x Rate of Interest
   - Subsequently = Opening Balance x Rate of Interest

i. Principal Factor

    i. Principal Not Given

        o Principal = Instalment – Interest

    ii. **Principal Given but Instalment unavailable and unequal**

        o Instalment = Principal + Interest

B. **Closing Balance Calculation**

    ♦ Opening Balance – Principal

Interest Table Format

	Hire Purchase Interest Calculation Method 2				
Period(s)	Opening Balance O/s	Interest Portion	Principal Portion	(Instalment)	Closing Balance O/s
1	(a)	(b)	(c)	(d)	(e)
Following/ Final Years					

The Opening Balance Column contains the following

♦ **Cash Price** at Beginning

♦ Subsequently the **Closing Balance** is carry forwarded in this column

Note: Interest of the last instalment must be rounded off if **principal** is **fixed or unavailable**.

10.6.2.1 Illustration

A. Interest Calculation based on Rate of Interest with Principal Factor

    i. Principal Not Given

    E Ltd purchased **machinery** from **T Ltd** on hire purchase based on the following details lets calculate the interest.

    ♦ Cash Price – Rs. 550000/-

    ♦ Down Payment – Rs. 100000/-

    ♦ Instalment – Rs. 141900 for 4 Years

    ♦ Rate of Interest Per annum – 10%

    ♦ Last Instalment Interest must be rounded off by Rs. 287.10/-

Interest Table

	Hire Purchase Interest Calculation Method 2				
Period(s)	Opening Balance O/s	Interest Portion	DP/Principal Portion	(Instalment)	Closing Balance O/s
1	550000		100000		450000
1	450000	45000	96900	141900	353100
2	353100	35310	106590	141900	246510
3	246510	24651	117249	141900	129261
4	129261	12639	129261	141900	0

Note: Closing Balance Calculation = Opening Balance – Principal

    i. Principal Given but Instalment unavailable and unequal

    Z Ltd purchased **equipment** from **A Ltd** on hire purchase based on the following details lets calculate the interest.

    ♦ Cash Price – Rs. 350000/-

♦ Down Payment – Rs. 50000/-

♦ Principal – Rs. 60000 for 5 Years

♦ Rate of Interest Per annum – 5%

Interest Table

	Hire Purchase Interest Calculation Method 2				
Period(s)	Opening Balance O/s	Interest Portion	DP/Principal Portion	(Instalment)	Closing Balance O/s
1	350000		50000		300000
1	300000	15000	60000	75000	240000
2	240000	12000	60000	72000	180000
3	180000	9000	60000	69000	120000
4	120000	6000	60000	66000	60000
5	60000	3000	60000	63000	0

Note: Closing Balance Calculation = Opening Balance – Principal

10.7 FULL CASH PRICE METHOD

In this method, the hire purchaser of goods is considered as the owner of the asset. Hence in this method, the asset purchased by the hire purchaser is recorded at full cash price, which is legally incorrect however, this is the most practical method used for accounting hire purchase or instalment

Now let us understand the accounting of hire purchase system using full cash price method following by the illustration

10.7.1 Accounting Journal Entries

Transactions	In the Books of Hire Purchaser		In the Books of Hire Seller	
Purchase of Goods	Asset A/c — To Hire Seller	Dr Cr	Not Applicable	
	(Note: Entry of asset must always be recorded on cash price)			
Sales of Goods	Not Applicable		Hire Purchaser A/c — To Hire Sales A/c	Dr Cr
	(Note: Entry of asset must always be recorded on cash price)			
Down Payment	Hire Seller A/c — To Cash/ Bank A/c	Dr Cr	Cash/ Bank A/c — To Hire Purchaser A/c	Dr Cr
Interest Due	Interest A/c Dr — To Hire Seller A/c	Dr Cr	Hire Purchaser A/c — To Interest A/c	Dr Cr
Transfer of Interest to P & L Account	P & L A/c — To Interest A/c	Dr Cr	Interest A/c — To P & L A/c	Dr Cr
Instalment Payment	Hire Seller A/c — To Cash/ Bank A/c	Dr Cr	Cash/ Bank A/c — To Hire Purchaser	Dr Cr
Depreciation	Depreciation A/c — To Asset A/c	Dr Cr	Not Applicable	
Depreciation Transfer to P & L A/c	P & L A/c — To Depreciation A/c	Dr Cr	Not Applicable	

Disclosure in Balance Sheet Using Full Cash Price Method

In the Books of Hire Purchaser Balance Sheet as at			In the Books of Hire Seller Balance Sheet as at		
Liabilities	Assets	Rs	Liabilities	Assets	Rs
	Fixed Assets			Current Assets	
	HP Asset at Full Price			Sundry Debtors	
	(-) Depreciation			Hire Purchaser	
	(-) Balance in Hire Seller A/c				

10.8 ILLUSTRATION

On 1st April, 2012. **Anil International Pvt Ltd** purchased machinery from **HIVE Machines & Instruments Ltd** on hire purchase systems, the details of the transactions are as follows.

- The **Cash Price** of the Machinery in the Market is Rs. 15,00,000/-
- The **Down Payment** mentioned was Rs. 2,00,000/-
- The **Instalment** amount is fixed to Rs. 4,10,000/- at each interval and paid on 31st March of Following Year. The deal would complete in **4 years**
- The **Rate of Interest is 10**% per annum
- **Anil International Pvt Ltd** charge **deprecation** the fixed asset @ 5% using straight line method.
- The Last instalment interest would be **rounding off** at the difference of Rs. 520/-

Let us calculate the interest

Interest Table

Periods	Effect	Particular	Amount
01/04/2011		Cash Price of Goods	1500000
	Less	Down Payment	200000
		Closing Balance O/s	1300000
	Add	Interest @ 10%	130000
		Payable	1430000
	Less	1st Instalment	410000
		Closing Balance O/s	1020000
	Add	Interest @ 10%	102000
		Payable	1122000
	Less	2nd Instalment	410000
		Closing Balance O/s	712000
	Add	Interest @ 10%	71200
		Payable	783200
	Less	3rd Instalment	410000
		Closing Balance O/s	373200
	Add	Interest Rounded Off	36800
		Payable	410000
	Less	4th Instalment	410000

Caption: Hire Purchase Interest Calculation Method 1

Total Interest = 340000/-

Let us take the same above illustration and use the alternative method for interest calculation.

On 1st April, 2012. **Anil International Pvt Ltd** purchased machinery from **HIVE Machines & Instruments Ltd** on hire purchase systems, the details of the transactions are as follows:

- The **Cash Price** of the Machinery in the Market is Rs. 15,00,000/-
- The **Down Payment** mentioned was Rs. 2,00,000/-
- The **Instalment** amount is fixed to Rs. 4,10,000/- at each interval and paid on 31st March of Following Year. The deal would complete in **4 years**
- The **Rate of Interest is 10**% per annum
- **Anil International Pvt Ltd** charge **deprecation** the fixed asset @ 10% using straight line method.
- The Last instalment interest would be **rounding off** at the difference of Rs. 520/-

Interest Table

Period(s)	Opening Balance O/s	Interest Portion	DP/Principal Portion	(Instalment)	Closing Balance O/s
1	1500000		200000		1300000
1	1300000	130000	280000	410000	975000
2	975000	102000	308000	410000	650000
3	650000	71200	338800	410000	325000
4	325000	36800	373200	410000	0

Caption: Hire Purchase Interest Calculation Method 2

Total Interest = 340000/-

Principal Calculation

- Principal = Instalment − Interest

Closing Balance Calculation

- Opening Balance − Principal

Journal Entries

In the books of Hire Purchaser (Anil International Pvt Ltd)

Date	Particulars		LF	Dr.	Cr.
01-04-12	Machinery A/c	Dr		1500000	
	To Hive Machines & Equipment Ltd A/c	Cr			1500000
	(Being goods bought on hire purchase basis)				
01-04-12	Hive Machines & Equipment Ltd A/c	Dr		200000	
	To Bank A/c	Cr			200000
	(Being downpayment made)				
31-03-13	Interest A/c	Dr		130000	
	To Hive Machines & Equipment Ltd A/c	Cr			130000
	(Made the interest due)				
31-03-13	Hive Machines & Equipment Ltd A/c	Dr		410000	
	To Bank A/c	Cr			410000
	(Being 1st Instalment paid)				
31-03-13	Depreciation A/c	Dr		150000	
	To Machinery A/c	Cr			150000
	(Being depreciation charged on fixed asset)				
31-03-13	Profit & Loss A/c	Dr		150000	
	To Depreciation A/c	Cr			150000
	(Being depreciation transferred to P&L A/c)				
31-03-14	Interest A/c	Dr		102000	
	To Hive Machines & Equipment Ltd A/c	Cr			102000
	(Made the interest due)				
31-03-14	Hive Machines & Equipment Ltd A/c	Dr		410000	
	To Bank A/c	Cr			410000
	(Being 2nd Instalment paid)				
31-03-14	Depreciation A/c	Dr		150000	
	To Machinery A/c	Cr			150000
	(Being depreciation charged on fixed asset)				
31-03-14	Profit & Loss A/c	Dr		150000	
	To Depreciation A/c	Cr			150000
	(Being depreciation transferred to P&L A/c)				
31-03-15	Interest A/c	Dr		71200	
	To Hive Machines & Equipment Ltd A/c	Cr			71200
	(Made the interest due)				
31-03-15	Hive Machines & Equipment Ltd A/c	Dr		410000	
	To Bank A/c	Cr			410000
	(Being 3rd Instalment paid)				
31-03-15	Depreciation A/c	Dr		150000	
	To Machinery A/c	Cr			150000
	(Being depreciation charged on fixed asset)				
31-03-15	Profit & Loss A/c	Dr		150000	
	To Depreciation A/c	Cr			150000
	(Being depreciation transferred to P&L A/c)				
31-03-16	Interest A/c	Dr	L.F	36800	
	To Hive Machines & Equipment Ltd A/c	Cr			36800
	(Made the interest due)				
31-03-16	Hive Machines & Equipment Ltd A/c	Dr		410000	
	To Bank A/c	Cr			410000
	(Being 4th Instalment paid)				
31-03-16	Depreciation A/c	Dr		150000	
	To Machinery A/c	Cr			150000
	(Being depreciation charged on fixed asset)				
31-03-16	Profit & Loss A/c	Dr		150000	
	To Depreciation A/c	Cr			150000
	(Being depreciation transferred to P&L A/c)				

In the books of Hire Purchaser (Anil International Pvt Ltd)

Vendor Account

	Hive Machines & Equipment Ltd A/c				
Date	Particulars	Amount	Date	Particulars	Amount
01-04-12	To Bank A/c	200000	01-04-12	By Machinery A/c	1500000
31-03-13	To Bank A/c	410000	31-03-13	By Interest A/c	130000
31-03-14	To Bank A/c	410000	31-03-14	By Interest A/c	102000
31-03-15	To Bank A/c	410000	31-03-15	By Interest A/c	71200
31-03-16	To Bank A/c	410000	31-03-16	By Interest A/c	36800
		1840000			1840000

Machinery A/c

Date	Particulars	Amount	Date	Particulars	Amount
01-04-12	To Hive Machines & Equipment Ltd A/c	1500000	31-03-13	By Depreciation A/c	150000
			31-03-14	By Depreciation A/c	150000
			31-03-15	By Depreciation A/c	150000
			31-03-16	By Depreciation A/c	150000
			31-03-16	By Balance b/d	900000
		1500000			1500000

Depreciation A/c

Date	Particulars	Amount	Date	Particulars	Amount
31-03-13	To Machinery A/c	150000	31-03-13	By Profit & Loss A/c	150000
31-03-14	To Machinery A/c	150000	31-03-14	By Profit & Loss A/c	150000
31-03-15	To Machinery A/c	150000	31-03-15	By Profit & Loss A/c	150000
31-03-16	To Machinery A/c	150000	31-03-16	By Profit & Loss A/c	150000
		600000			600000

Journal Entries

In the books of Hire Seller (Hive Machines & Equipment Ltd)

Date	Particulars		L.F	Dr.	Cr.
01-04-12	Anil International Pvt Ltd A/c	Dr		1500000	
	To Sales of Machinery A/c	Cr			1500000
	(Being goods sold on hire purchase basis)				
01-04-12	Bank A/c	Dr		200000	
	To Anil International Pvt Ltd A/c	Cr			200000
	(Being downpayment received)				
31-03-13	Anil International Pvt Ltd A/c	Dr		130000	
	To Interest A/c	Cr			130000
	(Interest receive due)				
31-03-13	Interest A/c	Dr		130000	
	To Profit & Loss A/c	Cr			130000
	(Being Interest transferred to P&L A/c)				
31-03-13	Bank A/c	Dr		410000	
	To Anil International Pvt Ltd A/c	Cr			410000
	(Being 1st Instalment received)				
31-03-14	Anil International Pvt Ltd A/c	Dr		102000	
	To Interest A/c	Cr			102000
	(Interest receive due)				
31-03-14	Interest A/c	Dr		102000	
	To Profit & Loss A/c	Cr			102000
	(Being Interest transferred to P&L A/c)				
31-03-14	Bank A/c	Dr		410000	
	To Anil International Pvt Ltd A/c	Cr			410000
	(Being 2nd Instalment received)				
31-03-15	Anil International Pvt Ltd A/c	Dr		71200	
	To Interest A/c	Cr			71200
	(Interest receive due)				
31-03-15	Interest A/c	Dr		71200	
	To Profit & Loss A/c	Cr			71200
	(Being Interest transferred to P&L A/c)				
31-03-15	Bank A/c	Dr		410000	
	To Anil International Pvt Ltd A/c	Cr			410000
	(Being 3rd Instalment received)				
31-03-16	Anil International Pvt Ltd A/c	Dr		36800	
	To Interest A/c	Cr			36800
	(Interest receive due)				
31-03-16	Interest A/c	Dr		36800	
	To Profit & Loss A/c	Cr			36800
	(Being Interest transferred to P&L A/c)				
31-03-16	Bank A/c	Dr		410000	
	To Anil International Pvt Ltd A/c	Cr			410000
	(Being 4th Instalment received)				

In the books of Hire Seller (Hive Machines & Equipment Ltd)

Customer Account

Anil International Pvt Ltd A/c

Date	Particulars	Amount	Date	Particulars	Amount
01-04-12	To Machinery A/c	1500000	01-04-12	By Bank A/c	200000
31-03-13	To Interest A/c	130000	31-03-13	By Bank A/c	410000
31-03-14	To Interest A/c	102000	31-03-14	By Bank A/c	410000
31-03-15	To Interest A/c	71200	31-03-15	By Bank A/c	410000
31-03-16	To Interest A/c	36800	31-03-16	By Bank A/c	410000
		1840000			1840000

Interest A/c

Date	Particulars	Amount	Date	Particulars	Amount
31-03-13	To Profit & Loss A/c	1500000	31-03-13	By Anil International Pvt Ltd A/c	130000
31-03-14	To Profit & Loss A/c	130000	31-03-14	By Anil International Pvt Ltd A/c	102000
31-03-15	To Profit & Loss A/c	102000	31-03-15	By Anil International Pvt Ltd A/c	71200
31-03-16	To Profit & Loss A/c	71200	31-03-16	By Anil International Pvt Ltd A/c	36800
		340000			340000

10.9 DEFAULT AND REPOSSESSION

In the hire purchase system, the agreement made between the hire seller and purchaser, state that if the hire purchaser makes default in the payment of instalments, the hire seller has the right to repossess the goods sold.

The purpose of hire purchase transaction is to transfer the ownership of goods to hire purchaser, only once the last payment is made. But if the hire purchaser default in making payment of instalment, the hire purchaser has to forfeit the earlier paid instalments, and the hire seller repossesses the goods either in full or partially.

The repossession of goods in full is known as **complete repossession** and if part of goods are repossessed then it is called as **partial repossession**.

In the partial repossession of goods by the hire seller are calculated at agreed price, hence the calculation of **agreed price** is based on the following points.

♦ Repossession of goods may be calculated on the basis of depreciation, the hire seller can charge rate of depreciation higher than normal rate applied by hire purchaser.

Note: Depreciation calculated by hire seller is only for calculation of partial repossession of good, hence the journal entries of depreciation must not be recorded in the books of hire seller since the advantage of depreciation of asset is already taken by hire purchaser.

♦ The agreed value may calculated on cash price or hire purchase price at certain rate.

♦ Any other agreed amount determined by mutual agreement between hire purchaser and hire seller.

Note: In the partial repossession both the parties, the hire seller as well as hire purchaser, does not close the account of each other in their respective books.

10.9.1 Accounting Treatment for repossession
In the books of Hire Seller

All the entries to be recorded as usual until the date of default	Regular Journal Entries	
Even at the period of default - Interest on goods as applicable	Hire Purchaser A/c To Interest A/c	Dr Cr
Transfer of Interest to P&L A/c	Interest A/c To Profit & Loss A/c	Dr Cr
In the event of default – Depreciation on **Partial Repossessed Goods**	Depreciation A/c To Repossessed Goods A/c	Dr Cr
The period of default. – If loss incurred in Goods Repossession.	Profit & Loss A/c To Hire Purchaser A/c	Dr Cr
The period of default. – If profit incurred in Goods Repossession	Hire Purchaser A/c To Profit & Loss A/c	Dr Cr

The period of default – **Repossession of Goods** & **Closing of Purchaser A/c**	Repossessed Goods A/c	Dr	
	To Hire Purchaser A/c		Cr
Any **expenses** made towards goods after repossession	Expense for Goods A/c	Dr	
	To Bank A/c		Cr
Transfer of expense to goods account	Repossessed Goods A/c	Dr	
	To Expense for Goods A/c		Cr
Sale of Repossessed Goods	Bank A/c	Dr	
	To Repossessed Goods A/c		Cr
Profit on Sale of Repossessed Goods	Repossessed Goods A/c	Dr	
	To Profit & Loss A/c		Cr
Loss on Sale of Repossessed Goods	Profit & Loss A/c	Dr	
	To Repossessed Goods A/c		Cr

In the books of Hire Purchaser

All the entries to be recorded as usual until the date of default	Regular Journal Entries		
Even at the period of default - **Interest** on goods as applicable	Interest A/c	Dr	
	Hire Seller A/c		Cr
Even at the period of default – **Depreciation** charged on Asset	Depreciation A/c	Dr	
	To Fixed Asset		Cr
Transfer of depreciation to Profit & Loss A/c	Profit & Loss A/c	Dr	
	To Depreciation A/c		Cr
If **loss** incurred in Submission of Goods	Profit & Loss A/c	Dr	
	To Asset A/c		Cr
If **profit** incurred in Submission of Goods	Asset A/c	Dr	
	To Profit & Loss A/c		Cr
The period of default – **Submission of Goods** & **Closing of Seller A/c**	Hire Seller A/c	Dr	
	To Fixed Asset A/c		Cr

10.9.2 Illustration – Complete Repossession

On 1st April, 2014, **Octogems Pvt Ltd** purchased Equipment from **Rantan Steel Ltd** on hire purchase systems, the details of the transactions are as follows

* The **Cash Price** of the Machinery in the Market is Rs. 4,00,000/-

* The **Down Payment** paid was Rs. 1,00,000/-

* The **Principal** amount is fixed to 1,00,000/- at each interval and instalment is paid on 31st March of Following Year. The deal would complete in **3 years**

* The **Rate of Interest is 5%** per annum

* **Octogems Pvt Ltd** charge deprecation the fixed asset @ 20% using **Straight Line Method**.

Octogems Pvt Ltd paid the first year instalment but unable to pay further instalments, Rantan steel Ltd took over the possession of equipment. On 31st March 2016, **Maintenance** of Rs. 6000 were incurred on equipment and thereafter on the same date, the equipment were sold for Rs. 2,20,000/-

Let us prepare interest calculation table, pass the necessary journal entries and prepare respective ledger accounts.

Interest Table

		Hire Purchase Interest Calculation Method 2			
Period(s)	Opening Balance O/s	Interest Portion	DP/Principal Portion	(Instalment)	Closing Balance O/s
1	400000		100000		300000
1	300000	15000	100000	115000	200000
2	200000	10000	100000	110000	100000
3	100000	5000	100000	105000	0

Total Interest = 30000/-

Journal Entries
In the books of Hire Seller (Rantan Steel Ltd)

Date	Particulars		L.F	Debit	Credit
01-04-14	Octogems Pvt Ltd A/c	Dr		400000	
	To Sales of Equipment A/c	Cr			400000
	Being goods sold on hire purchase basis				
01-04-14	Bank A/c	Dr		100000	
	To Octogems Pvt Ltd A/c	Cr			100000
	Being downpayment received				
31-03-15	Octogems Pvt Ltd A/c	Dr		15000	
	To Interest A/c	Cr			15000
	Interest receive due				
31-03-15	Interest A/c	Dr		15000	
	To Profit & Loss A/c	Cr			15000
	Being Interest transferred to P&L A/c				
31-03-15	Bank A/c	Dr		115000	
	To Octogems Pvt Ltd A/c	Cr			115000
	Being 1st Instalment received				

	Year of Default				
31-03-16	Octogems Pvt Ltd A/c	Dr		10000	
	To Interest A/c	Cr			10000
	Interest receive due				
31-03-16	Interest A/c	Dr		10000	
	To Profit & Loss A/c	Cr			10000
	Being Interest transferred to P&L A/c				
31-03-16	Repossession of Goods A/c	Dr		210000	
	To Octogems Pvt Ltd A/c	Cr			210000
	Being goods repossessed				
31-03-16	Maintenance of Equipments A/c	Dr		6000	
	To Bank A/c	Cr			6000
	Maintenance expenses incurred on the equipment				
31-03-16	Repossession of Goods A/c	Dr		6000	
	To Maintenance of Equipments A/c	Cr			6000
	Being equipment expenses added to the goods				
31-03-16	Bank A/c	Dr		220000	
	To Repossession of Goods A/c	Cr			220000
	Being profit on sale of repossessed goods acknowledge				
31-03-16	Repossession of Goods A/c	Dr		4000	
	To Profit & Loss A/c	Cr			4000
	Being profit on sale of repossessed goods acknowledge				

Customer Account

	Octogems Pvt Ltd A/c				
Date	Particulars	Amount	Date	Particulars	Amount
01-04-14	To Equipment A/c	400000	01-04-14	By Bank A/c	100000
31-03-15	To Interest A/c	15000	31-03-15	By Bank A/c	115000
			31-03-15	By Balance c/d	200000
		415000			415000
	Year of Default				
01-04-16	To Balance b/d	200000	31-03-16	By Repossessed Goods A/c	210000
31-03-16	To Interest A/c	10000			
		210000			210000

Stock Account

	Repossessed Goods A/c				
Date	Particulars	Amount	Date	Particulars	Amount
31-03-16	To Octogems Pvt Ltd A/c	210000	31-03-16	By Bank A/c	220000
31-03-16	To Maintenance of Equipments A/c	6000			
31-03-16	To Profit & Loss A/c (Profit on Sales)	4000			
		220000			220000

Journal Entries
In the books of Hire Purchaser (Octogems Pvt Ltd)

Date	Particulars		L.F	Debit	Credit
01-04-14	Equipment A/c	Dr		400000	
	To Rantan Steel Ltd A/c	Cr			400000
	Being goods bought on hire purchase basis				
01-04-14	Rantan Steel Ltd A/c	Dr		100000	
	To Bank A/c	Cr			100000
	Being downpayment made				
31-03-15	Interest A/c	Dr		15000	
	To Rantan Steel Ltd A/c	Cr			15000
	Made the interest due				

			Dr	115000	
31-03-15	Rantan Steel Ltd A/c				
	To Bank A/c		Cr		115000
	(Being 1st Instalment paid)				
31-03-15	Depreciation A/c		Dr	80000	
	To Machinery A/c		Cr		80000
	(Being depreciation charged on fixed asset)				
31-03-15	Profit & Loss A/c		Dr	80000	
	To Depreciation A/c		Cr		80000
	(Being depreciation transferred to P&L A/c)				
	Year of Default				
31-03-16	Interest A/c		Dr	10000	
	To Rantan Steel Ltd A/c		Cr		10000
	(Made the interest due)				
31-03-16	Depreciation A/c		Dr	80000	
	To Machinery A/c		Cr		80000
	(Being depreciation charged on fixed asset)				
31-03-16	Profit & Loss A/c		Dr	80000	
	To Depreciation A/c		Cr		80000
	(Being depreciation transferred to P&L A/c)				
31-03-16	Rantan Steel Ltd A/c		Dr	210000	
	To Equipment A/c		Cr		210000
	(Being goods submitted)				
31-03-16	Equipment A/c		Dr	30000	
	To Profit & Loss A/c		Cr		30000
	(Being loss incurred on submitting the goods)				

Vendor Account

Rantan Steel Ltd A/c

Date	Particulars	Amount	Date	Particulars	Amount
01-04-14	To Bank A/c	100000	01-04-14	By Equipment A/c	400000
31-03-15	To Bank A/c	115000	31-03-15	By Interest A/c	15000
31-03-15	To Balance c/d	200000			
		415000			415000
	Year of Default				
31-03-16	To Equipment A/c	210000	01-04-16	To Balance c/d	200000
			31-03-15	By Interest A/c	10000
		210000			210000

Fixed Asset Account

Equipment A/c

Date	Particulars	Amount	Date	Particulars	Amount
01-04-14	To Rantan Steel Ltd A/c	400000	31-03-15	By Depreciation A/c	80000
			31-03-15	By Balance c/d	320000
		400000			400000
01-04-16	To Balance b/d	320000	31-03-16	By Depreciation A/c	80000
			31-03-16	By Rantan Steel Ltd A/c	210000
				By Profit & Loss A/c (Loss on Submitting)	30000
		320000			320000

10.9.3 Illustration – Partial Repossession

On 1st April. 2014, **Moon Gold Enterprises** purchased Instruments from **Laser & Torrent Ltd** on hire purchase systems, the details of the transactions are as follows

* The **Cash Price** of the Machinery in the Market is Rs. 6,00,000/-
* The **Down Payment** paid was Rs. 1,75,000/-
* The **Instalment** amount is fixed to 1,34,000/- at each interval and instalment is paid on 31st March of Following Year. The deal would complete in **4 years**
* The **Rate of Interest is 10%** per annum
* **Moon Gold Enterprises** charge deprecation the fixed asset @ **20%** using straight line method.
* The Last instalment interest would be **rounding off** at the difference of Rs. **348.50/-**

Moon Gold Enterprises paid the first year instalment but unable to pay further instalments, **Laser & Torrent Ltd** agreed to leave some instruments and partially took over possession of

remaining instruments.

Laser & Torrent Ltd, taken over **60%** of the instruments after assessing it **on the basis of depreciation** and the **rate of depreciation** charged on instruments is **@ 30%** on annual basis using **Reducing Balance Method**.

Let us prepare interest calculation table, asset calculation table, pass the necessary journal entries in both, the books of hire purchaser and seller and prepare respective ledger accounts.

Interest Table

	Hire Purchase Interest Calculation Method 2				
Period(s)	Opening Balance O/s	Interest Portion	DP/Principal Portion	(Instalment)	Closing Balance O/s
1	600000		175000		425000
1	425000	42500	91500	134000	333500
2	333500	33350	100650	134000	232850
3	232850	23285	110715	134000	122135
4	122135	11865	122135	134000	0

Below is the calculation table of Asset Possessed by Seller and Retained by Purchaser and the difference in Net Asset on partial repossession

Hire Seller Valued the **Asset Possessed** – Rs. 600000/-

	In the Books of Hire Seller		
Year	Possession on Total Asset @ 60%	Depreciation @ 30%	Net Asset
1st Year	360000	108000	252000
2nd Year	252000	75600	176400

Difference in Net Asset on Partial Repossession – Rs. 600000/-

	In the Books of Hire Purchaser		
Year	Holding on Total Asset @ 60%	Depreciation @ 20%	Net Asset
1st Year	360000	72000	288000
2nd Year	288000	57600	230400

Hire Purchaser Valued the **Asset Retained** – Rs. 600000/-

	In the Books of Hire Purchaser		
Year	Holding on Total Asset @ 40%	Depreciation @ 20%	Net Asset
1st Year	240000	48000	192000
2nd Year	192000	38400	153600

Journal Entries

In the books of Hire Purchaser (Moon Gold Enterprises)

Date	Particulars		L.F	Debit	Credit
01-04-14	Instruments A/c	Dr		600000	
	To Laser & Torrent Ltd A/c	Cr			600000
	(Being goods bought on hire purchase basis)				
01-04-14	Laser & Torrent Ltd A/c	Dr		175000	
	To Bank A/c	Cr			175000
	(Being downpayment made)				
31-03-15	Interest A/c	Dr		42500	
	To Laser & Torrent Ltd A/c	Cr			42500
	(Made the interest due)				
31-03-15	Laser & Torrent Ltd A/c	Dr		134000	
	To Bank A/c	Cr			134000
	(Being 1st Instalment paid)				
31-03-15	Depreciation A/c	Dr		120000	
	To Instruments A/c	Cr			120000
	(Being depreciation charged on fixed asset)				
31-03-15	Profit & Loss A/c	Dr		120000	
	To Depreciation A/c	Cr			120000
	(Being depreciation transferred to P&L A/c)				

			Year of Default		
31-03-16	Interest A/c	Dr		33350	
	To Laser & Torrent Ltd A/c	Cr			33350
	(Made the interest due)				
31-03-16	Depreciation A/c	Dr		96000	
	To Instruments A/c	Cr			96000
	(Being depreciation charged on fixed asset)				
31-03-16	Profit & Loss A/c	Dr		96000	
	To Depreciation A/c	Cr			96000
	(Being depreciation transferred to P&L A/c)				
31-03-16	Laser & Torrent Ltd A/c	Dr		176400	
	To Instruments A/c	Cr			176400
	(Being goods submitted)				
31-03-16	Profit & Loss A/c	Dr		54000	
	To Instruments A/c	Cr			54000
	(Being loss incurred on submitting the goods)				

Laser & Torrent Ltd A/c

Date	Particulars	Amount	Date	Particulars	Amount
01-04-14	To Bank A/c	175000	01-04-14	By Instruments A/c	600000
31-03-15	To Bank A/c	134000	31-03-15	By Interest A/c	42500
31-03-15	To Balance c/d	333500			
		642500			642500
			Year of Default		
31-03-16	To Instruments A/c	176400	01-04-16	To Balance c/d	333500
31-03-16	To Balance c/d	190450	31-03-16	By Interest A/c	33350
		366850			366850

Instruments A/c

Date	Particulars	Amount	Date	Particulars	Amount
01-04-14	To Laser & Torrent Ltd A/c	600000	31-03-15	By Depreciation A/c	120000
			31-03-15	By Balance c/d	480000
		600000			600000
			Year of Default		
01-04-16	To Balance b/d	480000	31-03-16	By Depreciation A/c	96000
			31-03-16	By Rantan Steel Ltd A/c	176400
			31-03-16	By Profit & Loss A/c (Loss on Submitting)	54000
			31-03-16	By Balance c/d	153600
		480000			480000

Journal Entries

In the books of Hire Seller (Laser & Torrent Ltd)

Date	Particulars		L.F	Dr.	Cr.
01-04-14	Moon Gold Enterprises A/c	Dr		600000	
	To Sales of Instruments A/c	Cr			600000
	(Being goods sold on hire purchase basis)				
01-04-14	Bank A/c	Dr		175000	
	To Moon Gold Enterprises A/c	Cr			175000
	(Being downpayment received)				
31-03-15	Moon Gold Enterprises A/c	Dr		42500	
	To Interest A/c	Cr			42500
	(Interest receive due)				
31-03-15	Interest A/c	Dr		42500	
	To Profit & Loss A/c	Cr			42500
	(Being Interest transferred to P&L A/c)				
31-03-15	Bank A/c	Dr		134000	
	To Moon Gold Enterprises A/c	Cr			134000
	(Being 1st Instalment received)				
		Year of Default			
31-03-16	Moon Gold Enterprises A/c	Dr		33350	
	To Interest A/c	Cr			33350
	(Interest receive due)				
31-03-16	Interest A/c	Dr		33350	
	To Profit & Loss A/c	Cr			33350
	(Being Interest transferred to P&L A/c)				
31-03-16	Repossession of Goods A/c	Dr		176400	
	To Moon Gold Enterprises A/c	Cr			176400
	(Being 60% partial goods repossessed)				

Moon Gold Enterprises A/c

Date	Particulars	Amount	Date	Particulars	Amount
01-04-14	To Instruments A/c	600000	01-04-14	By Bank A/c	175000
31-03-15	To Interest A/c	42500	31-03-15	By Bank A/c	134000
			31-03-15	By Balance c/d	333500
		642500			642500
			Year of Default		
01-04-16	To Balance b/d	333500	31-03-16	By Repossessed Goods A/c	176400
31-03-16	To Interest A/c	33350	31-03-16	By Balance c/d	190450
		366850			366850

Repossessed Goods A/c

Date	Particulars	Amount	Date	Particulars	Amount
		Year of Default			
31-03-16	To Moon Gold Enterprises A/c	176400	31-03-16	By Balance c/d	176400
		176400			176400

PRACTICE EXERCISE

Q1. On 1st April. 2012, Soham Int Pvt Ltd purchased machinery from Titan Machines & Instruments Ltd on hire purchase systems, the details of the transactions are as follows.

- The Cash Price of the Machinery in the Market is Rs. 5,00,000/-
- The down payment mentioned was Rs. 1,00,000/-
- The Instalment is Rs. 1,26,000/- and paid on 31st March of Following Year.
- The Rate of Interest is 10% per annum
- The deal would complete in 4 years
- Soham Enterprises charge deprecation the fixed asset @ 20% using straight line method.
- The Last instalment interest would be rounding at the difference of Rs. 874/-

Pass the journal entries in the book of Hire Purchaser (**Soham Enterprises**), and prepare the **interest calculation** table and the following ledger accounts.

> **Vendors Ledger Account**
>
> **Fixed Asset Account**
>
> **Depreciation Account**

Pass the journal entries in the book of Hire Seller (**Titan Machines & Instruments Ltd**), and prepare the interest calculation table and the following ledger accounts.

> **Customer Ledger Account**
>
> **Interest Account**

Q2. On 1st April. 2014, Fly Kite Enterprises purchased machine from Birglass Tools Ltd on hire purchase systems, the details of the transactions are as follows

- The Cash Price of the Machinery in the Market is Rs. 2,50,000/-
- The down payment paid was Rs. 50,000/-
- The Principal amount is fixed to 50,000/- and instalment is paid on 31st March of Following Year.

- The Rate of Interest is 5% per annum
- The deal would complete in 4 years
- Octogems Pvt Ltd charge deprecation the fixed asset @ 20% using straight line method.

  Fly Kite Enterprises paid the first year instalment but unable to pay further instalments, **Birglass Tools Ltd** took over the possession of **machine**. On 31st March 2016, Maintenance of Rs. 5000 were incurred on machine and thereafter on the same date, the equipment were sold for Rs. 1,65,000/-

  Pass the journal entries in the book of Hire Seller (**Birglass Tools Ltd**), and prepare the **interest calculation** table and the following ledger accounts.

  Customer Ledger Account

  Repossessed Goods Account

Q3. On 1st April. 2014, Desert Sultan Pvt Ltd purchased Equipments from Toyo Steel Ltd on hire purchase systems, the details of the transactions are as follows

- The **Cash Price** of the Machinery in the Market is Rs. 5,00,000/-
- The **Down Payment** paid was Rs. 1,25,000/-
- The **Instalment** amount is fixed to 1,18,300/- at each interval and instalment is paid on 31st March of Following Year. The deal would complete in **4 years**
- The **Rate of Interest is 10%** per annum
- **Desert Sultan Pvt Ltd** charge deprecation the fixed asset @ **20%** using straight line method.
- The Last instalment interest would be **rounding off** at the difference of Rs. **7.20**/-

  Desert Sultan Pvt Ltd paid the first year instalment but unable to pay further instalments, **Toyo Steel Ltd** agreed to leave partial equipment with the purchaser and took over possession of remaining Equipments.

  Toyo Steel Ltd, taken over **60%** of the **Equipments** after assessing it **on the basis of depreciation** and the **rate of depreciation** charged on instruments is @ **30%** on annual basis using **Straight Line Method**.

  Prepare interest calculation table, asset calculation table, pass the necessary journal entries in both, the books of hire purchaser and seller and prepare respective ledger accounts.

Multiple Choice Questions

1. What is the buyer in the hire purchase system called as _____
   a. Dealer Purchaser   b. Broker
   c. Agent Buyer   d. **Hire Purchaser**

2. The excess of hire price over the cash price is called as
   a. Commission   b. **Interest**
   c. Brokerage   d. Penalty

3. The instalment amount paid is sum of _____ + _____
   a. **Principal + Interest**
   b. Principal + Closing Balance
   c. Interest + Penalty
   d. Cash Price + Hire Purchase Price

4. The price at which the goods can be purchased from the market at full payment
   a. Hire Purchase Price   b. Interest Price
   c. **Cash Price**   d. Instalments

5. Who reserves the right to repossess the goods at the event of default.
   a. Hire Purchaser   b. **Hire Seller**
   c. Government of India   d. Local Government

Review Questions

1. Once the last instalment is made by the hire purchaser, what would happen
   a. **Hire purchaser get the ownership of the goods**
   b. Hire seller take back the goods
   c. Hire seller depreciate the goods for the final time

2. Ever Instalment paid by the hire purchaser is treated as
   a. Loss to the company
   b. Profit to the company
   c. **Hire charge**

3. In the event of non-payment of instalment by the hire purchaser
   a. Hire purchaser would destroy goods and claim the amount from the insurance
   b. Hire purchaser would depreciate the assets at 100%
   c. **Hire seller would repossess the goods**

Chapter 11

Accounting for Inland Branches

LEARNING OBJECTIVES

After studying this chapter, you will understand:

- Different Types of Branches
- Systems of Accounting
- Recording Transaction in the Book of Dependent Branches
- Recording Transactions in the Bok of Independent Branches
- How to Prepare the Consolidated Profit & Loss Account
- How to Prepare the Consolidated Balance Sheet

11.1 INTRODUCTION

In order to increase sales or market their products in different locations, a business should make its products available to large territories or split the business in different parts or locations.

Numerous division of the business are located in different locations either in the same place or different place i.e., a business can be located in different part of the city like kormangala, Jayanagar and Indranagar in Bangalore city or different part of the country like Karnataka, Delhi, Kolkata, Assam or different countries like India, United Kingdom, Japan, U.S.A. These are known as branches and head office controls the activities of many branches.

Inland Branches are the branches located within the Country, Inland branches are also called as Home Branch or Domestic Branch.

11.2 PURPOSE OF BRANCH ACCOUNTING

The purpose of maintaining Branch accounts depends on the type of business and the requirement of the business concern which differ from business to business, the overall purpose of branch accounting in case of any business are given below:

1. **Profit or Loss**: Branch Accounts are maintained to know the profit or loss of the branch separately.

2. **Estimate the Progress and Performance**: By keeping the track of accounting details of Branch office, we can estimate the progress and performance of different branch offices and take the right business decision.

3. **Find out the Financial Position**: We can find out the financial position of branch at any given date.

4. **Auditing**: All Branch companies should maintained the accounting details for auditing purpose.

5. **Expansion of Business**: It helps in taking the decision whether the business has to be expanded or not.

11.3 TYPES OF BRANCHES

They are two types of branches in which the business transactions are recorded in the Books of accounts:

1. Dependent Branches: Dependent
2. Independent Branches
   a. Home Branch
   b. Foreign Branch

11.3.1 Dependent Branches

Dependent Branches doesn't maintains its books of accounts, they are maintained by its Head office.

Following are the main features of Dependent branch is given below:

1. **Full System of Accounting is Not Maintained:** As explained earlier in case of Dependent branches the books of accounts are maintained by the head office, but branch maintains details of Debtors Ledger and Stock Ledger. When the branch have permission to sell the goods on credit, then Debtors ledger are maintained to know the payable amount from Debtors and also a Stock Ledger is maintained to track the movement of goods from head office to branch office like goods received from head office and the balance of goods/stock in hand.

2. **Sometimes Branch Office are Permitted to Make Purchases:** Head office will supply the goods to Branch office on regular bases, sometimes the head office will allow the branch office to make purchases from local supplier and the payments for the purchases made by branch office will be made by head office.

3. **Remittance of Cash Collected by Branch Office to Head Office:** Cash collected from the cash sales or debtors are transferred to head office through local bank.

4. **Branch Expenses are Maintained by the Head Office:** Expenses incurred by the branch office like salary, rent, promotion expense etc., are paid by the head office through cheque for a particular period.

5. **Petty Cash is provided to Branch by Head Office:** Petty cash is provided to branch office by head office in order to meet their petty expenses and branch maintains the Petty cash book.

11.3.2 System of Accounting for dependent Branches

Head office will maintains the books of accounts of branch office. Based on the nature of business, size of business, volume of transactions etc., the head office will opt for any one of the following method to maintain the books of accounts of dependent branches.

I. Debtors System
II. Stock and Debtors System
III. Final Accounts System
IV. Wholesale Branch System

Let us understand how books of accounts of dependent branches are maintained in Debtors System.

11.3.2.1 Debtors System

This method is followed when the size of the branch is small. In this a branch account is maintained by the Head office and it is a nominal account and is prepared to calculate profit & loss for each branch. This method is also known as One Account System and is maintained as per the following simple system:

a. Branch account is debited with the opening balance or whatever the branch has in the beginning of accounting period like stock, debtors, petty cash, furniture, goods sent to branch account less returns etc.

b. Branch is debited, when head office send anything to branch during the accounting period like head office my send the cash to branch for the purchases made or for the expenses incurred by the branch.

c. Branch account is credited when head office receives anything from branch office like goods returned by the branch, cash remitted by branch etc.

d. Branch account is credited with the closing balance or whatever the branch has at the end of the accounting period like stock, debtors, petty cash etc.

The following are the Branch transactions which are recorded in the books of head office:

S.No	Branch Transactions	Particulars		L.F	Dr.	Cr.
		Accounting of Branch Transactions in the books of Head Office				
1	Goods supplied to branch office from head office	Branch A/c	Dr.		xxx	
		To Goods sent to Branch A/c				xxx
		(Being goods sent to branch)				
2	Goods returned by branch office to head office	Goods sent to Branch A/c	Dr.		xxx	
		To Branch A/c				xxx
		(Being goods returned by branch)				
3	Goods sent by branch to another branch with head office permission	Goods sent to Branch A/c	Dr.		xxx	
		To Branch A/c				xxx
		(Being goods returned by branch)				
4	Cheque or draft is received from the branch	Bank A/c	Dr.		xxx	
		To Branch A/c				xxx
		(Being remittance received from Branch)				
5	Expenses incurred by the branch office are paid by Head office	Branch A/c	Dr.		xxx	
		To Bank A/c				xxx
		(Being branch office expenses met by head office)				
6	Goods returned by branch debtors to head office directly	Goods sent to Branch A/c	Dr.		xxx	
		To Branch A/c				xxx
		(Being goods returned by branch debtors)				
7	Transfer of balance in goods sent to branch A/c	Goods sent to Branch A/c	Dr.		xxx	
		To Purchase A/c				xxx
		(Being transfer of balance in goods sent to branch)				
8	Branch asset at the end of accounting period	Branch Asset A/c	Dr.		xxx	
		To Branch A/c				xxx
		(Being adjustment entry for branch closing assets)				
9	Branch liabilities at the end of the accounting period	Branch A/c	Dr.		xxx	
		To Branch Liabilities A/c				xxx
		(Being adjustment entry for branch closing liability)				
10	For profit or loss Profit at branch transferred to profit & loss account	Branch A/c	Dr.		xxx	
		To General Profit & Loss A/c				xxx
		(Being branch profit transferred to P & L A/c)				
	Loss at branch transferred to profit & loss account	General Profit & Loss A/c	Dr.		xxx	
		To Branch A/c				xxx
		(Being branch Loss transferred to P & L A/c)				
11	At the end of the accounting year the assets and liabilities will appear in the balance sheet of head office and it has to be transferred to branch office in the beginning of the next accounting year. Transfer of Branch assets	Branch A/c	Dr.		xxx	
		To Branch Asset A/c				xxx
		(Being branch opening assets transferred to branch)				
	Transfer of Branch Liabilities	Branch Liabilities	Dr.		xxx	
		To Branch A/c				xxx
		(Being branch liabilities transferred to branch)				
					XXX	XXX

The Sample Branch Account format is given below:

Date 2016	Particulars	₹	Date 2016	Particulars	₹
		Branch Account			
	To Opening Balances			By Opening Balances	
	Stock	xxxx		Outstanding Expenses	xxxx
	Debtors	xxxx		Creditors	xxxx	XXXX
	Furniture	xxxx		By Bank	
	Petty Cash	xxxx		Collections from Debtors	xxxx
	Pre-paid Expenses	xxxx XXXX		Cash Sales (remittance)	xxxx XXXX
	To Goods sent to Branch A/c	xxxx		By Goods sent to Branch A/c (Goods returned to head office or returned by branch debtors or transferred to other branch)	xxxx
	To Bank (for payments made by head office on behalf of branch)	xxxx		By Closing Balances	
	To Closing Balances			Petty Cash	xxxx
	Outstanding expenses	xxxx		Furniture (at depreciation value)	xxxx
	Creditors	xxxx XXXX		Debtors	xxxx

To Profit (Transfer to general profit & loss account)			Pre-paid Expenses	xxxx	xxxx
			By Loss (Transfer to general profit & loss account)		xxxx

Note: If the debit side is more than the credit side then the branch office is under loss, if debit side is less than the credit side then the branch office is in profit.

Points need to be considered while recording the transactions in the Branch Account.

1. Head office should not record the following transactions in branch account.

   a. Surplus and shortage of stock

   b. Credit sales made by Branch

   c. Sales return made by branch debtors to branch (if the goods are return by branch debtors to head office then the entry should be recorded)

   d. Bad Debts, Discounts etc.

2. **Sale of fixed assets:** Brach can sell the fixed asset assets on cash and remit the amount to head office. In case of the branch sell the fixed assets on credit then the amount due will be shown as debtors at the branch at the end of accounting period. The net asset amount is shown at the end of accounting period and it is derived as shown below:

   Opening Balance + Purchase of Fixes Assets – Amount Realized on Account of Sale of Fixed Assets.

   No need of recording the separate entry for profit or loss made by the sale of fixed assets as it is taken automatically when the closing and opening balances are accounted in the branch account.

3. **Depreciation:** Depreciation of fixed assets is not shown in the Branch account but branch account is debited with the fixed assets value in the beginning of the accounting period and it is credited in the end of the accounting period and the difference that is depreciation is charged automatically.

   For Example:

   Fixed assets value in the beginning of the accounting period = 20,000

   Depreciation charged p.a 20%

   Now, in the beginning of the accounting period the branch account is debited with fixed asset value 20,000 and it is credited at the end of accounting period with fixed asset value as 18,000 and 2,000 is automatically charged as depreciation.

4. **Insurance claimed:** Amount received from the insurance company on account of damages incurred by the branch office will be remitted to head office.

5. **Petty Expenses:** Petty expenses incurred by the branch office is not recorded. The branch account is debited with petty cash opening balance and cash sent by head office to branch for meeting petty expenses and it is credited with

petty cash closing balance. Thus the petty cash expenses are automatically charged to the branch account.

For example:

Petty cash balance with branch account in the beginning of accounting period = 10,000

Petty Cash sent by head office to branch office to meet their petty expenses = 15,000

Petty expenses incurred by branch office = 20,000

Now, in the beginning of the accounting period the petty cash is debited with the value 25,000 (Opening balance + cash sent by head office) and it will be credited with the value 5,000 at the end of the accounting period.

Illustration 1: T&T Enterprises have its head office at Delhi and branch office at Karnataka, following are the transactions with head office at branch for the year ended 31st August, 2016.

Date 2016	Transactions
Sep. 1	Stock at branch ₹ 40,000
	Debtors at branch ₹20,000
	Petty Cash ₹ 5,000
	Goods supplied to branch office for ₹ 1,60,000
	Cash sales remittance from branch ₹ 11,000
	Realization of debtors ₹ 1,60,000
	Salary of ₹ 20,000 sent to branch
	Rent of ₹10,000 sent to branch
	Petty cash of ₹ 10,000 sent to branch
Aug. 31	Stock at branch ₹20,000
	Debtors at branch ₹ 10,000
	Petty Cash ₹ 10,000

Record the above transaction in the journal and prepare the Branch Account.

Solution:

	In the book of the T&T Head Office Journal Entries				
Date (2016)	Particulars		L.F	Dr.	Cr.
Sep. 1	Karnataka Branch A/c	Dr		65,000	
	To Branch Stock A/c				40,000
	To Branch Debtors A/c				20,000
	To Petty Cash A/c				5,000
	(Being Branch opening assets transferred to Branch A/c)				
Jan. 1 to Aug. 31	Karnataka Branch A/c	Dr		1,60,000	
	To Goods sent to branch A/c				1,60,000
	(Being goods sent to branch)				
Jan. 1 to Aug. 31	Bank A/c	Dr		11,000	
	To Karnataka Branch A/c				11,000
	(Being remittance received from branch)				
Jan. 1 to Aug. 31	Bank A/c	Dr		1,60,000	

	Particulars		₹	₹
	(Being realization of Debtors)			
Jan. 1 to Aug. 31	Karnataka Branch A/c	Dr.	20,000	
	To Salary A/c			20,000
	(Being salary sent to branch)			
Jan. 1 to Aug. 31	Karnataka Branch A/c	Dr.	10,000	
	To Rent A/c			10,000
	(Being Rent sent to branch)			
Jan. 1 to Aug. 31	Karnataka Branch A/c	Dr.	10,000	
	To Petty Cash A/c			10,000
	(Being Petty Cash sent to branch)			
Aug. 31	Branch Stock A/c	Dr.	20,000	
	Branch Debtors A/c	Dr.	10,000	
	Petty Cash A/c	Dr.	10,000	
	To Karnataka Branch A/c			40,000
	(Being Adjustment entry with branch closing assets)			
			4,76,000	4,76,000

The following is the branch account in the books of head office.

Karnataka Branch Account

Date (2016)	Particulars		₹	Date (2016)	Particulars		₹
Sep. 1	To Opening Balances b/d			Aug 31	By Closing Balances c/d		
	Branch Stock A/c	40,000			Branch Stock A/c	20,000	
	Branch Debtors A/c	20,000			Branch Debtors A/c	10,000	
	Petty Cash A/c	5,000	65,000		Petty Cash A/c	10,000	40,000
	To Goods sent to Branch A/c		1,60,000	Sep. 1	By Bank A/c		
	To Salaries A/c		20,000		Cash Sales	11,000	
	To Rent A/c		10,000		Debtors	1,60,000	1,71,000
	To Petty Cash		10,000		By Loss transferred to general profit & loss A/c		54,000
			2,65,000				265000

Note: In the above illustration debit balance is more than credit balance, hence the Karnataka branch account is showing loss.

Illustration 2: KK Enterprises have its head office at Mumbai and branch office at Kolkata, following are the transactions with head office at branch for the year ended 31ˢᵗ October, 2016, prepare branch account in the books of head office.

Date 2016	Transactions
Nov. 1	Stock at branch ₹ 12,000
	Debtors at branch ₹ 6,000
	Debtors at branch ₹ 6,900 as on Oct. 31
	Furniture at branch ₹ 2,200
	Petty Cash ₹ 700
	Salaries outstanding at branch ₹300
	Pre-paid fire insurance ₹ 3509
	Cash sales during the year ₹ 1,50,000
	Goods supplied to branch office for ₹ 1,00,000
	Cash sales remittance from branch ₹ 11,000
	Credit sales during the year ₹ 60,000
	Cash received from debtors ₹ 55,000
	Cash paid by branch office directly to head office ₹ 4,000
	Discount allowed to debtors ₹ 300
	Cash sent for the expenses incurred by branch office
	• Rent ₹ 4,000
	• Salaries ₹ 4,400
	• Petty Cash ₹ 3,000
	Goods Return by Debtors ₹4,000
	Goods returned by branch ₹ 3,000
	Stock as on Oct. 31 ₹ 7,000
	Petty Expenses at Branch ₹ 1,050
	Provide depreciation on furniture 10% p.a
	Goods costing 1,400 destroyed in accident and claimed ₹ 1,200 from insurance company.

Solution:

Kolkata Branch Account

Particulars	₹	Particulars	₹
To Opening Balances:		By Opening Balances:	
Branch Stock A/c	12,000	Outstanding Salaries A/c	300
Branch Debtors A/c	6,000	By Remittance	
Furniture A/c	2,200	Cash Sales	1,50,000
Petty Cash A/c	700	Cash Received from Debtors A/c	55,000
Pre-paid Insurance A/c	350	21,250	Cash paid by debtors directly to H.O	4,000
To Goods supplied to branch A/c		1,00,000	Received from Insurance Company	1,400	2,10,400
To Bank A/c			By Good sent to branch A/c (Return of goods by branch)	3,000
Rent A/c	4,000		By Closing Balances:	
Salary A/c	4,400		Branch Stock A/c	7,000
Petty Cash A/c	3,000		Branch Debtors A/c	6,900
Insurance A/c	800	12,200	Furniture A/c	1,980
To Net Profit	98,780	Petty Cash A/c	2,650	18,530
	2,32,230		2,32,230

Note: At the end Petty Cash Balance is calculated based on the information given below:

Petty Cash Opening balance is	700
Add: Petty Cash received from head office	3,000
Total Petty cash	**3,700**
Less: Petty Cash spent by Branch office	1,050
Petty Cash Closing Balance	**2,65**

Invoice Price Method:

♦ **Recording of Adjustment Entry Required in Head Office**

When the goods are sent to branch office by head office at Invoice price or selling price (Cost plus some profit percentage) and the branch should sell the goods at invoice price only.

In order to know the profit or loss made by the branch office, head office needs to record the adjustment entries as shown below:

Adjustment entries in the books of Head office		
Adjusting excess price of opening stock at branch		
Stock Reserve A/c	xxx	
To Branch A/c		xxx
(Being adjusted excess price of opening stock)		
Adjusting excess price of closing stock of branch or stock in transit at branch		
Branch A/c	xxx	
To Stock Reserve A/c		xxx
(Being excess of closing stock of branch adjusted)		

Based on the conservatism principle, no profit should be anticipated and all losses should be provided. Therefore it is mandatory to make a provision for the profit included in the unsold goods, because it will not earn any profit until sold.

Adjustment of excess price of goods sent to branch less returns made to head office		
Branch A/c	xxx	
To Stock Reserve A/c		xxx
(Being excess of closing stock of branch adjusted)		

♦ **Calculation of Loading or Excess Price**

For calculation of Loading or Excess Price or Markup, the following procedure needs to be followed.

Suppose the goods are supplied at Invoice price i.e. cost plus 20% profit. Consider cost is ₹ 100, profit is ₹ 25, selling price is 125 and the ratio of profit to selling price is 100/125. For the excess price value between invoice price and the cost price adjustments will be made based on the profit ratio 100/125 or 1/5 of the invoice price.

If the sales price is given with the percentage i.e., the percentage is given on sale price as 25%, then if the sales price is ₹ 100, profit will ₹ 25 and the cost will be ₹ 75 and the percentage on cost will be 1/3 of the cost or 25/75*100

11.3.2.2 Stock and Debtors System

This method is followed when the branch turnover is huge and also in this method more than one accounts are opened for various transactions at branch i.e., Head office should maintain a separate ledger accounts. For example Branch Stock, Branch Debtors, Goods supplied to Branch, Expenses incurred by Branch, Branch Assets and liabilities etc. Explanation about the each account is given below:

a. **Branch Stock Account:** In this account the transactions details like Goods received from head office, goods sold by branch office, goods returned to head office, goods returned by customers to the branch office etc. are recorded. It also provide the information regarding shortage of goods, excess of goods and closing stock.

b. **Branch Fixed Assets Account:** In this account transactions relating to fixed assets are recorded.

c. **Branch Expense Account:** In this account transaction relating to branch expenses are recorded i.e., summary of expenses incurred by branch like Discount, Bad debts etc.

d. **Branch Adjustment Account:** In this account transactions relating to goods sent to the branch, shortage or surplus at branch, opening and closing of stocks etc.., are recorded. This account is maintained to find out the gross profit.

e. **Branch Cash Account:** In this account all cash transactions of the branch is recorded.

f. **Branch Debtors Account:** In this account all transactions relating to debtors are recorded.

g. **Goods sent to Branch Account:** In this account transactions relating to goods movement to branch is recorded for example it will account the details of goods supplied to the branch and the goods returned by the branch to head office.

h. **Branch Profit & Loss Account:** This account is prepared in order to find out the profit and loss made by the branch office. Gross profit or loss is transferred to this account from branch adjustment account. This account is debited with all the expenses & loses and it is credited with all incomes and profit and the balanced amount will be the net profit or loss.

In case of Stock and Debtors System the following journal entries are recorded in the books of head office.

Accounting of Branch Transactions in the books of Head Office as per Stock and Debtors System					
S.No	Branch Transactions	Particulars	L.F	Dr.	Cr.
1	Goods supplied to branch office from head office (at invoice price)	Branch Stock A/c Dr		xxx	
		To Goods sent to Branch A/c			xxx
		(Being goods sent to branch at invoice price)			
2	Goods returned by branch office to head office (at invoice price)	Goods sent to Branch A/c Dr		xxx	
		To Branch Stock A/c			xxx
		(Being goods returned by branch at invoice price)			
3	Goods sent by branch to another branch with head office permission (This entry will be recorded as if branch has sent the goods to head office and from there it is transferred to another branch office) a. Branch A sent the goods to branch B	Goods sent to A Branch A/c		Dr	xxx	
		To A Branch Stock A/c			xxx
		Branch Stock A/c Dr		xxx	
		To goods sent to B Branch A/c			xxx
		(Being goods sent to other branch)			
4	For Discounts, Bad Debts etc.	Branch Expenses A/c Dr		xxx	

		To Branch Debtors A/c			xxx
		(Being expenses incurred)			
5	Expenses incurred by the branch office	Branch Expenses A/c	Dr.	xxx	
		To Bank A/c			xxx
		(Being branch office expenses)			
6	For abnormal losses or pilferage	Branch Adjustment A/c (enter amount of loading)	Dr.	xxx	
		Branch Profit & Loss A/c (enter shortage at cost)		xxx	
		To Branch Stock A/c (enter shortage at invoice price)			xxx
		(Being abnormal losses incurred)			
Note:	Reverse entry is recorded for surplus at branch and no entry should be accounted for normal loss of stock.				
7	Amount received from insurance company for abnormal loss	Branch Cash A/c	Dr.	xxx	
		To Branch Profit & Loss A/c			xxx
		(Being amount received from insurance company)			
8	Branch sold the goods on credit (at invoice price)	Branch Debtors A/c	Dr.	xxx	
		To Branch Stock A/c			xxx
		(Being sales made on credit by branch office)			
9	Branch sold goods on cash (at invoice price)	Cash A/c	Dr.	xxx	
		To Branch Debtors A/c			xxx
		(Being goods sold on cash)			
10	Goods returned by branch debtors to branch office (at invoice price)	Branch Stock A/c	Dr.	xxx	
		To Branch Debtors A/c			xxx
		(Being goods return by branch debtors to branch office)			
11	Goods returned by Branch Debtors to head office directly (at invoice price)	Goods sent to Branch A/c	Dr.	xxx	
		To Branch Debtors A/c			xxx
		(Being goods returned by branch debtors to head office)			
12	Transfer of Branch Expenses to branch profit & loss account	Branch Profit & Loss A/c	Dr.	xxx	
		To Branch Expenses A/c			xxx
		(Being branch expenses transferred)			
13	Adjustment of loading in the opening stock	Stock Reserve A/c	Dr.	xxx	
		To Branch Adjustment A/c			xxx
		(Being adjusted loading of opening stock)			
14	Adjustment of loading in the closing stock	Branch Adjustment A/c	Dr.	xxx	
		To Stock reserve A/C			xxx
		(Being adjusted loading of closing stock)			
15	Transfer of net profit at the branch	Branch Profit & Loss A/c	Dr.	xxx	
		To General Profit & Loss A/c			xxx
		(Being transfer of net profit at the branch)			
				xxx	xxx

Illustration 3: *Suraj Industries, Pune, has a Branch at Karnataka to which goods are sent at cost plus 25%. Branch makes credit and cash sales. Branch has to remit all cash received into the Head Office Bank Account at Karnataka and expenses incurred by head office are paid by the head office. From the following details prepare the accounts in the head office and find out the branch profits.*

Stock at Karnataka Branch on 1st August, 2016	10,000
Sundry Debtors at Karnataka on August, 2016	8,200
Stock at branch on 31st July, 2016	12,000
Goods received from head office at invoice price	70,000
Return of goods to head office at invoice price	2,200
Cash Sales	25,000
Credit Sales	37,000
Cash received from Sundry Debtors	33,000
Discount allowed to Sundry Debtors	700
Sales Return at Karnataka Branch	1,000
Rent at Karnataka Branch	2,000
Salaries at Karnataka Branch	7,000
Office Expenses	700
Bad Debts	500

Solution:

Karnataka Branch Stock Account in the books of Suraj Industries

Particulars	₹	Particulars	₹
To Balance b/d (Opening Stock)	3,000	By Cash Sales (Bank)	25,000
To Goods sent to Branch A/c	70,000	By Branch Debtors A/c (Credit Sales)	37,000
To Branch Debtors A/c (Returns)	1,000	By Goods sent to Branch A/c (Returns)	2,200
To Branch Profit & Loss A/c (Surplus)	2,200	By Balance c/d (Closing Stock)	12,000
	76,200		76,200

Karnataka Branch Debtors Account

Particulars	₹	Particulars	₹
To Balance b/d (Sundry Debtors)	8,200	By Bank A/c	33,000
To Branch Stock Account (Sales)	37,000	By Branch Profit & Loss A/c Bad Debts 500 Discounts 700	1,200
		By Branch Stock Account (Returns)	1,000
		By Balance c/d	10,000
	45,200		45,200

Karnataka Branch Adjustment Account

Particulars	₹	Particulars	₹
To Goods sent to branch A/c (Load on returns to H.O) (**Refer Below given calculation-1**)	440	By Balance b/d (Load in opening stock)	2,000
To Branch c/d (Load on closing stock) (**Refer calculation 2**)	2,400	By Goods Sent to Branch A/c (Load on goods sent)	14,000
To Branch Profit & Loss A/c	13,160		
	16,000		16,000

Karnataka Branch Expense Account

Particulars	₹	Particulars	₹
To Bank A/c		By Profit & Loss A/c	9,000
Rent	2,000		
Salaries	7,000		
Office Expenses	700		
	9,000		9,000

Karnataka Branch Profit & Loss Account

Particulars	₹	Particulars	₹
To Branch Expense A/c	9,000	By Branch Adjustment A/c	13,160
To Branch Debtors A/c (Discount)	7,00	By Branch Stock A/c	2,200
To Branch Debtors A/c (Bad Debts)	3,00		
To General Profit & Loss A/c	6,360		
	15,360		15,360

Goods Sent to Karnataka Branch Account

Particulars	₹	Particulars	₹
		By Karnataka Branch Stock	
To Branch Adjustment A/c	14,000	A/c	70,000
To Branch Stock A/c	2,200	By Branch Adjustment A/c	440
To Purchase A/c	54,240		
	70,440		70,440

Calculations:

1. **Load on return to Head office** = Return of goods to head office * 1/5

   = 2,200 * 1/5

   = 440

2. **Load on Closing Stock** = Closing Stock * 1/5

   = 12,000 * 1/5

   = 2,400

11.3.2.3 Final Accounts System

In this method profit and loss made by branches are found out by preparing the Branch Trading and Profit & Loss Account is prepared at cost price (i.e., cost of goods sent to the branch). Branch Trading and profit & Loss account is considered as memorandum account and will not form as a part of accounting system. Head Office may prepare the branch account and the nature of this account will be personal account as different from the branch account prepared by head office in case of Debtors System which is Nominal in nature. Hence the balances at the end of the accounting period represents the net assets at the branch (Assets – Liabilities at Branch)

Illustration 4: TIM Traders started branches at Chennai and Kerala as on 1st April, 2016. All goods are transferred by head office to branch office at cost plus 25 per cent. Head office pays all expenses incurred by the branch office. Cash collected by the branches are remitted to head office on daily bases. Each branch maintains its own sales ledger and sends the weekly statements to head office. The following are the details extracted from the weekly statements, sent by the different branches to head office for the half yearly period ended 30th September, 2016.

Particulars	Chennai (₹)	Kerala(₹)
Cash Sales made by branch	80,600	84,200
Credit Sales made by branch	1,27,200	1,12,000
Sundry Debtors	36,500	25,600
Sales Return	4,300	3,200
Rent and Rates	5,200	6,500
Bad debts	8,000	--
Salaries paid	18,000	20,000
General expenses incurred	4,600	3,500
Goods received from head office	1,52,000	1,27,000
Advertisement	9,500	7,200
Stock on 30th September, 2016	47,000	37,000

Prepare the branch accounts in the books of head office, showing the profit or loss for the accounting period and then prepare the Trading and Profit & Loss Account separately for each branch

Solution:

TIM Traders Branch Trading and Profit & Loss Account as on 30th September, 2016

Particulars	Chennai (₹)	Kerala (₹)	Particulars	Chennai (₹)	Kerala (₹)
To Goods sent to Branch (at cost pnse)	1,21,600	1,01,600	By Cash Sales	80,600	84,200
To Bad Debts	8,000		By Credit Sales	1,27,200	1,12,000
To Rent and Rates	5,200	6,500	Less Returns	4,300	3,200
To Salaries paid	18,000	20,000		2,03,500	1,93,000
To Advertisement	9,500	7,200	By Closing Stock (at cost price)	37,600	29,600
To General Expenses Incurred	4,600	3,500			
To Net profit to General Profit & Loss Account	74,200	83,800			
	2,41,100	2,22,600		2,41,100	2,22,600

Calculation: To find out the cost price of goods sent to branch follow the below given procedure.

Goods transferred to branch by head office is cost + 25%

Assume that the gods are invoiced at cost price 100 plus 25%

If the cost price is 100

Profit percentage is 25% of ₹ 100 i.e., ₹ 25

Selling price is 125 (100+25)

The ratio of profit to selling price is 25/125 0r 1/5

Therefore to find out the cost price for the above illustration take the ration 1/5

Invoice price = 1, 52,000

Profit = 30,400 (1, 52, 000 * 1/5)

Cost price = 1, 21,600 (1, 52,000 – 30,400)

Branch Accounts

Particulars	Chennai (₹)	Kolkata (₹)	Particulars	Chennai (₹)	Kolkata (₹)
To Goods Sent to branch account	1,52,000	1,27,000	By Cash Sales	80,600	84,200
To Salaries	18,000	20,000	By Collection from debtors (Refer calculation 3)	78,400	83,200
To Rent and Rates	5,200	6,500	By Goods Set to Branch A/c (Loading / Mark up) (Refer calculation 2)	30,400	25,400
To Advertisement	9,500	7,200	By Balance c/d Debtors & Stock	83,300	62,600
To General Expenses	4,600	3,500			
To Stock Reserve (Refer calculation 1)	9,400	7,400			
To Profit and Loss Account (Profit)	74,200	83,800			
	2,72,900	2,55,400		2,72,900	2,55,400

Calculations:

1. Calculation of stock reserve

   Stock Reserve of Chennai = 47,000 * 1/5 = 9,400 (Closing stock * 1/5)

   Similarly calculate stock reserve for Kolkata

2. Calculation of Goods sent to Branch A/c (Loading or mark up or excess price)

Loading = 1,52,000 * 1/5 = 30,400 (Goods sent to Branch office * 1/5)

3. Collection from debtors = Credit Sales - Sales Return - Sundry Debtors -Bad Debts

    = 1,27,200 - 4,300 - 36,500 - 8,000

    = 78,400

11.3.2.4 Wholesale Branch System

Manufacturers may sell the goods to the consumers through approved dealers or wholesalers or through their own branches. If manufacturers sells the goods directly to its branch office then it can earn more profit.

For example: Cost price of an item is ₹ 100 to a Manufacturer and he sells the same item at ₹ 130 to a wholesalers and then the goods are sold to consumers by retailers at ₹ 180, in this case the manufacturer will be able to earn only ₹ 30 as profit and wholesaler and other middlemen will take ₹ 50 as profit.

In case if the manufacturer sells the goods to its own branch then the overall profit will be earned by him i.e., ₹ 80 will be earned by Manufacturers.

If branch expenditure is less than the profit earned, then manufacturer will not earn any profit i.e., if the branch expenditure exceeds ₹ 50, then selling of goods through branch will not earn any profit, if the branch expenditure is less than ₹ 50, then the selling of goods through branch will be in profit.

Take the above example, if the branch expenditure come to ₹ 60, then the profit earned by manufacturer will be ₹ 20, then in this case manufacturer is earning less profit by selling the goods to its own branch. Head office prepares the branch account on this basis i.e., Invoice price is the cost price to the branch office instead of cost price to the head office, Hence the profit of the branch is found out on invoice price basis. If all the goods available in branch office are sold then there is no problem, if some of the goods remain unsold in the branch office, then these unsold goods should be priced at cost price by creating a stock reserve for unrealised profit (Difference between invoice price and cost price). The System of finding out the profit or loss at branch is known as Wholesale Branch System.

The following illustration will demonstrate Wholesale Branch System of accounting.

Illustration 5: T&T Bros. head office is located in New Delhi and branch office is located in Mumbai. The goods are sent to branch at 20% less than the Invoice Price which is cost plus 100%. Find out the profit made by the branch and head office based on the wholesale branch system.

Particulars	Head Office (₹)	Branch Office (₹)
Opening Stock (Cost/ Invoice Price)	30,000	15,000
Branch Expenses	30,000	6,000
Purchases	3,00,000	--
Good destroyed by accident (Invoice Price)	--	2,000
Sales at List Price	1,70,000	90,000
Goods sent to branch (Invoice price)	90,000	90,000

Solution:

Branch Stock Account

Particulars	₹	Particulars	₹
To Balance b/d (Opening stock)	15,000	By Sales (Cash/Debtors)	80,000
To Goods sent to Branch A/c	80,000	By Profit & Loss A/c (Goods Destroyed)	2,000
To Gross Profit c/d	18,000	By Balance c/d (Closing stock at invoice price) (refer below given calculation)	31,000
	1,13,000		1,13,000

Calculations:

If cost price = 100

List price = Cost + 100% = 100 + 100 = 200

Then Invoice price = 160 (200-40)

Cost of goods sold = 90,000*160/200 = 72,000

Calculation of Closing stock at branch (at invoice price

Closing Stock = Opening Stock + Goods from Head office - Cost of Goods Sold - Stock Destroyed

    = 15,000 + 90,000 - 72,000 - 2,000

    = 31,000

Branch Profit & Loss Account

Particulars	₹	Particulars	₹
To Goods Destroyed A/c	2,000	By Gross Profit b/d	16,000
To Branch Expenses A/c	6,000		
To Net Profit	8,000		
	16,000		16,000

Branch Profit & Loss Account

Particulars	₹	Particulars	₹
To Trading A/c	80,000	By Branch Stock A/c	80,000
	80,000		80,000

General Trading and Profit and Loss Account of Head Office

Particulars	₹	Particulars	₹
To Opening Stock	30,000	By Sales	1,70,000
To Purchases	3,00,000	By Goods sent to Branch	90,000
To Gross profit	1,18,750	By Closing Stock at cost price(Refer below given calculation)	1,88,750
	4,48,750		4,48,750
To Expenses	30,000	By Gross Profit b/d	1,18,750
To Stock Reserve (Refer below given calculation-2)	11,250	By Branch P&L A/c	8,000
To Net Profit taken to balance sheet	91,125	By Stock Reserve(Refer below given calculation-1)	5,625
	1,32,375		1,32,375

Calculations:

Closing stock at cost price (at head office) = Opening Stock + Purchases - Cost of Goods Sold - Cost of Goods sent to Branch

    = 30,000 + 3, 00,000 – (1, 70,000 * 100/200) – (90,000 * 100/ 600)

    = 30,000 + 3, 00,000 – 85,000 – 56,250

    = 1, 88,750

Stock Reserve adjustment Calculation: Closing and Opening Stock at branch office are appearing at Invoice price, now the head office have to adjust the unrealised profits

1. Stock Reserve (Opening Stock at Branch) = 15,000 * 60/160 = 5,625

2. Stock Reserve (Closing Stock at Branch) = 30,000 * 60/160
= 11,250

11.3.3 Independent Branches

Independent branches maintains its own books of accounts under double entry system and also it follows its own sales terms and policies. Apart from receiving the goods from head office, these branches can purchase the goods from suppliers or from market in short independent branches will maintain all the accounting transactions.

These branches prepare their own reports like Trial Balance, Profit & Loss Account and Balance Sheet and also it opens head office account in their books and it is debited whenever branch sends goods and cash to head office and also when the payments are made by the branch office (like payments made for purchase of assets and for losses of head office) on behalf of head office. Head Office is credited when branch office receives cash and goods from head office and also it is credited while recording for depreciation of branch fixed assets, profit earned by branch and charges made by the head office for providing services.

Similarly, the branch account will be maintained by the head office and the transactions will be maintained in the same way but it will be in reverse side.

Steps involved in preparation of independent branch accounts are as follows

1. Reconciliation Entries
2. Adjustment Entries
3. Incorporation/Consolidation of Branch Trial Balance in Head Office Book

11.3.3.1 Reconciliation Entries

Balance of head office account in branch books may not match with the balance of branch office account in the head office books. Following are the reasons for difference along with the accounting entry for reconciliation.

1. **Cash-in-transit:** Wile transferring the cash from head office to branch office and branch office to head office, they are chances that, at the end of the accounting period the cash may not have been received by the head office or branch office as the case may be, by this the balance of head office account will not match with the balance of branch office account. For reconciling the difference in balance a reconciliation entry can be recorded in the books of Head office or Branch office, but we cannot record the reconciliation entry in both the books.

Reconciliation entry in the books of Head Office

Particulars		Debit	Credit
Cash-in-transit A/c	Dr.	xxxx	
To Branch Office A/c			xxxx

Reconciliation entry in the books of Branch Office

Particulars		Debit	Credit
Cash-in-transit A/c	Dr.	xxxx	
To Head Office A/c			xxxx

2. **Goods-in-transit:** Wile transferring the goods from head office to branch office and branch office to head office, they are chances that, at the end of the accounting period the goods may not have been received by the head office or branch office as the case may be, by this the balance of head office account will not match with the balance of branch office account. For reconciling the difference in balance a reconciliation entry can be recorded in the books of Head office or Branch office, but we cannot record the reconciliation entry in both the books.

Reconciliation entry in the Books of Head Office

Particulars		Debit	Credit
Goods-in-transit A/c	Dr.	xxxx	
To Branch Office A/c			xxxx

Reconciliation entry in the Books of Branch Office

Particulars		Debit	Credit
Goods-in-transit A/c	Dr.	xxxx	
To Head Office A/c			xxxx

Note: Reconciliation entry cannot be recorded in both the books (Head Office Books and Branch Office books)

Illustration 6: Record the journal entries for reconciling the balances of head office and branch office from the following Trail Balance of head office and branch office.

	Trial Balance			
Particulars	Head Office		Branch Office	
	Debit (₹)	Credit (₹)	Debit (₹)	Credit (₹)
Current Accounts	1,00,000			70,000
Goods Received by/Sent to Branch		1,50,000	1,25,000	

Solution:

In the above illustration current account shows the different balances in head office and branch office and the difference amount is ₹ 30,000 (1, 00,000 - 70,000).

Goods received or sent account also shown the different balances in head office and branch office and the difference amount is ₹ 25,000 (1, 50,000 – 1, 25,000), by this we will come to know that out of ₹ 30,000, ₹ 25,000 is the difference in goods-in-transit and remaining amount of ₹ 5,000 is the difference in cash-in-transit. Now the following entries need to be recorded in the books of Head office or Branch office but not in both the books.

Reconciliation entry in the Books of Head Office

Particulars		Debit	Credit
Goods-in-transit A/c	Dr.	25,000	
Cash-in-transit A/c	Dr.	5,000	
To Branch Office A/c			30,000

Reconciliation entry in the Books of Branch Office

Particulars		Debit	Credit
Goods-in-transit A/c	Dr.	25,000	
Cash-in-transit A/c	Dr.	5,000	
To Head Office A/c			30,000

11.3.3.2 Adjustment Entries

Adjustment entries needs to be recorded at the end of the accounting year for few transactions like Depreciation account of branch office maintained by the head office and the expenses borne by the head office for the branch office, these transactions will take place between head office and branch office and adjustment entries has to be recorded for such transactions as shown below:

1. **Expenses borne by the head office for the branch:** Head office will provide services to branch office on regular bases and head office will charge for these services. **For example** head office will render administrative services to branch office and will charge sum of ₹ 10,000 to branch.

Adjustment entry in the Books of Head Office

Particulars		Debit	Credit
Branch A/c	Dr.	xxxx	
To Expenses (Administrative) A/c			xxxx

Adjustment entry in the Books of Branch Office

Particulars		Debit	Credit
Expenses Incurred by Head Office A/c	Dr.	xxxx	
To Head Office A/c			xxxx

2. **Depreciation account of branch maintained by head office:** When head office maintains the fixed asset account of branch office, then the following adjustment entries are required for depreciation on fixed assets:

Adjustment entry in the Books of Head Office

Particulars		Debit	Credit
Branch A/c	Dr.	xxxx	
To Branch Fixed Asset A/c			xxxx

Adjustment entry in the Books of Branch Office

Particulars		Debit	Credit
Depreciation A/c	Dr.	xxxx	
To Head Office A/c			xxxx

The following Illustration will demonstrate about the Adjustment Entries.

Illustration 7: Suka Enterprises have two branch one in Kolkata and other one is in Karnataka. Record the following transactions in the books of Head office (Suka Enterprises) and pass the necessary adjustment entries.

1. Kolkata Branch transferred goods to Karnataka Branch for ₹ 10,000

2. Depreciation of fixed assets (Branch) account are maintained by head office-Karnataka Branch ₹ 40,000 and Kolkata Branch ₹ 50,000

3. On 1st January 2016, Head Office sent the goods to Kolkata Branch for ₹ 20,000, but Kolkata Branch received the goods on 1st February 2016.

4. Head office charged ₹ 30,000 to Karnataka Branch for providing administrative services.

5. On 5th January 2016, Karnataka Branch remitted ₹ 50,000 to Head Office, but Head Office received the amount on 5th February 2016.

Solution:

Journal Entries in the Books of Head Office				
	Particulars		Debit	Credit
1	Karnataka Branch A/c	Dr.	10,000	
	To Kolkata Branch A/c			10,000
	(Being goods transferred from Kolkata branch to Karnataka branch)			
2	Karnataka Branch A/c	Dr.	40,000	
	Kolkata Branch A/c	Dr.	50,000	
	To Karnataka Fixed Asset A/c			40,000
	To Kolkata Fixed Asset A/c			50,000
	(Being fixed asset adjustment entry recorded for both the branches)			
3	Goods-In-Transit A/c	Dr.	20,000	
	To Kolkata Branch A/c			20,000
	(Being goods in transit)			
4	Karnataka Branch A/c	Dr.	30,000	
	To Administrative Expenses A/c			30,000
	(Being administrative expense charged to branch office)			
5	Cash-In-Transit A/c	Dr.	50,000	
	To Karnataka Branch A/c			50,000
	(Being cash in transit)			

11.3.3.3 Incorporation/Consolidation of Branch Trial Balance in Head Office Book

It is mandatory for the head office to prepare the consolidated Balance sheet at the end of the accounting period, because all the branches fall under one organization and shareholders and vendors will be interested in knowing the overall performance and position of the organisation, for this purpose it is necessary to consolidate the balances of different branches with head office. The process of preparing the consolidated Balance Sheet of the organisation is called as Incorporation of Branch Trial Balance in Head Office Book.

They are two ways to incorporate the branch Trial Balance in head office book as shown below

I. **Detailed Incorporation:** In this method all items of trading and profit & loss account are incorporated in the head office books and also Assets and Liabilities are incorporated. To prepare the consolidated Balance sheet the following entries are passed.

Detailed Incorporation					
S.No	Transactions	Explanation	Particulars	Dr.	Cr.
1	For incorporating the items showing under debit side of the Trading Account.	This transaction is recorded with the total value of items which are debited in Trading Account like Opening Stock, Net Purchases and Direct expenses Wages, manufacturing expenses etc.	Branch Trading A/c Dr To Branch A/c	xxx	xxx
2	For incorporating the items showing under credit side of the Trading Account	This transaction is recorded with the total value of items which are credited in Trading Account like Net Sales and Closing Stock etc.	Branch A/c Dr To Branch Trading A/c	xxx	xxx
3	For transferring gross profit to branch profit and loss account.	This entry is recorded in order to transfer the gross profit to P & L A/c	Branch Trading A/c Dr To Branch P & L A/c	xxx	xxx
4	For transferring gross loss to branch profit and loss account.	This entry is recorded in order to transfer the gross loss to P & L A/c	Branch P & L A/c Dr To Branch Trading A/c	xxx	xxx
5	For incorporating the items showing under debit side of the Branch P & L Account	This transaction is recorded with the total value of items which are debited in Branch Profit and Loss Account like Rent, Commission, Salary, Depreciation, Bad Debts etc	Branch P & L A/c Dr To Branch A/c	xxx	xxx
6	For incorporating the items showing under credit side of the Branch P & L Account	This transaction is recorded with the total value of items which are credited in Branch Profit and Loss Account like Commission earned, Discount Received etc	Branch A/c Dr	xxx	

			To Branch P & L A/c		xxx
7	For transferring net profit to general profit and loss account of head office.	This entry is recorded in order to transfer the net profit to General or Head office P & L A/c	Branch P & L A/c Dr To General or Head Office P & L A/c	xxx	xxx
8	For transferring net loss to branch profit and loss account.	This entry is recorded in order to transfer the net loss to P & L A/c	General or Head Office P & L A/c Dr To Branch P & L A/c	xxx	xxx
9	For incorporating assets of branch after adjustments, if any	While recording this entry each asset need to be debited individually	Branch Asset (Individually) A/c Dr To Branch A/c	xxx	xxx
10	For incorporating liabilities of branch after adjustments, if any	While recording this entry each liability need to be credited individually	Branch A/c Dr To Branch Liabilities (Individually) A/c	xxx	xxx

The branch accounts will be closed in the head office books because of these incorporation entries, then in the beginning of next accounting year, the assets and liabilities will be transferred to the branch.

The following entries are recorded for transferring the assets and liabilities to the branch.

Transferring Assets and Liabilities to Branch Office

Transferring Assets and Liabilities to Branch Office					
S.No	Transactions	Explanation	Particulars	Dr.	Cr.
1	Transferring of branch assets to branch	This entry is recorded to transfer the branch assets to branch at the beginning of accounting year	Branch A/c Dr To Branch Assets A/c (Being transfer of branch assets to branch)	xxx	xxx
2	Transferring of branch liabilities to branch	This entry is recorded to transfer the branch liabilities to branch at the beginning of accounting year	Branch Liabilities A/c Dr To Branch A/c (Being transfer of branch assets to branch)	xxx	xxx

The following illustration will demonstrate how the branch accounts are incorporated in the head office books of account.

Illustration 8: *Following is the Trial Balance of Karnataka branch office as on 31ˢᵗ March, 2016. Incorporate the Karnataka branch account with head office by giving the journal entries, after incorporating assets and liabilities show the branch account in head office books.*

Trial Balance
as on 31ˢᵗ March, 2016

Particulars	Debit (₹)	Credit (₹)
Opening Stock	40,000	
Manufacturing Expenses	20,000	
Wages	50,000	
Purchases	90,000	
Rent	14,000	
Salaries	20,000	
General Expenses	15,000	
Cash-In-Hand	12,000	
Goods Received from Head Office	25,000	
Purchase Returns		2,000
Sales		1,60,000
Discount Earned		2,000
Debtors	25,000	
Creditors		15,000
Head Office Account		1,23,000
Total	**3,11,000**	**3,11,000**

Rent Outstanding is ₹ 1,000 and Closing Stock at Branch is ₹ 40,000, Depreciation of 15% to be provided on Branch furniture of ₹ 10,000 and 20 % on Branch Machinery of ₹ 60,000.

Solution:

Journal Entries in the Books of Head Office

Date (2016)	Particulars		L.F	Dr.	Cr.
Mar. 31	Karnataka Branch A/c	Dr.		13,500	
	To Branch Furniture A/c				1,500
	To Branch Machinery A/c				12,000
	(Being depreciation charged to branch)				
Mar. 31	Karnataka Branch Trading A/c	Dr.		2,14,000	
	To Karnataka Branch A/c				2,14,000
	(Being the total of stock, wages, goods received from H.O, manufacturing expenses and wages debited to branch trading A/c)				
Mar. 31	Karnataka Branch A/c	Dr.		2,00,000	
	To Karnataka Branch Trading A/c				2,00,000
	(Being the total of Branch Stock-40,000 and Sales-1,60,000 credited to branch trading A/c)				
Mar. 31	Karnataka Branch P. & L. A/c	Dr.		23,000	
	To Karnataka Branch Trading A/c **(Refer the below given calculation-1)**				23,000
	(Being gross loss transferred)				
Mar. 31	Karnataka Branch P. & L. A/c	Dr.		63,500	
	To Karnataka Branch A/c **(Refer below given calculation-2)**				63,500
	(Being total of branch expenses transferred to branch P. & L. A/c)				
Mar. 31	Karnataka Branch A/c	Dr.		2,000	
	To Karnataka Branch P. & L. A/c				2,000
	(Being discount earned credited to Branch P. & L. A/c)				
Mar. 31	General Profit & Loss A/c	Dr.		84,500	
	To Karnataka Branch P. & L. A/c (**Refer below given calculation- 3**)				84,500
	(Being net loss transferred to head office profit and loss account)				
Mar. 31	Karnataka Cash A/c	Dr.		12,000	
	Karnataka Stock A/c	Dr.		40,000	
	Karnataka Debtors A/c	Dr.		25,000	
	To Karnataka Branch A/c				77,000
	(Being transfer of all branch assets to head office)				
Mar. 31	Karnataka Branch A/c	Dr.		16,000	
	To Branch Creditors A/c				15,000
	To Branch Outstanding (Expenses) A/c				1,000
	(Being transfer of all liabilities to head office books)				

Calculations:

1. Gross Profit/Loss = Sales – Cost of goods sold (Cost of goods sold = Beginning Inventory + Direct Expenses + Purchases – Ending Inventory).
   = 1, 60,000 – (40,000 + 95,000 + 88,000 – 40,000)
   = 1, 60,000 – 1, 83,000
   = 23,000 (It is a loss because revenue is less than the cost)

2. Branch Expenses as per the above illustration = Salaries + Depreciation + General Expenses + Rent
   = 20,000 + 13,500 + 15,000 + 15,000
   = 63,500

3. Net Profit or Loss = Gross Loss + Indirect expenses – Income (Discount earned)
   = 23,000 +63,500 – 2,000
   = 84,500 (It is a loss because expenses are more than incomes)

Karnataka Branch Account in Head Office Books

Date (2016)	Particulars	₹	Date (2016)	Particulars	₹
Mar. 31	To Balance b/d	1,23,000	Mar. 31	By Karnataka Branch Trading A/c	2,14,000
Mar. 31	To Branch Furniture A/c (Depreciation)	1,500	Mar. 31	By Karnataka Branch P. & L. A/c (total branch expenses)	63,500
Mar. 31	To Branch Machinery A/c (Depreciation)	12,000	Mar. 31	By Branch Assets	77,000
Mar. 31	To Karnataka Trading A/c (Stock + Sales)	2,00,000			
Mar. 31	To Karnataka Branch P. & L A/c	2000			
Mar. 31	To Branch Liabilities	16,000			
		3,54,500			**3,54,500**

II. **Abridged Method:** In this method a Memorandum Account is prepared i.e., Branch Trading and Profit & Loss Account is prepared as a Memorandum account and the entries are recorded to transfer the net profit or loss in the head office books. Head Office will not record any transaction for incorporating branch assets and liabilities because branch account in books of head office will show the balance equal to net worth.

The following illustration will demonstrate, how to prepare the Branch Trading and Profit & Loss Account

Illustration 9: *Saha Group of companies opens a new branch in Karnataka and it trades independently. The following are the transactions of the branch for the year ended 31ˢᵗ March, 2016. Prepare the Branch Trading and Profit & Loss Account and branch account in the books of head office.*

Transactions	
Transactions	₹
Goods received from Head office	22,000
Purchases from Market	20,500
• On Credit - ₹ 16,500	
• On Cash - ₹ 4,000	
Sales to Customers	31,600
• On Credit – ₹ 26,000	
• On Cash - ₹ 5,600	
Cash paid to Creditors	16,200
Cash received from Customers	32,400
Expenses Paid by Branch	10,950
Credit purchase of machinery by branch	5,500
Cash received from head office in the beginning	7,000
Remittance to head office	13,000

After incorporation of branch Trial Balance, we have taken the following into consideration.

i. Branch fixed assets accounts are maintained in Head Office Books.

ii. Branch Closing stock is ₹ 14,000

iii. Write off depreciation on machinery at 7 per cent per annum

iv. A remittance of ₹ 4,000 from branch to the head office is in transit.

Solutions:

Karnataka Branch Trading and Profit and loss account in the books of H.O as on 31ˢᵗ March, 2016				
Particulars	₹	Particulars	₹
To Goods Received from Head Office	22,000	By Credit Sales	26,000
To Credit Purchases	16,500	By Cash Sales	5,600
To Cash Purchases	4,000	By Closing Stock	14,000
To Gross profit c/d	3,100		
	45,600		45,600
To Expenses	10,950	By Gross profit b/d	3,100
To Depreciation on machinery (5500*7% = 385)	385	By Net Loss Transferred to General (H.O) P & L A/c	8,235
	11,335		11,335

Karnataka Branch Account				
Particulars	₹	Particulars	₹	
To Cash	7,000	By Machinery		5,500
To Goods supplied to branch	22,000	By Remittance	13,000	
To Branch Machinery (Depreciation)	385	Less: Cash-in- Transit	4,000	
				9,000
		By General (H.O) Profit & Loss A/c		8,235
		By Balance c/d (Assets - Liabilities) (Refer below given calculation-I)		6,650
	29,385			29,385

Calculation for Assets - Liabilities

1. Assets = Closing Stock + Cash in Hand + Cash in Transit

    = 14,000 + (7,000 + 5,600 + 32,400 – 16,200 – 10,950 – 4,000 – 13,000) + 4,000

    = 14,000 + 850 + 4,000

    = 18,850

    Liabilities = Creditors for Machinery +Advance from Debtors + Sundry Creditors

    = (5,500) + (32,400 – 26,000) + (16,500 - 16,200)

    = 5,500 + 6,400 + 300

    = 12,200

    Now: Assets – Liability = 6,650

Illustration 10: *Khan Group of Companies started a business on 01-04-2016 with head office at Karnataka and a branch office at Mumbai. Complete purchases were handled by head office were the goods were processed before sale and there are no loss or wastages in processing. Branch will handled only the processed goods received from head office and the goods were sent to branch at processed cost plus 10%.All sales made by head office or branch office were at same gross profit of 25% on their respective cost.*

Trial Balance as on 31ˢᵗ March, 2016				
Particulars	Head Office		Branch Office	
	Debit (₹)	Credit(₹)	Debit (₹)	Credit(₹)
Capital		3,20,000		
Drawings	63,000			
Purchases	19,79,500			
Cost of Processing	51,500			
Goods Sent to Branch		9,25,000		
Sales		12,81,000		8,20,000
Administrative Expenses	1,40,000		15,000	
Selling Expenses	51,000		7,200	
Branch Current Assets	3,90,300			
Debtors	3,10,600		1,14,600	
Creditors		6,03,900		21,800
Bank Balance	1,53,000		78,000	
Head Office Current Account				2,62,500
Goods Received From Head Office			8,81,000	
	31,41,400	31,34,900	10,95,800	11,04,300

Additional Information is given below:

1. As on 01-03-2016, Head Office sent the goods to branch office for ₹ 45,000, but branch office did not received the goods till 01-04-2016.

2. As on 01-03-2016, Branch office sent the remittance of ₹ 85,300 Head office, which was not received till 01-04-2016

3. Branch disclosed the shortage of ₹ 21,000 (at selling price to the branch)

4. As on 31-03-2016, head office showed the cost of unprocessed goods for ₹ 1,01,000

    Prepare the columnar Trading and profit & loss account with combined form and also prepare the consolidated Balance sheet of the business as on 31-03-2016.

Solution:

Trading and Profit & Loss Account of Khan Group of Companies as on 31st March, 2016

Particulars	Head Office	Branch	Total	Particulars	Head Office	Branch	Total
To Purchase	19,79,500		19,79,500	By Sales	12,81,000	8,20,000	21,01,000
To Cost of Processing	51,500		51,500	By Goods sent to branch A/c	9,25,000		
To Goods Received from Head Office		8,81,000		By Stock Shortage (at selling price) i.e , 21,000*1/5		16,800	16,800
To Gross Profit c/d	3,40,291	1,64,000	6,86,471	By Goods in Transit			45,000
				By Closing Stock Processed Goods (Refer calculation 1 a & b)	64,291	2,08,200	2,72,491
				Unprocessed Goods	1,01,000		1,01,000
	23,71,291	10,45,000	27,17,471		23,71,291	10,45,000	25,36,291
To Administrative Expenses	1,40,000	15,000	1,55,000	By Gross Profit b/d	3,40,291	1,64,000	6,86,471
To Selling Expenses	51,000	7,200	58,200				
To Stock Shortage		16,800	16,800				
To Stock Reserve (Refer calculation 2)	24,910		24,910				
To Net Profit	1,24,381	1,25,000	2,49,381				
	3,40,291	1,64,000	5,04,291		3,40,291	1,64,000	6,86,471

Consolidated Balance Sheet of Khan Group of Companies as on 31st March, 2016

Liabilities	₹	₹	Assets	₹	₹
Capital	3,20,000		Closing Stock:		
Add: Net Profit	2,49,381		Processed Stock:		
	5,69,381		Head Office	64,291	
Less: Drawings	65,000		Branch Office	2,08,200	
		5,04,381		2,72,491	
Creditors:			Less: Stock Reserve (Refer calculation 2)	20,820	2,51,671
Head Office	6,08,900		Unprocessed Goods		1,01,000
Branch Office	21,800		Bank Balance: Head Office	1,53,000	
		6,30,700	Branch Office	78,000	2,31,000
			Goods in Transit (45,000 - 4,090) (Refer Calculation 2)		40,910
			Cash-in-Transit		85,300
			Debtors:		
			Head Office	3,10,600	
			Branch Office	1,14,600	4,25,200
		11,35,081			11,35,081

Calculations:

1. Closing Stock Calculation:		
a) Stock at head office (19,79,500 + 51,500 - 1,01,000) =		19,30,000
Less: Cost of goods sold at branch ₹ 9,25,000 *100/110 =	8,40,909	
Cost of goods sold = 12,81,000 *100/125 =	10,24,800	18,65,709
Processed stock at head office =		64,291
b) Stock at Branch office:		
Goods received from head office =		8,81,000
Less: Invoice value of goods sold (8,20,000 *100/125) =	6,56,000	
Invoice value of shortage of stock (21,000 *100/125)=	16,800	6,72,800
Stock Branch (at invoice price)		2,08,200
Less: Stock Reserve (2,08,200 *10/110)		20,820
Processed stock at Branch office at cost =		1,87,380

2. Stock Reserve Calculation:	
Branch stock unrealised profit (2,08,000 *10/110)	20,820
Goods-in-Transit unrealised profit (45,000 *10/110)	4,090
	24,910

KEY TAKEAWAYS

- Inland Branches are the branches located within the Country, Inland branches are also called as Home Branch or Domestic Branch.

- Depended Branch and Independent Brach are the two types of branch in which books of accounts are maintained.

- Dependent Branches doesn't maintains its books of accounts, they are maintained by its Head office.

- Independent branches maintains its own books of accounts under double entry system.

PRACTISE EXERCISES

Section A: Review Questions

1. What is Branch Accounting?
2. Explain the purpose of Branch Accounting?
3. What is dependent Branch?
4. What is Independent Branch?
5. What does Goods-In-Transit mean?
6. What does Cash-In-Transit mean?

Section B: Multiple Choice Questions

Select the most appropriate answer from the choices given below:

1. _____ maintains its own book of accounts and sales policies.
   - a. Dependent Branch
   - b. Independent Branch
   - c. Domestic Branch
   - d. Head Office

2. _____ doesn't maintains its books of accounts.
   - a. Dependent Branch
   - b. Independent Branch
   - c. Domestic Branch
   - d. Head Office

3. Debtor's System is one of the system of accounting for
   _____.
   a. Dependent Branch   b. Independent Branch
   c. Domestic Branch   d. Head Office
4. How many types of systems of accounting available for
   dependent branches?
   a. 3   b. 2
   c. 4   d. 1

Section C: Practical Questions

1. Mukta Enterprises have its head office at Karnataka and
   branch office at Mumbai, following are the transactions
   with head office at branch for the year ended 31st August,
   2016.

Date 2016	Transactions
Sep. 1	Stock at branch ₹ 50,000
	Debtors at branch ₹30,000
	Petty Cash ₹ 15,000
	Goods supplied to branch office for ₹ 1,70,000
	Cash sales remittance from branch ₹ 21,000
	Realization of debtors ₹ 1,70,000
	Salary of ₹ 30,000 sent to branch
	Rent of ₹20,000 sent to branch
	Petty cash of ₹ 20,000 sent to branch
Aug. 31	Stock at branch ₹30,000
	Debtors at branch ₹ 20,000
	Petty Cash ₹ 20,000

Record the above transaction in the journal and prepare
the Branch Account under Debtor's System of Accounting.

2. SUK Traders started branches at Delhi and Kolkata as on
   1st April, 2016. All goods are transferred by head office to
   branch office at cost plus 25 per cent. Head office pays all
   expenses incurred by the branch office. Cash collected by
   the branches are remitted to head office on daily bases. Each
   branch maintains its own sales ledger and sends the weekly
   statements to head office. The following are the details
   extracted from the weekly statements, sent by the different
   branches to head office for the half yearly period ended
   30th September, 2016.

Particulars	Chennai (₹)	Kerala(₹)
Cash Sales made by branch	90,600	94,200
Credit Sales made by branch	137,200	1,22,000
Sundry Debtors	46,500	35,600
Sales Return	14,300	13,200
Rent and Rates	15,200	16,500
Bad debts	18,000	--
Salaries paid	28,000	30,000
General expenses incurred	14,600	13,500
Goods received from head office	1,62,000	1,37,000
Advertisement	19,500	17,200
Stock on 30th September, 2016	57,000	47,000

Prepare the branch accounts in the books of head office,
showing the profit or loss for the accounting period and
then prepare the Trading and Profit & Loss Account
separately for each branch as per Final Accounts Systems.

3. Ashok Bros. head office is located in New Delhi and branch
   office is located in Kolkata. The goods are sent to branch at
   20% less than the Invoice Price which is cost plus 100%.
   Find out the profit made by the branch and head office
   based on the wholesale branch system.

Particulars	Head Office (₹)	Branch Office (₹)
Opening Stock (Cost/ Invoice Price)	30,000	15,000
Branch Expenses	30,000	6,000
Purchases	3,00,000	--
Good destroyed by accident (Invoice Price)	--	2,000
Sales at List Price	1,70,000	90,000
Goods sent to branch (Invoice price)	90,000	90,000

4. Record the journal entries for reconciling the balances of
   head office and branch office from the following Trail
   Balance of head office and branch office.

Particulars	Head Office Debit (₹)	Head Office Credit (₹)	Branch Office Debit (₹)	Branch Office Credit (₹)
				Trial Balance
Current Accounts	1,10,000			80,000
Goods Received by/ Sent to Branch		1,60,000	1,35,000	

5. TK Enterprises have two branch one in Mumbai and other
   one is in Delhi. Record the following transactions in the
   books of Head office (TK Enterprises) and pass the
   necessary adjustment entries.
   a. Mumbai Branch transferred goods to Delhi Branch for
      ₹ 10,000
   b. Depreciation of fixed assets (Branch) account are
      maintained by head office-Delhi Branch ₹ 40,000 and
      Mumbai Branch ₹ 50,000
   c. On 1st January 2016, Head Office sent the goods to
      Mumbai Branch for ₹ 20,000, but Mumbai Branch
      received the goods on 1st February 2016.
   d. Head office charged ₹ 30,000 to Delhi Branch for
      providing administrative services.

   On 5th January 2016, Delhi Branch remitted ₹ 50,000 to Head
   Office, but Head Office received the amount on 5th February
   2016.

Chapter 12

Goods and Services Tax (GST)

12.1 INTRODUCTION

India is a federal country where both the Centre and the States have been assigned the powers to levy and collect taxes through appropriate legislations. Both the levels of Government have distinct responsibilities to perform according to the powers prescribed in the Constitution

Accordingly,

* The centre can levy of excise duty on the manufacture of goods and service Tax on rendering of services.
* The state can levy VAT on the sale of goods

Introduction of the CENVAT and Value Added Tax (VAT) at the Central and the State level has been considered to be a major step – an important breakthrough – in the sphere of indirect tax reforms in India. If the CENVAT and VAT were a major improvement over the existing Central Excise duty at the national level and the Sales Tax system at the State level, then the Goods and Services Tax (GST) will mark a significant progress – the next logical step – towards a complete indirect tax reform in the country.

12.2 WHAT IS GST?

GST is a tax on goods and services, with comprehensive and continuous chain of input credit set-off from Manufacturer to Distributor to Retailer till it reaches the end customer. It is essentially a tax, only on the value addition at each stage. Through the input tax credit mechanism, a supplier at each stage is permitted to set-off the GST paid on the purchase of goods and services against the GST to be paid on the supply of goods and services.

The final consumer will thus pay only the GST charged by the last dealer in the supply chain, since the set-off benefits can be availed through all the different stages.

12.2.1 Dual Concept GST

Dual Concept GST is a model of GST in which both federal (center) and provincial (state) governments will levy GST separately, rather than the center alone levying taxes and sharing their revenues with the states.

Dual GST is preferred in countries where there is a federal structure of the government. This is because in a federal system, states would be independent in their revenue sources and they don't have to rely on the Centre to share the revenues.

Since India is a federal country, where both the Centre and the States have been assigned the powers to levy and collect taxes, the GST model to be implanted in India is Dual GST.

Under this system, tax is administered, collected and shared by both the Centre and States based on the nature of transaction (Within a state or interstate).

12.3 WHY GST

The current indirect tax system has multiple taxes (Central Levy: Excise Duty, Service Tax, Various Cess and State Levies:- VAT, Entry Tax, Octroi, Luxury Tax, Entertainment taxes, Purchase Tax etc.) - at different rates - at multiple points (at the time of manufacture, trade, rendering services, and so on.). This has led to several inefficiencies and limitations.

In the year 2005, VAT was introduced with a similar objective - to overcome the cascading effect (tax on tax) of sales tax - by providing the setting-off the tax paid on purchases with the tax collected. Similarly, CENVAT, an improvised system over Central Excise has a similar set-off mechanism to remove the cascading effect

But both the CENVAT and the State VAT have certain limitations.

One of the major limitations is the cascading effect of tax. Under the current tax regime, when Excise Duty is charged by the manufacturer on billing to a Dealer, the Input Tax credit cannot be claimed by the dealer. This then becomes a cost to the dealer. Similarly, the Central Sales Tax (CST) charged on interstate purchases is non-creditable (Input Tax credit is not available), leading to a break on the input tax credit chain, and leading to taxes forming a part of the product cost.

GST allows for seamless flow of tax credit, and eliminates the cascading effect of all the indirect taxes in the supply chain - from manufacturers to retailers, and across state boarders.

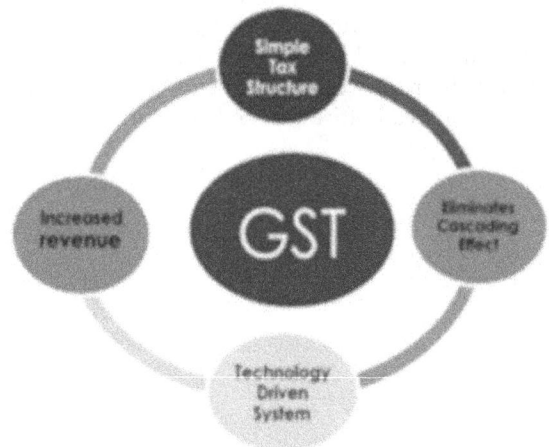

12.4 STRUCTURE OF GST

On every supply of goods and services, a tax component of the Centre and State will be applicable.

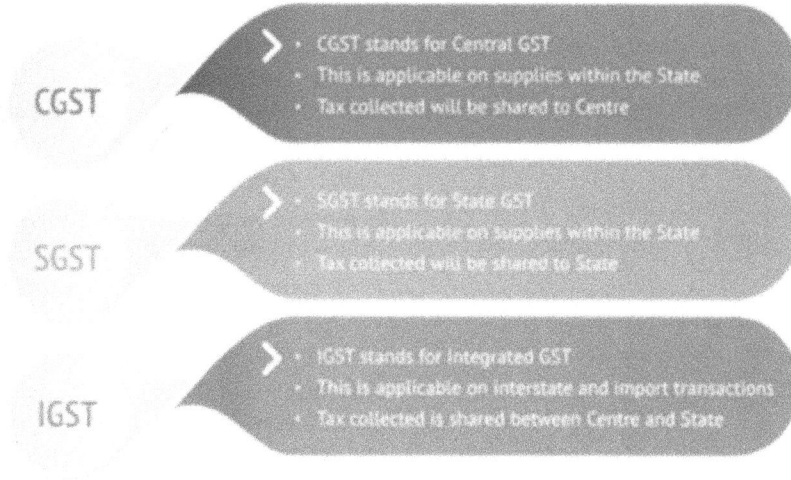

12.5   TAXES SUBSUMED UNDER GST

As shown in the image above, all the central taxes are subsumed under Central GST (CGST), state taxes under State GST (SGST), and the Central Sales Tax, and CVD and SAD applicable on imports are subsumed under the Integrated GST (IGST)

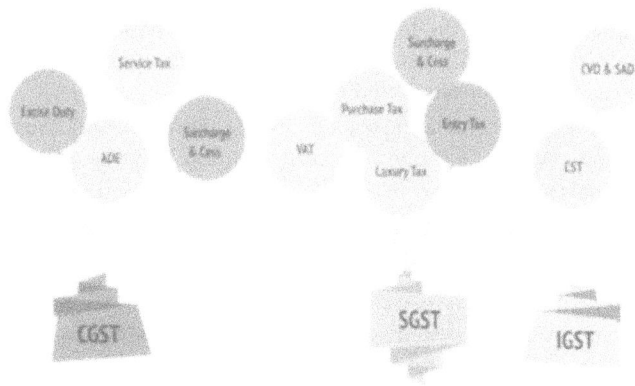

12.6   REGISTRATION

Registration under GST is a 15 digit PAN based registration. GSTIN is the registration number allocated post registration.

State Code		PAN										Entity Code	Blank	Check Digit
1	2	3	4	5	6	7	8	9	10	11	12	13	14	15

Structure of GSTIN

12.6.1   Registration Threshold Limit

*Special Category States - Arunachal Pradesh, Assam, Jammu and Kashmir, Manipur, Meghalaya, Mizoram, Nagaland, Sikkim, Tripura, Himachal Pradesh and Uttarakhand

The turnover threshold considered here is aggregate pan-India turnover for a business entity, and not state-wise. Turnover (Aggregate) includes the value of:

1. Taxable Supplies
2. Exempt Supplies
3. Export supplies

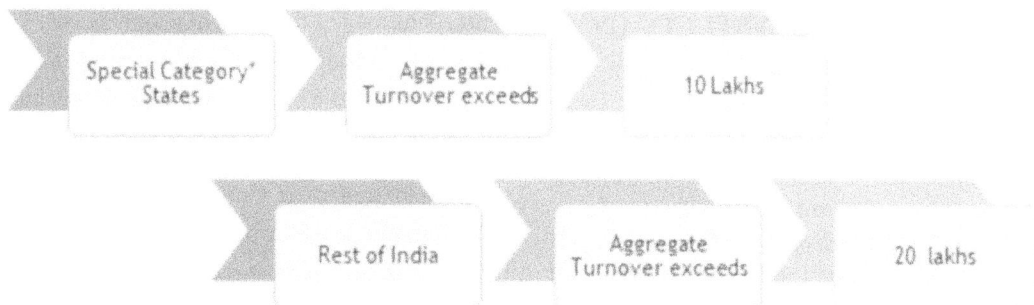

12.6.2   Existing Dealers Registration

Existing dealers who have already registered under the existing indirect taxes system, like VAT, Central Excise and Service Tax, will be auto migrated to GST, and will be given provisional registration. Upon submitting the required documents and details, final registration will be granted.

The state wise enrollment of existing dealer registration started in phased manner.

12.7   COMPOSITION TAX PAYER

To ease the process of compliance for small dealers in the states, the composition scheme is provided. In GST also, a similar benefit will be extended to small dealers, who can opt for compliance under the composition scheme. In GST, this is referred to as 'Composition Levy' and the registered taxable person who is allowed pay tax at a certain percentage of the turnover during the year is called the Composition Tax payer.

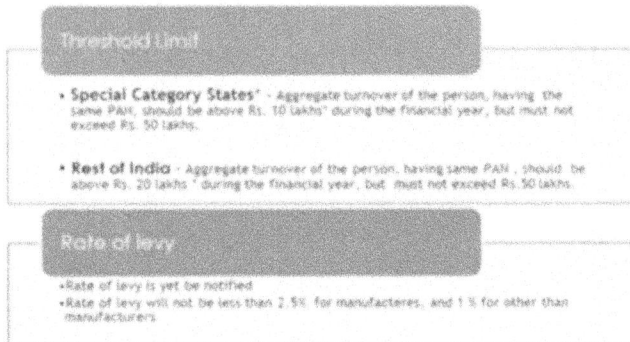

Apart from the threshold limit, there are various other conditions are also critical in determining the eligibility for composition levy. The following are few conditions

* **Cannot be engaged in supply of services**
* **No Interstate supplies**
* **Cannot be engaged in the manufacture of specific notified goods**

12.8   SUPPLY OF GOODS AND SERVICES

The taxable event under GST is the supply of goods and/or services. All taxes such as Central Excise, Service Tax and VAT/CST will be subsumed under GST, and the concept of manufacture of goods, sale of goods, and provision of services will no longer be relevant

The term Supply includes all forms of supply such has sale, barter, exchange, lease, license, disposal, supplied or to be supplied, for a consideration, in the course of or for furtherance of business.

However, there are specific types of supplies mentioned in the law which need to be considered as supply even without a consideration.

12.9   CONCEPT OF MIXED AND COMPOSITE SUPPLY

12.9.1   Mixed Supply

The supply of two or more individual supplies of goods or services, or any combination of goods and services, by a taxable person, for a single price, is called Mixed Supply.

In Mixed Supply, the combination of goods and/or services are not bundled due to natural necessities, and they can be supplied individually in the ordinary course of business

Consider a kit which contains a tie, a watch, a wallet, and a pen, as a combo, for Rs. 4,500/-

To calculate the tax liability on Mixed Supply, the tax rate applicable on the goods or services attracting the highest rate of tax, in the combination of goods and services, will be considered.

12.9.2   Composite Supply

Composite Supply of goods and services is made by a taxable person to a recipient, and:

* It comprises two or more supplies of goods or services, or
* A combination of goods and services, which are naturally bundled and supplied, in the ordinary course of business.

This means that the goods and services are bundled owing to natural necessities. The elements in a Composite Supply of goods and services are dependent elements on the *'principal supply'* of goods or services.

What is Principal Supply?

The pre-dominant element in the supply of goods or services, forming part of composite supply, is principal supply, and any other dependent supply, forming part of composite supplies, are secondary to principal supply.

For example, Sale of Laptop with Bag.

This is a composite supply because laptop bag is natural requisite to carry the laptop. But if the customers opts for a multipurpose bag like backpack bag, it is not a composite supply since it is not naturally bundled.

For purpose of calculating tax liability, the rate of tax applicable on the principal supply of such goods and services will be effected on the composite supply

12.10   PLACE OF SUPPLY

To determine the applicable taxes, the place of supply plays a vital role. This is because GST is a **destination based consumption tax system**, unlike most of the existing indirect tax systems, which are origin based.

Under the GST regime, tax revenues will reach the state where consumption or supply happens. This means goods and/or services are taxed in the state in which they are consumed. Hence, determining the place of supply is very important:

* To know taxable jurisdiction where tax should reach.
* To determine whether the transaction is intrastate which is subject CGST + SGST or interstate which subject to IGST.

In determining the nature of transaction, you always need to apply the logic of the place of supplier and place of supply

12.10.1 Intrastate Supply

If the place of supplier and place of supply are the same state, it is intrastate supply, and the tax charged will be CGST + SGST.

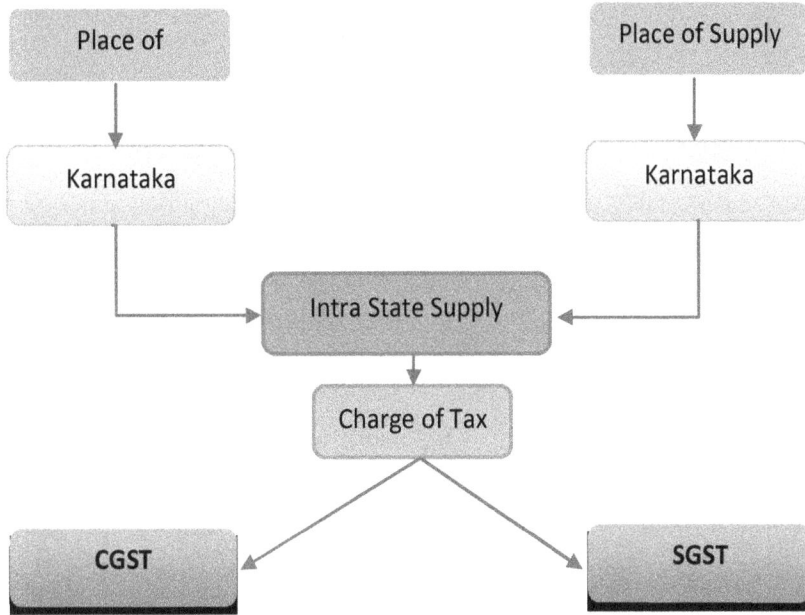

12.10.2 Interstate Supply

If the place of supplier and place of supply are different states, it is interstate supply, and the tax charged will be IGST.

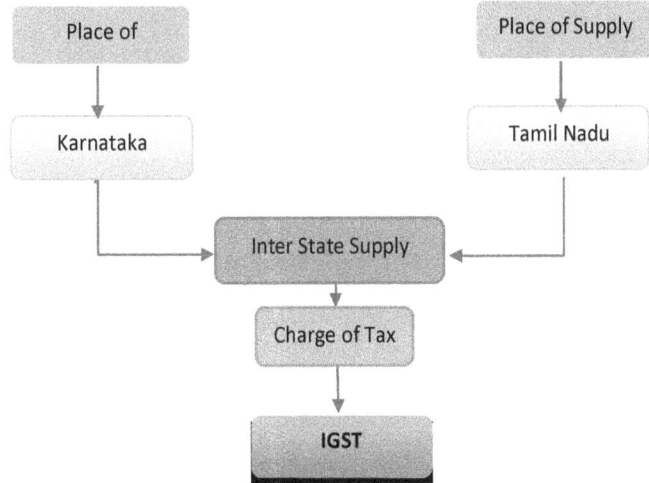

The place of supply for goods involving movement, no movement of goods and supply through agent are different. Similarly, for supply of services, separate provisions are defined for supply of service for B2B and B2C.

12.11 TIME OF SUPPLY OF GOODS AND SERVICES

12.11.1 Forward Charge on Supply of Goods

Liability of GST (CGST and SGST or IGST as applicable) arises during either of the following, whichever is earlier:

Note: The date on which the payment is made shall be the date on which the payment is entered in the books of accounts of the recipient or the date on which the payment is debited in his bank account, whichever is earlier

Forward charge on supply of service

Liability of GST (CGST and SGST or IGST as applicable) arises on one of the following dates, whichever is earlier.

12.12 VALUE OF SUPPLY

Under GST, the value of taxable supply of goods and services will be the transaction value. Transaction value refers to the price actually paid or payable for the supply of goods and services

Let us understand this with an example

A-1 Spare Ltd sells spare parts to Rev Automobiles for Rs. 6,000. The MRP of the spare parts is Rs. 10,000. The invoice that is issued to Rev Automobiles is illustrated below:

Invoice					
Sl.No	Description of goods	Qty	Rate	Per	Amount
1	Spare Parts	1	6,000	No	6,000
	CGST @ 9%				540
	SGST @ 9%				540
	Total	1			7,080

As per the above example, the transaction value is RS.6, 000 on which a GST of 18% is charged.

12.13   INVOICING

Invoicing is an important aspect of tax compliance for every business. It is necessary to be aware of the rules of invoicing under GST. Let us understand these in detail.

In the GST regime too, two types of invoices will be issued:

1. **Tax invoice:** When a registered taxable person supplies taxable goods or services, a tax invoice is issued. Based on the rules of the details required in a tax invoice

2. **Bill of Supply :** Bill of Supply is to be issued by a registered supplier on supply of exempted goods or services or if Supplier is paying tax under the composition scheme

For supply of goods, three copies of the invoice are required – Original, Duplicate, and Triplicate. For Supply of Services, 2 copies – original and duplicate are required to be issued.

12.14   INPUT TAX CREDIT CLAIM

Under the GST regime, input tax credit can be availed by every registered taxable person on all the inputs used or intended to be used in the course or furtherance of business. Under GST, to avail input credit on the supply of goods or services, all of the following conditions need to be satisfied to avail input credit:

♦ The dealer should be in possession of the Tax Invoice/Debit or Credit Note/Supplementary Invoice issued by a supplier registered under the GST Act.

♦ The said goods/services have been received.

♦ Returns (**Form GSTR-3**) have been filed.

♦ The tax charged has been paid to the government by the supplier.

12.14.1 Input Tax Credit Set off

On every transaction within a state, a component of Central GST (CGST) and State GST (SGST) will be applicable. Integrated GST (IGST) is for interstate transactions. Let us understand how to set off the input credit against each of these components in the order as prescribed by the GST Law.

Input Tax Credit	Set off against liability
CGST	CGST and IGST (in that order)
SGST	SGST and IGST (in that order)
IGST	IGST, CGST, SGST (in that order)

12.15   RETURNS

With GST in place, it does not matter whether you are a trader, manufacturer, reseller or a service provider. You only need to file GST returns.

Let us understand different types of return forms in GST

All the forms are required to be e-filed. The details of each form are listed below along with details of applicability and periodicity.

12.15.1 Regular Dealer

Form Type	Frequency	Due Date	Details to be furnished
Form GSTR-1	Monthly	10th of the succeeding month	Furnish details of outward supplies of taxable goods and/or services effected
Form GSTR-2A	Monthly	On 11th of the succeeding month	Auto populated details of inward supplies made available to the recipient, on the basis of **Form GSTR-1** furnished by the supplier
Form GSTR-2	Monthly	15th of the succeeding month	Details of inward supplies of taxable goods and/or services claiming input tax credit. Addition or modification in **Form GSTR-1** should be submitted in **Form GSTR-2**
Form GSTR-1A	Monthly	20th of the succeeding month	Details of outward supplies as added, corrected or deleted by the recipient in **Form GSTR-2** will be made available to the supplier
Form GSTR-3	Monthly	20th of the succeeding	Monthly return on the basis of finalization of details of outward supplies and inward supplies

		month	along with the payment of amount of tax
Form GST ITC-1	Monthly	--	Communication of acceptance, discrepancy or duplication of the input tax credit claim
Form GSTR-3A	--	15 days from default	Notice to a registered taxable person who fails to furnish return
Form GSTR-9	Annually	31st Dec of next fiscal	Annual Return - Furnish the details of the ITC availed and GST paid which includes the local and interstate transactions and import/exports.

12.15.2 Composite Dealer

Return Type	Frequency	Due Date	Details to be furnished
Form GSTR-4A	Quarterly	--	Auto-populated details of the inward supplies made available to the recipient registered under the composition scheme, on the basis of the FORM GSTR-1 furnished by the supplier.
Form GSTR-4	Quarterly	18th of succeeding month	All outward supplies of goods and services, including auto-populated details from Form GSTR-4A and tax payable details. Details of any additions, modifications, or deletions in Form GSTR-4A should also be submitted in Form GSTR-4.
Form GSTR-9A	Annual	31st Dec of next fiscal	Consolidated details of the quarterly returns filed along with tax payment details.

12.16 TRANSITION TO GST

While it is important to know the fundamentals of GST, it is also very critical for you to understand the transition provisions available, and take the necessary actions to ensure a smooth transition to GST, and leverage on transition benefits. You will need to review your accounting and reporting procedures, procurement, logistics decisions, and so on, in advance, to avail the appropriate input tax credit.

12.16.1 Closing Balance of Input Tax credit

The business registered under current can carry forward the balance CENVAT credit and Input Vat credit available on the last day, prior to date on which GST is implemented, as input credit.

What does this mean?

- The closing balance of CENVAT credit and Input Vat Credit should reflect in the last return filed by you, and
- It should be allowed as input tax credit under GST

The closing cenvat credit will be carried forwarded as CGST Input Credit and Input Vat will be carried forwarded as SGST input credit.

12.16.2 Unavailed Cenvat and Vat credit on capital Goods

The unavailed CENVAT and Input VAT credit on capital goods will be allowed to carried forwarded, if these conditions are satisfied:

- Under the current statute, CENVAT and input VAT are allowed as input tax credit.
- It is admissible as input tax credit in GST.

12.16.3 Availing the Input Credit Held in Closing Stock

The input tax credit (CENVAT, input VAT, entry tax and Service Tax) held in the closing stock of inputs (raw- materials), semi-finished goods, and finished goods can be availed in the following Scenario:

- Not liable to be registered under the current law, but are liable for registration under GST
- Engaged in the manufacture or sale of exempted goods or services
- First stage dealer or a second stage dealer or a registered importer

◆   Composition Dealer switching to Regular Dealer

However, there are conditions that you need to meet to be eligible to avail input tax credit held in your closing stock.

12.16.4 Goods returned to the place of business on or after implementation of GST

Duty Paid Goods returned

The goods on which duty had been paid under the current law and are returned by a customer (not registered under GST) after implementation of GST, the supplier will be allowed for refund of duty paid such return. Only those returns which are removed prior to 6 months from date of implementation of GST and are returned within 6 months from date of implementation of GST will be eligible for refund.

If duty paid goods are returned by registered taxable person, it will be considered as supply and GST will be levied on such return.

Exempt Goods returned

The goods which are exempt under the current law and are returned after implementation of GST, no tax will be levied, if the goods so returned are removed prior to 6 months from date of implementation of GST and are returned within 6 months from date of implementation of GST. If goods are returned after a period of 6 months, tax will be levied on such return.

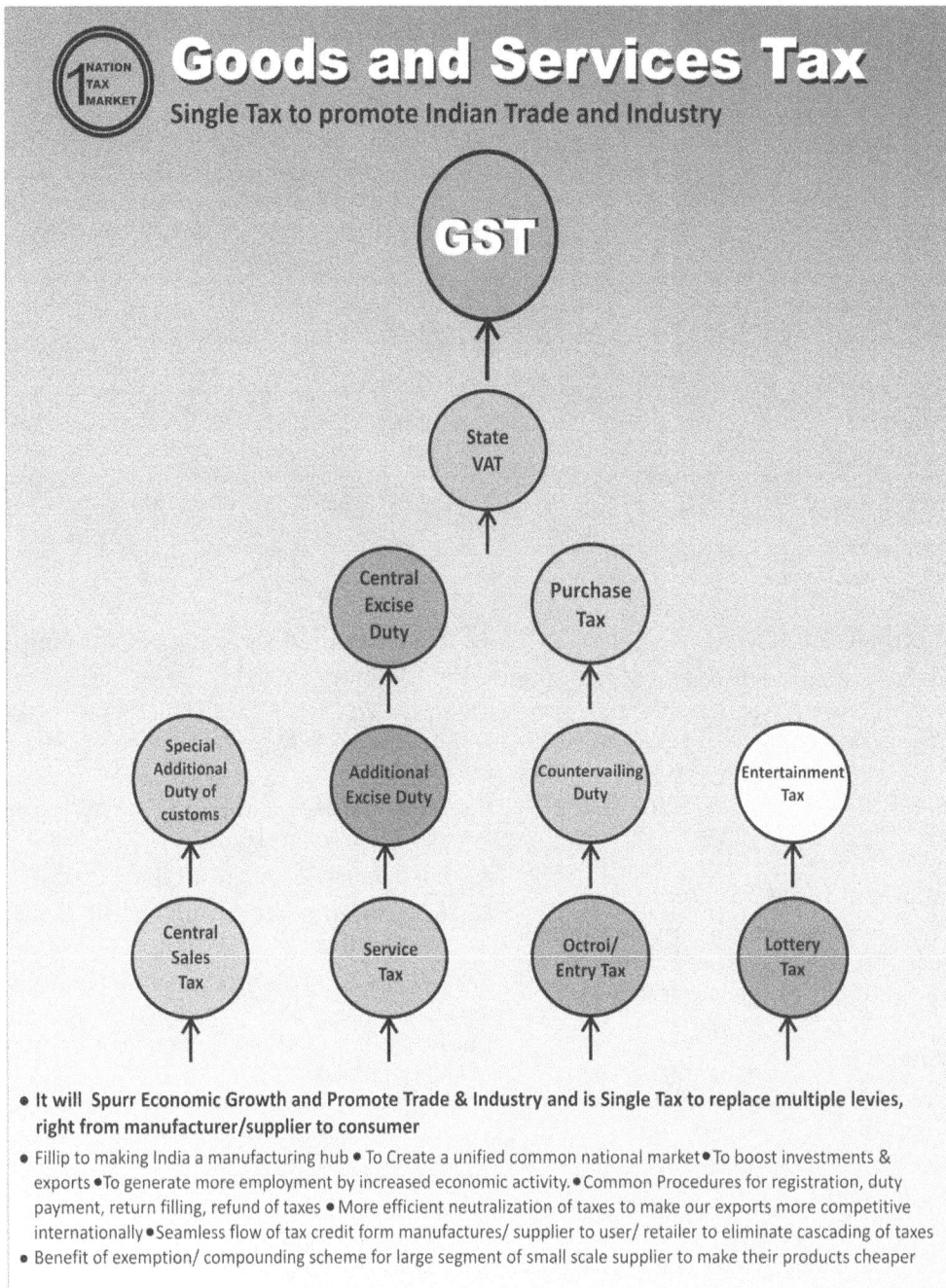

- It will Spurr Economic Growth and Promote Trade & Industry and is Single Tax to replace multiple levies, right from manufacturer/supplier to consumer
- Fillip to making India a manufacturing hub ● To Create a unified common national market● To boost investments & exports ●To generate more employment by increased economic activity. ●Common Procedures for registration, duty payment, return filling, refund of taxes ● More efficient neutralization of taxes to make our exports more competitive internationally ●Seamless flow of tax credit form manufactures/ supplier to user/ retailer to eliminate cascading of taxes
- Benefit of exemption/ compounding scheme for large segment of small scale supplier to make their products cheaper

Chapter 13

Payroll Administration

LEARNING OBJECTIVES

After studying this section you will be able to understand how to:

* Create Pay Heads
* Create Employees
* Define Salary Details
* Process and Pay Salary
* Manage Provident Fund Deductions and Contribution

13.1 INTRODUCTION

The term payroll refers to a series of accounting transactions involved in the process of paying employees for the services rendered after taking all the statutory and non-statutory deductions into account, in conformance with the terms of employment, company policy and the law of the land i.e., payment of payroll taxes, insurance premiums, employee benefits and other deductions.

Payroll Administration is the process of managing the compensation of employees based on the number of hours worked by employees and it is the process of keeping the track of worked hours, commission earned by employees, statutory deductions and contributions and also it ensures that the company policies are adhering to employment laws.

13.2 FEATURES OF PAYROLL

* It is fully integrated with accounts to give you the benefits of simplified payroll processing and accounting.
* It has user defined classifications and sub-classifications for comprehensive reporting. This may be related to the employees, employee groups, pay components, departments etc.
* It provides the facility to create user-defined earnings and deductions pay heads.
* It allows flexible and user-definable criteria for simple or complex calculations
* It allows unlimited grouping of payroll master
* It supports user-defined production units i.e., attendance/production/ time based remuneration units.
* It provides a flexible payroll processing period.
* It provides comprehensive cost center as well as employee-wise costing reports.
* It provides auto-fill facility to expedite the attendance, payroll and employer contributions processes.
* It ensures an accurate and timely salary processing, employee statutory deductions & employer statutory contributions with the help of predefined processes.
* It facilitates an accurate computation and deduction of ESI, EPF, professional tax, income tax, gratuity etc.

* It helps in the generation of statutory forms & challans for EPF, ESI, and income tax as prescribed.
* It allows drill-down facility to voucher level for any kind of alteration.
* It facilitates computation of arrears pertaining to prior period(s).
* Processing payments using the e-payments capability in Tally.ERP 9

13.3 ACTIVATION OF PAYROLL

In Tally.ERP 9, we can activate payroll feature and administer the payroll activities like keeping track of working hours, commission earned by employees, statutory deductions and contributions and also it manages the compensation based on the number of hours worked by Employees. In Tally.ERP 9, we can generate instant payroll reports like payroll statement, pay slip, pay head break up etc.

Scenario

Sky Lark Pvt. Ltd. deals in trading of Furniture's and it has expanded its business into multiple regions. To maintain proper sales process, the company has hired many sales executives and to maintain sales executive's compensation/payroll details, the company installed Tally.ERP 9 software.

To maintain payroll details in Tally.ERP 9, we need to create the company and activate Payroll feature

Activity: Create the following company in Tally.ERP 9:

* *Company Name: Sky Lark Pvt. Ltd.*
* *Address: #52, 8th Cross, Mahim Tech Park, Bengaluru- 560001*
* *Financial year begins from: 01-04-2016*
* *Books beginning from : 01-04-2016*

To activate payroll in Tally ERP 9, follow the steps given below:

Step 1: Activation of Payroll in Accounting Features

1. Go to **Gateway of Tally > F11: Company Features >** Press **F1: Accounting Features**

2. Set **Maintain payroll** to **Yes**

3. Set **Maintain more than one payroll or cost category** to **No**

   The **Accounting Features Screen** appears as shown below (Figure 13.1)

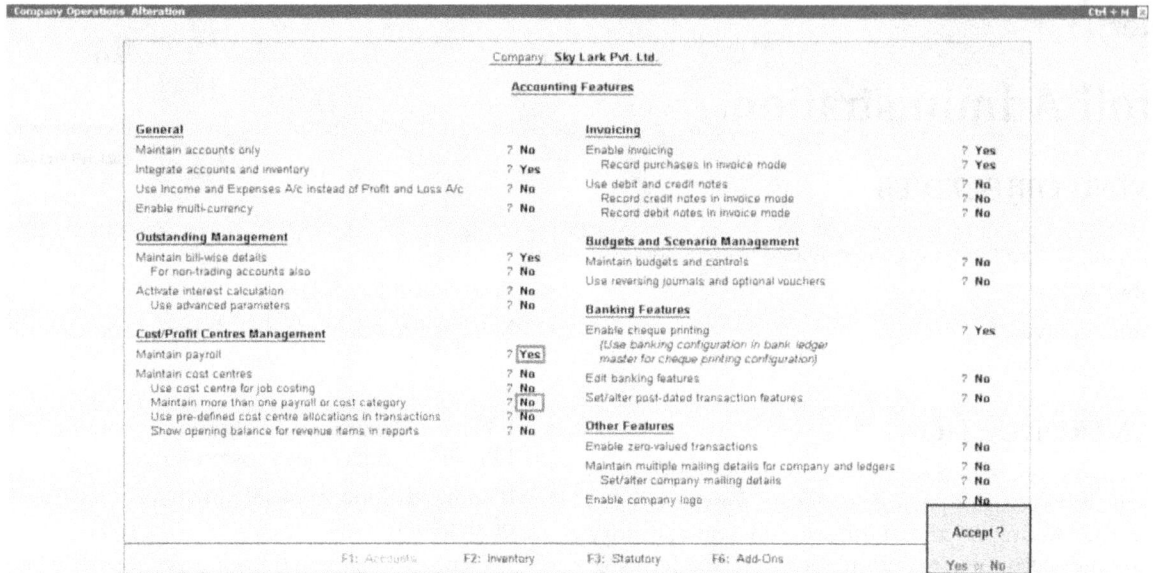

Figure 13.1: Accounting Features Screen

4.   Accept the screen

Note: The option Maintain more than one payroll or cost category is set to Yes, when separate cost categories are created to allocate employee cost. In cases, where only one cost category i.e., primary cost category is used to allocate multiple cost centres, this option may be set to No.

Step 2: Activate Payroll in Statutory & Taxation Features

1.   Go to **Gateway of Tally > F11: Company Features >** Press **F3:Statutory & Taxation**

2.   Set **Enable payroll statutory** to **Yes**

3.   **Set/alter payroll statutory details** to **Yes**

    The **Company Operations Alteration Screen** appears as shown below (Figure 13.2)

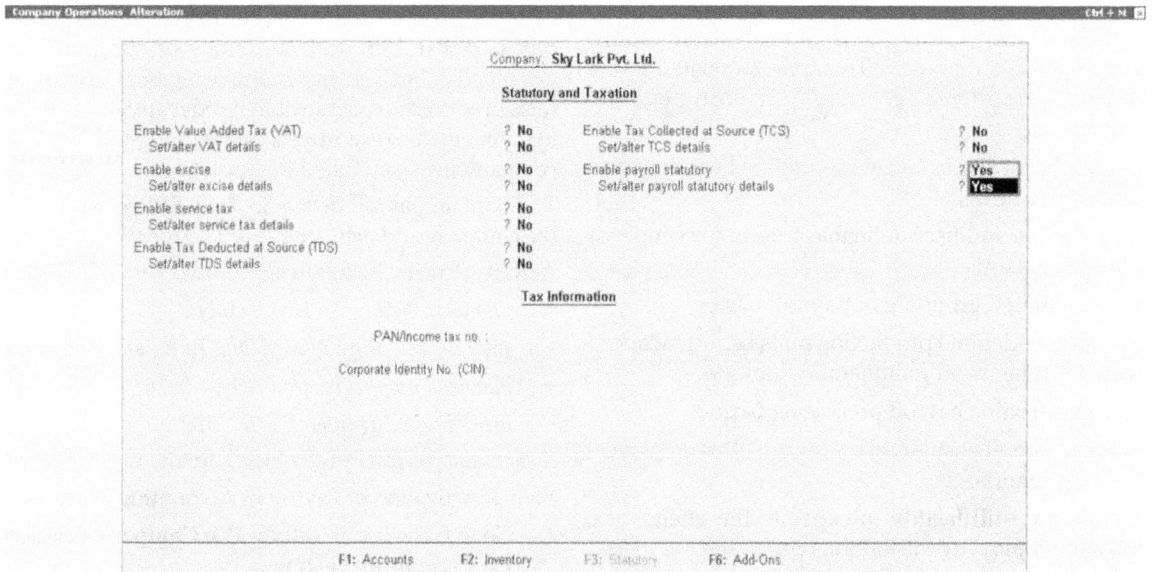

Figure 13.2: Statutory and Taxation Screen

4.   In the **Payroll Statutory Details** screen, enter the **Provident Fund, Employee State Insurance, National Pension** **Scheme and Income Tax** details of the company as shown below (Figure 13.3):

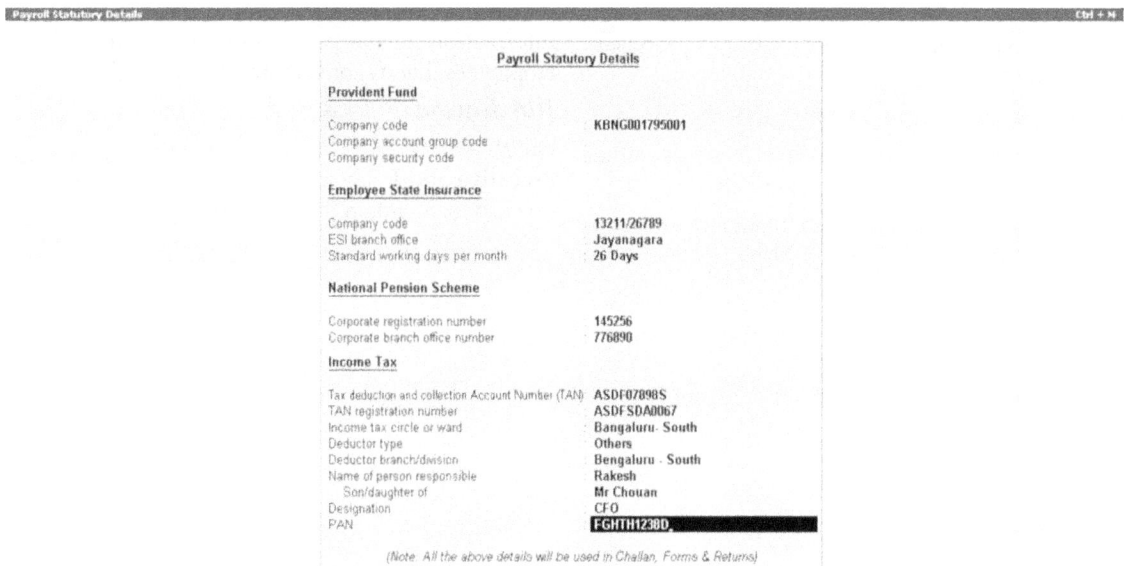

Figure 13.3: Payroll Statutory Details Screen

5. Accept the screen

Explanation of Payroll Statutory Details

1. **Provident Fund**

   • **Company code:** This field denotes the provident fund code of the company allotted by the department.

     PF Department has specified the format for entering the company **PF Account Number**. The format is as shown below:

Region Code	Office Code	Est Code	Extension Code
[KN]	[BNG]	ˉ digits	3 digits

   Example: Company PF Account Number to be entered as **KNBNG0001795001**

   • **Company account group code:** This field denotes the provident fund group code of the company allotted by the department.

   • **Company security code:** This field denotes the security code of the company allotted by the department.

2. **Employee State Insurance**

   • **Company code:** This field denotes the ESI code of the company allotted by the department

   • **ESI branch office:** This field denotes the nearest ESI office under whose jurisdiction, the company is situated.

   • **Standard working days (per month):** This field denotes the consistent pay period to be considered for ESI calculation. If this field is left blank, the calculation is done based on the calendar days in each month

3. **National Pension Scheme**

   • **Corporate registration number:** Specify the corporate registration number as allotted by the central record keeping agency (CRA) during registration.

   • **Corporate branch office number:** Specify the corporate branch office number allotted by the central record keeping agency (CRA) during registration

4. **Income Tax**

   • **Tax deduction and collection Account Number (TAN):** Specify the 10 digit **TAN** assigned to the employer.

   • **TAN registration number:** Specify the TAN registration number provided when **TAN** is registered on **TIN**

   • **Income tax circle or ward:** Specify the name of the income tax circle, to which the employer is associated

   • **Deductor type:** Select government for **Central or State Government companies**. For all other companies, select **Others**

   • **Deductor branch/division:** Enter the branch/division name.

   • **Name of person responsible:** Enter the name of the person responsible for TDS deduction in the company

   • **Son/daughter of:** Enter the responsible person's father's name

   • **Designation:** Specify the official designation of the responsible person.

   • **PAN:** Mention the PAN number of the person

13.4 PROCESSING BASIC PAYROLL IN TALLY.ERP 9

Tally.ERP 9's payroll features require minimal effort for accurate payroll processing. It takes five easy steps to process payroll and generate payslip in Tally.ERP 9

Essentially, payroll involves the calculation of amounts due to an employee on the following basis.

- on hourly wages
- pay on a fixed basis such as a certain amount per week, per month and so on
- pay to sales persons on commission
- reimbursement of expenses such as travel expenses, either as paid by the employee or based on per item rate
- pay on the number of pieces produced/manufactured/sold

It is therefore essential to quantify the following payroll information for the purpose of computation of payments to employees. Let us consider the following illustration.

Illustration: Processing of payroll in Tally.ERP 9

On 01-04-2016, Sky Lark Pvt. Ltd., hired 5 employees as sales executive and following is the Monthly salary structure of 5 executives, maintain the following structure in Tally.ERP 9

Employee Name	Basic Pay	HRA	Conveyance	PF Deduction 12%	PF Contribution 12%	
					EPS	EPF
Abhinav Kumar	20,000	40%of Basic Pay	800	12%	8.33%	3.67%
Bhaskar Pandey	22,000	40%of Basic Pay	800	12%	8.33%	3.67%
Chetan Singh	23,000	40%of Basic Pay	800	12%	8.33%	3.67%
Dhiru Rokaya	25,000	40%of Basic Pay	800	12%	8.33%	3.67%
Elena D Souza	15,000	40%of Basic Pay	800	12%	8.33%	3.67%

To maintain the above salary structure/ details of employees in Tally.ERP 9, follow five steps given below:

1. **Create Employee Master:** In this step, we will create the employee details like Name of employee, date of birth, joining date, address, bank details and statutory details etc. **For example:** In this step we create employees masters like Abhinav, Bhaskar, Chetan, Dhiru & Elena

2. **Create Payroll Units:** In this step, we will create units of measure **for example:** work can be measured based on time or quantity. Hence we will be creating the payroll unit like **hour.**

3. **Create Pay Heads:** In this step the salary components constituting an employee's pay structure i.e., Pay Head is created in Tally.ERP 9. **For Example:** Basic Pay, Conveyance, PF, HRA etc.

4. **Define Salary:** In this step, the salary details like its calculation details or formula will be defined. **For Example:** HRA should get calculated as 40% on Basic Pay, Dearness Allowance should get calculated as 30% on Basic Pay etc.

5. **Process and Pay Salary:** In this step, the payroll transactions are recorded for processing the salary. **For Example:** Recording of Attendance Voucher, Processing of Salary, Processing of PF and Making Salary Payment etc., will be recorded in Tally.ERP 9

13.4.1 Creation of Employee Master

The Employee master records employee information – department, date of joining, date of leaving, ID number, designation, location, function, employee bank details, statutory details, and passport & visa details and so on.

The Employee master is used to record the employee information. In Tally.ERP 9, the following employee masters can be created:

- Employee Category Master
- Employee Group Master
- Employee Master

Employee Category Master

An **Employee Category** provides an additional level to classify employees in a logical manner. This is in addition to the employee group available by default.

Employee categories option will be available only if the option **Maintain more than one payroll or cost category** is enabled in F11: Company Features>F1: Accounting Features.

Employee Group Master

Businesses with multiple departments, divisions, functions or activities may create the required employee groups and classify individual employees under a specified group.

For example, you can create the salary structure based on the department or function such as Production, Sales, and Administration soon, or by designation such as Managers, Supervisors, and Workers.

Note: By enabling the option "Define salary details" in the employee group creation, we can define the salary structure for the employee group. If the salary structure for the group is same then salary can be defined in employee group creation.

Employee Master

In Employee Master, we can create individual employee masters, with or without grouping them, under the employee group master.

In Tally.ERP 9, you can record all the necessary information of the employees in the employee masters Tally.ERP 9 also allows you to enter the Statutory, Expat and Contract details of the employees.

Note: Tally.ERP 9 allows you to configure the settings like statutory, expat & contract details from the employee creation screen, by clicking F12: Configure. You can enable "Provide passport and visa details to Yes "and "Provide contract details to Yes", to get expat details in employee creation screen.

Let us create the Employee Master by following the procedure given below:

Creation of Employee Master

- Go to **Gateway of Tally > Payroll Info. > Employees >** under **Single Employee >** Select **Create**
- Fill in the details as shown below (Figure 13.4)

  The **Completed Employee Creation Screen** appears as shown below (Figure 13.4):

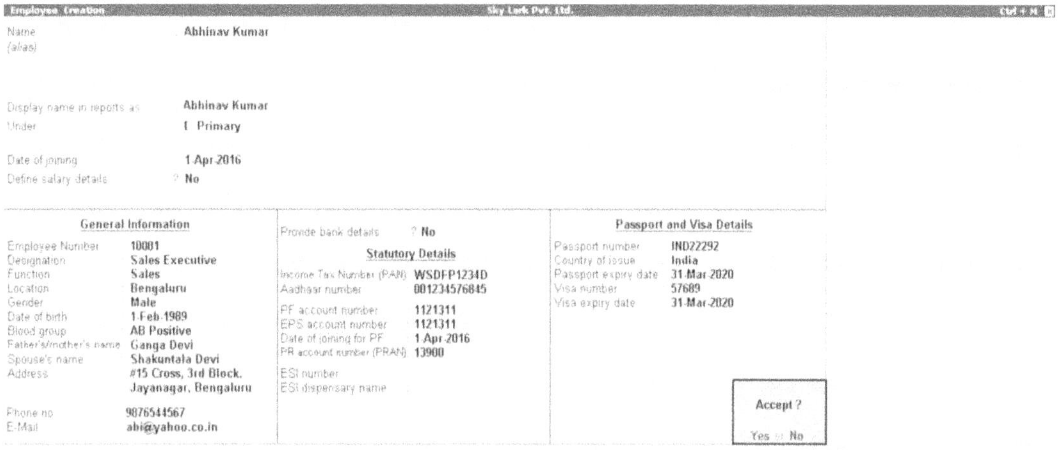

Figure 13.4: Employee Creation Screen

- Accept the screen

Note: ◆ The date of resignation/retirement option will be available only on the employee alteration screen. After you enter the date of resignation/retirement, you can also select a reason for leaving.
- Enable the option – Provide bank details to Yes and provide the bank information like, account number, IFS code, MICR code, bank name and branch.

Activity: Similarly create the following **Employee** masters under Primary and enter the **Date of joining** as 1-4-2016.

- *Bhaskar Pandey*
- *Chetan Singh*
- *Dhiru Rokaya*
- *Elena D Souza*

13.4.2 Creation of Payroll Units

The salary paid to an employee is computed based on work done by an employee, which is measured in terms of time or quantity.

In Tally.ERP 9, work done can be quantified using the **"Payroll Unit"**.

A payroll unit is similar to unit of measure used in the inventory module. You can create simple as well as compound payroll units measured on attendance/production types such as time, work or quantity.

Simple Unit Creation

Go to **Gateway of Tally > Payroll Info. > Units (Work) > Create**

Hours	
Against the Field	Actions to be Performed
Type	Accept the default option; i.e.: Simple
Symbol	Enter Hrs
Formal Name	Enter Hours
Number of Decimal Places	Enter 0

Note: In Tally.ERP 9, we can create Compound Unit from, Gateway of Tally > Payroll Info. > Units (Work) > Create > Press Backspace > Select Type of Unit as Compound.

13.4.3 Attendance/Production Types

An **Attendance/Production Type** is used to record the attendance and production data. Based on the various components (pay head), you may need to define multiple attendance/production types.

Examples for attendance types are present or absent, and examples of production types are hours worked, or number of pieces produced.

An **Attendance/Production Type** is associated with a pay head in an employee's pay structure. Attendance/Production types may also be defined in hierarchical groups whereby attendance types having a common unit are combined under logical groups.

Example: Present Days can have present and leave with pay as sub-groups

The Attendance/Production Type may be:

*   **Attendance/Leave with Pay:** should be used to record positive attendance and leave with pay

    For example: **Present, Sick Leave**, etc.

*   **Leave without Pay:** should be used to record negative attendance

    For example: Absent, Leave without Pay etc.

*   **Production:** should be used to record the production details

    For example: Piece Production, Overtime Hours, etc

*   **User Defined Calendar Type:** should be used to create user defined calendar which can be later used to specify the variable number of days for each month.

    For example: 25 days in January, 24 days in February, 26 days in March, etc

Follow the below given procedure to create attendance master

Attendance Type Creation

Go to **Gateway of Tally > Payroll Info. > Attendance/Production Types > Create**

Present	
Against the Field	Actions to be Performed
Under	Select Primary
Attendance type	Select Attendance/Leave with Pay
Period Type	By Default it will take as **Days**

Absent	
Against the Field	Actions to be Performed
Under	Select **Primary**
Attendance type	Select **Leave without Pay**
Period Type	By Default it will take as **Days**

Note:
*   You can also create various attendance type, for example Earned Leave (EL), Casual Leave (CL). But instead of selecting primary in under field, need to select as present.
*   We can create User Defined Calendar type: This can be used to compute the per day salary based on the variable days for each month. For example:

25 days in January will mean that salary will be calculated for 25 days and not for 31 days

13.4.4 Creation of Pay heads

The salary components constituting an employee's pay structure is called a **Pay Head**. A pay head may be an earnings for the employee, or a deduction which is recovered from his/her salary. The value of these pay heads could be either fixed or variable for each payroll period.

For example: Basic Pay is a fixed pay component, whereas variable pay, bonus, etc., are variable components.

Pay Heads may be broadly considered as earnings and deductions from an employee's point of view. However, these pay heads would still be expense and liability from the employer's view point.

Some examples of earnings pay heads are basic salary, dearness allowance, house rent allowance, etc. Some examples of deductions pay heads are Employees' Provident Fund (EPF), Employees' State Insurance (ESI), Professional Tax, Income Tax etc., some of the examples for contribution pay heads are EPS, EPF etc.

The essential pay heads required to be created to process the salaries of the employees of Sky Lark Pvt. Ltd., are as follows:

*   **Basic Pay**
*   **House Rent Allowance**
*   **Conveyance**
*   **Employees PF Deduction @ 12%**
*   **Employers EPS Contribution @ 8.33%**
*   **Employers EPF Contribution @ 3.67%**
*   **EDLI & Administration charge**

Let us now see how these pay heads are created in Tally.ERP 9.

1.   **Creation of Earning Pay Heads**

Basic Pay

*   Go to **Gateway of Tally > Payroll Info. > Pay Heads > Create**

Basic Pay	
Against the Field	Actions to be Performed
Pay head type	Select **Earnings for Employees**
Income type	Select **Fixed**
Under	Select **Indirect Expenses**
Affect net salary	Select **Yes**
Name to be displayed in payslip	By Default **Basic Pay** appears
Use for calculation of gratuity	Select **No**
Set/Alter Income Tax Details	Set to **No**
Calculation type	Select **On Attendance**
Attendance/leave with pay	Select **Present**
Calculation period	Select **Months**
Basis of calculation (per day)	Select **As per Calendar Period**
Rounding Method	Select **Normal Rounding**
Limit	Enter **1**

The **Completed Basic Pay head Creation Screen** appears as shown below (Figure 13.5):

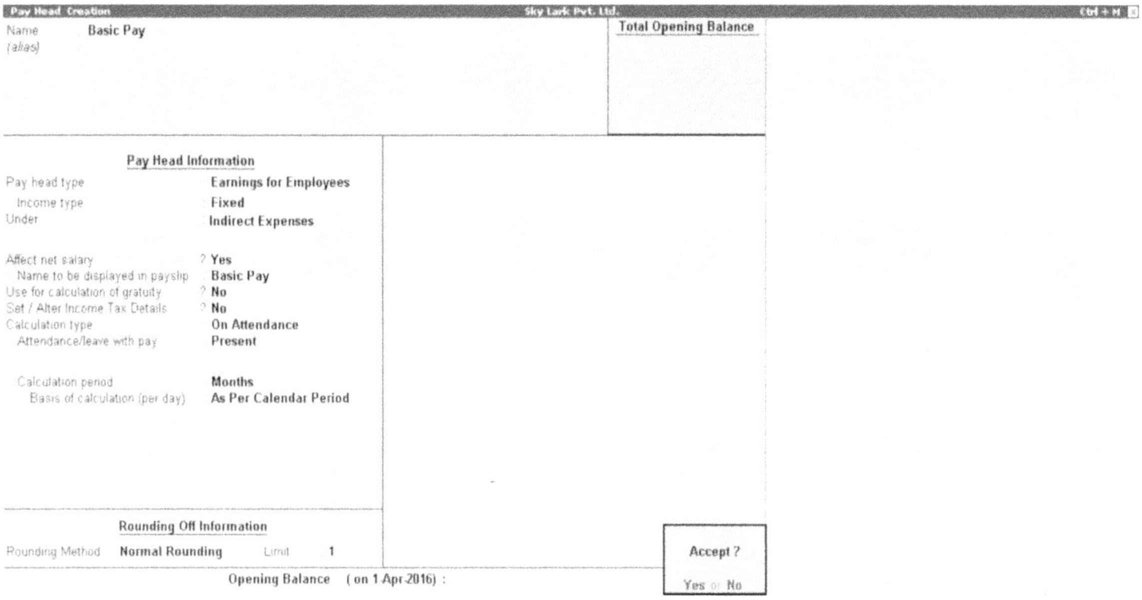

Figure 13.5: Basic Pay Creation Screen

- Accept the screen

House Rent Allowance

- Go to **Gateway of Tally > Payroll Info. > Pay Heads > Create**

House Rent Allowance	
Against the Field	Action to be Performed
Pay head type	Select Earnings for Employees
Income type	Select Fixed
Under	Select Indirect Expenses
Affect Net Salary	Select Yes
Name to be displayed in payslip	Enter HRA
Use for calculation of gratuity	Select No
Set / Alter Income Tax Details	Set to No
Calculation type	Select As Computed Value
Calculation period	Months will be selected as default
Rounding Method	Select Normal Rounding
Limit	Enter 1
Compute	Select On Specified Formula
Compute on Specified Formula	
Function	Add Pay Head appears as default
Pay Head	Select Basic Pay
Effective From	Enter 01-04-2016
Slab Type	Select Percentage
Value Basis	Enter 40%

The **Completed House Rent Allowance Pay Head** **Creation Screen** appears as shown below (Figure 13.6):

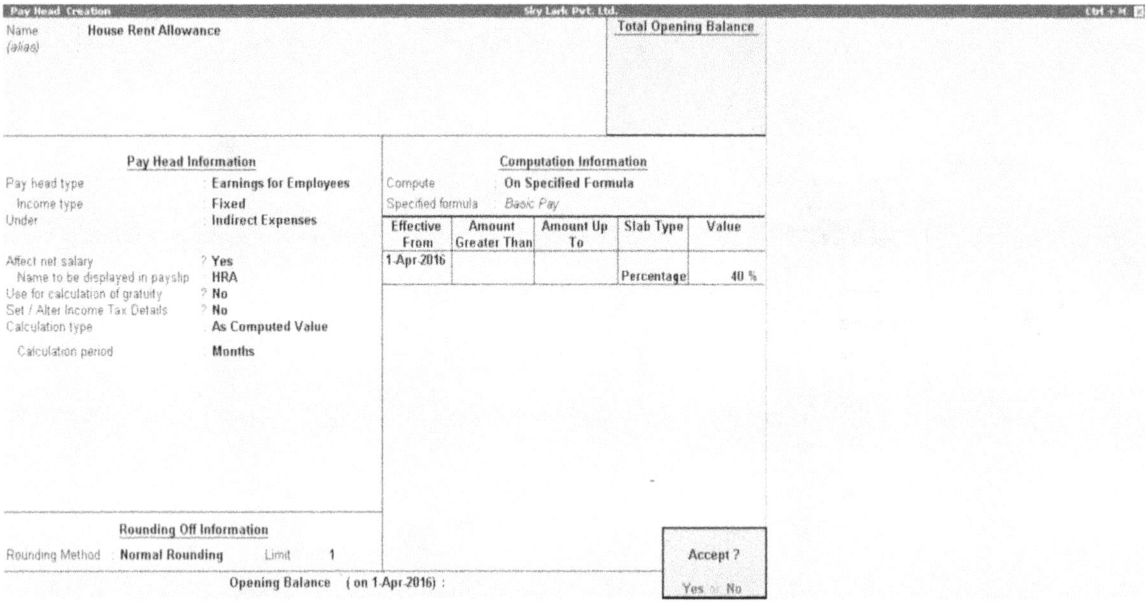

Figure 13.6: HRA Pay Head Creation Screen

- Accept the screen

Conveyance

- Go to **Gateway of Tally > Payroll Info. > Pay Heads > Create**

Conveyance	
Against the Field	Actions to be Performed
Pay head type	Select **Earnings for Employees**
Income type	Select **Fixed**
Under	Select **Indirect Expenses**
Affect net salary	Select **Yes**
Name to be displayed in payslip	Let it be as **Conveyance**
Use for calculation of gratuity	Select **No**
Set/Alter Income Tax Details	Set to **No**
Calculation type	Select **Flat Rate**
Calculation period	Select **Months**
Rounding Method	Select **Normal Rounding**
Limit	Enter 1

The **Completed Conveyance Pay Head Creation Screen** appears as shown below (Figure 13.7):

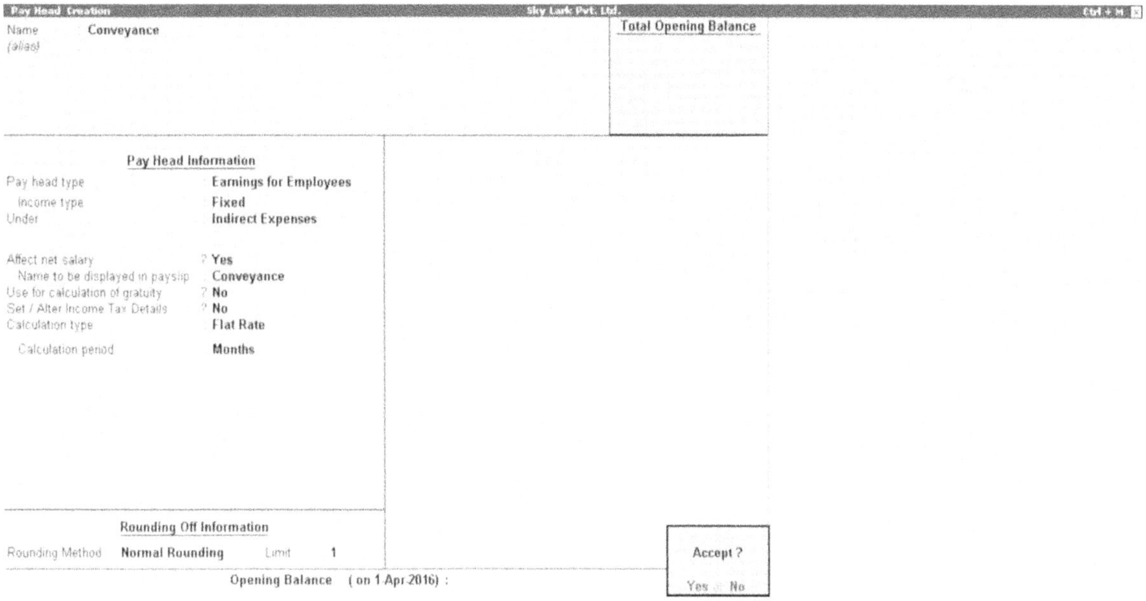

Figure 13.7: Conveyance Pay Head Screen

- Accept the screen

2. **Creation of Statutory Deduction Pay Head**

Employee PF Deduction @ 12%

- Go to **Gateway of Tally > Payroll Info. > Pay Heads > Create**

Employees PF Deduction @ 12%	
Against the Field	Actions to be Performed
Pay head type	Select Employees' Statutory Deductions
Statutory pay type	Select PF Account (A/c No. 1)
Under	Select Current Liabilities
Affect net salary	Select Yes
Name to be displayed in payslip	By Default it take as Employee's PF Deduction @ 12%
Rounding Method	Select Normal Rounding
Limit	Enter 1
Compute	Select On Specified Formula
Computation on Specified Formula	
Function	By Default Add Pay Head appears
Pay Head	Select Basic Pay
Effective From	Enter 01-04-2016
Slab Type	Select Percentage
Value Basis	Enter 12%

The **Completed Pay Head Creation Screen** for the pay head Employee's PF Deduction appears as shown below (Figure 13.8):

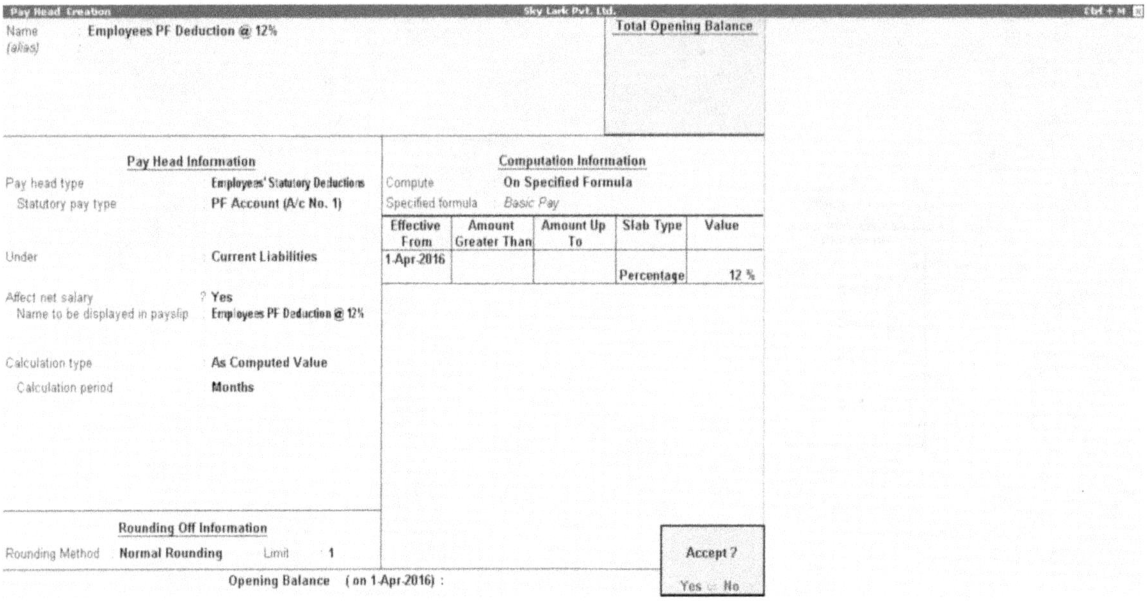

Figure 13.8: Employee's PF Deduction@12% Pay Head

- Accept the screen

Note:
- PF is a statutory deduction. It is deducted on Basic + Dearness Allowance
- DA is provided only in government departments.
- Employee's PF account number is of 7 digits which has to be provided in employee master.
- Any employee who wants to en-cash his PF amount, he can draw the total amount using of Form 10 C & Form 19

3. **Creation of Statutory Contribution Pay Heads**

Employers EPS Contribution @ 8.33%

- Go to **Gateway of Tally > Payroll Info. > Pay Heads > Create**

Employers EPS Contribution @ 8.33%	
Against the Field	**Actions to be Performed**
Pay head type	Select **Employer's Statutory Contributions**
Statutory pay type	Select **EPS Account (A/c No. 10)**
Under	Select **Indirect Expenses**
Affect net salary	Select **No**
Rounding Method	Select **Normal Rounding**
Limit	Enter **1**
Compute	Select **On Specified Formula**
Computation on Specified Formula	
Function	By Default **Add Pay Head** appears
Pay Head	Select **Basic Pay**
Effective From	Enter **01-04-2016**
Amount Up To	Enter **15,000**
Slab Type	Select **Percentage**
Value Basis	Enter **8.33%**
Amount greater Than	By default it will be taken as **15,000**
Amount Up To	**Leave it blank**
Slab type	Select **Value**
Value basis	Mention the amount as ₹ **1,250**

The Completed **Employers EPS Contribution @ 8.33% Pay Head Creation Screen** appears as shown below (Figure 13.9):

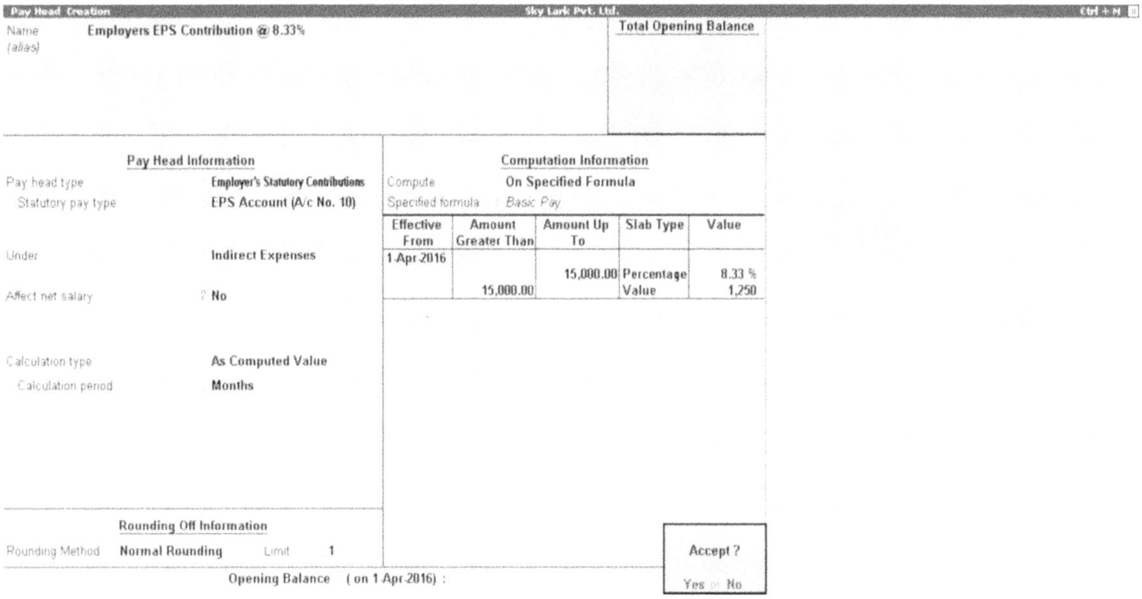

Figure 13.9: Employers EPS Contribution @ 8.33% Pay Head Creation Screen

◆ Accept the Screen

Note: ◆ EPS (Employee Pension Scheme) is an arrangement by which an employer and an employee pay into a fund that is invested to provide the employee with a pension on retirement.
   ◆ Employer's share to pension fund is limited to 8.33% of the workman's salary (Basic and DA) subject to a maximum of ₹ 15,000. Therefore, the monthly pension fund contribution per employee will be limited to ₹ 1,250 i.e., 8.33% of ₹ 15,000.

Employers PF Contribution @ 3.67%

◆ Go to **Gateway of Tally > Payroll Info. > Pay Heads > Create**

Employers PF Contribution @ 3.67 %	
Against the Field	Actions to be Performed
Pay head type	Select Employer's Statutory Contributions
Statutory pay type	Select PF Account (A/c No. 1)
Under	Select Indirect Expenses
Affect net salary	Select No
Rounding Method	Select Normal Rounding
Limit	Enter 1
Compute	Select On Specified Formula Add Pay Head : Employee's PF Deduction @ 12% Subtract Pay head : Employer's EPS Contribution @ 8.33%

The Completed **Computation on Specified Formula Screen** appears as shown below (Figure 13.10):

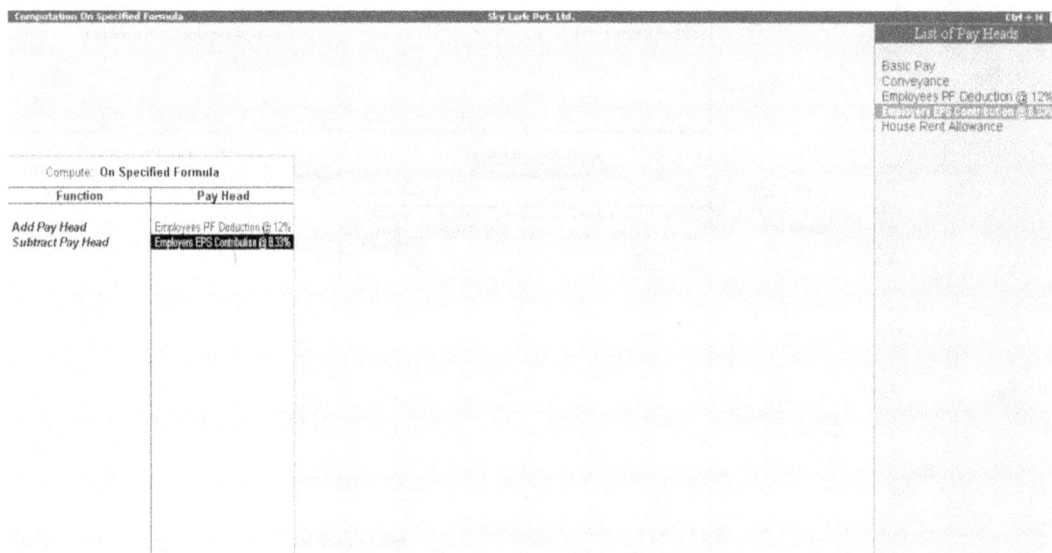

Figure 13.10: Computation on Specified Formula Screen

- Press **Enter** from the above screen
- In **Slab Type** field, select as **Percentage**
- In **Value field** enter as **100%**

The completed **Employers PF Contribution @ 3.67% Pay Head Creation Screen** appears as shown below (Figure 13.11):

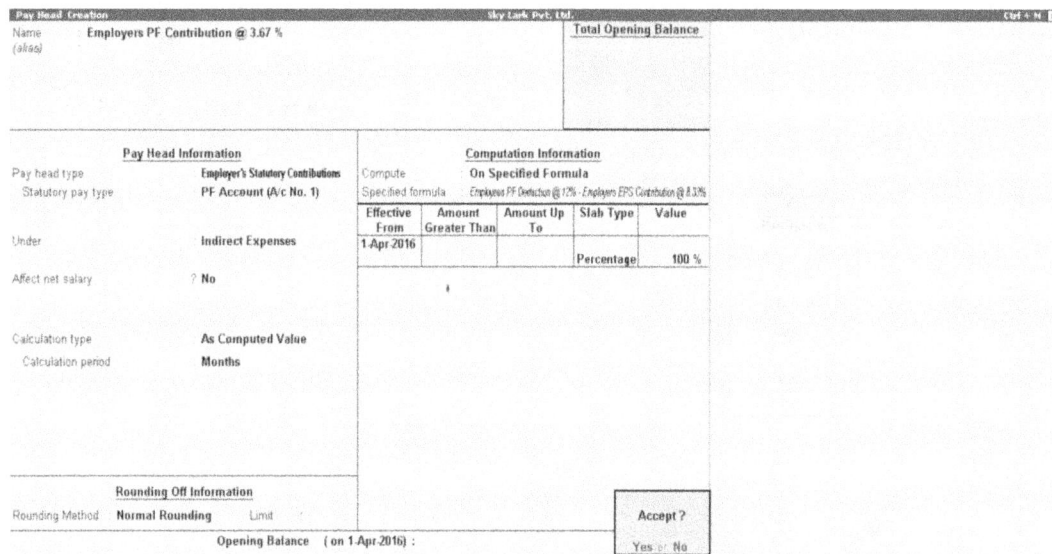

Figure 13.11: Employer PF Contribution @ 3.67% Pay Head Creation Screen

- Accept the screen

4. **Liabilities Masters (Pay heads)**
   - Go to **Gateway of Tally > Payroll Info. > Pay Heads > Create**

The **Completed Salary Payable Pay Head Creation Screen** appears as shown below (Figure 13.12):

Salary Payable	
Against the Field	Actions to be Performed
Pay head type	Select **Not Applicable**
Under	Select **Current Liabilities**

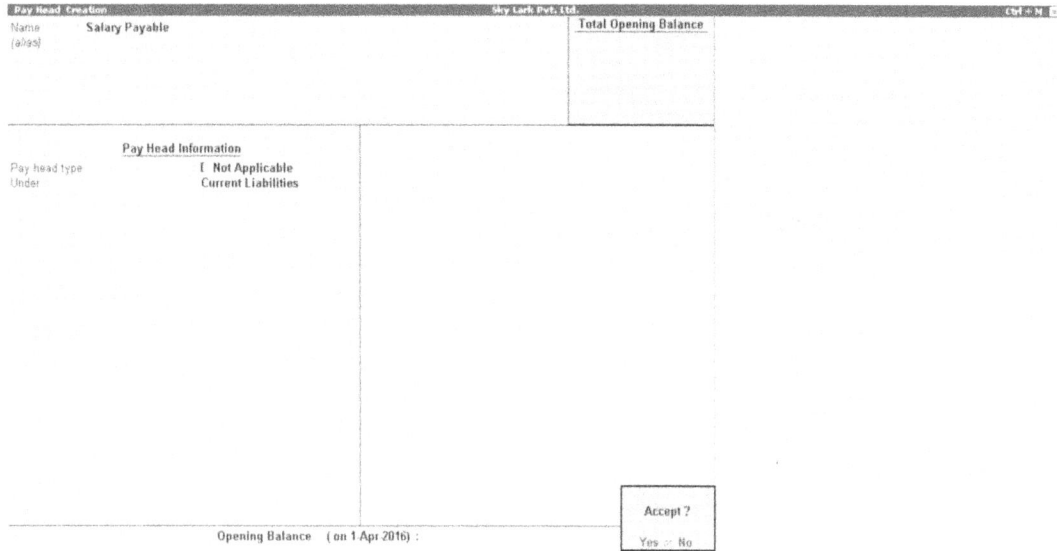

Figure 13.12: Salary Payable

- Accept the screen

13.4.5 Defining Salary Details for an Employee

The pay structure for an employee can be defined in Tally.ERP 9 using the Salary Details option.

1. Go to **Gateway of Tally > Payroll Info. > Salary Details > Define > Select Abhinav Kumar**

2. Specify the details based on the screen shown below (Figure 6.164)

The **Completed Salary Details Screen** appears as shown below (Figure 13.13)

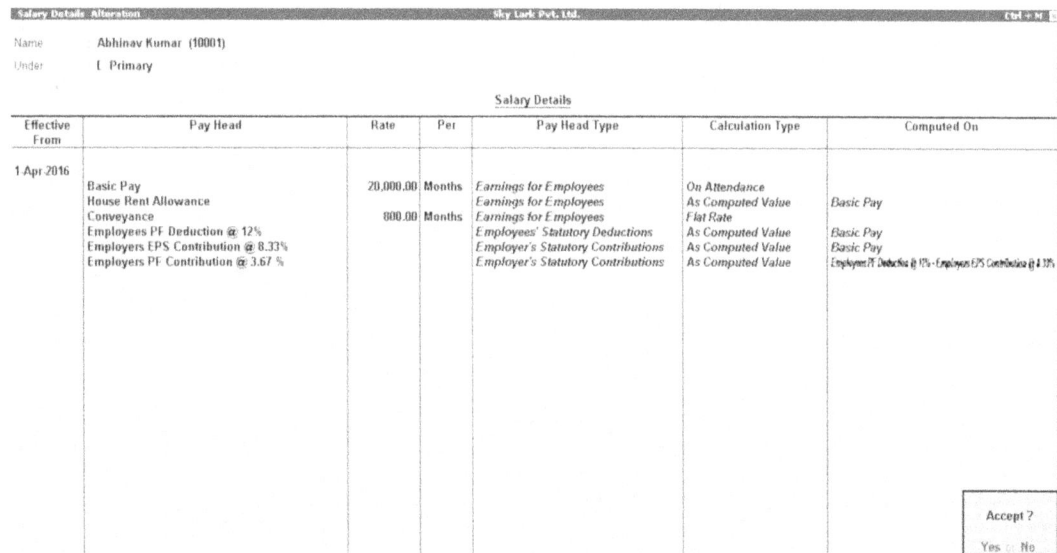

Figure 13.13: Salary Details-Abhinav Kumar

3. Accept the screen

Activity: Similarly define salary details for following employees by referring to the illustration table:

- *Bhaskar Pandey*
- *Chetan Singh*
- *Dhiru Rokaya*
- *Elena D Souza*

13.5 SALARY PROCESSING

Once the Salary Structures are defined for all the employees in Tally.ERP 9, then at the end of every month the company can record the payroll transactions to process the salary. Following section will explain how different types of payroll transactions are maintained in Tally.ERP 9.

Illustration: Processing of different types of payroll vouchers in Tally.ERP 9

On 30-4-2016, process the salary for all the employees based on the Attendance details given below. Salary for the month of April should be paid to all the employees on 01-05-2016.

Employee Name	Present (Days)	Absent (Days)
Abhinav Kumar	29	1
Bhaskar Pandey	28	2
Chetan Singh	30	0
Dhiru Rokaya	30	0
Elena D Souza	30	0

As per the illustration, salary process comprise of the following Vouchers:

♦ Recording of attendance voucher

♦ Processing of salary payable

♦ Processing of statutory pay heads

♦ Processing of employers EDLI & PF admin charges

♦ Payment of salary to employees

♦ Payment of Provident Fund to PF Department

Step 1: Recording of Attendance Voucher

To process the salary, firstly we require to calculate the attendance of the employees. Attendance voucher allows you to enter attendance, overtime, leave or production details. You can enter separate vouchers for each day or a single voucher for a given pay period, say a month, with aggregated values.

1. Go to **Gateway of Tally > Payroll Vouchers >** Press **Ctrl+F5: Attendance**

2. Click **F2: Date** or press **F2** and change the date to **30-04-2016**

3. Record the attendance voucher for the employees

    The **Attendance Voucher Creation Screen** appears as shown below (Figure 13.14):

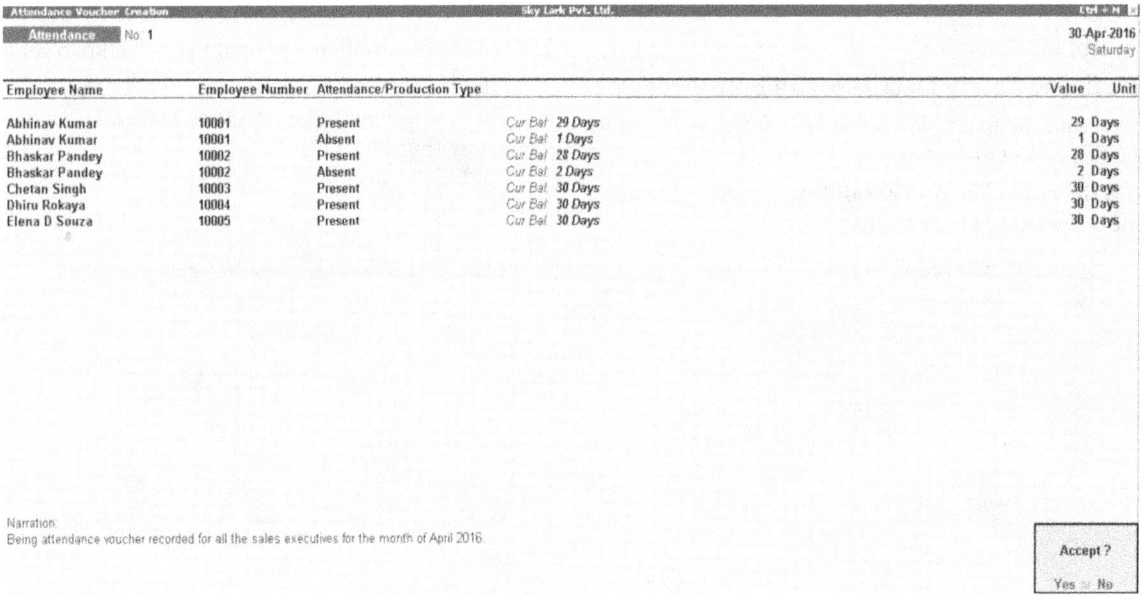

Figure 13.14: Attendance Voucher Screen

4. Accept the screen

Note: Attendance Voucher can also be created using the auto fill option. To use this option, Press Alt + A.

Activity: Create a ledger Kotak Mahindra Bank under Bank Accounts with an opening balance of ₹ 10, 00,000.

Step 2: Processing of Salary Payables to All Employees

The salary can be directly paid from the payroll vouchers or the payroll vouchers can be used to create the liability and the salary can be paid using the payment voucher. Before we make the payment of the salary using a payment voucher, we have to calculate the salary.

To process the salary of all the employees follow the steps given below:

1. Go to **Gateway of Tally > Payroll Vouchers > Ctrl+F4: Payroll**

2. Press **Alt+A** for **Payroll Autofill**

3. In **Process for** field select as **Salary**

4. Enter the From and To dates **01-04-2016 to 30-04-2016**

5. Select **All Items** from the **List of Employees/Group** or select particular employee to process salary for one employee

6. Select Sort by as **Employee Name**

7. Select the **Salary Payable** ledger from the **List of Ledger Accounts** as shown below (Figure 13.15):

Figure 13.15: Auto fill screen for Salary Payable

The **Payroll Voucher Creation for Salary** appears as shown   below (Figure 13.16)

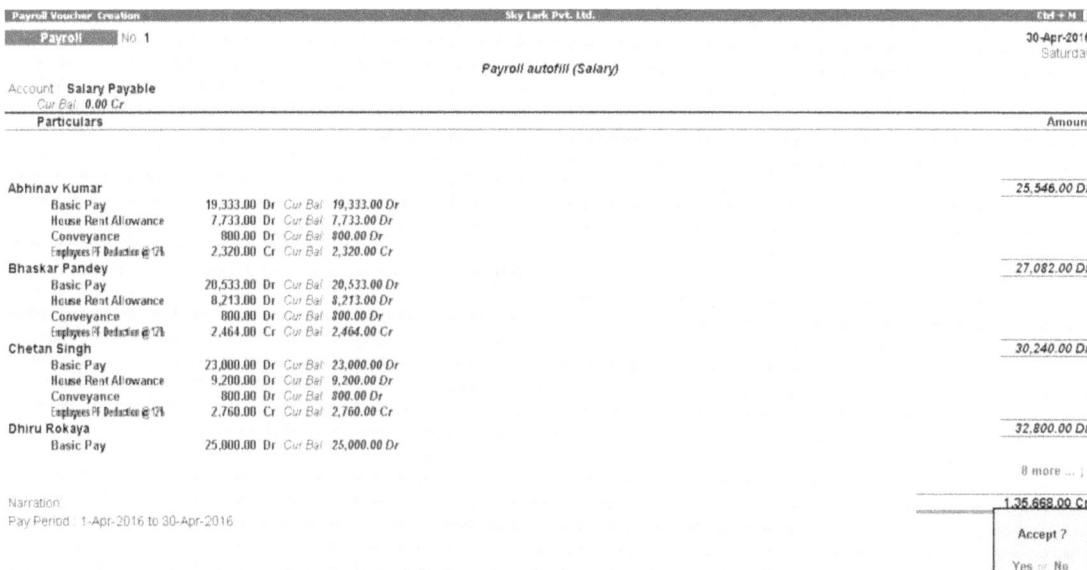

Figure 13.16: Payroll Voucher – Salary payable

8. Accept the screen

The salary of a month for each employee is based on the **Salary Details** defined for them and also based on the attendance for that month which is captured in the attendance voucher.

Step 3: Processing of Statutory Pay Heads

Provident Fund

Let us see how **Employer Contribution** towards provident fund is processed in Tally.ERP 9. The following illustration shows how PF is processed for the employee

To process the Provident Fund of the employee Abhinav Kumar,

1. Go to **Gateway of Tally > Payroll Vouchers**
2. Press **F2** to change the Date to **30-04-2016**

3. Press **Alt+A** for **Payroll Auto Fill**
4. Select PF Contribution in **Process for** field
5. Enter the From and To date as 01-04-2016 to 30-04-2016
6. Select **All Items** for the **Employee/Group**
7. Select sort by as **Employee Name**
8. Select **PF Payable** from the List of Ledger Account (If the PF Payable ledger is not created, press Alt+C from Payroll ledger field and create PF Payable ledger >Select Pay Head Type as Not Applicable > Take it under Current Liabilities)

The **Payroll Voucher Creation for PF Payable** appears as shown below (Figure 13.17):

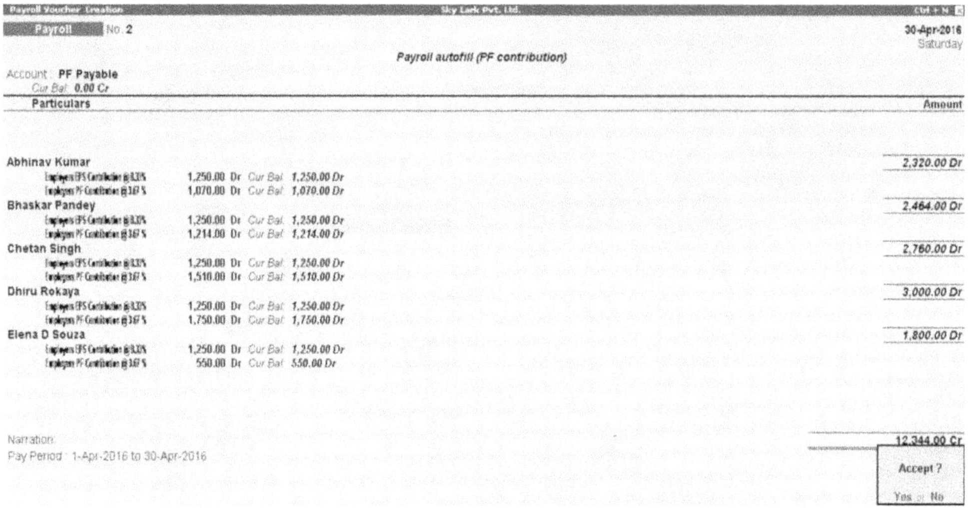

Figure 13.17: PF Contribution Voucher Creation Screen

9. Accept the screen

Step 3: Processing of Employer EDLI & PF Admin Charges

EDLI: Employee Deposit Linked Insurance is a scheme which is amended in the year 1976. It is insurance on PF deposit. This scheme pays a lump sum payment to the insured nominated beneficiary in the event of death due to accident, illness or accident.

All employees who join employee provident scheme are covered by EDLI Scheme and the EDLI Contribution rate is 0.5%. EDLI Contribution will be calculated on PF gross (PF gross refers to the value of pay heads used for A/c. No. 1 (employee PF @ 12%) pay head.)

Administrative charges: These are the charges collected by the government in order to maintain the PF and EDLI account. It's a charge paid by the employers to maintain the PF and EDLI account.

Employer PF administrative charges, EDLI contribution & EDLI Administrative charges are calculated based on the PF gross at 0.85%, 0.5% and 0.01%.

The minimum charges payable for Employer PF administrative and Employer EDLI administrative is configured as ₹ 500 and ₹ 200 respectively.

Let us create the employer's other charges Pay Heads and then process the employer's EDLI & PF admin charges:

1. **Creation of Employer's other Charges Pay Heads**

EDLI Contribution – Account Number 21

Go to **Gateway of Tally > Payroll Info. > Pay Heads > Create**

EDLI Contribution @ 0.50%	
Against the Field	**Actions to be Performed**
Pay head type	Select **Employer's Other Charges**
Statutory pay type	Select **EDLI Contribution (A/c No.21)**
Under	Select **Current Liabilities**
Affect net salary	Select **No**
Calculation type	By default it will take **As Computed Value**
Calculation Period	By default it will take as **Months**
Computation Info	
Compute	By default it will take as **On PF Gross.**
Effective From	Enter **01-04-2016**
Amount Upto	**Leave it Blank**
Slab Type	Select **Percentage**
Value Basis	Enter **0.50%**

Creation of EDLI Admin charges- Account Number 22

EDLI Admin Charges @ 0.01%	
Against the Field	Actions to be Performed
Pay head type	Select **Employer's Other Charges**
Statutory pay type	Select **EDLI Admin Charges (A/c No.22)**
Minimum Rs 2/Employee?	Set to **No**
Under	Select **Current Liabilities**
Affect net salary	Select **No**
Calculation type	By default it will take **As Computed Value**
Calculation Period	By default it will take as **Months**
Computation Info	
Compute	By default it will take as **On PF Gross.**
Effective From	Enter **01-04-2016**
Amount Up To	Leave it **Blank**
Slab Type	Select **Percentage**
Value Basis	Enter **0.01%**

Note:
- When the option minimum ₹ 2/employee is set to Yes, the EDLI Admin Charges for each employee will be minimum ₹ 2.
- The minimum charges payable for Employer PF Administrative and Employer EDLI Administrative is configured as ₹ 500 and ₹ 200 respectively

Creation of PF Admin charges – Account number 2

PF Admin Charges @0.85%	
Pay head type	Select **Employer's Other Charges**
Statutory pay type	Select **Admin Charges (A/c No.2)**
Under	Select **Current Liabilities**
Affect net salary	Select **No**
Calculation type	By default it will take **As Computed Value**
Calculation Period	By default it will take as **Months**
Computation Info	
Compute	By default it will take as **On PF Gross.**
Effective From	Enter **01-04-2016**
Amount Up To	Leave it **Blank**
Slab Type	Select **Percentage**
Value Basis	Enter **0.85%**

Note: Employer's Other Charges pay heads will not be included in the salary details for the employees as this is an employer related expenses and needs to be handled separately.

Create Expense Ledger

Go to **Gateway of Tally > Accounts Info > Ledgers > Create**

PF Admin Expenses	
Against the Field Name	Action to be Performed
Under	Select Indirect Expenses
Inventory values are affected	Set No

2. **Process the PF Admin Charges**

To process the Employer PF Admin Charges follow the steps given below:

1. Go to **Gateway of Tally > Accounting Vouchers >Press F7: Journal**

2. Press **F2** to change the Date to **30-04-2016**

3. **Press Ctrl+O** for **Other Charges Auto Fill**

4. In the **Other Charges Auto Fill** screen, enter the From and To date as **01-04-2016 to 30-04-2016**

5. Select Employee group **All Items** for the **Employee/ Group**

6. Select **PF Admin Expenses** in the **Expense Ledger** field

7. In **Admin Charges (A/c No.2),** select **PF Admin Charges**

8. In **EDLI Contribution (A/c No.21**), select **EDLI Contribution @ 0.50%**

9. In **EDLI Admin Charges (A/c No.22**), select **EDLI Admin Charges @ 0.01%**

The **Other Charges Auto Fill** screen appears as shown below (Figure 13.18):

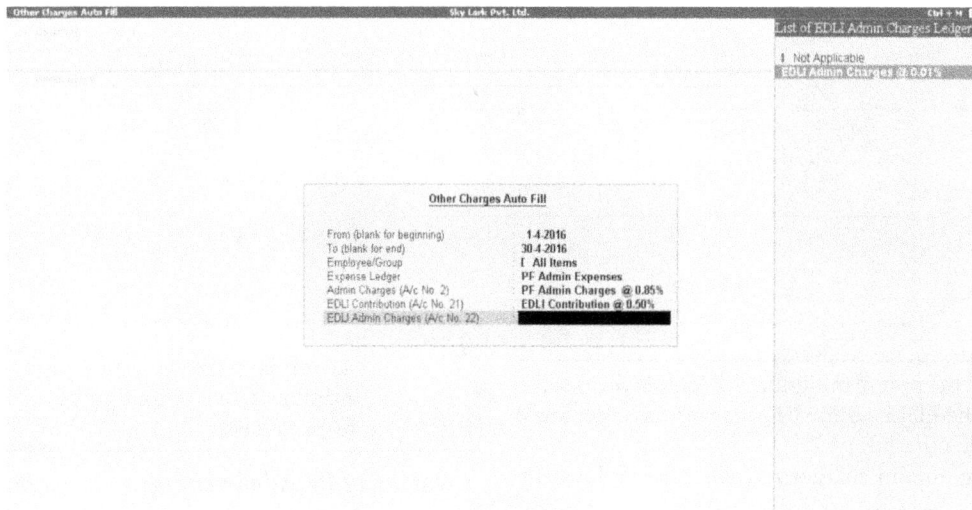

Figure 13.18: Other Charges Auto Fill Screen

10. The **Admin Charges** will be calculated for all the employees automatically.

The completed **Journal Voucher** appears as shown below (Figure 13.19):

Figure 13.19: Journal Voucher-Other Charges

11. Accept the screen

Note:	• PF Admin Charges, EDLI Contribution and EDLI Admin Charges is calculated as per latest change and it is calculated on PF Gross as defined
	• In the above case the total PF Admin charges calculation is above ₹ 500. If PF Admin charges were below ₹ 500, then the employer have to remit minimum of ₹ 500. For example: if the total admin charges come up to ₹ 480, then it will take as ₹ 500

Step 4: Record Salary Payment

To make the Salary Payment, follow the steps given below:

1. Go to **Gateway of Tally > Accounting Vouchers >Press F5:Payment**
2. Press **F2** to change the Date to **01-05-2016**

3. Press **Alt+A** for **Payment Autofill**
4. **Process for** select as **Salary Payment**
5. Enter the From and To date **01-04-2016 to 30-04-2016**
6. Enter the **Voucher Date** as **01-05-2016**
7. Select **All Items** from the **List of Employees/Group**
8. Select **Payroll Ledger** as **Salary Payable**
9. Select **Kotak Mahindra Bank** ledger from the List of Ledger Accounts
10. Set the option **"Use Mode of Payment/Transaction Type"** to **No**
11. Accept the **Bank Allocations** screen

The **Completed Accounting Voucher Creation Screen** for Salary Payment appears as shown below (Figure 13.20)

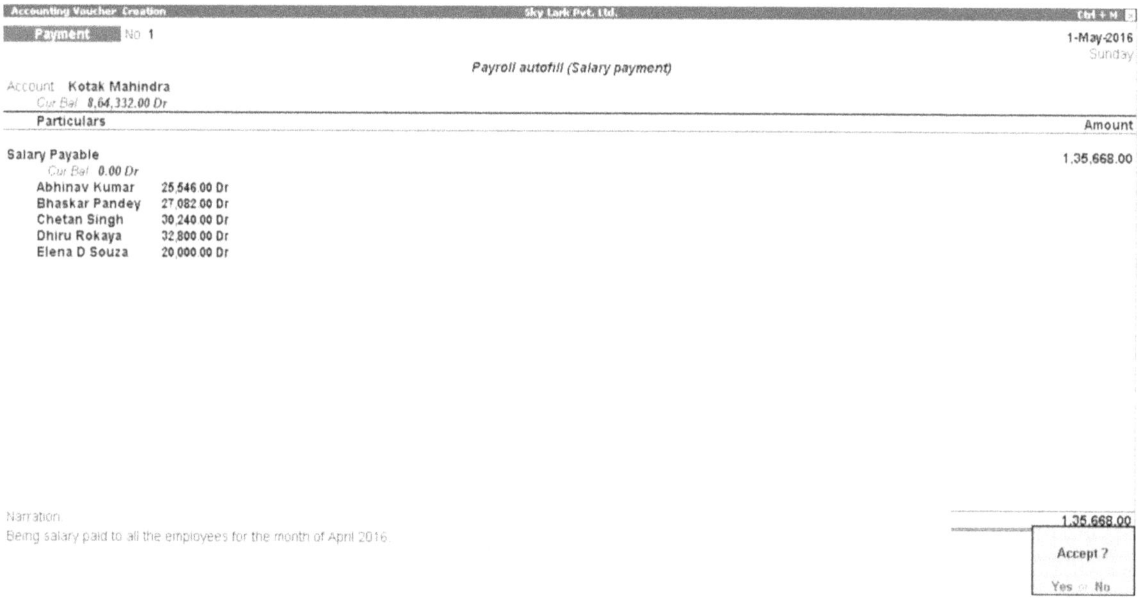

Figure 13.20: Salary Payment

12. Accept the screen

This completes the processing of payroll in Tally.ERP 9. In this section we have learnt how different salary structure of all the employees is defined by creating employee master, earning pay head, deduction pay head and contribution pay head.

13.6 PAYROLL REPORTS

In Tally.ERP 9, we can generate reports instantly once the salary is processed, we can generate following reports like:

*   Statement of Payroll:
*   Attendance Sheet
*   Attendance Register
*   Expat Reports
*   Statutory Reports

13.6.1 Generating Pay Slip in Tally.ERP 9

A **Pay Slip** is a document issued to an employee that lists each component of earnings and deductions, and the net amount paid to an employee for a given pay period. It provides details on how the net amount has been arrived at.

The **Pay Slip** option in Tally.ERP 9 facilitates the users to view the pay slip for individual employees, configure the content and appearance based on the requirement and then print or e-mail the pay slip. To view the pay slip, follow the steps given below:

1. Go to **Gateway of Tally > Display > Payroll Reports > Statements of Payroll > Pay Slip > Single Pay Slip**
2. Select **Abhinav Kumar**
3. Press **F2:Period** and enter the period as 01-04-2016 to 30-04-2016

The **Pay Slip Screen** appears as shown below (Figure 13.21):

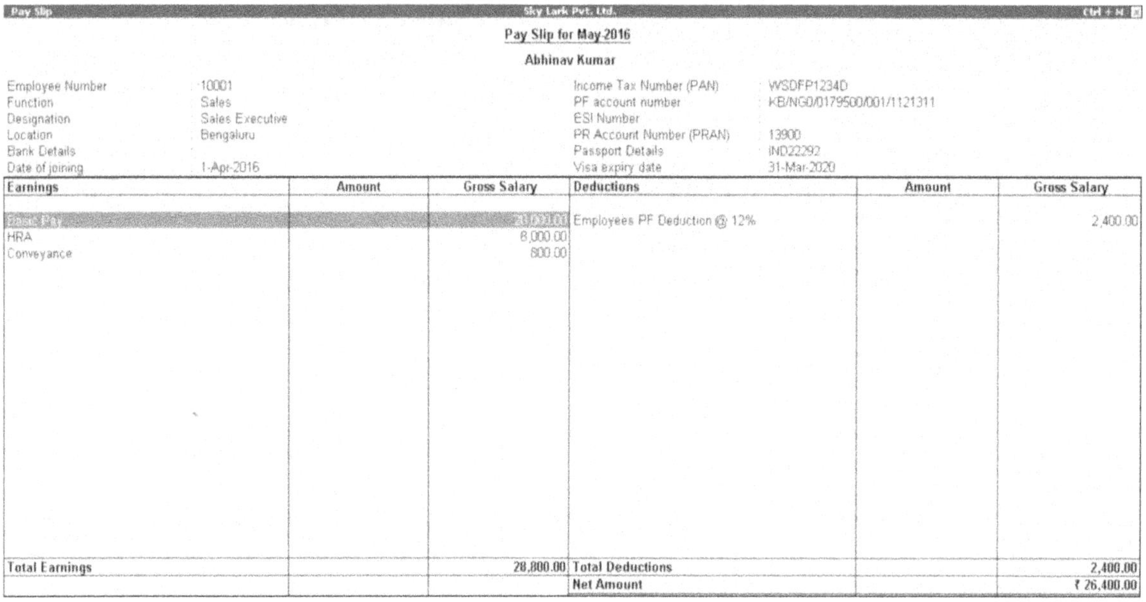

Pay Slip | Sky Lark Pvt. Ltd. | Ctrl + M

Pay Slip for May 2016

Abhinav Kumar

Employee Number	: 10001	Income Tax Number (PAN)	: WSDFP1234D
Function	: Sales	PF account number	: KB/NG0/0179500/001/1121311
Designation	: Sales Executive	ESI Number	:
Location	: Bengaluru	PR Account Number (PRAN)	: 13900
Bank Details	:	Passport Details	: IND22292
Date of joining	: 1-Apr-2016	Visa expiry date	: 31-Mar-2020

Earnings	Amount	Gross Salary	Deductions	Amount	Gross Salary
Basic Pay		20,000.00	Employees PF Deduction @ 12%		2,400.00
HRA		8,000.00			
Conveyance		800.00			
Total Earnings		28,800.00	Total Deductions		2,400.00
			Net Amount		₹ 26,400.00

Figure 13.21: Pay Slip

In the above pay slip you are getting the earnings and deduction details, to get contribution details in the pay slip, press **F12: Configure** from the above screen (Figure 13.21) and enable the option **Show Employers Contribution.** In F12: Configure, we can enable many options like vertical pay slip, employees details, attendance details etc.

Similarly, we can generate Pay sheet, Payroll statement, Payroll register, employee profile, employee head count etc. from statement of payroll option.

13.6.2 Generating Attendance Sheet in Tally.ERP 9

The following Attendance/Production related reports can be generated in Tally.ERP 9:

- Attendance Sheet
- Attendance Register

Attendance Sheet

The Attendance Sheet report is similar to pay sheet report, and displays a pre-formatted report with columns, related to your attendance/production data. To view the attendance sheet,

1. Go to **Gateway of Tally > Display > Payroll Reports > Attendance Sheet**
2. Press **F2:Period** and enter the from date as **01-04-2016** and **to** date as **30-04-2016**

The **Attendance Sheet** appears as shown below (Figure 13.22):

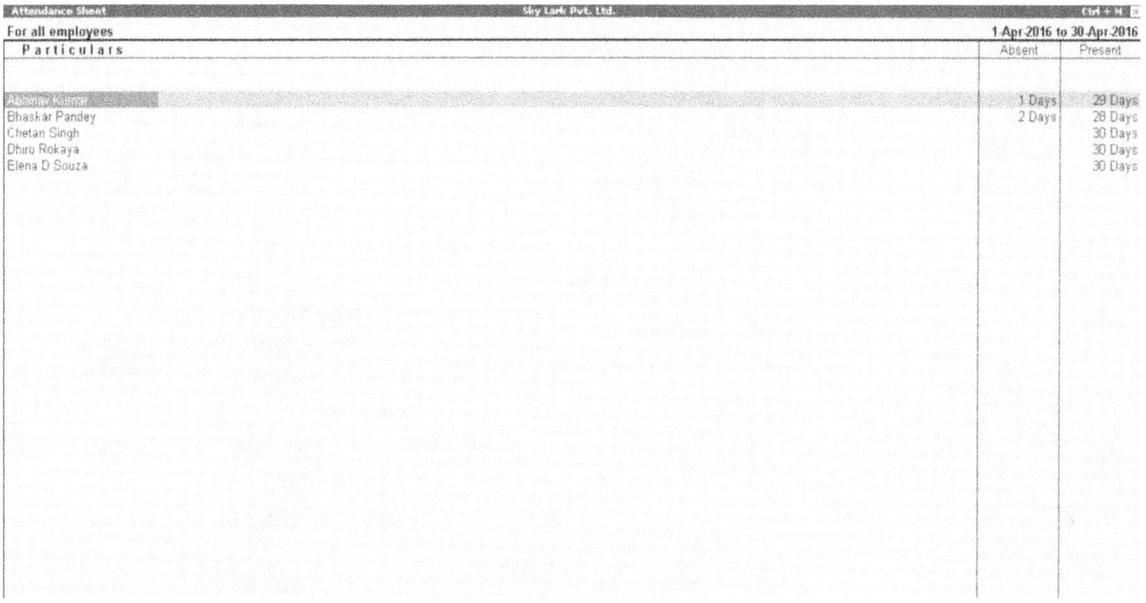

Attendance Sheet | Sky Lark Pvt. Ltd. | Ctrl + M

For all employees — **1-Apr-2016 to 30-Apr-2016**

Particulars	Absent	Present
Abhinav Kumar	1 Days	29 Days
Bhaskar Pandey	2 Days	28 Days
Chetan Singh		30 Days
Dhiru Rokaya		30 Days
Elena D Souza		30 Days

Figure 13.22: Attendance Sheet

In the above report (Figure 13.22), we will get the details of attendance of all the employees with present and absent details.

> **Note:** Similarly, we can generate the following reports:
> * Attendance Register: it displays the summary report of the attendance voucher
> * Expat Reports: it displays the passport and visa expiry details.

13.6.3 Generating Payroll Statutory Summary Report in Tally.ERP 9

In Tally.ERP 9, we can generate Statutory Reports like Summary, Provident Fund, Employee State Insurance, and Professional Tax, National Pension Scheme, Gratuity and Income Tax details.

To generate payroll statutory summary report, follow the steps given below:

1. Go to **Gateway of Tally > Display > Payroll Reports > Statutory Reports > Summary**
2. Press **F2:Period** and enter the from date as **01-04-2016** and **to** date as **30-04-2016**

The **Payroll Statutory Summary Report Screen** appears as shown in below (Figure 13.23)

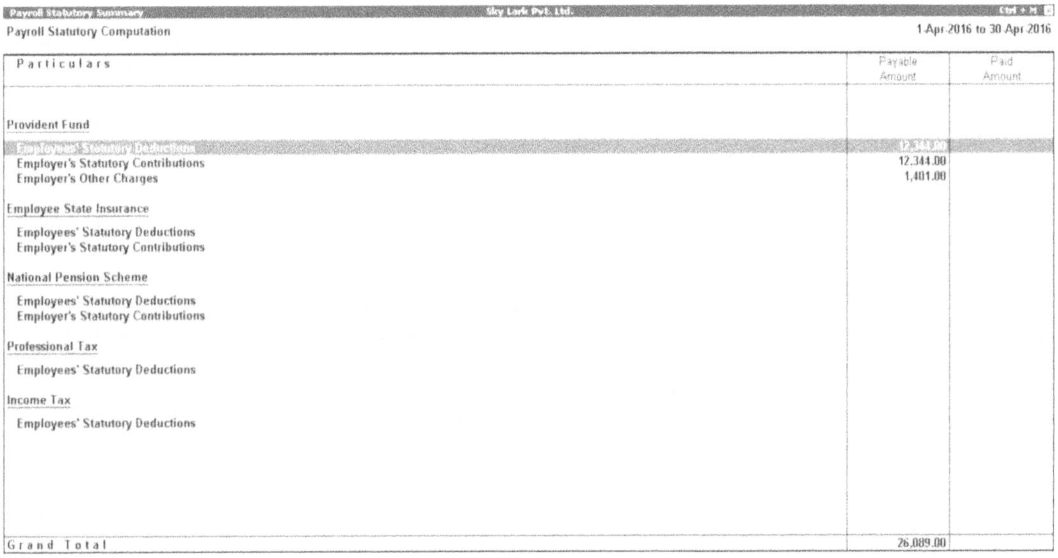

Figure 13.23 Payroll Statutory Summary Report Screen

In the above report (Figure 13.23), we can view the details of Provident Fund, because we have defined the details of PF deduction and contribution in the salary details of employees. Further drill down to get the details of employee wise PF Deduction and contribution details.

In the same report, we can view the detail summary of Employee State Insurance, National Pension Scheme, Professional Tax & Income Tax details. If the same is defined in the salary details of employees. In this case we have defined only the provident fund details, hence we are getting on PF details.

PRACTICE EXERCISE

Section A: Review Questions

1. Define Payroll
2. What are the steps to implement Payroll in Tally.ERP 9?

Section B: Objective Questions

1. From where can we activate payroll features?
   a. F11>F1   b. F11>F2
   c. F11>F1&F2   d. F11>F1&F3
2. PF is calculated on?
   a. Basic   b. Basic & HRA
   c. Basic & DA   d. Basic, DA & HRA
3. EDLI contribution is:
   a. Earnings for employee
   b. Employee's statutory deduction
   c. Employer's statutory deduction
   d. Employer's others charges
4. What is the rate of percentage for PF Calculation?
   a. 12%   b. 12.5%
   c. 15%   d. 15.5%
5. EPS contribution rate is?
   a. 8.33%   b. 3.67
   c. 8.67%   d. 3.33%

www.ingramcontent.com/pod-product-compliance
Lightning Source LLC
Chambersburg PA
CBHW080538220326
41599CB00032B/6308